Herodotus in Context

Herodotus called his work an enquiry and wrote before 'history' was a separate discipline. Coming from Halicarnassus, at the crossroads between the Persian and Athenian spheres of influence, he combined the culture of Athens with that of the more pluralistic and less ethnocentric cities of east Greece. Alive to the implications of this cultural background for Herodotus' thought, this study explores the much neglected contemporary connotations and context of the *Histories*, looking at them as part of the intellectual climate of his time. Concentrating on Herodotus' ethnography, geography and accounts of natural wonders, and examining his methods of argument and persuasion, it sees the *Histories*, which appear virtually without antecedents, as a product of the late fifth-century world of the natural scientists, medical writers and sophists – a world of controversy and debate.

ROSALIND THOMAS is Reader in Ancient History at Royal Holloway, University of London. She is the author of *Oral Tradition and Written Record in Classical Athens* (1989) and *Literacy and Orality in Ancient Greece* (1992).

D1343067

Herodotus in Context

Ethnography, Science and
the Art of Persuasion

Rosalind Thomas

Royal Holloway, University of London

CAMBRIDGE
UNIVERSITY PRESS

CAMBRIDGE UNIVERSITY PRESS
Cambridge, New York, Melbourne, Madrid, Cape Town, Singapore, São Paulo

Cambridge University Press
The Edinburgh Building, Cambridge CB2 2RU, UK

Published in the United States of America by Cambridge University Press, New York

www.cambridge.org
Information on this title: www.cambridge.org/9780521662598

First published 2000
First paperback edition published 2002

A catalogue record for this publication is available from the British Library

ISBN-13 978-0-521-66259-8 hardback
ISBN-10 0-521-66259-1 hardback

ISBN-13 978-0-521-01241-6 paperback
ISBN-10 0-521-01241-4 paperback

Transferred to digital printing 2006

Contents

Acknowledgements

Many friends and colleagues have helped, directly or indirectly, with this book. Various people read parts of it, or gave their reactions to versions in seminar form: I would like to express my warmest appreciation to Ineke Sluiter for her comments on the whole manuscript, to Michael Trapp and Lene Rubinstein for their enthusiasm and critical comments, and Geoffrey Lloyd who read part of the manuscript and offered astute criticism at an earlier stage. Of the many others who offered advice or encouragement, I should mention particularly Sally Humphreys, Ahuvia Kahane, Ann Hanson and Wesley Smith for their advice on medical matters, Richard Bett and Istvan Bodnar. The Center for Hellenic Studies in Washington D.C. gave me a fellowship for 1994/5, and this, with the generous support of the Directors Deborah Boedeker and Kurt Raaflaub, offered the calm and peace to complete the bulk of the work. Royal Holloway gave me a sabbatical to complete it. An invitation from L'Ecole des Hautes Etudes en Sciences Sociales and the Centre Louis Gernet in Paris gave me the opportunity to try out the ideas at an advanced stage, and complete further work on the manuscript: in particular, I owe much to François Hartog, Catherine Darbo-Peschanski, Pauline Schmitt-Pantel and Andreas Wittenburg. I would also like to thank Pauline Hire, my copy-editor, Linda Woodward, and the anonymous referees for Cambridge University Press. Finally, I thank my family and Michael.

References and texts

In the notes I use the Harvard system of author and date with the sole exception of modern commentaries. For greater ease of reference, commentaries are referred to by the name of the scholar and a reference to the commentary in question: thus commentaries by Stein, for example, Asheri, A. Lloyd, etc. will be clearly signalled in the notes.

For works in the Hippocratic Corpus, the best modern texts, used here where available, are listed below. The only complete edition is the nineteenth-century edition of Littré, *Hippocrate*. W. H. S. Jones' edition (1923–31), for the Loeb Classical Library, maintains a reference system similar to Littré's, of line-numbering within each chapter. Where possible, I use more recent texts (Budé series and the *Corpus Medicorum Graecorum* (= *CMG*)); otherwise the Littré and Jones texts. Littré references (Littré volume + page + line) are signalled with a capital L after the reference. For the more recent texts, I use their system of subdividing chapters (either by line or other subdivision); the general division into chapters is usually similar to that found in the Loeb editions but subdivisions within chapters vary between editors. The following are the main modern texts used:

Airs, Waters, Places (= *Airs*)
Hippocrate, Airs, Eaux, Lieux, vol. ii.2, Budé series: text, translation and commentary by J. Jouanna (Paris 1996). (Note that there is also an edition of *Airs* by H. Diller, in the *CMG* series, *Hippocratis De aere aquis locis, CMG* i 1.2 (Berlin 1970).)

On the Art (= *Art*), also known as *On the Art of Medicine*
Hippocrate, Des Vents – De l'Art, vol. v.1, Budé series: text, translation and commentary by J. Jouanna (Paris 1988).

On Breaths (= *Breaths*)
Hippocrate, Des Vents – De l'Art, vol. v.1, Budé series: text, translation and commentary by J. Jouanna (Paris 1988).

Ancient Medicine (= *Anc. Med.*)
Hippocrate, L'Ancienne Médecine, vol. II.1, Budé series: text and translation and commentary by J. Jouanna (Paris 1990).

Epidemics I and III (= *Epid. I and III*)
Hippocrates, vol. I, Loeb Classical Library, translation and introduction by W. H. S. Jones (Cambridge, Mass., 1923).

On Generation/Nature of the Child/Diseases IV (= *Gen/Nat. Child/Dis. IV*)
Hippocrate, De la Génération, De la Nature de l'Enfant, Des Maladies IV, Du Foetus de Huit Mois, vol. XI, Budé series: text, translation and notes by R. Joly (Paris, 1970).

On the Nature of Man (= *Nat. Man*)
Hippocrate, Nature de l'Homme, text, translation and commentary by J. Jouanna, *CMG* vol. I 1.3 (Berlin, 1975).

Regimen (= *Regimen*)
Hippocrate, Du Régime, text, translation and commentary, R. Joly with collaboration of S. Byl, *CMG* I. 2.4 (Berlin, 1984).

Regimen in Acute Diseases (= *Acut.*)
Hippocrate, Du Régime des maladies aiguës, vol. VI.2, Budé series: text and translation by R. Joly (Paris, 1972).

On the Sacred Disease (= *Sacr. Dis.*)
Hippocrates, vol. II Loeb Classical Library, translation and Introduction by W. H. S. Jones. Jones' chapter divisions are used; but reference is also made to the text of H. Grensemann, *Die hippokratische Schrift 'Über die heilige Krankheit'*: text, Introduction and Commentary (Berlin, 1968).

Note also:
Diseases of Women I and *II* (= *Mul. I, Mul. II*)
The Littré text is used.

1   Introduction

Herodotus' *Histories* present his readers with a bewildering array of subjects, a total history and description of the known world. The narrative traces the relations between Greeks and barbarians from mythical times and the sixth-century Lydian conquest of the Asian Greeks, to their culmination, the Persian invasions of Greece in the early fifth century by the Great King. Within and alongside this narrative are digressions which describe almost the entire known world. As areas come under Persian attack – Lydia, Egypt, Libya, for example – their geography, customs and sometimes their history, are described, often at immense length. Herodotus shifts from being geographer, to historian to anthropologist. He moves effortlessly from describing the nature of the Scythian land mass to the customs of the various peoples within it. The furthest reaches of the world find a place – North Africa beyond the Straits of Gibraltar, India and the central Asian Steppes. He was, and still is, considered the father of history. But improbable tales also abound – Cicero calls them *fabulae* – and from antiquity he has been accused of lying. There is a mixture of credulity and wonder alongside an apparently careful measuring of evidence. He has also been claimed as the first anthropologist. In other words, as is well recognized, the *Histories* in all their breadth seem to spring up with little in the way of antecedents. As Momigliano put it famously, 'There was no Herodotus before Herodotus'.[1] Neither the Homeric epics nor Hecataeus' dry works on geography and genealogy at the turn of the sixth and fifth centuries[2] are quite enough to 'explain' the achievement of the *Histories*.

Herodotus must have been pursuing his research in the decades of the highest pinnacles of Athenian power (450s to 420s) and in a period when that power was justified by Athenians through their contribution to the Persian defeat, but he ceases his narrative strictly at the end of the Persian

---

[1] Momigliano (1966) 129; Cicero *De Legibus* I 5.
[2] As with most fragmentary writers he is probably attributed with far more than he can reasonably bear, and the Hecataean remnants are especially austere: see n. 68 below.

Wars, on the very verge of the creation of the Delian League by Athens in 478 BC. The *Histories* have always been an essential source for archaic Greek history (pre-470s) and the Persian Wars themselves, and in that sense Herodotus seems a writer of the past, immersed in events long before his own time. Yet he is also a figure of the mid to late fifth century. He was travelling within the massive boundaries of the Persian empire, and writing (down to the 420s) at a time of important intellectual developments in 'science', natural philosophy and the art of argument. The mixture of the traditional and the modern in the *Histories* is often remarked. This book attempts to examine the *Histories* as part of the intellectual developments of the mid and late fifth century. It attempts to ask how far Herodotus' work should be seen as part of those developments – developments both in understanding the physical world, natural philosophy and medicine, and in the means of persuasion – rather than to an earlier and more traditional world to which his use of oral traditions links his narrative so closely. And it tries also to analyse them more explicitly as part of the world of East Greece, the Greek cities of the Eastern Aegean crouched on the edge of the Persian empire, between the Persian spheres of influence and the Athenian.

One example illustrates the contemporary late fifth-century angle that can sometimes be found in Herodotus' descriptions of ethnography. Egyptian religious practices fascinated Herodotus. In the midst of his description of their religious habits and in particular their cleanliness, Herodotus mentions certain Egyptian taboos surrounding behaviour in temples. 'Almost all other people, except for the Egyptians and the Greeks, couple in temples and enter such places after coupling without having washed, believing that human beings are just like the other beasts.' All other beasts and birds behave in this way inside temples, for, 'If this were not pleasing to the divinity, then animals would not do this either.' However, Herodotus concludes, 'I do not agree with those who now defend their practice in this way' (II 64) (οὗτοι μέν νυν τοιαῦτα ἐπιλέγοντες ποιεῦσι ἔμοιγε οὐκ ἀρεστά).

Considering that his initial theme was Egyptian cleanliness, we may wonder at the comparatively lengthy aside on what other peoples are prepared to countenance in their temples and the kind of justification taken from the animal world. Herodotus asserts that he does not accept this: those who now argue like this are not to his liking. Why does Herodotus tell us this? What should his audience think at this point? We start with this example because it is a particularly vivid case where Herodotus gives an emphatic opinion of his own about a matter which had strong resonances in the second part of the fifth century. One of the elements of the new education parodied in Aristophanes' *Clouds* is precisely the way an appeal to behaviour in the animal kingdom may be made to justify human behaviour. Pheidippides tried to use this tactic against his father to justify beating him: the rooster and other animals fight their fathers, he insists, and the animals are no different from us except that they don't issue decrees. 'Why, then', his father retorted, 'since you imitate the rooster in everything, don't you eat dung and sleep on a perch?' (*Clouds* 1421–31). Quite so. This kind of argument was closely associated with the 'new education' of the so-called sophistic generation, with the nature–culture controversy so fashionable at the time, and with the type of clever arguments Pheidippides was hoping to learn in order to move up in the world. Pheidippides appealed to the animal kingdom as if to 'nature' and therefore to something that could be seen as fundamental and right; his father gave the essential deflationary retort. Such ideas go on being discussed and disliked, the appeal to nature being especially closely associated with immorality and hedonism.[3]

Similarly, I would suggest, with Herodotus' remarks about the behaviour of birds and beasts in temples, and the attempt to use these to justify similar human behaviour. This section in Book II seems too reminiscent of the kind of argument parodied in the *Clouds*, too close to the sort of appeal to the animal kingdom that Plato (for one) so disliked, for one not to suspect that Herodotus in a quiet way is referring to such ideas – and quietly, but explicitly, signalling his distaste.

The passage raises several issues which will form central themes of this book. It implies that Herodotus was familiar with at least some of the radical arguments of the 'Greek Enlightenment' of the second half of the fifth century, as we know from other sections of the *Histories*, and that he might know of them while at the same time dismissing them. It raises sharply the possibility that at least some of his ethnographical enquiries were carried out with a quite clear awareness of certain of the new ideas that began to circulate during that period. Indeed it suggests that there may be more of such awareness, lying beneath the text or alongside his long narrative sections, than is immediately apparent. It also illustrates the presence of semi-hidden controversy, or at the least, quiet but explicit assertions of Herodotus' opinions which contrast with his more indirect and suggestive method of making links in his narrative sections.

---

[3] See Kerferd (1981a), ch. 10 and Guthrie (1971), ch. 4, esp. 99–101 for some arguments on the 'necessity' of following nature. Cf. Plato *Rep.* 586a1–b4 on the unthinking and beast-like pursuits of the common man; *Gorgias* 482c4–486d1 for examples of where the arguments from nature may lead.

The *Histories* do have a contemporary context, though they relate events of long before, and it is argued here that it is that contemporary world which must do much to clarify their background, whether it is the intellectual world of the natural scientists (*physiologoi*), 'sophists' and doctors, or the milieu of the Homeric rhapsodes which deserve more focus – or simply the Greek world of the mid to late fifth century. Some of these ideas may seem difficult to reach, or perhaps one might doubt that he could have had access to new ideas so fast. Yet in a world in which intellectual communication is not necessarily dominated by the (slow) publication of books, but can happen instantly in oral colloquia or electronically by computer or telephone, we can perhaps better appreciate the possible importance of the contemporary world, as opposed to the world of the preceding twenty or fifty years, in forming a written work. While not forgetting their more traditional features and sources, I argue here that the *Histories* as we have them could not have come into being without the intellectual developments of the mid to late fifth century; that Herodotus needs to be seen more overtly than he usually is, as part of the world of Ionian and east Greek 'science' of the latter part of the fifth century. While not necessarily radical, he shared many of the interests and knew of some of the ideas that are visible in those conventionally known as the sophists and in early medicine (and by 'sophists', for the time being, I mean simply those principal thinkers such as Protagoras and Prodicus, usually denoted by this title). It is argued that the overt methodology, the combative style and the way in which Herodotus tries to persuade his audience that he has the appropriate authority, belong inseparably to that period; and that the orality of the *Histories* is not only that of the oral narrator (perhaps in the tradition of oral storytellers), but also in the more geographically and ethnographically oriented sections, the orality of the oral performance lecture.

The areas we consider further by way of introduction concern the following: whether Herodotus is essentially 'archaic', either in his story-telling or in his intellectual debts – that is, a writer who is essentially a product of early fifth- or late sixth-century Greek culture; the need for contemporary context for understanding his methods and ideas; his cultural background, the condition of Asia Minor and the relevance of travelling intellectuals.

Herodotus' intellectual and cultural milieu

Herodotus' intellectual context has of course been treated before, but it seems ripe for renewed and more extensive discussion. A common complaint in many works on Herodotus is that he is misleadingly regarded as rather naive.[4] Or even if it may be accepted that there are elements in Herodotus reminiscent of preoccupations of late fifth-century thinkers, the implications are not examined at any length, and he is frequently regarded as overwhelmingly 'archaic', an essentially traditional thinker and storyteller whose work bears more comparison with Homer and the lyric poets than with the writers and thinkers of his time. Much recent work has looked at his narrative techniques, the skilful way in which he wove together the various tales and traditions into a narrative thread which subtly directs his audience in a certain direction.[5] It has been suggested with elegant economy that Herodotus was the last in a long line of Ionian prose storytellers,[6] or that he was a *logios*, a professional oral storyteller of narratives of the past, perhaps similar to the guardians of the past described by anthropologists of Africa;[7] or that he was more of a storyteller than a historian.[8]

Yet Herodotus' 'orality' – a slippery term at the best of times – is not sufficient to divorce him from the mid to late fifth-century world. And concentration upon his narrative techniques seems to have a tendency to archaize the *Histories* in a way which makes it virtually impossible to accommodate much of what he does elsewhere. It implicitly treats Herodotus as more old-fashioned than the period in which all agree he was still writing. Besides, the 'origins' of a genre (here, storytelling) are in danger of becoming a dominant explanation of the genre which he was writing so much later. The more traditional role of the poet in preserving fame is echoed by Herodotus in his clear intention to preserve memories (Proem), and there are other unmistakeable Homeric resonances within the narrative of the Persian invasion; yet we also find him offering a critique of Homer and the 'Homeric' texts in a manner characteristic of the Homeric criticism in both Thucydides and amongst the participants portrayed in some Platonic dialogues.[9] Alongside his well-recognized piety towards matters divine, in Book II we find him attempting to date the gods, or more precisely to fit the gods, the Egyptian traditions about the gods and the Greeks' discovery of these gods, into the long chronology of human history that he has himself devised (II 3.2–4; 43–5; 49–58; 143–6).

---

[4] From Nestle back in 1908.
[5] See e.g. Lang (1984); Erbse (1992); Boedeker (1988).
[6] Murray (1987).
[7] Evans (1991); cf. also Nagy (1987).
[8] Erbse (1992) most recently.
[9] Cf. Thucydides' rationalization of Homer in his Archaiologia; Hdt. II 53 on Homer's contribution to Greek knowledge of the gods; II 113–20 on Helen and the Trojan War. (Richardson (1975) deals more with the fifth-century exponents of Homeric allegory.) Xenophanes was also critical of Homer's account (e.g. DK 21, B11, 12), but within a poetic mould.

The extensive presence of folk-tales, and of travellers' tales of exotic nature, tend, it is true, to give an air of traditionalism or archaism to some of Herodotus' narrative – the stories of Polycrates' ring or of Cyrus' up-bringing, for instance, to take the most obvious, contain motifs which recur again and again in folk-tales all over the world. But it seems im-portant to distinguish, insofar as one can, the kind of tales, traditions or folk-tales, which were likely to be available to any enquirer like Her-odotus, and Herodotus' own use of them.[10] It seems likely that many tales and traditions were still in circulation at the time he wrote them down (that does not, of course, mean that they were necessarily accurate memories of the past). Provided one does not take the view that Her-odotus made up most of his narrative, it is then possible to say that he may have changed the emphasis, inserted the tales into larger, more meaningful narratives and historical patterning,[11] but to a large extent the repeated story-motifs may be a product of the traditions he picked up rather than his own creation. Anyone recording traditions is liable to change them in the process, even if this is a danger which is consciously being avoided,[12] but it would be going too far to say that they are in any serious sense new 'inventions'. He must have been at the mercy of his sources to some extent. Traditions which have been passed down over generations without fixed form are likely to conform ever more closely to the successive interests of new generations.[13] The nature of those sources should presumably tell us something about the period (mid-fifth century and later) in which such traditions were still remembered, and sometimes they may tell us more about the reasons for their being remembered than about the period they purport to record.[14] Inevitably they leave their traces in the *Histories*. But the presence of oral tradition there raises as many questions about the present as about the past.

Herodotus' intellectual affinities are perhaps most often connected by scholars with the generation of the 'Ionian Enlightenment' of the late sixth century (or earlier). Herodotus mentions Thales and Pythagoras, after all, as well as Hecataeus. The sensitive study by Gould, for instance, sees his important predecessors as Xenophanes, Pythagoras, Heraclitus,

---

[10] Fowler (1996) is excellent on this; also Murray (1987) and (1993), 22–8; note also Luraghi (forthcoming).

[11] Cf. Erbse (1992) for the creation of historically meaningful narratives; on story-motifs, Aly (1921), and Griffiths (1987), (1989).

[12] See esp. Vansina (1985); also the earlier edition of (1973), Henige (1974).

[13] See pertinent remarks by Murray (1987) on the clear improvement of Herodotus' infor-mation for the later periods.

[14] See Thomas (1989): ch. 5 stresses that Herodotus must have used his informants – and several different ones – quite carefully.

the 'Milesians', and Hecataeus.[15] Xenophanes' hint of cultural relativism, criticism of Homer, his scepticism about anthropomorphic gods, are often brought into play. But the fragments of Xenophanes are inevitably frustrating. He belonged perhaps to the generation of Herodotus' grandfather, and these questions all continue to be live issues in later decades. Other Presocratics are occasionally mentioned, especially Anaxagoras, though one senses that Herodotus was not much interested in the nature of being on the abstract level on which Anaxagoras discusses it.[16] Certain sophists are also sometimes mentioned, most obviously Protagoras,[17] but the implications remain unpursued. A pioneering article by Lateiner has recently analysed in detail certain affinities between Herodotus and the early medical writers, a connection noted before in more general terms.[18] More frequently, however, it seems still to be assumed, at least in print, that these later developments in Greek intellectual life are irrelevant for Herodotus: again and again the *Histories* are pushed back to represent a more archaic form of thought, a more primitive form of writing. That view may be plausible – and it would be foolish to imply that there was nothing of the archaic world in the *Histories* – but in that case we should adjust our picture of late fifth-century Greece to accommodate such a writer who was active at least until the early years of the Peloponnesian War (mid 420s). It is perhaps the polymorphous nature of the *Histories* which seem in some respects to defy categorization, which makes it much more difficult to see Herodotus within his contemporary world than Thucydides.[19] Moreover, coming from East Greece, Herodotus hailed

---

[15] Implied, Gould (1989), 8. Of Halicarnassus, he says (p. 7), 'It was also, as Herodotus' own work shows, part of the thought-world that had been created already in the sixth century BC by the philosophical and scientific thinkers who worked in Miletus ... and in other Ionian Greek cities.'

[16] A. Lloyd (1975) has an important section on Herodotus' intellectual affinities (ch. 4, esp. 156–70 on Presocratic speculation); for detailed comparison of method, D. Müller (1981); Nestle (1908) is still the fullest discussion. Immerwahr emphasizes the importance of the Heraclitean concept of balance between strife and cooperation (1966, 152–3); also (1956), 280: 'The rationalism of Herodotus follows the modes of thought of the Presocratic philosophers in its insistence on proportional relationships and analogy' – adding that it is all the more remarkable that he developed 'the tool of true historical causality to a large extent'; Pippidi (1960) stresses archaic mentality. See also ch. 5, pp. 135–6 below on the Nile.

[17] E.g. Dewald and Marincola (1987); Lateiner (1989) – both in passing. The main treatments still remain Nestle (1908), Dihle (1962a), (1962b). Further refs. in nn. 52, 53.

[18] Most often in connection with *Airs*. See Lateiner (1986), and (1989), less emphatically; G. E. R. Lloyd (1966) on Herodotus' use of analogy and inference; see also G. E. R. Lloyd (1979) for some use of Herodotus; earlier works compare Herodotus and *Airs* in particular (Nestle (1938), 25–7, for brief discussion of climate and ethnic character): for which see ch. 3.

[19] For Thucydides, cf. Finley (1942) and (1967), Hornblower (1987). Hunter (1982), 283f., suggested a comparison between Herodotus and Thucydides in their relation to contemporary intellectual currents as 'a task for the future'.

from a world that was less monoglot and considerably less unified culturally and politically than fifth-century Athens – we need perhaps to think more adventurously about the intellectual and social milieu in which we place him. Hartog suggested tentatively that Herodotus occupied a position half way between the sophist, who sold knowledge, and the rhapsode who sang Homeric verse, 'but the relation of Herodotus to these groups has not been tackled'.[20] A recent article by Fowler (1996) may point to a similar way forward in its conclusion that Herodotus was really a *sophos*, a sage or man of wisdom.

The contemporary context has considerable importance for any interpretation of what he was trying to do, and how his *Histories* could be interpreted. In the lively and continuing debate about Herodotus' methods of research, closely allied with that on his reliability, there is often little attempt to see such questions in a fifth-century context.[21] For instance, the controversy over whether Herodotus was an accurate and a conscientious researcher (not necessarily the same thing) may be conducted at a bitter level.[22] Yet in Fehling's work on Herodotus' 'source-citations', there is a striking absence of almost any contemporary cultural context. The reliability of Herodotus' information is often initially judged by nineteenth- or twentieth-century standards of what he should have seen, and described, if he had visited a certain site. If Herodotus has failed by such a twentieth-century test, then, it is argued, he has made it up, and the fact that he attributes such and such a belief to Lydians or Egyptians only shows that these attributions too are totally fictional.[23] There is little attempt in such discussions to ask what might have been acceptable or 'true' to fifth-century Greeks, and comparisons are made with ancient literature of a much later date and later stage of cultural development. Similarly, as was pointed out by Cobet, it is difficult to believe that Herodotus should be producing a clever literary parody, equipt with seemingly accurate

---

[20] Hartog (1988), 361.
[21] Lateiner (1986), exceptional in recent work on Herodotus' method; also D. Müller (1981), who compares his method with that of the natural philosophers (but not medical works); Corcella's thoughtful study (1984), emphasizes the natural philosophers, esp. Anaxagoras (and the gulf in conceptions about man and gods between Herodotus and sophists). Schepens (1975), on source theory, e.g., makes no connection with developments outside historiography, though he cites Heraclitus' preference for 'the eyes' as sources over 'the ears'.
[22] E.g. Fehling (1989); Pritchett (1993).
[23] Cf. also Armayor (1978) on Herodotus' supposed visit to the Black Sea; also (1980), (1985). Pritchett counter-attacks partly by arguing that certain phenomena *are* well attested, but also points out the obvious methodological flaw, that Fehling does not ask what kinds of things Greeks at the time were *prepared* to believe. Cf. also Thomas (1996).

source-citations, of a literary genre (i.e. history) that did not yet exist.[24] The controversy, stimulating as it has been, serves to highlight the need for more appreciation of Herodotus' intellectual milieu.

It is also particularly problematic, tempting though it is, to see the *Histories* against the later development of history writing. It is generally accepted that 'history' as a genre did not yet exist when Herodotus wrote, and it is a platitude that *historie* (literally 'enquiry') for Herodotus did not yet mean 'history', yet it always deserves reiterating. For if this is so, then it is misleadingly teleological to compare Herodotus only with a long line of historians, Hecataeus as a possible protohistorian, then Thucydides, and so on. Indeed such comparisons may in any case be pursuing only certain selected elements of the genre of ancient historiography; Hellenikos of Lesbos, after all, also wrote on Egypt, Scythia, and Persia as well as on the mythical and recent past.[25] Large sections of the *Histories* deal entirely with geography, ethnography and the culture of the known world. We misrepresent the *Histories* by seeing them primarily (or only) against the story of the development of history-writing.

What, then, is his contemporary world? Let us turn to Herodotus' origins in Asia Minor, and what that may imply for his cultural and intellectual allegiances.

East Greece and the travelling intellectual

Herodotus' home town, Halicarnassus, was a Greek city, in which Greeks and the non-Greek Carians seem to have intermingled. In Greek terms its inhabitants were Dorian in origin but to judge from surviving inscriptions it was Ionic in language and culture.[26] While it lay to the south of Ionia proper, it belonged with the other Greek cities of that coast as part of the intellectually and culturally thriving Greek communities of 'East

---

[24] Cobet (1974); note also the important remarks of Dewald and Marincola (1987), 26–32 and Marincola (1987), 126; Corcella (1984), 65–7 n. 32; Hornblower (1987), 17 ff.; Erbse on 'Fiktion und Wahrheit' (1991). Luraghi (forthcoming) is an important deconstruction of the 'source-citation' issue. For Fowler (1996, 86), 'He did not invent his sources; he discovered the *problem* of sources.'

[25] Cf. *FGrH* 4, F53–5, 173–6, 64–5, 185–7, etc.: his relation to Herodotus is hard to gauge; for what it is worth, Porphyry thought he cribbed his *Barbarika nomima* from Herodotus and Damastes (F72). Cf. Hornblower (1994a) 55–6 on the problem of treating historiography as a 'succession' or *diadoche* (cf. also his Commentary vol. II, 19–38 on Thucydides and Herodotus); note also Humphreys (1997) for stimulating remarks on the history of historiography.

[26] See the mid-fifth-century law from Halicarnassus in Ionic script, ML 32.

Greece'; Herodotus wrote in the Ionic dialect.[27] It was an area which had been first under Persian rule along with the Ionian cities to the north – Halicarnassians had to fight for Xerxes in the Persian Wars (Hdt. VII 99) – then again with the Ionian cities under the rule of the Athenian empire. Halicarnassus appears frequently, along with Cos, on the Athenian tribute lists. This might imply that that whole area, Ionian and Dorian, was a cultural backwater and poverty-stricken also, as has in fact been argued, in which case, we would have to envisage Herodotus turning with relief to the intellectual excitements of Athens. He was after all in exile for much of his life according to the biographical tradition. It might also imply that all he gained intellectually from the Ionian tradition harked back to the now elderly ideas of the early natural philosophers like Thales or Heraclitus. But this does not do justice to what we can glean from the admittedly difficult evidence from 'East Greece', that is, the western seaboard of Asia Minor, in the fifth century.[28] Closely related is the question of the vitality and energy of poets, writers and thinkers from that part of the world, and the possibility of their mobility.

Both areas deserve more analysis here since they subtly and implicitly percolate discussions of the *Histories* and modern Athenocentrism tends to underestimate the importance of East Greece. In simplified terms, such a view sees Athens not only as the centre of intellectual life, as indeed it was, but also the only place where intellectual activity is thriving in the second half of the fifth century; Ionia is in terminal decline since the Persian conquest, the members of its sixth-century 'Ionian Enlightenment' disperse to the West, the coast of Asia Minor stagnates culturally and economically and while Athens is a ferment of activity, the rest of the Greek world is in danger of being ignored. This assumption is visible in the common idea, for instance, that what little knowledge Herodotus had of current natural philosophy and sophistic ideas, could only have been gleaned at Athens (or alternatively at Thurii, an Athenian-led colony); and that other writers or poets can only come into their element when

---

[27] See the excellent picture of Halicarnassus and its culturally mixed character between Greeks, Carians and Persians, in Gould (1989), ch. 1. On Asia Minor more generally in the fifth century: Cook (1961) and (1962), Balcer (1985), (1991), with remarks below, pp. 14–15; Hornblower (1982a) and (1994c), ch. 8a; Hanfmann (1953); articles in *REA* 87 (1985); Mitchell (1989–90) on recent archaeological discoveries.

[28] If he really spent many years in Thurii, it is remarkably hard to see much in the *Histories* that might derive from the West Greek world; Pythagoras was widely known, and the geography of the western Mediterranean is conspicuous by its near absence. How and Wells, vol. I, 8–9 offer some evidence that Herodotus returned from Thurii to Athens.

they arrive in Athens.[29] Yet this blatantly distorts the evidence we have and ignores the fact that our predominantly Athenian evidence means that our searchlight only uncovers extensive evidence when it is trained on Athens. There is a nice moment in the narrative of the Persian Wars, after the first Persian retreat, where ambassadors from Ionia are to beseech the mainland Greeks to cross over to Ionia, but for these mainland Greeks, even Delos seems impossibly distant. 'All beyond that seemed to the Greeks full of danger; they had no experience of these places and thought they were full of Persian soldiers; as for Samos, it seemed to them as far as the Pillars of Heracles' (VIII 132.3). This reads like a quiet rebuke to mainland Greeks for their ignorance of the Asian side of the Aegean.

Let us start with the travelling thinkers. Not only did intellectuals travel extensively in this period, but even our relatively slight evidence indicates that Athens was only one of several stops made by some of these men, thus that they had not needed Athens exclusively to support their activities. The Platonic dialogues, for instance, are often set at the point when a 'foreign' natural philosopher or sophist has just arrived in Athens. The picture Plato paints is presumably plausible even if it is not strictly historical in every detail. Zeno and Parmenides, for instance, come to Athens for the Great Panathenaia; incidentally, Zeno's writings also arrive in Athens for the first time when they visit (*Parm.* 127b–d). In the *Protagoras*, Protagoras is pictured as having recently arrived in Athens, and the last time he was there was a few years back (*Protag.* 309d3, 310e5). It is striking that some of the sophists come to Athens not as a cultural centre, but on specific political business. Gorgias' famous visit in 427 was initially as part of an embassy; Prodicus is said to have been on many embassies from his home city of Keos to Athens.[30] These men are often fully active and important citizens of their own polis, far from the image of 'citizens of the world' of some later philosophers. Their presence in Athens might, therefore, be primarily as a representative of a more or less submissive member state of the Athenian empire. Some of the antagonism to the sophists may have been fuelled by the very fact that they were foreigners, albeit Greek ones.[31] The natural philosopher Melissos was a citizen of Samos, one of the most powerful islands in the Athenian league, and he was a general in a sea battle against Pericles in 441/0, part of the disas-

---

[29] For the need to have Herodotus at Athens (or Thurii), cf. e.g., Nestle (1908), 15–16, Dihle (1962a), Wells (1923); cf. Athenocentrism of Pohlenz (1953). Herodotus is now seldom regarded as pro-Periclean: see Fornara (1971a) on the problems; Strasburger (1955); Gould (1989), ch. 1; cf. Ostwald (1991) who restates the case.

[30] See esp. Kerferd (1981a) who stresses extent of travelling, p. 23: pp. 42–3 for Protagoras.

[31] Ostwald (1992), esp. 368, stresses the non-Athenian complexion of the sophists.

trous Samian revolt (Plut. *Per.* 26–8; cf. DK 30 A3). The fact that intellectuals of the time might visit Athens does not imply necessarily that they were wholehearted supporters of Athenian politics.

The sophists in Plato are frequently portrayed in what we might call the pied-piper image: they travel around the cities and remove the young men from their cities and families. Protagoras is made to admit the potential awkwardness when a stranger finds his way into great cities, persuading the flower of youth to leave their families and join him (*Protag.* 316c5 ff.). The sophist travels round with a bevy of pupils (*Protag.* 315a6–7). Similarly, according to Socrates in the *Apology*, 'There is Gorgias of Leontini and Prodicus of Keos and Hippias of Elis, who go the rounds of the cities and are able to persuade the young men to leave their own citizens by whom they can be taught for nothing' (*Apol.* 19e2–20a2).[32] Gorgias himself is said to have taught also in Argos, where he was disliked (DK II 425.26), and went to Thessaly where, according to Socrates' acid remark, he was 'embuing the Aleuadai with love of wisdom' (*Meno* 70a–71b, esp. 70b2–3). Democritus probably travelled extensively – though presumably not to teach – if we can follow fragment 299: 'I covered more territory than any other man in my time, making the most extensive investigations, and saw more climes and countries and listened to more famous men.'[33] He also said, famously, 'I came to Athens and no one knew me' (DK 68, B116).

This suggests that the period was one in which intellectuals, and not only the sophists gathering their crop of pupils, visited many cities in the Greek world – of which Athens was only the most powerful. Other cities benefited – or suffered – from the visits of philosophers. Even the Spartans, after all, listened to Hippias' learned lectures. Athens was far from being the only city who could host such visitors. At least some of the major sophists visited her on political missions; others were exiles. Herodotus was presumably another of such travelling intellectuals.

Many of these natural philosophers and sophists came from East Greece and were part of an Ionian tradition which still flourished in the second half of the fifth century. It is far from clear that all the prominent East Greeks moved west to Sicily or else to Athens, as has been suggested.[34] Melissos the Eleatic philosopher was, as we have seen, a native

---

[32] Other evidence: *Meno* 92b3 (Anytus thinks cities should drive them out, whether they are citizens or *xenoi*); 91c2; *Soph.* 223d5.

[33] DK 68, B 299, which Guthrie seems to accept as genuine: p. 387, n. 1. Cf. also B 246 and A1 (ch. 35), 9, 12, 13, 16.

[34] Cf. Emlyn-Jones (1980, 170): 'A reason for the lack of distinction in the cultural life of fifth-century Ionia may have been the migration of the majority of her more remarkable citizens to Athens,' a view echoed by Cook (1961); or with the exception of Melissos, 'all the distinguished Ionians about whom we have any information, migrated to Athens' (Emlyn-Jones p. 172). But is this permanent migration or simply travelling?

of Samos. Euthydemos and Dionysodoros, professional teachers of wisdom, were originally from Chios: they are supposed to have joined the Thurii venture but returned to mainland Greece in exile.[35] There is no tradition of emigration for the mathematician Hippokrates of Samos or for Hippon of Samos, a philosopher who revived Thales' first principle of water; nor for Archelaos of Miletus, said to have been Socrates' teacher. Oinopides, mathematician and astronomer (DK 41), came from Chios. The famous Anaxagoras, from Clazomenae on the Ionian coast, certainly spent some time in Athens, a friend, we are told, of Pericles, but he seems to have ended his life in Lampsakos, perhaps expelled from Athens.[36] If we consider the great Ionian diaspora in the Aegean, Protagoras was from Abdera in northern Greece, as was Democritus: Abdera was a colony founded in Thrace first by the Ionian city of Clazomenae, then by Ionian Teos. We might add the natural philosopher Diogenes, though not strictly Ionian, who was a native of Apollonia, probably the city of that name in Phrygia. And lest Clazomenae be thought stripped of cultural respectability by Anaxagoras' departure to Athens, Plato's *Parmenides* begins with the visit of Cephalus of Clazomenae who has come to Athens to meet someone he met there last time, Antiphon, and he introduces a group of fellow countrymen from Clazomenae who are all described as lovers of philosophy. Other figures who are less immediately concerned with philosophy include Hippodamus of Miletus, who designed the Piraeus, wrote on the ideal state, and stayed in Athens, but was not a permanent immigrant – and incidentally is later described as having extravagantly long hair and elaborate ornaments.[37] Somewhat earlier, Ion of Chios, poet and philosopher, was certainly on close terms with some Athenians, but there is no evidence of emigration to Athens.[38] He stays in Chios.

Herodotus' home city seems to have been Ionian in culture as we have seen; Herodotus wrote in the Ionic dialect, as was appropriate for a serious work in prose, and often measured his achievements against 'the

---

[35] Accepted by Kerferd (1981a, 53), citing the evidence in R. K. Sprague, *Older Sophists* (1972), 294–301.

[36] Demetrius of Phaleron claimed he stayed in Athens for thirty years, generally thought implausible: see Guthrie (1965), 266f., 322f.

[37] Arist. *Pol.* II 1267b22–30, where Aristotle also says dismissively that he wanted to be considered learned (*logios*) 'on the whole of nature'. See Burns (1976), for a thorough re-examination of the evidence. Like Herodotus, curiously, he is connected with Samos as well as Thurii by the very late sources. The confused testimony of Schol. *Eq.* 327 says he had a house in the Piraeus.

[38] See Huxley (1965a) on Ion of Chios – who sees him as a counter-balance to Athenian cultural activity, simply visiting Athens, as indeed the *Epidemiai* would suggest: the *Epidemiai* include visits of Athenian generals, including Sophocles, to Chios: Athen. 13.603e–604d (= *FGrH* 392, F6).

Ionians'. Just opposite Halicarnassus lay the island of Cos, which became associated with the early medical writings of the Hippocratic Corpus, and the peninsula of Cnidus.[39] Hippocrates himself was from Cos – and while we cannot be sure about the geographical whereabouts of the other early medical writers preserved under his name, we can at least assume that this area of East Greece also had important associations with developments of natural philosophy and medicine. Like Halicarnassus, Cos was Dorian in its Greek origin, but the Hippocratic writers wrote in Ionic and had links with other natural philosophers. It is perhaps the marginalization of medicine that accounts for the way this important group tends to be omitted from general surveys of East Greece. The idea, then, that East Greece was culturally defunct or denuded by the second half of the century does not bear close examination: the Ionian tradition of natural philosophy, of rational enquiry into the nature of the world, continued and indeed developed in the period.

Finally, however, it should be mentioned that the archaeological evidence of fifth-century Ionia is scarce and confusing, and this has been thought to back up a picture of desolation, extreme poverty, even 'a life of urban pauperization'. Cook's grim picture of Ionian destitution was based largely on the archaeological record alongside interpretations of the quota lists. But the archaeological evidence is not only very patchy, often still unpublished, or not even yet found; it is also inconsistent with the data on tribute paid to Athens from this area, which implies that many cities could afford large amounts.[40] Cook supposed that cities in the Persian empire who became members of the Athenian alliance would pay double amounts of tribute to both Persians and Athenians, but the evidence is rather circumstantial.[41] Herodotus' remark that the Persian assessment of tribute by Artaphrenes remained valid down to his own day (VI 42.2) is most plausibly interpreted by Oswyn Murray to mean simply what it says – that the *assessment* of tribute has remained the same, a kind of hanging assessment should cities admit to being subject to the Persians again, not that the actual tribute is still necessarily being paid by these cities to Persia

---

[39] For Cos, see Sherwin-White (1978).

[40] Cook (1961) – quotation at p. 17; some provisos in Boardman (1964), reviewing Cook (1962); Meiggs (1972), 269–71. For data on amounts of tribute paid to Athens, Meiggs (1972, 327) gives an increase for the Ionian-Carian area in 425 from c. 110T (= talents) to c. 500T (cf. for Hellespontine area, c. 85T to 250–300T). Miletus alone paid 10T, though Meiggs does not think this much. In Thucydides, Ionian exiles urge the Spartan Alcidas to encourage an Ionian revolt from Athens since this would 'deprive Athens of her chief source of revenue' (III 31).

[41] Cook (1961); cf. Hornblower (1994c), ch. 8a on Asia Minor; also Balcer (1985), 39; and the articles in *REA* 1985, esp. Briant (1985); Descat (1985); Petit (1985); Sekunda (1985). Hunt (1947) on *pyrgoi* and 'feudal survivals in Ionia' relies mainly on evidence from around Teos.

under a double tax burden.[42] Cities such as Colophon and Clazomenae appear in the literary record as active, not to mention factious in the late fifth century (e.g. Thuc. III 34).

The clichés about Ionian extravagance also hardly back up this archaeological picture of depression, though clichés can, admittedly, be wildly out of date if they are evidence for anything more than prejudice.[43] In addition, Herodotus, who ought to know, gives no impression in his accounts that this area of the world was lacking in vitality or wealth. Certainly he indicates that its submission to the Persians and its failure in the Ionian revolt made some dints to Ionian self-esteem; Miletus was actually destroyed. But in the famous remark about Ionian status in the eyes of the other Greeks often quoted to show this low self-regard, Herodotus actually seems to imply that Ionian prestige in his time was higher than it had been. Speaking of the first conquest of Ionia by Persia in the mid sixth century, he stresses Ionian weakness: he continues, 'The other Ionians, and the Athenians, avoided the name, not wanting to be called Ionian, and even now (ἀλλὰ καὶ νῦν) most of them, it seems to me, are ashamed of it' (I 143.3). He goes on to say that the twelve 'pure' Ionian cities gloried in the name. Some Ionians, then, have always been proud. For the others, he implies that the stocks in Ionian prestige have actually risen in his time.

A central argument of this book, then, is that it is too narrow to see Herodotus in terms of an 'Ionian tradition' of historiography, though the precedent and subject choices of Hecataeus obviously have some influence.[44] Nor can his links lie exclusively with the traditional habits of

---

[42] Murray (1966), accepted by (e.g.) Lewis (1977), 87; de Ste. Croix (1972), 313. It is possible that Herodotus refers to the rate as collected by Athenians, but if so, surely he'd make this clearer. Cook also suggested that the Persian tribute would be paid by individual landowners rather than the cities, but this city–territory division Murray sees, surely rightly, as impractical and unusual (1966, 143). The same hanging assessment might apply to the cities 'given' to individuals by the Persian king if the cities tried to join Athens. Whether there was a *legal* and formal separation of city from its territory in Asia Minor so early is dubious: see Hornblower (1994c), 211, with Lewis (1977), 105, 122 and de Ste. Croix (1972), 313–14. It is not unusual to punish a city by removing some of its territory, as the Persians did to punish Miletus after its revolt (Hdt. VI 20), or as Athens did to her allies: but this does not necessarily entail complete formal separation of city from territory.

[43] For Ionia and its relation to Athens, Connor (1993a); Geddes (1987); Alty (1982), 7 ff. on Ionian low status; also Emlyn-Jones (1980).

[44] Cf. Murray (1972) on Herodotus and Hellenistic culture: suggesting that the Herodotean legacy he traces is part of the Ionian tradition of historiography which includes cultural with political history and 'failed to distinguish' the genres of geography, ethnography. The best example of this tradition, which naturally combines geography and ethnography, seems to be Herodotus – and Hecataeus. What I would emphasize more is the role of an Ionian tradition of 'science' (for want of a better word), which does not look at the past, in this tradition.

Ionian culture. Herodotus can also be seen more enthusiastically and more positively as within the milieu of Ionian science – that is, natural philosophy and medicine – and part of Ionian science of the mid and late fifth century, not simply of the sixth century. The tradition of Ionian natural philosophy still thrives in the latter half of the fifth century, East Greece is the home of Hippocratic medicine, and in addition to Hellenikos of Lesbos, many of the well-known sophists are also from East Greece, as well as from areas colonized by East Greeks. This tends to be lost sight of in generalizations about sixth-century Ionia. I hope to show that in many respects the *Histories* are a part of this Ionian intellectual world of the fifth century, a world which has to look towards Athens as the economic and cultural centre of the Aegean, and which is politically dependent upon Athens, but which has by no means lost its cultural independence.

Approaches and methods

Let us look more closely in this final section at some general points concerning Herodotus' relation to earlier and contemporary thinkers, in particular (i) some remarks about previous work, and where this book differs; (ii) certain problems in conventional source-criticism in dealing with questions of intellectual milieu; (iii) the problem of a rigidly linear schema for intellectual history; and (iv) the use of the early Hippocratic essays which will feature prominently in later discussion.

The intellectual background of Herodotus has of course been much discussed. It was particularly in the early decades of this century that Herodotus' intellectual affinities and the various intellectual influences upon him were most adventurously explored. Nestle's long essay of 1908, which is still the most thorough survey, worked through the main early philosophers from Thales and Anaximander,[45] to Xenophanes, Anaxagoras[46] and then those writers conventionally called sophists, Protagoras, Gorgias, Prodicus and Antiphon. He explored every possible avenue of influence, but the method, inevitably at that time, concentrated on explicit, specific links between one writer and another, an exclusively literary connection and one exerted through the famous names, in a manner

[45] Thales (Nestle (1908, 6)): a wise statesman at I 170.3, whose family Herodotus thinks is Phoenician in origin; eclipse and drainage of Halys, I 74–5; his theory about the Nile mentioned anonymously, II 20.2. Note also Nestle (1942), 503–14.

[46] Detailed comparison with Presocratic method by D. Müller (1981); Wells (1923), very brief; some other works which treat the Presocratic angle at n. 16 above. Momigliano (1966), 211–20, also implies (211–12) that Herodotus' main debt is to Hecataeus and Xenophanes. Cf. also Diels (1910) on early philology.

which we may feel over-scholastic today and excessively tied to certain (extant) literary texts – an attempt to work out who Herodotus had read, as it were, who among the great thinkers had influenced him.[47] Nestle tends to assume, for instance, that any antithesis in Herodotus is Gorgianic, including, apparently, the description of Themistocles' speech at VIII 83.1, where he is said to set the stronger arguments against the weaker (see below, ch. 8).[48] Or the sentiment given to Mardonios that the Greeks, being all of the same language, should settle their differences by negotiation not war (VII 9 β 2) he immediately compared with Gorgias' not very original declaration about the importance of union against the barbarians.[49] Certain ideas are acute and illuminating, other are somewhat far-fetched, for instance when he traces Herodotus' emphasis on the great turnings of fortune ultimately to Heraclitus (with a glance also at Prodicus' pessimism), despite admitting that many other Greeks shared the same view.[50]

This is a method which concentrates upon finding precise relations between one text and another, and therefore between one particular author and another. It also tends, at least implicitly, to explain Herodotus via an earlier writer. While such links may be interesting, such a search for intellectual 'borrowings' tends to make the *Histories* seem not simply archaizing, but a mélange of other men's ideas. It tends to remove from view the question of what Herodotus was intending to convey in his own right, and what his audience may have been meant to understand. It may also be added that much of this kind of research (though not Nestle's) was interested primarily in establishing the chronological priority of the texts in our corpus. This is most clear, for instance, in the many discussions of the relation between Herodotus and the Hippocratic essay *Airs, Waters, Places*,[51] and the assumption was that publications, and therefore ideas, succeeded each other in a neat linear way (further below). It is difficult to countenance this now. We need constantly to remember the obvious fact that a mass of other literature existed which has not survived to this day;

---

[47] Medicine is mentioned only briefly: see Nestle (1938), 25–7, and (1942), 508–9. He also assumes (1908, 15–16) that Herodotus would have to be in Athens – or Thurii – to meet Protagoras (and hear sophistic *epideixeis*).

[48] For Gorgias, Nestle (1908), 19–20. Contrast, however, J. Finley, on antithesis in Thucydides (1967); Pritchett (1975) on antithesis, esp. 100 ff.

[49] Philostr. *VS* I 9.4–5 = DK 82, A1.

[50] Nestle (1908), 9 for Heraclitean 'influence', and 20–1 for links with Prodicus. (A. Lloyd's Commentary (1975) and particularly A. Lloyd (1990), has a highly Heraclitean interpretation of Herodotus' world view.) Cf. also Nestle's use of Plato's *Cratylus* to argue that Herodotus' interest in the meaning of words can be traced back to Heraclitus (1908, 9–11).

[51] For works on *Airs* and Herodotus and their relationship: see ch. 3 below.

also, that ideas could spread by other means than the written word, and that they could be discussed, approved, disliked, without written publication. Though self-evident, it deserves spelling out since it has wide implications for the *Histories*. It should be possible to think of certain ideas as in rather wider circulation than implied by their existence in one or other writer. The example with which we began this chapter involves ideas in circulation, rather than an exact dialogue between Herodotus and Aristophanes about fraudulent analogies from the animal kingdom.

Other important treatments of Herodotus' intellectual style show how certain mid- to late fifth-century issues surface in the *Histories*. Heinimann's seminal work on *Nomos und Physis*, and their perceived relationship in Greek literary and intellectual history, has much discussion of the *Histories* and he tried to establish the exact relationship between Herodotus, *Airs*, and the later sophistic writers.[52] Alan Lloyd's *Introduction* to his monumental commentary on Book II has an important and suggestive discussion of modes of argument and broad characteristics of method and approach, which he loosely characterizes as those of the Presocratics.[53] We may add that Democritus especially remains a tantalizing but probably very important figure. There are more precisely targeted discussions of various elements loosely regarded as sophistic. The constitutional debate in which the Persian conspirators speak successively in favour of setting up a democracy (Otanes), an oligarchy (Megabazos) and a monarchy (Darius) is couched in terms which are easily and plausibly linked with the constitutional discussions and perhaps set debates of the mid- to late fifth century (III 80–3). They reflect contemporary concerns and it is tempting to associate them with the ideas of Protagoras.[54] The story of Darius' 'experiment' with customs of burial amongst different peoples seems to present us with a vivid illustration of 'sophistic relativism' (III 38.2–4). Darius enquires of Greeks and of Indians how much money it would take to induce them to treat their dead parents as the other group treated theirs. The story is much quoted in philosophical discussions of the sophistic period, and it is often mentioned in work on Herodotus, but with less comment on the possible oddity of finding this

---

[52] Heinimann (1945); note also Heinimann (1976) on sophistic *technai*; also Pohlenz (1953).

[53] A. Lloyd (1975), ch. 4, with 156ff. on 'Herodotus and Pre-Socratic speculation'; Herodotus' theories about religion show he is 'firmly in the current of Pre-Socratic discussions of such matters', by which Lloyd means rational discussion of the mid- to late fifth century, whether within natural philosophy or thinkers like Protagoras or Prodicus.

[54] The bibliography on the constitutional debate is immense: see Lasserre (1976); Harvey (1966); Lateiner (1984); Stroheker (1953/4); see also commentary by Asheri and Medaglia (1990), ad loc.; Demont (1994b), esp. 81–5, on the form of the three-way debate.

most extreme illustration of the relativity of customs in an historian not usually thought to be in the vanguard of sophistic relativism.[55]

Similarly with the important debate between Demaratus and Xerxes in Herodotus' seventh book (VII 101–4), where the Persian king and Spartan exile discuss at length and from different points of view the likelihood of the Greeks being able to resist Persia. Analysed brilliantly by Dihle in an article entitled 'Herodot und die Sophistik', still the most important recent treatment of his sophistic tendencies, the argument is couched in terms which circle around reliance on nature and the strength of custom or *nomos*, and Dihle saw it as a debate between the older Ionian rationalism and a more sophistic emphasis on *nomos*. It is the latter, as the audience would all know, which turns out to be on the winning side. We shall have reason to return to this; for the time being, it is enough to comment that this analysis – and Herodotus' own abstract analysis through these speeches – does not seem to attract as much scrutiny as it might had it appeared in Thucydides' *History*.[56] And if it is accepted that Herodotus shows knowledge of some central sophistic reasoning in this passage, what are the implications for the rest of his *Histories*? Are these in effect isolated instances of abstract intellectual reasoning, a momentary toying with new ideas, in what is otherwise a mass of traditional storytelling – or do they imply we should read the rest somewhat differently?[57] It seems implausible that Herodotus would have maintained such views (as above) in a double-glazed insulation from the rest of his enquiries.

This is also the place to raise the related issue of linear intellectual development and its application to the *Histories*, since it will recur frequently in what follows and may sometimes be implicit in discussions of Herodotus. The idea of linear development in Greek literature and historiography is perhaps often unconscious but nonetheless tyrannical. The assumption that one author clearly builds upon (or against) another, and the related search for whether author A comes after author B, because A

---

[55] See ch. 4 below.

[56] Dihle (1962a); he begins by putting the general case for Herodotus being influenced by the sophists; note also (1962b). Cf. Dewald (1987), 152: 'We now recognize that as a thinker Herodotus is a member of the generation of Sophocles and Protagoras,' citing Dihle, Hunter (1982) and Hartog (1980), pointing out that there are acutely important problems posed by all this (Dewald and Marincola (1987), 35–7, tend more towards the influence of 'Presocratic philosophers and Ionian natural scientists'). Cf. Corcella (1984), 239–43.

[57] Other scholars who accept 'sophistic' elements in Herodotus: Lasserre (1976); Burkert (1990), sees connections with Protagoras which could be taken further; cf. also Burkert (1985a); Lateiner (1989) – fleeting remarks about sophists (e.g. 19) and scepticism, p. 245 n. 1; Dornseiff (1933) on sophistic *paignia* in Herodotus; Pelliccia (1992). A recent close reading of Herodotus' language is Kurke (1995).

knows something of B, has been dominant in certain strands of Herodotean scholarship and can sometimes produce strange interpretations. The question of who preceded whom can establish a particular approach to our evidence that continues to direct and dominate discussion even when those questions are no longer being asked (compare also Jacoby's manner of explaining the combination of geography and history in the *Histories* by means of Herodotus' biographical – and linear – development). The interactions of ideas within philosophy, after all, or between medicine and philosophy, can be highly complex and not neatly linear.[58] Moreover, though the schema is undoubtedly important in many contexts, it tends to assume a modern (but pre-Internet) model of the circulation of ideas, in which one writer writes a book which is published, then circulated, and which then invites criticism, answering articles, and books which build upon it. Yet in the fifth century, even towards its end, it is unlikely that ideas circulated only via the distribution of written texts: one need only think of any Platonic dialogue where a natural philosopher or sophist becomes available for devastating demolition by Socrates by his presence in Athens or his performance of public lectures, whether or not he has already published a written work (as of course several did). People moved around, ideas moved with them, lectures and display performances were part of the 'publication' – in its very literal sense – as well as full written texts. While this may seem obvious – and this is not in the least to diminish the importance of the written texts themselves – the implications for Herodotus are broad-ranging. As the controversy about the publication date of the *Histories* indicates, we seem to have a combination of equally striking indications that Herodotus' *Histories* either referred to dateable events or were known in Athens by a certain time, and the indications are contradictory.[59] The most plausible explanation, it would seem, if all these cases are in fact clear signs of Herodotean influence, is that his ideas and material and composition were becoming known before the whole *Histories* began to be circulated, written out, in their final form.[60]

[58] Cf. for example, Kahn (1981), on 'The origins of social contract theory', on the *longue-durée* of Milesian natural philosophers; and below, ch. 5.

[59] Aristophanes *Ach.* 523 ff. on the start of the war, is perhaps a parody of Hdt. I 1–5; cf. *Ach.* 85–7, 92 on oriental customs; cf. the end of Sophocles' *Antigone*; Eurip. *Cresphontes* fr. 449N. But the strongest arguments derive from Herodotus' own oblique references to events early in the Peloponnesian War (mainly VI 98.2 (Artaxerxes), VII 235 (Cythera), VII 137 (execution of envoys in 430 BC), IX 73.3). Jacoby (1913), col. 233 took Hdt. VI 91.1 (on Aegina) to give a *terminus ante quem* of 424 BC. Cf. Fornara (1971b) and (1981); Cobet (1977); Sansone (1985) – a compromise, but neglecting the tight ring composition of the whole; Evans (1979). Cf. also Lattimore (1958).

[60] Sansone (1985) suggested that he wrote Bks. I to the beginning of V first, and 'published' those books from the 420s; Evans (1979) suggests tentatively that he 'published' roll by roll till the 420s.

However, it is abundantly clear that there is also a danger of over-rigid categorization for a period in which there was little separation of disciplines. Lateiner's apt criticism of attempts to see traces of specific philosophers in the *Histories* is that such attempts 'suggest more about the range of fifth-century intellectual interests and lack of compartmentalization than demonstrate borrowings'.[61] It is increasingly clear that there are few demarcations between the various groups who may be categorized by modern scholars as Presocratics, natural philosophers, sophists, doctors – even if you accept, for instance, the distinction that sophists share their wisdom for money, the interests and methods of prominent individual sophists, as conventionally labelled (e.g. Protagoras, Prodicus) are by no means entirely distinct from some of the *physiologoi* or natural philosophers or from certain writers in the Hippocratic Corpus.[62] From the point of view of understanding Herodotus' background, this makes the analysis – and even the terms of the analysis – even more complicated. But at least we do not need to be limited to searching for 'borrowings', as the dangers of the linear schema make clear. In this study we concentrate more on analysing types of argument, approaches, and language, as well as specific instances of knowledge or theory, trying by comparison with other non-historical branches of writing to make some suggestions about intellectual affinities and, to use a deliberately vague term, the milieu to which Herodotus' enquiries might have belonged in the fifth century, while yet allowing Herodotus the degree of traditionalism we would all recognize in his work. This is also a way of asking how the fifth-century audience might have taken the *Histories* in a period before historiography was an established genre, and perhaps of answering the question Momigliano raised, who were the historians' audiences.[63]

Medicine is a case in point, and we turn finally to some preliminary remarks about the relevance of the medical corpus to a study of Herodotus. Scholars have noted common knowledge, material, or factual information, which appear both in the *Histories* and in the Hippocratic Corpus; others have emphasized that the careful amassing of evidence, the careful attention to the evidence of the senses, is shared by both – the reliance on autopsy, experience, sight, rather than on abstract theorizing, contrasts with some of the methods of the natural philosophers.[64] But the

---

[61] Lateiner (1989), 245 n. 1
[62] See G. E. R. Lloyd (1987), 92–3, for instance; for the meaning of '*sophistes*' before Plato, see below, ch. 9.
[63] Momigliano (1978).
[64] For common knowledge, particularly Althoff (1993a); Jouanna (1992); Demont (1988) and next chapter. On methods: Lateiner (1986) for common empirical bent; empirical emphasis shared by D. Müller (1981), who, however, made the contrast between Herodotus and the Presocratics.

Hippocratic Corpus tends to be studied by historians of medicine and science. Those working on early Greek science and medicine seem more ready to look to Herodotus than the other way round: G. E. R. Lloyd, in particular, brought aspects of Herodotus into his discussion of the development of Greek science, though this was tantalizingly brief.[65] Lateiner's article of 1986, already mentioned, was the most thorough examination of the terminology and language used in both, going far beyond the comparison more usually found between *Airs, Waters, Places* and the *Histories* – and he showed in particular that they shared a similar language of witnessing, evidence, autopsy. He argued that they shared a similar empirical method, 'a shared epistemological response' to their material.

This study attempts to take these hints and suggestions further. In looking at the early medical works, one is still not safely ensconced in a neatly defined area of clear 'scientific research' based entirely on empirical evidence. Some works, particularly the *Epidemics*, were innovative in their careful collection of observable data, but not all treatises were such clear and impressive anticipations of the scientific quest for knowledge based on observable and testable evidence. As G. E. R. Lloyd has shown, these early writers were themselves trying to define themselves as practising a separate art or *techne*. Moreover the arguments of the author of *On the Art*, which argues energetically that medicine is a *techne*, and not merely philosophical speculation, imply that this precise claim can hardly have been accepted by all observers. There was still a problem of separating disciplines which were not necessarily or clearly separate. Early medicine as illustrated in early Hippocratic works is often hard to distinguish from natural philosophy, either in its interests or in its methods of argument (see chapter 5, pages 153–61). Many concerned themselves with issues which were hardly confined to the pursuit of health, issues such as climate, the status of evidence, the rejection of magical cures, the difficulty of determining anything about what is invisible. In their reliance on certain types of argument (analogy, polarity), the medical writers can be seen to lie well within the same philosophical fold as the natural philosophers; they too were dependent on theoretical constructions which were not necessarily based on visible, observable evidence. Other Hippocratic essays look so sophistic (and so unconcerned with the main issues of human health) that they have long been thought to be the work of sophists rather than doctors. As is more readily agreed now, the strong rhetorical bent

---

[65] G. E. R. Lloyd (1966) brought in Herodotus' use of analogy and inference alongside the Hippocratics; cf. also (1979) especially; (1987) to lesser extent.

and style to some of these works is likely to be just as appropriate to the needs of medicine at the time as for anything else: they are probably as much part of the medical world as the more empirically based works such as *Epidemics I and III*. Against the poor quality of any medical knowledge, doctors had to build their ideas from theoretical argument as well as experience, and above all they needed to persuade. Without the secure seal of status from a professional qualification, a doctor had to convince to gain patients; other rival theories and competing cures existed, not to mention quacks and magicians. The institution of public doctors, of which we first hear in Aristophanes' *Acharnians* (1030–2), required in effect public appointment by laymen.[66] Indeed the very fact that *On the Art* and *Breaths* were included in the medical corpus, though obviously sophistic in style, may tell us something about the disparate nature of early medical writings and the lack of fixed boundaries between 'medicine' and other areas. This further suggests that the early medical works may give us evidence for more than medical methodology and language in a relatively narrow sense, the common style of intellectual discourse of the time.

This has exciting implications for a study of Herodotus. Myres called Herodotus the only fully surviving Presocratic.[67] But the earlier medical essays preserved in the Hippocratic Corpus are in some sense contemporary with Herodotus and they are complete in themselves, whole essays rather than tantalizing fragments chosen by later commentators or epitomators. This enables us to see how a whole argument or theory is being built up, and it means that we can at least avoid the pitfalls and traps laid by the fragmentary and often ambiguous remains of other prose writers earlier than or even contemporary with Herodotus, whether the prose genealogists or the late fifth-century sophists.[68] Herodotean scholars have given *Airs* much attention, but the other earlier essays have been almost

---

[66] For the persuasive side to medicine, G. E. R. Lloyd (1979), esp. 86–125; Jouanna (1984b); Jouanna (1992), 116 ff., and his editions of *Anc. Med.*, *Art* and *Breaths*; Kudlien (1974); Lloyd (1987); cf. also Laín Entralgo (1970); ch. 8 below.

[67] Myres (1953), 43: 'In the collection of facts about Man, and in the interpretation of them, Herodotus is the only "Pre-socratic" writer who is preserved in full' (he assumes (*ibid.*) the Hippocratic doctrines, e.g. about climate, are later than Herodotus; and thinks (the later) Hippocrates is responsible for any explicit doctrine even though Herodotus has relevant observations: pp. 44–5).

[68] Cf. Hecataeus of Miletus, seen by Jacoby (1912) as rationalizer of myths and exponent of scientific methods, who anticipated and foreshadowed the more empirical and 'scientific' element in Herodotus (followed by K. Müller (1972) on ethnography). But the fragments as we have them, and indeed later testimony, hardly support this picture (see ch. 2, n. 53 below). Contrast Erbse's sceptical remarks (1992), ch. 5, esp. 173. Note the important new study of Fowler (1996) on Herodotus' prose contemporaries (those in *FGrH*).

totally neglected.[69] They are too important to be left exclusively to the history of medicine.[70]

There may seem, however, to be insuperable problems with the relative dates of all these writers. How can one really bring into interpretations of the *Histories* essays from the Hippocratic Corpus which are not only anonymous, placed under the name of Hippocrates, but difficult to date with any certainty, and many certainly dating to the fourth century? To take authorship first, this is not a problem for our purposes.[71] A particular essay does not need to be by Hippocrates himself for it to form possible and useful comparative evidence. Moreover, the very fact that the essays are by a range of writers means that they give us a wider range of styles and theories, a richer background, than we might otherwise have.

The matter of dating is more difficult and its relevance depends what one is looking for. For the Hippocratic Corpus itself, dating of the essays has to be approximate, and it tends to be determined according to content, doctrine, relation to known authors, and, occasionally, style. Besides, the medical tradition obviously goes back further than the first writings. But it should be said that much earlier work on the essays was preoccupied with trying to determine which were 'genuine' and by Hippocrates, thus dating was simply subordinate or pressed into the service of this other aim. Moreover, some dating proceeded on the assumption that such and such an essay had to be later than Herodotus – particularly evident in the discussions of *Airs* – without much careful examination of the *Histories* themselves. It may also be haunted by the 'linear development fallacy' – as will again be clear in the claims that *Airs* is 'more scientific' and *therefore* later than the *Histories*. Style and language are important, but seem to have received less attention – given the state of the texts of many Hippocratic essays, many still only reprinted in the old Littré edition, this is hardly surprising.[72] Some recent work, however, is particularly valuable in giving stylistic analysis or evaluation alongside discussion of the

---

[69] With the exception of Lateiner (1986); cf. also Thomas (1993), a preliminary study, and (1997).

[70] As Nutton remarks (1991), 26.

[71] On the 'Hippocratic problem', see esp. Edelstein (1935); Edelstein (1939); G. E. R. Lloyd (1975b); Jouanna (1992); Smith (1979).

[72] Note that some essays are also composite; and there is the important question of how much earlier material or doctrine is recorded in the treatises, esp. interesting in the case of the gynaecological treatises.

theories, particularly the recent Budé editions of *Airs, Waters, Places, On the Art, Breaths, On Ancient Medicine*.[73]

It is therefore clearly impossible to proceed on the basis of any exact idea that a certain essay was published a certain number of years after (or before) Herodotus published his work. But there are other ways of progressing. Conventional source criticism helps where we are dealing with pieces of information, but as we shall see (chapter 2), it does not always work convincingly, especially where we may be dealing with a body of material from which both Herodotus and Hippocratic authors seem to draw (not always drawing on exactly the same material). What we can do with greater plausibility is use the Hippocratic essays as a further point of comparison with Herodotus, and use them in several different ways. We shall be looking at this in more depth in some later chapters, and a summary may be helpful here. For instance, similarities in points of method may suggest something about the intellectual milieu or context in which Herodotus was putting his *Histories* together. Or we may look for the style of thought, habits of argument, frameworks within which material evidence is understood. Similarities in presentation – in the concoction of a theory or an argument – may imply important conclusions about the audience for whom Herodotus was writing, the type of people he thought he needed to persuade, the methods he thought necessary to convince. Occasionally it may even be revealing if a demonstrably later essay has some point of contact – the very fact that it is later may give us a far wider horizon from which to judge Herodotus' own attempts. We are unnecessarily constrained by confining ourselves to works demonstrably earlier (and fragmentary), or contemporary, if that leaves us with little understanding of what continued to be said or written about (for instance) ethnography or the natural world.

That said, we will mainly be using a group of Hippocratic essays which for various reasons do indeed seem to be earlier than the bulk of the Corpus, the essays dated variously by different scholars, with a range from about 430 BC or slightly earlier, to about 400 BC. They are the following: *Airs, Waters, Places*, generally agreed to be very early, partly because of its similarity with Herodotus; *On the Art* and *Breaths*, both mannered, regarded as sophistic in style, and often thought not to be by a medical specialist; *Ancient Medicine*; *On the Sacred Disease*; *On the Na-*

---

[73] Note also Lonie's detailed edition of *On Generation/Nature of the Child/Diseases IV*; and Jouanna's edition of *On the Nature of Man* in *CMG* – with commentary. Note the *CMG* edition, coming out gradually. Ph. van der Eijk (1997) surveys the 'rhetoric of ancient scientific discourse', with suggestions for (much needed) further research on style and context.

ture of Man, attributed to Polybus in antiquity; *On Generation/Nature of the Child/Diseases IV*; *Epidemics I and III*, the earliest of the *Epidemics*; and *Regimen in Acute Diseases* and *Regimen*, used far less. A few others will make intermittent appearances (see list of texts used for each of these essays at pp. vii–viii). In fact it is precisely in these earlier essays where the style and language are noticeably more similar to that of Herodotus, which tends to confirm their earlier provenance.[74]

Herodotus' *Histories* continue to astound his audiences in the breadth of their interests, subject matter and sympathies. The debates about his factual accuracy or inaccuracy will continue, new archaeological evidence continues to prompt reassessment. There has been much recent work on the intellectual and cultural developments of the fifth century and later which makes it more possible and also more attractive to look afresh at the question of Herodotus' intellectual or cultural affiliations and background. Here we concentrate on those areas where there are important points of contact with the natural philosophy, medicine, and the sophists of the fifth century; and with his methods of argument, his language of truth. Comparison with contemporary 'science' is immensely valuable since it enables us better to retreat from twentieth-century assumptions about what Herodotus should have considered plausible and observe how his contemporaries went about proving to their satisfaction that what they said was the truth. The inclusion of Hippocratic medicine makes possible a shift of perspective; medical texts enable one to compare what prose style on technical subjects, and subjects trying to grasp at the truth, might have been like. It is against this general milieu of debate, 'scientific' and philosophical exposition, the *koine* of Greek intellectual life in the second half of the fifth century, that Herodotus' work may at least partially be seen – or so I would wish to argue. We seem in fact to find such methods and connections particularly prominent, not so much in the narrative sections about the past and the last books where the story of the Persian Wars gathers momentum, though even there frequent digressions are inserted, but in the sections treating the ethnography and geography of the known world. In the end, I hope we will be able to understand in more

---

[74] Dating: see Jouanna's helpful summary (1992), Appendix 3 – he tends to be happier about placing treatises in the fifth century than some others. Other discussions of dating: see particularly Heinimann (1976), 138–40, n. 32 on dating of *On the Art* and *Ancient Medicine* to fifth century on stylistic and other grounds; also Lonie (1981), *Hippocratic Treatises* ... 71 on dating of *Gen./Nat. Child/Dis. IV* to Peloponnesian War on grounds of style, habits of thought and argument, relation to *Airs* and *Sacred Disease*, and to Democritus. G. E. R. Lloyd tends to date the essays later. Cf. Longrigg (1963), 159 ff., for problematic assumptions used in dating *Ancient Medicine*. On the puzzling work *On Sevens*, previously dated to before 400, see Mansfeld (1971).

depth and with better clarity both how Herodotus' *Histories* 'fit in' to some of the intellectual currents of his day, and also why, despite establishing the genre of history, they still cannot be categorized in any modern terms.

Let us turn to the striking evidence for Herodotus' interest in matters relating to medicine, health and cures, and for detailed knowledge on his part of certain elements of Hippocratic medical theory. This raises immediate questions about the circumstances in which such familiarity could have been fostered, and the intellectual atmosphere of East Greek cultural life.

2   Medicine and the ethnography of health

In this chapter, we look at the detailed evidence for Herodotus' acquaintance with certain ideas usually associated with the early medical writers (pages 29–42). These will show, I hope, that Herodotus' enquiries are often either informed by certain Hippocratic ideas, or running parallel to them. In the process, it becomes clear how Herodotus' observations and 'research' may be influenced by wider theory, indeed how misleading it may be to suppose that Herodotus (or the medical writers) could engage in theory-free observation in these areas. In the second part (pages 42–68) we explore the further implications of this: first, the presence of controversy on such matters within Herodotus' *Histories*. Then we turn more explicitly to the role of ethnography – or any material concerning non-Greek peoples – in the medical works; and to the extent that Herodotus' ethnography intersects with the structures, frameworks or material visible in the medical writings. These last two questions are so closely interrelated that it is simplest to deal with them simultaneously, via an examination of Libya and of Scythia in the medical works and in the *Histories*. Here we will find further curious cases where material in the *Histories* and material in the early medical writers seem to be like disparate parts of the same jigsaw. It is not always so much that we find exact correspondence of facts or content, but rather, connections in subject matter or suggestive similarities in approaches and interests. In certain areas, Herodotus' ethnography has a community of interests and outlook with other enquiries into nature; we can occasionally even see him engaging in some sort of hidden debate with such theories. The following case studies will show how implausible it is to separate Herodotus from contemporary and later ethnography (including medical ethnography). I argue, among other things, that Herodotus' view of Libya and of Scythia, indeed his very choice of those areas for extended discussion, was influenced in part, at least, by their presence and importance in certain medical theories; that his researches also formed part of these, rather than passive borrowings from another discipline, and that they were structured by ideas and schemata that were familiar from the natural philosophers and doctors.

We will also find that ethnographic material and speculation have a role in early Greek science which stands somewhat apart from the preoccupations with Hellenism, Greek identity and Greek conflict against the barbarian that emerge from studies of the barbarian in Greek tragedy and fifth-century Athens. This implies that there are further twists and intricacies in the Greeks' relations to the barbarian world.

The whole chapter also deals implicitly with the issue of what is credible. The evidence of the medical writers and natural philosophers gives us a different perspective on what the Greeks of the fifth and early fourth century may have been prepared to believe of the outside world. The kinds of 'facts', or evidence, that are adduced, the relation of observable data and theory, all suggest that the lines of credulity and plausibility were often very different from those of the modern scholar. This is hardly surprising, but the implications for our reading of Herodotus may be underestimated. The chapter will end with some suggestions on the attraction of the exotic in these areas.

Medicine in Herodotus

Herodotus' *Histories* show considerable interest in doctors, medicine and health, and there is a strong strain of what one might call the ethnography of medicine and health. We are given in various places the whole spectrum of health care. Certain Indians, for instance, make no attempt at any cure and have no medical skill at all (III 100): they are vegetarians and, in contrast to the generally friendly reputation of modern vegetarians, take the sick to a deserted place to die and no one cares for either the dead or the sick. The Padaeans solve the problem of illness, as it were, by sacrificing anyone who falls sick and devouring the flesh before it is spoilt; in this way, few reach old age (III 99). The Massagetai offer up for sacrifice those who grow old, thinking this the happiest end, but do not eat those who die of disease (I 216.2–3); the Issedones wait till the father has died (IV 26).

Considerably higher on the scale of medical care, the Babylonians, he insists, incredibly, practise the market-place cure, laying out their sick for any advice that might be available (I 197). At the other end of the spectrum, Persian medical skill is noted (I 138, VII 181), and the Egyptians are singled out as having, remarkably, only doctors who are specialists (II 84). The highly specialized medicine of Egypt contrasts with the way the Scythians believe a king's illness is caused by false oaths and dealt with by soothsayers (IV 68–9). Much of the narrative of Book III is generated by the action of doctors: for it is the advice and the grudge of an Egyptian eye-doctor which is given as the immediate cause of Cambyses' invasion of Egypt (III 1), the action of Democedes via Atossa which is supposed to alert Darius to the possibility of conquering Greece (III 133 ff.). The story of Democedes of Croton (III 129 ff.), summoned by Darius to cure his injured foot, is in many ways a tale about the superiority of Greek medicine over others – the 'Greek cures' Democedes uses, as opposed to the methods of the Egyptian doctors who only succeeded in making things worse. It is interesting that Herodotus bothers to note so much about medical practice in general. The author of *On Ancient Medicine* also comments on those who do not use doctors, 'barbarians and some Greeks' (ch. 5.2 J).

Moreover, Herodotus in his own person has views on matters which would be classed as medical and physiological, from the causes of the dark skin of the Egyptians (II 22.3 – the effect of heat) to the relative skull-thickness of Persians and Egyptians (III 12).[1] He has an account and explanation of the 'female disease' of the Scythians, the ailment by which many Scythian men become impotent and live like women (I 105.4; also IV 67.2). He notes the way the Persians isolate anyone with leprosy and scrofula (I 138). The madness and possible epilepsy of Cambyses (to which we return) is discussed (III 33), as well as various other mental disorders.[2] We meet the Agrippaioi who are hairless men (IV 23.2) and are told of the black semen of Indians and certain Ethiopians (III 101). The latter statement incidentally has to be refuted scornfully by Aristotle.[3] We will meet others shortly.

There is, then, a large amount of sheer medical and physiological detail in Herodotus' *Histories*. It is also worth dwelling on the implications of the fact that Herodotus is happy to proffer explanations and opinions, which if we take his text at face value at least, are offered as his own. These are not simply observations or traditions picked up by him. He has his own speculations about the causes of Cambyses' madness (III 33–8), or the nature of Cleomenes' behaviour (VI 84), and the cause of the Scythian female disease (I 105.4). He produces, notoriously, what seems to be a pseudo-scientific examination, and then theory, of skull-thickness from some highly unconvincing enquiries at the battlefield of Pelusium (III 12).

---

[1] For medical elements in Herodotus, cf. Dawson (1986) with notes by Harvey (Dawson simplifies circumstances); cf. also Brandenburg (1976), with surprising omissions; Moeller (1903); Nestle (1938), esp. 25–8, briefly; also Nestle (1908), 12–14; Jouanna (1992), 319–27; Demont (1988); Huyse (1990); Althoff (1993a).

[2] Other examples of mental disorders: III 145; V 85.2; VII 43.2, panic; Cleomenes perhaps mad: V 42.1; VI 75.1; VI 84 (with Harvey on Dawson (1986), 94). General medical allusions: VII 88, Pharnuces and his horse. See Dawson for blindness and injuries (p. 94).

[3] *Hist. Anim.* 523a17–20; *Gen. Anim.* 736a10–14.

When we look more closely, we may begin to glimpse a level of abstraction or theorizing that is too great to be explained simply as the result of neutral 'fieldwork' of any kind, and which either bears close resemblance to specific Hippocratic theories, or seems to show an interest in medical or physiological matters which could well belong to a similar range of enquiries by others.

Let us look briefly at the famous speculations about skull-thickness (III 12). Herodotus wishes us to believe that he realized, on the battlefield of Pelusium, from the skulls lying around, that Persian skulls were thin, easily broken, and Egyptian skulls were strong – and he accepts what he implies is the 'local explanation', that Egyptians grew thicker skulls because they had shaven heads, and because of the heat. In fact the same cause (*aition*) will also explain why the Egyptians are less bald than any other men:

... because the Egyptians shave their heads from early childhood, and the bone of the skull (*osteon*) is thickened by the sun. This is also the reason (*aition*) why they do not become bald. For you will see fewer bald men in Egypt than anywhere else. (3.12.2–3)

He is, he says, persuaded, and he says he noted a similar phenomenon at Papremis (III 12.4).

Many scholars have tried to restore credibility to Herodotus' ingenious and tendentious discussion. There is particular debate on whether he really picked up a local explanation, local wisdom, or foisted upon the locals his own view – or at the most extreme, whether he invented the whole tale.[4] It is also hard to see how he could even have observed the phenomenon at all, for modern medical explanations are somewhat tendentious (for a recent explanation, by means of calcified bone, see Althoff (1993)). Some scholars have, of course, doubted whether he could have observed such skulls or even been to Pelusium at all. The point I would prefer to emphasize here, however, is that Herodotus gives us an account of his curiosity about this physiological phenomenon, and that he attempts an explanation. Whether or not it was really derived from the locals, it is still an attempt to explain, to say something about the skulls of (in this case) Persians and Egyptians. He wants his audience to see him as doing some kind of research on his own account, and research that would accord well with the concerns of those interested in nature. Moreover it is

---

[4] For Pelusium, see Althoff (1993a), esp. 3 ff. – sensible discussion, inclined towards local information. Also A. Lloyd, Commentary ad loc.; Fehling (1989), 28 ff., one of Fehling's first cases of 'fabricated observation'; *contra*, Pritchett (1993), 29 ff. Cf. IX 83.2 on Persian skeletons (skull without suture, other wonders), with Harvey's note on Dawson (1986).

only one of the more awkward of his observations and cannot be seen in isolation.

The other interesting aspect is that his explanation accords exactly with what one might call one of his 'theoretical frameworks' of explanation elsewhere, which is that climate has a crucial effect on the nature of mankind, and so do their customs.[5] The skulls are thickened both by the sun, thus presumably by heat, and by the habit of having shaven heads. We have here a combination of nature (*physis*) and custom (*nomos*) in the creation of human appearance that can be exactly paralleled in the phenomenon of the Makrokephaloi in *Airs, Waters, Places* – those long-headed men who acquired elongated heads first by human agency, then by nature itself which takes over (ch. 14). In other words the theory or explanation, used so firmly by Herodotus elsewhere, may perhaps have helped interpret the observation or given 'data'.[6] This raises the complex issue of the relation of theory to observation – to what extent do people see what they think they ought to? This interest in physiology would be most obviously shared by those of the early medical circles, and the *physiologoi*.

Theory and observation are inextricably mixed up in other expressly medical observations of Herodotus, and here we can see clear evidence of specifically Hippocratic medical theory in the *Histories*. Once we note the presence of current medical theory, it becomes less clear where 'observation' ends and theory starts. We will return later to the relationship of theory to observation, though as we will see, one cannot really separate them at any level of the discussion. The presence of Hippocratic ideas may help resolve some of these difficulties.

One of the most important tenets of Hippocratic medicine was that there were natural causes to illness and health. *On the Sacred Disease* aimed to show that there were always physical explanations for illness, even for epilepsy or 'The Sacred Disease', and that no disease was any more 'sacred' than another. At first sight we would think Herodotus' view of disease left a large part for divine agency, and so could not possibly share any features with so naturalistic a thesis. The well-known Hippocratic insistence upon natural and not divine causes for disease seems in some cases to be quite absent from Herodotus' view of disease, for he

---

[5] Fehling (1989), 28 cites *Airs* rapidly: 'Greek theoretical speculation' related to *Airs*, put 'into the mouths of his avowed sources'. But Fehling exaggerates the extent to which Herodotus says he was guided by local Egyptians. Herodotus simply says, 'I saw a great marvel, having learned of it from the local inhabitants,' and he quotes vaguely Egyptian agreement with the cause given (Fehling *himself* elaborates and spins out the story, p. 29; note also (p. 29): 'The obvious starting point for the whole story is a Greek supposition that the bones of northern peoples must be softer than those of southern peoples' – but in any case we are dealing here with Egyptians and *Persians*!).

[6] Here I differ fundamentally from Fehling.

accepts that disease may be sent by the divine as punishment or retribution. So in the remarkable story of early Cretan history that he inserts to explain why the Pythia advised the Cretans to stay neutral in the Persian Wars: the anger of Minos is somehow connected with a plague and famine, and a double depopulation (VII 171). However, this traditional account is of the distant legendary era and Herodotus leaves Minos' role somewhat hazy.

The madness of Cleomenes, king of Sparta, is more clear (VI 84). The Argives say it is punishment for his sacrilegious acts, the Spartans, interestingly, attribute a physical cause, seeing it as the result of his regrettable habit of drinking too much unmixed wine. But Herodotus here expressly declares his view that it was a penalty (*tisis*) for wronging Demaratus (VI 84.3), accepting a divine cause of some illness or disease, as he does for the disease and the collapse of the school roof in Chios (VI 27).

More interesting is the case of the Scythian 'female disease', Scythian impotence. At first glance, Herodotus seems to countenance a divine explanation of which the author of *Airs, Waters, Places* would disapprove. Herodotus calls it the 'female disease', mentions the sufferers, the Enarees, and the Scythians' explanation that it was the result of a sacrilegious act, the plundering of the temple of Aphrodite at Ascalon (I 105.4). He implicitly agrees with the Scythians, and later mentions the divinatory powers of these men (IV 67, 2: οἱ δὲ Ἐνάρεες οἱ ἀνδρόγυνοι). *Airs* on the other hand gives a detailed physical explanation (ch. 22), yet the overall approach is not as different as one might expect. For the author of *Airs* agrees with the Scythians themselves that the disease is divine (*theia*), but like the author of *On the Sacred Disease*, he thinks that no disease is more divine than any other, but that they have natural causes, and indeed launches into a polemical explanation of this: 'I *too* [with the Scythians] think that these diseases are divine, and so are all others, and none is more divine or more human than any other but all are alike, and all divine. Each has a natural cause and none arises without its natural cause' (ch. 22.3 J). There is a natural explanation which he then gives, both very detailed and far more complex than Herodotus' brief note. Herodotus, then, knows of a disease which features in a Hippocratic discussion; he refers to it as if it were reasonably well known, and he accepts a divine explanation, which the medical author seems almost to accept; the medical author differs in appending physical causes, natural causes, while agreeing that the disease is 'divine'.[7]

---

[7] For an interesting medical discussion, see Lieber (1996). Cf. Ph. van de Eijk (1990) and (1991) on natural causes and the divine in *Sacr. Dis.* and *Airs*; Ballabriga (1986); Arist. *Eth. Nic.* VII 1150b14–15 mentions the hereditary softness of the *Royal* Scythians; *Airs* too stresses it as a disease of the wealthy. Cf. also pp. 179–80 below for divine influence.

Herodotus' acceptance that disease may come as divine retribution does not convey the whole picture and it is increasingly noted by scholars in the field of early medicine that Herodotus did know of specific ideas in Hippocratic medicine (see chapter 1, pages 21–2 above). He seems, moreover, to be participating in this kind of research on his own account. Let us look at further examples.

(i) First the case of Cambyses' madness (III 33). When Herodotus talks about Cambyses' madness, he mentions as a possible explanation that Cambyses is said to have had epilepsy:

> Thus was Cambyses mad against his own kindred, whether because of the Apis bull, or because of some other of the many calamities which tend to fall upon men; for they say that Cambyses suffered by heredity (ἐκ γενεῆς) from a terrible disease, the disease which some call 'sacred'. For it is not likely that the mind should remain healthy when the body is suffering from a great illness.

In his careful use of the expression, 'the disease which some call sacred' (νοῦσον ... τὴν ἱρὴν ὀνομάζουσί τινες), Herodotus is surely making a clear allusion to perhaps the most famous thesis of the Hippocratic school, the theory that diseases have natural causes, and that the 'Sacred Disease' is no more sacred than others (see note 7). This is rather unexpected. He had mentioned earlier that the Egyptians thought Cambyses went mad directly because of the sacrilegious murder of the Apis bull, and he implied there that he agreed (III 30.1: 'as the Egyptians say'). Herodotus' mention of the Apis bull tends to attract more modern attention, but in this later chapter the bull is apparently set aside, as are Persian strictures about wine (III 34).[8] This is one place where Herodotus seems unwilling to dwell upon divine retribution, the element of the exotic and supernatural which he may accept elsewhere.

What he does linger over (with explanatory γάρ) is the interpretation we know to be Hippocratic, for he notes the *hereditary* nature of epilepsy. This was something that the *Sacred Disease* was most concerned to argue, putting 'the sacred disease' alongside all others in the fact that it might have a hereditary origin (the phrase used is κατὰ γένος, ch. 5.8 Jones = 2.4 G). I have translated Herodotus' own expression (ἐκ γενεῆς) as inferring the hereditary nature of the disease, since in normal usage

---

[8] At III 30.1, after Cambyses' killing of Apis, Herodotus says, 'Cambyses, so the Egyptians say, went mad because of this injustice.' Emphasis on wine (III 34) in Romm (1992), 58; G. E. R. Lloyd (1987), 23–4, n. 73, assumes that the Apis bull and epilepsy are on equal footing as explanations; cf. also Georges (1994), 187, for over-emphasis on Apis; Munson (1991) (oblique). Nestle (1908), 12–14 noted link with *Sacr. Dis.*; Erbse (1992), 51–2: epilepsy only an explanation for first step to insanity.

it should mean literally 'by descent', 'from the family', and since in both places where Herodotus uses it, he seems to imply a hereditary characteristic.[9]

Then Herodotus suggests a link between diseases of the body and those of the mind, so linking Cambyses' epilepsy with his madness: 'for it is not likely that the mind should remain healthy when the body is suffering a great illness'. This view of causation, seeing madness as perhaps partly caused by the physical illness, is reminiscent of Hippocratic appreciation of their patients' mental states. *On the Sacred Disease*, for instance, has much on the relation of the disease to the patients' mental and emotional states. Even the bare and brutal lists of symptoms in *Epidemics III* make note of symptoms like fear, depression, rambling.[10] Herodotus' remark may simply be an intelligent observation on his part: but even in that case we must recognize that it would not look out of place in a Hippocratic text, and that Herodotus is thinking along much the same lines, especially in the recognition of heredity, and the relation of physical ill-health and mental well-being.[11]

(ii) Libyan health. The Libyans are the healthiest people in the world, according to Herodotus (IV 187.2–3), and the Egyptians are the next healthiest (II 77.2–3). Here we may glimpse another Hippocratic controversy, indeed the possibilities for Hippocratic 'influence' seem to be even greater here than has been suggested. Herodotus tells us that it is the habit of at least some Libyans in North Africa, to cauterize the veins (*phlebes*) at the top of the heads or in the temples of their children, in order to prevent mucus or phlegm (*phlegma*) descending from the head:

---

[9] The other occurrence is at IV 23.2, the Agrippaioi who are bald ἐκ γενεῆς: both are usually translated as 'from birth', and LSJ takes both to denote 'time of birth', in a separate category from most usages of *genos*. 'From birth' strongly implies heredity in any case, even more obviously for the utterly bald Agrippaioi, but there seems no good reason to reject the literal meaning of ἐκ γενεῆς here – 'from the family', i.e. by inheritance. See von Staden (1990), on hereditary disease; he cites Hdt. III 33 (and IV 23.2) as an 'Ionic' parallel for the meaning of ἐκ γενεῆς as 'since the time of birth' (p. 94), but does not note that the Herodotean context is medical. Cf. Pigeaud (1983) on innate characteristics (mainly on *Airs*).

[10] Ch.13, 15–16 J = 10.5 G: 'a seizure is also caused by fear of the mysterious'; and esp. chs. 17–18, on emotional states and madness, all related to the brain. Cf. *Epid. III* 1, case 11; cf. *III* 17, case 15. Cf. also the appreciation of mental states in *On Regimen*. Cf. Pigeaud (1980) on mind and soul (much on *Sacr. Dis.*). *Sacr. Dis.* talks mainly about mental states leading to the disease, but only implies that the causes of epilepsy would cause madness too (chs. 17–18); I would stress the sheer linkage between mind and body: the physical factors affecting the mind in *Sacr. Dis.* also affect the body (phlegm etc.).

[11] Cf. Hdt. III 134.3*, the *phrenes* grow alongside the body (with Nestle (1908), 12). Cf. von Staden (1990) on patients' need to combine with doctors in fighting disease.

It is because of this that they say they are the healthiest. For the Libyans are truly the most healthy of all men that we know. Whether this is really the reason why they are the healthiest, I cannot exactly say, but they are indeed the healthiest. (IV 187.3)[12]

He adds a final remark about the use of goats' urine to mitigate the effects of the cauterization, the spasms that the children might suffer (187.3).

As with the Pelusian skulls, this has been a battlefield between those who think he found data for this Libyan practice, and those who think, at the most generous, that he has foisted an *interpretatio Graeca* on some ethnographic observations.[13] Did he pick up a genuine Libyan practice, or invent one? However, it is unlikely that the question can be posed so simply, for the observation, whatever it was, has been overlaid or interpreted through what are surely Hippocratic eyes.

What is striking here is that Herodotus is at least using technical vocabulary of the Hippocratics and accepting their preoccupations with the adverse effects of mucus in the head. As Althoff has shown, the early Hippocratic texts have strong opinions on mucus in the head (in Herodotus its bad effects are assumed, which is interesting in itself). *On the Sacred Disease* (ch. 6 ff. J = 3 ff. G), for instance, sees phlegm flowing from the brain as a main cause of epilepsy. *Airs* (ch. 3) talks about cities 'exposed to the hot winds' causing mucus in the head, and later deals with 'phlegm descending from the brain because of moistness of (phlegmatic) constitutions' (ch. 10. 6 J). Later in *Airs* in fact (ch. 20), we find the Scythians attributed with a similar practice of cauterization because of the moistness of their constitution. So Herodotus' remarks about the Libyans express the type of preoccupation with phlegm that is to be found in early medical writing – and also a solution, cauterization, that is attributed in another work, *Airs*, to the Scythians. Herodotus' text also provides, on conventional dating, the earliest case of phlegm appearing as a humour.[14]

---

[12] καὶ διὰ τοῦτο σφέας λέγουσι εἶναι ὑγιηροτάτους. εἰσὶ γὰρ ὡς ἀληθέως οἱ Λίβυες ἀνθρώπων πάντων ὑγιηρότατοι τῶν ἡμεῖς ἴδμεν· εἰ μὲν διὰ τοῦτο, οὐκ ἔχω ἀτρεκέως εἰπεῖν, ὑγιηρό-τατοι δ' ὦν εἰσί.

[13] On IV 187.2–3: Macan has parallels – see note ad loc.; Gsell (1915) 157, cited by A. Lloyd (1990, 240), only refers to Rawlinson's Commentary ad loc., and Tissot, *Géographie* I, 479, for cauterization in modern folk medicine; Pritchett (1993), 88 cites modern examples, though aware of Greek medical interest. Fehling listed this (1989), 90, under 'Passages with simple source citations, in which the fabrication is capable of proof', since 'Greek theory lies behind this'.

[14] See Lonie (1981), note on *Diseases* IV, ch. 35 (ad loc.) and pp. 277–9 on phlegm generally.

This is one of the places where Jacoby and Heinimann could only envisage a Hecataean origin for Herodotus' medical knowledge – but the more contemporary interest is properly attested and must be more plausible, as suggested by Althoff.[15] There is simply no evidence that any of this came from Hecataeus. The simplest and most economical solution is that Herodotus here reflects the interests of contemporaries. Herodotus is at least couching his remarks in terms which are strongly reminiscent of Hippocratic medicine (we will return to the Hippocratic preoccupation with Libya).

I would also add that it is not clear which element in Herodotus' account is actually raw observation, and where the theory begins – can we say what Herodotus actually observed (if he did observe something) or what his informant saw? Was it the practice of cauterization itself, or did he also find out the reason for the practice as well, that is, the pre-existing belief about mucus? The explanation Herodotus gives – mucus prevention – might simply have been assumed to be the obvious aim by a puzzled Greek observer, rather than an original Libyan belief.

(iii) Egyptian health (II 77.2–3). The picture becomes more involved when we return to the good health of the Egyptians. At II 77, we are told that the Egyptians are the most healthy after the Libyans. Rejecting the Egyptians' own explanation that this is because of their use of purgatives, 'believing that all diseases originate from what one eats' (ἀπὸ τῶν τρεφόντων σιτίων, 77.2), Herodotus declares that their excellent health is derived from the fact that Egypt has few changes in season. Illnesses tend, he insists, to be caused by changes in the seasons:

And in any case the Egyptians are the healthiest of all people after the Libyans because of the seasons, as it seems to me, since the seasons do not change; for it is with changes that diseases are particularly prone to occur, and most especially during changes of the weather/seasons. (II 77.3)[16]

He then describes their diet.

There has been some consternation at Herodotus' statement on Egyptian good health. Is it true or not? But that is not perhaps the best question – and in any case how could someone possibly tell, given the scientific

---

[15] See Althoff (1993a); also Mansfeld (1980a), Appendix who also assumes this is a case of *interpretatio Graeca*, and sees it (as II 77.2) as reflecting Cnidian doctrine (attributed to Euryphon in Anon. Lond. – phlegm a factor in all diseases); against Heinimann (1945), 172 ff.

[16] εἰσὶ μὲν γὰρ καὶ ἄλλως Αἰγύπτιοι μετὰ Λίβυας ὑγιηρέστατοι πάντων ἀνθρώπων τῶν ὡρέων ἐμοὶ δοκέειν εἵνεκεν, ὅτι οὐ μεταλλάσσουσαι αἱ ὧραι· ἐν γὰρ τῆσι μεταβολῆσι τοῖσι ἀνθρώποισι αἱ νοῦσοι μάλιστα γίνονται, τῶν τε ἄλλων πάντων καὶ δὴ καὶ τῶν ὡρέων μάλιστα. (II 77.3)

and social conditions of the fifth century?[17] There is in any case a Hippocratic background here, which alters the perspective, and probably a somewhat elaborate medical controversy. For Herodotus' observation about changes in weather has been noted by scholars of medicine and others as reminiscent of the Hippocratic belief that changes of weather and climate were of cardinal importance in health. The essay *Airs, Waters, Places* expounded elaborate theories about the effect of climate on health. Even the bare listing of symptoms and cases in *Epidemics I and III* is always careful to note the season and the weather. *Sacred Disease* has much about changes in the weather: for example in a passage about times of risk for an attack of epilepsy, the winter is the most dangerous time for the old but 'in summer the risk is least, as there are no sudden changes (*metabolai*)' (ch. 13. 33–4 J = 10.9 G; cf. ch. 11 = 8 G, epileptic fits). The later compilation of *Aphorisms* opens the section on the seasons with, 'It is chiefly the changes of the seasons (Αἱ μεταβολαὶ τῶν ὡρέων) which produce diseases, and in the seasons the great changes from cold or heat, and so on according to the same rule' (IV 3.1L). Herodotus is elsewhere very aware of the importance of weather change;[18] he also assumes here that all change will have an effect on health.

So when he declares that the absence of changes in the seasons is the cause of Egyptian good health, he seems to be voicing a Hippocratic view.[19] What is more, Herodotus also contradicts, in effect, the Egyptians' own view about disease, that all diseases are caused by food, producing in its place his own (and Hippocratic) claims about changes in the seasons – his view is emphasized by the expression 'I think' (ἐμοὶ δοκέει). He has appended his own view about the cause of health in a distinct tension to the Egyptians' own views. In other words we are glimpsing here a segment of a debate about the causes of good health and the effects of the seasons. This was a debate which was of vital concern to the Hippocratic doctors; it was also one to which Herodotus evidently felt he could contribute.

---

[17] For relation to Egyptian health, A. Lloyd, Commentary ad loc. For Egyptian medicine, see A. Lloyd (ad loc.) and von Staden (1989), ch. 1, with emphasis on what Greek medicine may have learned from Egypt. For II 77: noted by Nestle (1908); see also Kudlien (1967), 128 ff.; Althoff (1993a) 10; A. Lloyd, Commentary ad loc. (p. 333), who stresses that Egyptian medicine *does* take seasons into account: but cf. A. Lloyd (1975), Introduction pp. 165–6, where he sees Hippocratic influence; Jouanna (1992), 323; Pritchett (1993), 88 – citing Phillips (1973), 15. Cf. Mansfeld (1980a), Appendix, esp. 389.

[18] E.g. III 106.1, good mixture of seasons; I 142 on Ionia; cf. also on a grander scale, IX 122, VII 102. Nestle (1938), 25–8 on climate and ethnicity, and comparison mainly with *Airs. Water*: Hdt. III 23.2 on Ethiopians, and *Airs* 7–9.

[19] Jouanna, Comm. on *Airs* p. 25, thinks, however, that the idea that illness is linked to changes of season is common knowledge, citing Thuc. VII 87 and Pindar.

In fact there are further hints of controversy here, for the view attributed to the Egyptians about food causing disease was actually one held by certain Greek doctors, the so-called Cnidian school. It has been suggested by Mansfeld that the Egyptian view about food given here by Herodotus was Greek too, and specifically Cnidian: but perhaps following the easy temptation to 'archaize' Herodotus, he takes it for granted that Herodotus' text is indicative only of the older doctrines of Greek intellectual life (i.e. Cnidian in this case rather than Hippocratic), sees Herodotus' own view in the *Egyptian* one given, and neglects the fact that Herodotus then proceeds to present his favoured theory, which is Hippocratic in tenor. If Greek doctors were arguing about the relative importance of food or of climate in the presence of disease, then we may be seeing here in miniature a controversy that could only be of intense concern to anyone in the later fifth century interested in Greek medical theories.[20]

(iv) Diet. Another case where medical theory may lie below the surface of Herodotean narrative has been discussed interestingly by Demont.[21] He has argued that when one looks more closely at Herodotus' account of the retreat of Xerxes' army, the famine and disease that are described on the way evince an awareness of Hippocratic theories about change of regimen (VIII 115 and 117): Herodotus makes a logical link between the food, water and general conditions the army encountered, and the famine, plague and dysentery they suffer. At ch. 115, we are told, they eat grass and the bark and leaves from trees 'whether cultivated or wild' when they run out of corn to plunder (it is presumably significant that they eat *wild* things). At Abydos they eat more food than they had on the way, they have a change of water, and there is no '*kosmos*', so many more die (VIII 117.2):

ἐνθαῦτα δὲ κατεχόμενοι σιτία [τε] πλέω ἤ κατ᾽ ὁδὸν ἐλάγχανον, οὐδένα τε κόσμον ἐμπιπλάμενοι καὶ ὕδατα μεταβάλλοντες ἀπέθνησκον τοῦ στρατοῦ τοῦ περιεόντος πολλοί.

There they obtained more abundant corn than they had yet obtained on their march, and they ate their fill without any discipline (*kosmos*), and had a change of water, so that many perished who had so far survived.

Physical, natural and, in effect, medical explanations are being offered which bear close similarity to the analysis of disease caused by regimen in *Diseases II* (2.55 J), which describes a disease arising, apparently, from excess of drink, rich food, or a change of water; or by a change in regimen in *Ancient Medicine* ch. 10. Primitive food brings on disease and death, as

---

[20] Cf. Jouanna (1980); Mansfeld (1980a), Appendix, esp. 389.   [21] Demont (1988).

was so vividly described in *Ancient Medicine* (ch. 3).[22] The doctrine of contagion was not recognized by the Hippocratic writers.[23] Herodotus' account, like the other passages already discussed, seems, then, to involve assumptions about illness and health which can again be connected with current medical theory.

Where does all this get us? These examples suggest some kind of 'link' between Herodotus and contemporary medicine – he knows of certain specific theories which feature both in his ethnography and in the early medical works. In the most recent study of Herodotus' general medical knowledge, Althoff, while affirming the unimportance of Hecataeus here, seems reluctant to decide whether Herodotus was using the medical writings directly or whether the borrowing was the other way round. He also discusses the possibility of folk-wisdom, though this must inevitably remain very uncertain, and affirms principally that Herodotus was clearly familiar, even closely familiar, with Hippocratic methods.[24] But there seem to be more indications, more connections, than he sees. Secondly, it seems that the intricacy of the passages discussed in detail above suggests also that Herodotus himself was attempting to participate at some level in the debates that were current, as well as showing knowledge of them. It is perhaps not simply a matter of a one-way borrowing. There may also be some difficulty in drawing a strict line between Hippocratic and folk medicine. We cannot concentrate only on statements that to our eyes are very obviously medical, for given the Greek medical association of health and disease with climate, and for that matter the poor 'scientific' basis of some Greek medicine, elements which may to us resemble 'folk-wisdom' may well have been part of serious medical theory or fully part of a more 'professional' medical practice. Scholars do occasionally dismiss possibly relevant remarks on the grounds that they are not medical.[25] But at this early stage of medical expertise, it may be impossible to be sure that what looks like popular knowledge is not also 'professional'.

[22] Demont emphasizes the distinction between communal and individual disease (1988, 12) – but the historian of an army's retreat is likely to be most concerned with *mass* communal famine and disease. Note also: Grmek (1983b), 285–96, for Herodotus' medical knowledge elsewhere; and (1983a).

[23] Whereas Thucydides did: *Nat. Man* 9 (and Celsus, *de Medicina* 1.10) recommends that one find a different climate in time of pestilence, or breathe in less by resting a lot. Noted by Poole and Holladay (1979); for further debate, Solomon (1985), and Holladay (1987).

[24] While Althoff (1993a) concentrates on specific passages, the wider milieu or implications deserve more attention, given that we are at a point at which neither 'medicine' nor 'history' have a totally autonomous existence as disciplines. He hints (p. 15) that some of these conceptions are too general to be securely pinned to Hippocratic work, but much Hippocratic theory uses more general ideas (e.g. effect of heat).

[25] E.g. Althoff (1993a), 12–13, on the 'folk-psychology' concerning the link of bravery and weather.

There are other instances of Hippocratic terminology. For instance in Herodotus' description of the Egyptian doctors who, he says, are all specialists, he mentions eye-doctors, doctors for the head, teeth, intestines, and 'doctors for the invisible diseases' (II 84: οἱ δὲ τῶν ἀφανέων νούσων). This latter category is unmistakeably Hippocratic (e.g. *Art*, ch. 10.1 J, and ch. 6 below). The very way Herodotus stresses the specialisms in Egypt implies a contrast with Greek doctors.

The Greek doctor Democedes has to treat Atossa's tumour (III 133.1): the word *phuma* here is listed by Liddell and Scott as the first occurrence in the sense of 'diseased growth', and it occurs thereafter in the Hippocratic Corpus (e.g. *Anc. Med.* 22.8, 9 J; cf. also *Timaeus* 85c1). We also meet *phlebes*, or veins, in a strange and often misunderstood passage on Scythian mare's milk (IV 2.1), and in the passage discussed above on the Libyans (IV 187.2). Phlegm (φλέγμα) occurs in the same Libyan description. Elsewhere we meet bile (IV 58: from grass); and certain other humours, including phlegm and *ikmas* (to which we return below, p. 49), not to mention 'beavers' testicles', supposedly a Scythian remedy for gynaecological complaints (IV 109.2: see section on Scythia below).

The tale of Democedes, a Greek from Croton captured as a slave, is redolent with the language of the *techne*, 'the art', the expression used by medical writers to refer to the art of medicine (III 129f.). The Persian king Darius calls Democedes to his presence, in the hope that he can cure Darius' foot, and the question he asks Democedes is 'Do you know the art?' – τὴν τέχνην εἰ ἐπίσταιτο (III 130.1). Democedes at first evades the matter, but he seems to Darius to be 'behaving artfully' – τεχνάζειν, a wonderful pun on *techne* – and Darius produces the torturing equipment (130.2). So backtracking rapidly, Democedes explains 'that he does not know it truly, but having met with a doctor, he has a poor knowledge of the *techne*' (φὰς ἀτρεκέως μὲν οὐκ ἐπίστασθαι, ὁμιλήσας δὲ ἰητρῷ φλαύρως ἔχειν τὴν τέχνην). The context of the whole episode makes it obvious that the medical art is what is meant (similarly with *techne* in 129.3, where it seems to refer to Democedes' 'skill'), yet the failure to qualify *techne* at any point, the way Darius asks simply 'Do you know the art?', is strongly reminiscent of the language of the Hippocratics, especially, of course, of *On the Art* (*Peri Technes*). Here, *the techne* was most definitely the art of medicine; medicine is the art *par excellence*.[26]

As we have seen so far, then, Herodotus is not only conscious enough of the subject of health to include it as a regular item in his ethnographical descriptions; he is aware of certain ideas associated with early medical

---

[26] Cf. the importance attributed to the way *Anc. Med.* had 'a developed notion of medicine as an art, τέχνη': see (e.g.) G. E. R. Lloyd (1963), 126.

writers. Herodotus' *Histories* contain a surprising quantity of information on the ethnography of health and medicine, from cannibalistic treatment of the dead to Scythian or Libyan medical techniques. These remarks seem not to be the result merely of coincidence, or of an all-embracing curiosity on Herodotus' part, for in some cases at least he seemed to be following paths of enquiry and preoccupations which were recognizable in medical works; there were distinct Hippocratic resonances. These pre-occupations went beyond the familiar interest in the relation between climate and ethnic character. This implies very strongly indeed that Herodotus' enquiries were more or less contemporary to certain of the ideas visible in early medicine; that the conventional attempts to date his work as earlier, and therefore utterly uninformed by the medical theories (or even by *Airs*), are not supported by the evidence; and that some of Herodotus' ethnography might be partially created with the help of certain interests and ideas current in medical circles.

The ethnography of health: Scythia and Libya

We may then go further and consider in more depth (a) the extent to which ethnographic material, information and theories feature in these medical works; and (b) the extent to which Herodotus' enquiries intersect with the pursuit of ethnography in these works, thus to what extent he is following the same intellectual route. For, to take the first question, there is a thin but determined strand of ethnographical enquiry (or material) visible in the medical discussions beyond *Airs, Waters, Places*. *Airs, Waters, Places* is familiar with its theory about climate affecting health, and its attempt to link climate with ethnic character; but it is not alone. Ethnographic material is important for Herodotus' contemporaries and near contemporaries interested in nature and health. We may wonder why and where medical writers in particular turn to ethnography. What questions or preoccupations prompted them to do so, and where does this 'medical' ethnography belong in fifth-century medical or physiological enquiries? It is also important to remember that the *physiologoi* may have had some interest in non-Greek peoples: certainly they almost all discussed the causes of the Nile's unusual summer flooding, though that is admittedly a meteorological puzzle, not one of human nature. Democritus spoke of peoples and places beyond the Greek world.

Secondly, there are striking respects in which Herodotus' ethnographic descriptions intersect with medical writings, and the implications are suggestive. As we shall see, some cases can fall under the title of ethnography of health again. In others we are drawn away from health as such and find important similarities between Herodotus and medical writers where what is at issue is the polar grid of the hot and the cold, the wet and the dry, a grid which the medical work used but which may have its roots (also) in the speculations of the natural philosophers, and which would surely not have been unfamiliar to a natural philosopher.

The issues and questions involved are very complex, and worth pursuing precisely for that reason. For we are able to get away from the usual and simple comparison of the *Histories* with *Airs* – it is clear, as we will see, that *Airs* was only one treatise which reflected a wider and deeper interest in a use of ethnographic material on the part of a few medical writers.[27] Study of *Airs* and Herodotus is often, in any case, bedevilled by ideas, often going round in circles, that data on foreign peoples either moved from Herodotus to *Airs*, or from *Airs* to Herodotus, depending on one's attitude to either, or that they must both have a common source, usually named as Hecataeus.[28] But this does not account for the evidence we actually have. There must have been much other information and pseudo-information about foreign peoples available to Herodotus and medical writers, both written and unwritten. Heinimann suggested long ago that there was a rich ethnographic and medical literature already in existence,[29] but he did not pursue this and ended up suggesting that Hecataeus was Herodotus' source.[30] As for other information, there were Greek colonists strung around the Mediterranean, along the Libyan coast beyond Cyrene and into the West, and into the Black Sea where Miletus had sent numerous colonies.[31] Not only had Hecataeus long ago written his *Periodos Ges* in the form of a voyage around the Mediterranean, but

---

[27] For concentration on Herodotus and *Airs* for picture of fifth-century ethnography, cf. K. Müller's handbook (1972), which mainly follows Jacoby; Trudinger (1918); Georges (1994). Byl (1995) focuses on geographical names and familiarity in the Hippocratic Corpus (remarking that it is roughly similar to Herodotus', p. 228).

[28] On the various theories (e.g. Pohlenz, Nestle), see now Jouanna's excellent survey in his edition and commentary on *Airs*, pp. 79–82. Jacoby and Heinimann tend to see Hecataeus as a source (e.g. Heinimann (1945), 177, who noted the slightly polemical tone of Hdt. II 77.3 (ἐμοὶ δοκέειν), but seemed to think the polemic was simply internal to the text).

[29] He also pointed out that the disagreement over priority of either *Airs* or Herodotus 'is symptomatic of a method which wishes to establish a priority of thought from the desire for secure chronological clues . . .' (1945, 173); cf. A. Lloyd (1975), also, on the wealth of other information: Introduction, p. 134.

[30] E.g. Heinimann (1945), 179–80. Cf. Jouanna's new edition of *Airs* (pp. 54–71, esp. 59f.) for clear implications of *Airs* and Herodotus that there were other sources.

[31] Hellanikos, younger contemporary of Herodotus, also wrote an *Aigyptiaka* and *Scythiaka* (*FGrH* 4, F53–5, 64–5) as well as a *Persika*. For Greek knowledge of geography, recent archaeological evidence is most illuminating, showing now an extensive network of traders, travellers, colonists, other forms of exchange, across the Mediterranean and into the Black Sea: Boardman (1980) and Descoeudres (1990); note also the lead letters from merchants in the Black Sea, e.g. Bravo (1974); and Sherk (1992), 235–6, Graf (1974), on Olbia; Graham (1982), 122–30.

slaves from the more 'barbarous' areas actually inhabited the Greek world and some of the most common were Phrygians, Thracians, Scythians and Carians.

If there was far more interest in ethnographic material in this period, and we have access to some of it, then there are some exciting implications. It means we may approach the subject of ethnography, and of Greek attitudes to other peoples, from a rather different angle from recent discussions which have tended to stress, rather, the Greek use of the foreign, 'the other', to contrast with and emphasize their own qualities, a xenophobic discourse which loved to see non-Greeks as weak and inferior. It is in the medical writers that we see ethnographical material used by those interested in the nature of the world, in *physis* and in the truth about the world. They thus raise questions about the role of ethnography in the search for knowledge about nature and the nature of man. What do we do when we find intersections between this and Herodotus' ethnography? It is particularly in his descriptions of non-Greek peoples that one may suspect that Greek preoccupations and obsessions have moulded the material, informed his observations. It has been claimed influentially, for instance, that he virtually created his observations of other peoples via a 'rhetoric of inversion', that is, creating an inverted image of 'the other' from Greek customs.[32] Certainly he looked on with the eyes of a Greek observer, intrigued by those elements which ran counter to Greek experience – and it is hard to see how he could do anything else. So certain Greek ideas of normality may have coloured his account. But what *kind* of ideas or preoccupations may have guided these interpretations? The possibilities are usually left very general.[33] I argue here that his ethnography bears the stamp not simply of Greek interests in general, but that they are informed by certain ideas, theories and lines of thought visible also in the medical writers and enquirers into nature. The ideas via which the non-Greek world is observed are considerably wider than is often suspected – not to mention that the criteria for what is considered credible may also be judged accordingly.[34] We are not necessarily dealing with 'sources' in the traditional sense of written, literary sources, but with a set of preoccupations, ways of seeing the ethnographic 'evidence' which seem driven in part by the methods and categories visible in some of the medical treatments of ethnography. The ethnography of health is concerned with *physis* and sameness, general human characteristics and processes of

---

[32] Hartog (1988); Cartledge (1993).

[33] See esp. Gould (1989) and Redfield (1985); also A. Lloyd (1975), Introduction, on 'intellectual affinities'.

[34] Cf. however, Fehling's remark to the opposite effect: (1989), 97.

human health and disease, rather than with ethnic difference for its own sake. This seems very different from the clichés about barbarians which we find, for instance, in much Athenian literature.[35] In the medical works and natural philosophy, the barbarian peoples brought into play are seen as part of a grand schema which assumes the sharing of a common nature, rather than the gulf between Greeks and others.

Controversy

In Herodotus we see not only data, *logoi*, which relate somehow to medicine or health, but evidence that, in some places, he was engaging in some sort of controversy or debate on the matter of health, and that in some important respects, his ethnography has taken over, or shares, some of the same structures and interests.

We looked briefly at the medical controversy in miniature visible in Herodotus' remarks on Egyptian health (II 77), where two conflicting views about the cause of disease are presented. Whether or not the Egyptians really believed that disease was caused by food, it was striking that Herodotus gave us first a theory which was held by certain Greek doctors, and then his own affirmation that the seasons were really the cause, a view which accorded exactly with a prominent Hippocratic theory. Moreover, his presentation of Egyptian health was couched in terms of conflicting views.

Similarly with the good health of the Libyans. We seem to have a hint here of a controversy lying just below the surface of Herodotus' text. For he was insistent on the matter of their excellent health (IV 187): 'And it is because of this [i.e. cauterization] that they say they are the healthiest. For the Libyans are truly (ὡς ἀληθέως) the most healthy of all the people we know; whether it is because of this, I cannot exactly say, but they are indeed the healthiest.' Then there was the life-saving remedy of goats' urine in case of spasms. Why was he so keen on Libyan health? He insists that it is his own view that they are indeed the healthiest, that it is the real truth; the manner in which he admits some kind of doubt as to the *exact* contribution of cauterization to this healthiness, only serves to strengthen his insistence on their superb health.[36]

The main reason for his emphasis, I would suggest, is not simply that it

---

[35] See esp. E. Hall (1989); Saïd (1991); Diller (1962); also Fondation Hardt vol. xxxv on *Hérodote et les peuples non-grecs* (1990); Nippel (1990).

[36] For Libya, see A. Lloyd (1990), 239–42; discussion, 245–53 (cf. p. 253: 'finally, there was also a literary tradition of some antiquity culminating in Hecataeus on which Herodotus drew'); Pritchett (1993), 254 ff.; – neither of whom note Hippocratic interest in Libya; also Corcella's commentary (1994); Gsell (1915).

is his own discovery, but that Libyan health was discussed by others, and that the reasons for their health were a matter of debate. In fact Libyan health crops up in the treatise *On the Sacred Disease*, with a hint, though surely ironic, at exactly the opposite verdict. In an ironic passage making fun of various quack remedies for epilepsy, avoidance of goat meat and goat skin is mentioned (ch. 2.35ff. J = 1.22 G): 'So', the author adds, 'I suppose that no Libyan dwelling in the interior can enjoy good health', since they are entirely dependent upon the goat. Why are Libyans singled out? The remark seems to imply that we all know, of course, that Libyans *are* healthy. Either the Libyans were agreed to have excellent health, or there was some medical opposition to the idea, and certainly controversy about the causes. But evidently their health was a matter of discussion in the Hippocratic circle. Again, then, in Herodotus, we seem to be glimpsing hints of a larger debate of the time about the health of the Libyans, and the causes of that health, a small section of which emerges briefly into the text of Herodotus, and which is signalled by Herodotus' insistent style at that point.

For Libyans crop up elsewhere in the early essays of the Corpus, including the well-known *Airs, Waters, Places*. *Prognostic* ch. 25 (II 190.1 L) insists, for instance, that the symptoms of the ailment in question would be 'the same in Libya, Delos and Scythia': the choice of places used to make the point that similar symptoms would be found universally is interesting. Delos houses the major Ionian cult of Delian Apollo and is a central focus of the Ionian world; Libya and Scythia were evidently areas of the world which belonged to any discussion involving the ethnography of health. In *Diseases IV*, the author mentions almost casually a certain Libyan practice to underline his point about the toughness of the stomach: 'Indeed the Libyans, or most of them, use the hides of their domestic animals as garments, and their stomachs as sacks: the stomach is a strong thing' (ch. 56.4 J). Libya also featured in *Airs, Waters, Places*, though there is unfortunately no detail left (ch. 13.1 D; 12.7 J); there was also a comparison, mostly lost, of Scythia and Egypt, and the second half of the essay tries to use these main areas to connect ethnic character with climate.

In other words certain major barbarian peoples seem to have featured in medical discussion in the late fifth century: 'Libya' – meaning north Africa, but not Ethiopia – was prominent, along with Scythia and Egypt. We will return to this striking selection again (chapter 3). The Hippocratics concentrate upon certain areas, omitting many others. Why? It is striking that Herodotus also looks at exactly the same areas in some depth. Who is borrowing from whom? What are the aims here? Let us concentrate more closely on Libya and Scythia. We will see a further intertwining of Herodotean material and interests, and ideas that occur in the medical works.

Libya and the humours

Libya offers an extreme example of two of the four favourite opposites used by natural philosophy and medicine: the hot and the dry, as opposed to the cold and the wet. It may also bear some relation to one or other theory about the humours, theories about the constituents of the body. These constituents had to be in balance for health, and they were thought variously by different medical writers, to consist of phlegm, blood, yellow bile and black bile (*Nature of Man*); or fire (which is hot and dry) and water (cold and wet) as in *Regimen*; or the hot, cold, wet and dry, the theory attacked by *Ancient Medicine*; or the 'powers' suggested instead by the same author, which included salt and bitter, sweet and acid, astringent and insipid (*Anc.Med.* ch. 14). The humours advanced by *On the Nature of Man* are characterized by their relation to the hot/cold spectrum – for example phlegm is very cold – and the balance is affected by the successive seasons which cause, by their similarity, one or other humour to become dominant (ch. 7). Humours may also be affected, as we will see, by the land and climate. The medical vision seems to include Libya, and it seems to put it within this general polarized grid.

We recall that Libya attracted some discussion in *Airs, Waters, Places*, but that the Libyan section itself was lost. However, a curious and suggestive discussion of Libya also occurs in the work *On Regimen*, which may possibly fill in some more of the background of this medical ethnography and even what is missing from *Airs*. Its second book (starting ch. 37) turns to the situation and nature of various districts, which a doctor must understand. There are obvious similarities in the approach of the author of *Airs, Waters, Places* (to which we return), but here in *Regimen* we have the advantage of an analysis of Libya still remaining in the preserved text. Indeed it is striking that Libya is mentioned almost immediately, and as the extreme example of the hot and dry country:

The way to discern the situation and nature (θέσιν καὶ φύσιν) of various districts is as follows. The southern countries are hotter and drier than those lying towards the north, because they are closer to the sun. The races (ἔθνεα) of men and plants (τὰ φυόμενα) in these countries are of necessity drier and hotter and stronger than those in the opposite areas. For instance, compare the Libyan *ethnos* with the Pontic one, and also the peoples nearest to each other. (*Regimen* ch. 37.1 J)

So Libya and the Pontus region are opposites again, as we found hinted at in *Prognostic* (above, page 46), and Libya is being used as the extreme example of the very hot and very dry.[37] The claim of dryness, heat and strength corresponds so exactly to what is said in the surviving parts of *Airs* about the Scythians, that one may be able to guess that this picture of the strong, dry Libyans was not dissimilar to that of *Airs* which has been lost.[38] The ethnography remaining in *Airs* had much to say on the extreme dampness of the Scythians, and the various effects (including low fertility) that this had (chs. 18–22; cf.15). We seem to have a mirror image across the two works of a symmetrical world with symmetrical human characteristics: the wet flabby Scythians, rather effeminate, some of them even suffering from the female disease (though this also receives a more precise sociological explanation), and the dry, hot Libyans who are strong (note also that the Scythian–Egyptian antithesis visible in *Airs* is absent in *Regimen*). It was a frequent refrain in Hippocratic medicine that the female body was wet, the male dry and hot, and the same principle seems to have been applied to ethnic character and climate.

However, it is not necessary to suggest that this section in *Regimen* corresponded in any sense to the lost sections in *Airs* to find in it important further evidence of medical discussion of Libya. The dating of *Regimen* may be somewhat later; it is usually dated to the end of the fifth century or first half of the fourth.[39] But that does not diminish the interest of its ethnography: there seem to be surprising correspondences with Herodotus, and these may be the result of a common approach to ethnography, or other earlier medical works, but they seem at least to reflect a similar intellectual framework. Herodotus' insistence that the health of the Libyans was indeed the best of all may be related to this idea in *Regimen* of hot, dry Libyans, and we recall that Herodotus had mentioned the practice of cauterization to stop the phlegm descending from the head, which, given that phlegm is cold and wet, could only help dry them out and heat them up further.[40] The insistence of *Regimen* on the strength of the Libyans seems related to the idea that they were dry and very hot. Perhaps it was against – or alongside – such ideas that Herodotus wanted to stress that cauterization might be a factor in their health.

There seem, then, to be just visible lines of correspondence between the

---

[37] This adjective, 'Pontic', is the only occurrence of Pontus as such in the Hippocratic Corpus; 'Pontic' also used of some kind of nut bearing tree, κάρυα, for an ingredient at *Mul.* II 208, VIII 402.20 L.

[38] At least this is more plausible than some of the more extreme speculations made by some modern scholars. See ch. 3, n. 31 for some illegitimate (and ethnocentric) reconstructions of sections on Egypt and Libya: esp. Backhaus (1976); cf. Lévy (1981), 66, on the author's supposed 'condemnation of extremes'.

[39] As Jouanna (1992); for Joly, see n. 41 below.

[40] Note the Scythians in *Airs* had tried to dry themselves out by cauterization; thus cauterization is important in both authors.

picture of *Airs* and that of *Regimen* ch. 37, and indications of a complex of ideas not fully represented in the texts we now have.[41] There are also further indications of a debate that may have lain under the surface of Herodotus' keenness on Libyan health, a debate to which he could add a contribution.

The interrelationships of all these ideas emerge further from the remarks a little later in *Regimen*, on the nature and power of winds in Libya (ch. 38). Winds in general, the author says, differ according to the places through which they blow, though all winds have a cooling and moistening nature. The winds from the south get dried up by the sun:[42]

Therefore in the nearest countries it must import such a hot and dry quality (δύναμις), as it does in Libya. For there it parches the plants (τὰ φυόμενα) and insensibly dries up the human inhabitants (καὶ τοὺς ἀνθρώπους λανθάνει ἀποξη-ραίνων). For it cannot get ἰκμάς from the sea, nor from any river, and so it drinks up the moisture from the living animals and from the plants. (ch. 38.4 J)

So the south wind in Libya has passed over no sea or river, as it would have if it had crossed the Mediterranean (thus becoming hot and wet); therefore the plants and inhabitants become dried up.[43]

The presence of the expression *ikmas* (ἰκμάς) is interesting here, and especially in conjunction with a description of Libya. This may enable us to disentangle a further complex of ideas in this medical ethnography. *Ikmas*, meaning some sort of moisture, had a use in Greek before this period,[44] but it seems to acquire a technical or semi-technical sense in the medical works. For instance the author of *Diseases IV* talks of plants which will only grow in one place and no other. The author has just re-

---

[41] On links between *Airs* and *Regimen* see Joly (1960), 93–6, on chs. 37 and 38; and bibl. there, esp. Pohlenz (1938); Edelstein (1931). Joly thought *Regimen* after *Airs* but mentally often 'of an earlier age', i.e. the age of the *physiologoi*; he argues against a simple dependence of *Regimen* on *Airs* on the grounds that *Regimen* recalls more the *a priori* ideas of the Presocratics, who did discuss geography, and (for Joly) *Airs* reacted to that; also on grounds of style and method. Cf. also Joly on *Regimen*, CMG I 2.4 (1984), 262 f. Jouanna's edition of *Airs* (1996, 77–9) has brief comparison, esp. on winds; cf. Joly (1960), 95 also, on winds.

[42] However, he seems to think things get colder again further south, later in ch. 38. This perhaps indicates an idea of a global world, possibly from Anaxagoras: Joly (1960), esp. 95.

[43] Note however, that the earlier discussion in *Regimen* was simply about lands to the south, not the wind. Cf. the negative attitude of *Sacr. Dis.* to the south wind (ch. 16): for it would make things 'dull instead of bright, hot instead of cold, wet instead of dry', even moistening the brain; the north wind – with opposite effects – was the healthiest. Herodotus' whole discussion of the Nile Flooding (II 24–7) also involves Libya and what happens when the sun passes near it.

[44] Homer, *Iliad* XVII.392, used of oily leather; also Aeschylus frag. 229 Radt (Sisyphus): καὶ θανόντων, οἷσιν οὐκ ἔνεστ' ἰκμάς (Radt's reading) – where *ikmas* is apparently the liquid content which distinguishes the living from the dead.

marked on the good situation of both Ionia and the Peloponnese, and the general context is a discussion of growth and nutrition, on how humans drew the four humours from their food and drink, and then (ch. 34), how plants in the earth drew from the earth the humour they needed (with like attracting like), 'so that each plant draws from the earth nutriment (τροφήν) such as the plant itself is' (Lonie's transl.):

One cannot grow silphium, though many have tried, either in Ionia or in the Peloponnese, but it grows in Libya by itself (αὐτόματον). For neither in Ionia nor in the Peloponnese is there the kind of *ikmas* to nourish it. (ch. 34.3)[45]

Ikmas here cannot merely mean 'moisture', in the sense of water, for it is not moisture alone which is the difference at issue between the plant-growing capacities of Libya, Ionia and the Peloponnese; the author qualifies it with 'this kind of *ikmas*'. As the author put it just before, 'A plant will not even begin to sprout, if it does not have its natural humour (*ikmas*). Ionia and the Peloponnese are very well situated in relation to the sun and the seasons, and the sunshine is quite sufficient there for the plants' (ch. 34.2 J). So *ikmas* here denotes some kind of nutrient-giving moisture, perhaps as Lonie and Joly have taken it, a 'humour' – a humour to nourish the plant (as above, ch. 34.3). The four humours in man were also ἰκμάδες; plants drew humours from the soil, and plants provide a model for the human body also.[46] Two main senses of *ikmas*, partly overlapping, are distinguished by Lonie: (a) 'moisture present in sub-stances, usually organic, which is not necessarily apparent but may be-come so by being exuded or drawn out'; and (b) 'moisture regarded especially as nutriment'. In other words, it may not necessarily be as technical as the translation 'humour' implies, perhaps rather, sometimes, some kind of special juice or moisture.[47] At least, however, the question of nutriment, which might involve humours, was linked to the question of what plants grew where, and thus their geographical distribution.

So geography is again being brought in to wider discussions about the nature of growth, and Libya with its monopoly on silphium, serves as an outstanding example of the importance of *ikmas* or 'humour'. Lands have *ikmas*, as well as humans. All our discussions involve Libya: for the author of *Diseases IV*, only Libya had the right *ikmas* for silphium; for

[45] ἐν δὲ τῇ Λιβύῃ αὐτόματον φύεται· οὐ γὰρ ἔστιν ἐν τῇ Ἰωνίῃ οὐδὲ ἐν Πελοποννήσῳ ἱκμὰς τοιαύτη ὥστε τρέφειν αὐτό (ch. 34.3 J).

[46] Cf. *Nat. Child* ch. 27 on *ikmas* for plants compared with that for children; cf. also *Nat. Child* ch. 22.1–2; formation of plants, chs. 22–7, with Lonie (1981), 211–16; cf. pp. 260–6 on the four humours in *Gen./Nat. Child/Dis. IV*, and related texts. *Nat. Man* 6.3 J has a less developed analogy with plants.

[47] Lonie (1981), 269f. Here I am indebted to the comments of G. E. R. Lloyd.

the author of *Regimen II*, the land of Libya is the driest and hottest because of the nearness of the sun and, as he says later, the south wind draws out the ἰκμάς from living animals and plants, since it cannot draw it from sea or rivers.

This is where we should return to Herodotus. He provided 'the earliest recorded use' of Lonie's second sense of *ikmas*,[48] and this example also, curiously, occurs in a description of Libya. Speaking of the furthest reaches of Libya, where the houses are made of salt, and there is no rain at all, he adds (Hdt. IV 185.3):

Beyond this ridge, the area toward the south and into the interior of Libya, the land is desert (*eremos*), without water, without animals, without rain, and without trees (καὶ ἄνυδρος καὶ ἄθηρος καὶ ἄνομβρος καὶ ἄξυλός), and there is no *ikmas* in it (καὶ ἰκμάδος ἐστὶ ἐν αὐτῇ οὐδέν).

So in the desert part of Libya there is no *ikmas* at all: he is hardly commenting merely that there was no water, indeed he has just said Libya was waterless – *ikmas* is something more. This is some more valuable type of moisture which gives life and nutrition. While it might take little insight for Herodotus to note the excessive dryness of Libya, the peculiar combination of the technical term *ikmas* with a discussion of Libyan dryness seems more than coincidental. It is also worth noting here how Herodotus mentions several times, at scattered intervals, plants that are wild or which grow 'spontaneously' (αὐτόματος) – showing an interest in the natural distribution of plants, which as we saw in *Diseases IV*, could be a topic closely allied to the issue of special juices necessary for growth (see chapter 5, p. 153).

Herodotus sees *ikmas* in humans also. For in the gruesome tale of Polycrates' death by hanging (III 125.4), the daughter's dream is fulfilled: Polycrates' body is washed by Zeus, and 'anointed by the sun by losing its *ikmas* from the body' (ἐχρίετο δὲ ὑπὸ τοῦ ἡλίου ἀνιεὶς αὐτὸς ἐκ τοῦ σώματος ἰκμάδα). He seems to mean some more important substance than mere moisture, though Polycrates is admittedly dead, and in the context the process envisaged seems similar to that of the south wind in Libya drawing up *ikmas* from living animals and plants. In *Airs* also, the author talks of the sun being able to draw out a specific part of *ikmas*, 'the thinnest and lightest part of the *ikmas*' even from men.[49]

A further twist to all this, however, is that *ikmas* is not an exclusively

---

[48] Lonie (1981), 263; Powell (*Lexicon*, 1938) interpreted *ikmas* in Herodotus simply as moisture.

[49] *Airs* 8.4 J: καὶ ἐκ αὐτῶν τῶν ἀνθρώπων ἄγει τὸ λεπτότατον τῆς ἰκμάδος καὶ κουφότατον. There follows the proof, the man sweating under the cloak, where the sun is drawing up the sweat. Lonie assumes (1981, 270) *ikmas* means sweat here.

medical term, and it should at least be mentioned that there is strong overlap and interaction between medical writers and fifth-century *physiologoi*, particularly in the subject of generation. The biologically important idea of *ikmas* probably had a wider currency in the period. *Ikmas* was a fashionable enough concept to be parodied in Aristophanes' *Clouds*, where Socrates talks of 'the *ikmas* of the mind' (τὴν ἰκμάδα τῆς φροντί-δος): probably a parody of Diogenes of Apollonia, who was very fond of the concept.[50] Commentators on *Gener./Nat. Child/Diseases IV* have suggested that the medical author's discussion shows some relation to or influence of Diogenes, especially in the realm of botany and in particular in the common concept of *ikmas* being 'pulled up' (with ἕλκειν) that we find in *Diseases IV*, ch. 34.[51] Democritus too may have talked of *ikmas* in connection with the growth of horns, as he also discussed silphium.[52] But amidst these inconclusive and fragmentary sources, we may note that no modern discussions really take into account the Herodotean (and non-fragmentary) evidence, or focus upon the specifically geographical complexion of the treatments in the medical writings and Herodotus, where *ikmas* in a particular area of the world is at stake. This serves, perhaps, to draw together Herodotus and the Hippocratic works. Herodotus' careful noting of Libya's lack of the life-giving moisture, or of plants which grow spontaneously only in certain places, may have a central place in the controversies and discussions of the latter part of the fifth century.

Several points seem, then, to be emerging. We have a series of remarks which imply that Herodotus seems to be using *ikmas* in the semi-technical sense visible in the Hippocratic corpus, as 'humour' or nutrient moisture. It is also striking that exactly the same processes are deduced for the human inhabitants as for the land – certainly in the medical writers, and very possibly in Herodotus (the Polycrates tale). It seems probable that for all of these writers, humans have *ikmas* as well as land and plants, and that the processes are deduced as analogous. Moreover, the subject of Libya seems to focus the attention on the presence or absence of *ikmas*,

[50] *Clouds*, 233; also 236: see Dover's note, Commentary on *Clouds*, ad loc. In the doxographical tradition on Diogenes, the word *ikmas* appears three times; according to Theophrastus, he thought it hampered the intellect: DK 64, A 19 (DK II p. 56, line 14) (Theophrastus); A 18 (Nile connection), A 33.

[51] Joly stresses (Budé edn, p. 22) that *Dis. IV*, ch. 34 esp. is influenced by Diogenes: he suggests also that Diogenes uses in a 'façon privilégiée' the words *ikmas* and ἕλκειν, like the Hippocratic author. But cf. also Lonie, Commentary pp. 263 ff., on possible relations to Empedocles, Anaxagoras or Democritus: essentially inconclusive, he prefers a 'network' with preference for Democritus as the source.

[52] DK 68, A 153, 155; silphium: A 99a.

the life-giving nutrient, the mysterious type of humour which Libya but nowhere else could provide for silphium but which was dried out from humans and plants by the south wind there, and which (finally) was completely absent according to Herodotus, in the desert area of Libya. All these remarks (in Herodotus and medical writers) seem to converge; they seem to belong to the same milieu, the same intellectual framework, and to imply the same problems. It is tempting to think – though this is pure speculation – that Libya served in the medical (and possibly physiological) discussions on humours, growth and generation, as an extreme case study, an example for the action or effect of 'humour', given that it could provide both silphium and also at its extremes an almost total absence of any moisture at all. Its status as an extreme, even perhaps as 'a wonder', lent it special status in the enquiries into nature.[53]

Herodotus' image of Libya is not confined to its hot dryness, and further hints of physiological ideas emerge. The excessive dryness of Libya is stressed repeatedly, it is true. Even ethnographic observations and anecdotes in Herodotus convey this: the Psylloi disappeared when they foolishly decided to march against the south wind which had dried up all their reservoirs (IV 173; possibly connected with the character of Libya as bare, ψιλῆς:175.2); the Atarantes curse the sun because it burns up the people and the country (184.2). But Herodotus also gives us careful observations about the land of Libya, the inhabitants, life-style, and the kind of cultivation and wildlife that is supported in the great catalogue of Libyan wildlife, where Libya is clearly regarded as able to support an immense variety of wild animals (191). His emphasis on the huge variety of types of animals in Libya, represented by the great 'catalogue' of animals, may be following the same line of thought visible much later in Aristotle's references to the 'polymorphous' nature of Libyan animals and the tantalizing mutilated reference to 'polymorpha' in connection with Libya in *Airs*.[54] In his Scythian *logos*, Herodotus contrasted the effect of Scythian cold on animal growth unfavourably with the heat of Libya (IV 29–30), and emphasized that horns did not grow in Scythia because of the cold. Egypt

---

[53] It is thus illegitimate to assume with Jacoby (followed by Heinimann (1945), Appendix, on IV 187) that all this comes from Hecataeus. Note also that the place names attested as clearly coming from Hecataeus (and most fragments *are* names) bear remarkably little relation to those which occur in Herodotus' account of Libya – an important methodological point. With so little correspondence between Herodotus and the *securely* attested Hecataean fragments, I doubt one can assume a close, cosy correspondence with the lost parts. Trenchant and plausible remarks in Erbse (1992), esp. 172–3, against much use of Hecataeus by Herodotus.

[54] Arist. *Hist. Anim.* VII (VIII) ch. 28, 606b; *Airs* ch. 12.7 J.

does not abound in wild animals, he says, 'even though it is next to Libya' (II 65.2). It is interesting that he sees Libya and Scythia – as opposed to other pairs – as climatic opposites; they are part of a climatic grid.[55] The implication is that he was used to seeing the heat of Libya in a more complicated manner than simply as something that burned everything up: heat had a beneficial effect on growth after all (see chapter 5, pp. 150–2 for further discussion of horns). In other words, we are told a great deal about the natural resources of Libya, its heat, climate, fertility, animals, and we are told in a way which continues the image of Libya as very hot and dry in a manner reminiscent of the scientific or medical writers.[56] Herodotus' detailed enquiries into Libyan geography go far beyond popular clichés.

We find a circuit of ideas, then, which have fascinating implications: Libya, seen as very hot and dry, raised the question of *ikmas* and why certain plants could grow there but nowhere else. Libyan health (and reasons for that health) was an issue in the midst of the medical works; whether or not some of these ideas derived ultimately from other writers, it is reasonably clear that Libya and its ethnography (however heavily selective) were of importance. This may be why Herodotus devoted a long section to an account of Libya; not merely because Hecataeus dealt with it, but because it was of contemporary concern to those seeking an understanding of *physis*.[57] Herodotus' text seems to fit into this same mesh, with its complex of data and ideas on Libyan health, Libyan heat, *ikmas*, climate and the proliferation of animal types, and the contrasts between Libya and Scythia, the hot and dry versus the cold and wet. His section on Libya should be seen as a contribution to the discussions on nature by contemporaries interested in nature and the nature of man.

Scythia

Scythia has received more attention from those interested in Herodotean or in medical ethnography. Scythia does after all receive the bulk of the surviving ethnographical descriptions in *Airs, Waters, Places*, and it already had a role in earlier Greek literature and society, which ranged

---

[55] See good analysis of comparisons between Libya and Scythia in Erbse (1992), 171 ff. (though he does not apparently note this climatic grid).

[56] The quality of the soil is compared unfavourably with that of 'Europe' and 'Asia', with the single exception of the Cinyps region (IV 198–9), a broad generalization similar to the grand comparisons between Asia, Europe and Libya in some of the medical writings.

[57] Cf. A. Lloyd (1990), 252: 'Libyans interested him as quintessentially βάρβαροι, i.e. they were, in so many respects, different from Greeks.'

from the idealizing to the practical.[58] Homer mentioned 'the noble Hippemolgoi' or 'horsemilkers', but not Scythians as such, Hesiod mentioned 'horsemilking Scythians',[59] and the Greek idea of Scythian justice or wisdom was personified in the Scythian sage Anacharsis. He reappears in Herodotus and seems to constitute one of the main reasons why Herodotus exempts the Scythians from his devastating claim that the inhabitants of the Pontic region are the least wise of all men (IV 46.1: 'within the Pontos').[60] The Scythians managed like the Greeks to repel the Persians, a quality hinted at in the *Eumenides* (700–3) where Athena boasts of founding an institution for Athens to guard the city such as no other men have, 'neither the Scythians nor the Peloponnesians'.[61]

On the other hand, Scythians were notorious among Greeks for drinking pure wine, hence the expression, as Herodotus explains, for 'taking wine Scythian style', ἐπισκύθισον (Hdt. VI 84.3), though whether or not this was thought to have the same effect on the Scythians as the Spartans thought it had had on Cleomenes (madness: VI 84) is unclear. Herodotus may have been correcting current idealization when he declared that they only had one admirable thing, namely, their method of dealing with aggressors (IV 46.2). The Scythians were free, to a large extent nomadic, and the anti-type of the polis;[62] 'the Greeks furnish an absent model', in Lateiner's felicitous phrase.[63] The expedition of Darius and Scythian resistance in Herodotus prefigured in many ways the Athenians' resistance to Xerxes, as has often been noted,[64] though it must be admitted that the most striking similarities, apart from the Scythians' attempt to rouse re-

---

[58] See Lévy (1981), and bibl. there; Hartog (1988) above all on Herodotus; Lateiner (1989), 155–7; E. Hall (1989); Corcella (1994), Commentary, esp. pp. xii–xiv, which stresses extensive contacts between Greek and Scythia, *contra* Armayor. Recent discussion by Erbse (1992). For recent archaeological discoveries, see Rolle (1989); Rolle *et al.* (1991); Rudenko (1970); for Scythian funeral customs, Thordarson (1988). There is increasing knowledge about Greeks on the north coast of Black Sea: see e.g. Graham (1982), 122–30 on Pontus.

[59] *Iliad* XIII 3–7: the Mysians, noble Hippemolgoi and Abioi, 'most just of men'; Hesiod, *Cat. Women*, frag. 150 M–W, vv. 15–16.

[60] Cf. Hdt. IV 76–7, on Anacharsis, including his visit to Sparta. A possible earlier ref. in Pherecydes, *FGrH* 3, fr. 174 is of doubtful authenticity (West 1988, 210).

[61] Lévy (1981), 61: not a ref. to Scythian good government; matched by Herodotus' verdict (IV 46.2–47.1).

[62] Most extensively developed by Hartog (1988), who argues that they are to a large extent a creation in the mirror image of the Athenians.

[63] (1989), 157 (for Lateiner the ethnography is to explain why the Greeks defeated Persia, p. 146). For a longer analysis of the relation of the ethnography and geography to the historical events, see Erbse (1992), 157–79.

[64] See Immerwahr (1954), 24–6 on the crossing of the Hellespont; Legrand (1932); Saïd (1981); Hartog (1988), esp. ch. 2.

sistance among their neighbours, lie in the behaviour of the Persian king as he makes preparations and crosses the great division between the continents. Darius' idealization in the *Persae* against the figure of Xerxes seems to require the downplaying of Darius' own forays into Europe, first against the Scythians, then against the Athenians. It was the Scythian success, a success, moreover, that lay in Europe, that may be the reason why the image of Persian history given by Darius in the *Persae* had to omit the Scythian expedition.[65]

In ethnographic terms, Scythia in Herodotus is balanced in several ways by Egypt: its remarkable rivers set against the Nile, its situation 'opposite' Egypt, its status as youngest of nations, while Egyptians thought they were the oldest, and so on.[66] But modern discussions of the Greek 'image' of Scythia have tended to neglect the more obviously intellectual or scientific dimension in Scythia's role, the part Scythia plays in those enquiries that were more interested in physical, medical and physiological characteristics than in moral and intellectual attributes, and the fact that in many ways Scythia's natural opposite was Libya rather than Egypt.[67] Herodotus' account is relevant on this level too: there are obvious correspondences, for example, between Herodotus and *Airs* in their knowledge of the Scythian 'Female Disease', though *Airs* has much to say, while Herodotus refers to it as if it were well known.[68] The common subject matter in both authors of the Sauromatai, Amazons, and the Scythian nomadic lifestyle are familiar (*Airs* chs. 17–19). If Herodotus' vision is informed partly by general Greek views and prejudices about Scythia, the Greek cultural grid as Gould puts it, it seems also to be informed by certain Greek medical or physiological interests.

One enters here into a maze of enquiries into sources, debts and influences along the lines of conventional literary source criticism. The question of what role Scythia had, if any, in Greek 'science', is crucial. It might easily be assumed that any data on foreign peoples found in *Airs* (or other medical works) must have derived from Herodotus. More recent specialists in medicine who have noted the correspondences are sometimes reluctant to decide whether Herodotus was using the medical writings

[65] See Saïd (1981), 17–38; and *Persai* 759–86.
[66] See above all Hartog (1988), e.g. 17, 28 ff. on its climate; cf. Trüdinger (1918), 14–34 on the correspondences between the two *logoi*; Lateiner (1989), 155–7.
[67] E.g. Lévy's discussion (1981) of the Scythian 'mirage' concentrates on broad characteristics like 'savagery', and moral qualities, rather than the physical explanations that are equally important. Harmatta (1990), briefly on Scythians within general pattern of *oikoumene*; K. Müller (1972).
[68] On the Anarieis/Enarees, see p. 33 above. The practice of incision behind the ear, in *Airs* ch. 22.5 J crops up also in *Generation* 2.2: see Joly (1966), 209–10 on *Anarieis*.

directly or whether the medical writers used him, preferring a general idea of familiarity.[69] In any case Herodotus – and other Greeks – were in a position to find out about Scythians from elsewhere in Greece, even Athens.[70] If we agree that Herodotus is picking up and engaging in certain controversies visible also in Hippocratic works, then something more interesting and focused than mere familiarity is involved.

For instance a vivid and detailed description of the making of Scythian mare's cheese occurs in the work *On Generation/Nature of the Child/ Diseases IV* (ch. 51.2), where the author tries to explain the agitation of humours in the body, and it bears some resemblance to Herodotus' description of horse-milking at the start of his Scythian *logos* (IV 2). The very fact that this elaborate and technical description can be introduced at all as a parallel for the agitation of humours would suggest the knowledge of this technique was very much alive and well in the circle of the medical writers and their audiences of the latter part of the fifth century. We may also note, again, the connection between a discussion of humours and ethnography.

But we may go rather further. The treatise in which Scythian mare's milk occurs, *Diseases IV*, has been dated in the most recent study, on the grounds of style and argument, to the period of the Peloponnesian War.[71] The author discusses the way the disturbance of the humours and the heating of the fluid in the human body create disease (ch. 51.1). An immediate analogy is made with the Scythian treatment of mare's milk and the way the Scythians turn it into cheese, *hippake* (51.2), and there follows the close description of exactly what they do. The essential characteristic of the cheese-making is the dual movement of ingredients as they separate:

This condition is similar to what the Scythians do with mare's milk. They pour it into wooden bowls and agitate it; when it is agitated, it becomes foamy and separates; and the fatty part, which they call butter, being light is separated and rises to the surface, The heavy and thick portion settles downwards; they separate this off and dry it, and when it is coagulated and dry, they call it mare's milk cheese (*hippake*). The whey of the milk remains in the middle. (ch. 51.2: Lonie's transl.)

There is more detail in the Hippocratic author about the physical process of cheese-making, more attention in Herodotus to the slaves who prepare the milk (IV 2). Herodotus describes how the Scythians blind all their slaves, to use them in preparing their milk. The slaves put pipes into the genitalia of the animals, blowing into the tubes through the veins, thus forcing the udders down, while others are doing the milking:

---

[69] Cf. Althoff (1993a).   [70] As Asheri points out for the Thracians (1990).
[71] Lonie (1981).

Now the Scythians blind all their slaves, to use them in preparing their milk. The plan they follow is to thrust tubes made of bone, not unlike our musical pipes, up the vulva of the mare, and then to blow into the tubes with their mouths, some milking while the others blow. They say they do this because when the veins of the animal are full of air, the udder is forced down. The milk thus obtained is poured into deep wooden casks, about which the blind slaves are placed, and then the milk is stirred round. That which rises to the top is drawn off, and considered the best part; the under portion is of less account. Such is the reason why the Scythians blind all those they take in war; it arises from their not being tillers of the ground but a pastoral race. (IV 2)

The parallels in language and style were noted, for example by Lonie, but he takes it that 'the Scythian information in that work [*Dis. IV*], as in Herodotus, probably goes back to Hecataeus', following Heinimann.[72] This observation cannot survive close scrutiny.[73]

Firstly, we may note that Scythian mare's cheese makes other appearances, and it was obviously something of a curiosity. It is mentioned in a fragment of Aeschylus' *Prometheus Unbound*, for instance, as a characteristic of the Scythians, as well as later writers, and it makes a brief appearance in *Airs* itself, though *Airs* was clearly not a 'source'.[74] Scythian mare's milk seems to be regarded as a major peculiarity of the Scythians for anyone who happened to be interested in Scythia in the first place. It makes its appearance very early on indeed in Herodotus' own account of Scythia. The tribe of 'horsemilkers' are mentioned in the *Iliad*, after all. Knowledge about Scythian milking of mares by itself did not have to derive from Hecataeus.[75] Contact between Greeks, especially those of Ionia and the Black Sea, and Scythians, had been healthy since the seventh century, with numerous Milesian colonies, and no doubt exchange of slaves.[76]

As for the essay *Diseases IV*, this, then, is another medical work where ethnography makes an appearance, a further hint that ethnographic material was in some form part of the corpus of information, or possible information, possible exempla, available to medical thinkers. It is, after all, an extraordinary analogy to use if Scythia and Scythian practices were not part of their common parlance – as Lonie put it, 'The example is

---

[72] *Hippocratic Treatises*, pp. 339f., on ch. 51.2.
[73] Note Alan Griffiths' interesting analysis (forthcoming) of the slave element of this 'grim dairy tale' in terms of Greek story-telling – not incompatible with the analysis here.
[74] Aesch. fr. 198 N: ἀλλ' ἱππάκης βρωτῆρες εὔνομοι Σκύθαι; *Airs*, ch. 18.4 J: καὶ ἱππάκην τρώγουσι· τοῦτο δ' ἐστὶ τυρὸς ἵππων.
[75] Cf. *Iliad* XIII 5; Hesiod frag.150 M–W, 15; possibly mentioned by Hecataeus, *FGrH* 1, fr.185, but this is unclear. Cf. also for *hippake*: Theophrastus, *HP* 9. 13. 2; Pliny, *NH* 28. 131 (cf. 133–4) and 205. Lonie (1981, 339–40) thinks coincidences in language between *Diseases IV*, Herodotus, Pliny and Theopompus, suggest a common source.
[76] See remarks in Corcella (1994), Introduction to Commentary, xii–xiv.

rather recherché', even though it offered a particularly close analogy.[77] Scythian making of mare's cheese, the separating of substances in this precise instance, does not seem to be the most obvious way of illustrating a complex point about the disturbance of humours unless the example or at least the culture were part of the discussion about nature.

This by itself makes it unlikely that this piece of information – or any other information about Scythians – came straight from Hecataeus: even if Hecataeus had anything to say on this Scythian practice, the interest is clearly a live one. One may guess that with the author of *Airs* and Herodotus intent on examining Scythia, there was much more than merely antiquarian repetition of Hecataeus at work here.

But the relation to Herodotus is problematic. One might expect Herodotus to be the obvious source for the author of *Diseases IV*, but he cannot be: he does not even provide the name of *hippake*, he has much to say about the method of milking which does not occur in the medical writer, and less about the process of separation and making of the cheeses (though the process envisaged is clearly the same). We seem to be seeing in both these descriptions reflections of a practice which was currently known and discussed. Perhaps we can be more confident of the idea that Scythia was a subject fashionable in circles of medicine and enquiries into *physis*.

All of this fails, however, to deal with the puzzling and bizarre details that occur in Herodotus in the course of his description of how the blind slaves milk the horses by blowing through a tube made of bone put into the mare's genitals, 'some milking while others blow' (IV 2.1). Indeed he goes so far as to explain this practice:

φασὶ δὲ τοῦδε εἵνεκα τοῦτο ποιέειν· τὰς φλέβας τε πίμπλασθαι φυσωμένας τῆς ἵππου καὶ τὸ οὖθαρ κατίεσθαι.

They say they do it for the following reason: the veins (φλέβας) of the horse are filled with air (distended/puffed) and the udder is extended.

It is understandable why this passage, with its bizarre and untoward description, a method of milking which would amaze any dairy farmer, is usually passed over discreetly. We may wonder if this is yet another occasion where we are seeing in action some sort of assumption about air in the veins which may have some relation to a medically oriented Greek account – whether or not it corresponded to any Scythian practice.[78]

---

[77] Lonie (1981), 84. Lonie seems unhappy about a source in Hecataeus; cf. p. 339: 'There was obviously some description of its [*hippake*] manufacture current, apart from both the present passage and Herodotus 4, 2.'

[78] Cf. note of Corcella, Commentary on IV 2.2 on possible modern milking parallels. This neglects the explanation given by Herodotus.

Phlebes recur again in Herodotus' statement about the causes of Libyan health (IV 187), and it is perhaps useful to note that in the medical writers, *phlebes* are not veins in the modern medical sense but can be thought to carry all sorts of substances through the body: indeed the author of *Diseases IV* itself continues with his description of the agitation and morbid humours ranging around the body, creating disease, and describes how 'the veins (*phlebes*) become overfilled (ὑπερπίμπλανται), and being exceedingly full they cannot release until they have enough space to do so' (ch. 51.8, Lonie's transl.).

This latter, medical, description of *phlebes* becoming full and unable to release their contents may be another indication of the kind of milieu and intellectual framework in which the curious 'Scythian' milking practices could make sense, although perhaps only to a Hippocratic doctor or someone familiar with the Hippocratic theory of veins. For amongst the elaborate network of veins and passages thought to exist in the human body and linking up specific organs – communication is a dominant function – there is a particular set for women mentioned by the author of *Nat. Child* which connect the womb and the breasts.[79] The author is trying to explain how it is that a mother's milk starts to appear when the embryo starts to move around: pressure is the answer, exerted on the womb by the growing child, and the veins between the breasts and the womb. The conclusion is inevitable that the milk which can reach the breasts can also reach the embryo in the womb:

A small quantity [of fatty substance, i.e. milk] goes to the womb as well, through the same vessels (φλέβια): for the same vessels and others similar to them extend alike to the breasts and the womb. When it arrives in the womb, it has the appearance of milk, and the embryo uses a small quantity; while the breasts are filled with it and swell (οἱ δὲ μαζοὶ δεχόμενοι τὸ γάλα αἴρονται πιμπλάμενοι). (21.4, Lonie's transl.)

Here we encounter not only the communication highway between breasts and womb, but the idea of pressure from the swollen breasts further affecting the womb, and even some of the same vocabulary that appeared in the strange tale about Scythian mare's milk.[80]

We may suspect, then, though it cannot of course be proved, that Herodotus' account belongs to some kind of physiological milieu which has an interest in ethnography; at the very least that the ethnography has been passed through a Hippocratic filter. He knows of the essential upwards and downwards motion which is so particular to the Hippocratic analogy,

---

[79] *Nat. Child* 21.4 J.
[80] Cf. also 21.5: these veins become wider when the child sucks. Lonie on 21.4 notes other Hippocratic refs.; cf. Appendix, pp. 87–97 on vascular system.

and the assumption about veins also suggests perhaps a medical milieu. It is an oddly medical or pseudo-scientific explanation for something so ordinary as milking, even milking a horse. To someone with Hippocratic inclinations or knowledge, however, the method might seem a startlingly sensible or 'scientific' way of approaching the business.

It was the Hippocratic account which relayed the details of the dairy products, including the name of the cheese (ἱππάκην, ὀρρὸς, βούτυρον), and which analysed the essential separation with the upward and downward movement. Herodotus knew of this, but devoted his attention to the process of milking itself with the peculiar feature of the tubes. Perhaps, then, what we are seeing are two sides of the same coin. The Hippocratic writer's use of Scythian ethnography seems to be part of a wider use of ethnography on the part of certain medical writers. Herodotus gives us another angle on the Scythian mare's milk, but reflects similar assumptions about the movement of matter in strikingly Hippocratic form, and perhaps shares some of the Hippocratic or medically-oriented information (or pseudo-information) about Scythians with those primarily pursuing questions about the nature of man.

If we combine the implications of this with the obviously extensive attention to Scythia given by the author of *Airs*, we seem to have indications of a steady level of knowledge – perhaps curiosity is a better word – about Scythia and Scythian customs, used in the medical treatises. The evidence is less strikingly varied or extensive than it is for Libya, and it does not cross so many works. *Airs* gives by far the most elaborate description, but the strand of Scythian ethnography in medical writing is wider than that by itself would suggest – the author of *Diseases IV* could hardly use a Scythian analogy for something so important as the humours, if ethnographic examples taken from Scythia were totally unfamiliar. The precise analogy for the humours is explained sufficiently to stand on its own, but why take such an elaborate analogy from Scythia in the first place?

The confidence with which these Hippocratic writers turned to Scythian customs may be unexpected, but it is underlined by the contrast with the appearance of those more exotically fabulous northern people, the Amazons, who appear once in the Corpus. The author of *On Joints* was discussing the dislocation of joints when he brought in as (apparently) a merely anecdotal detail, the Amazonian practice of dislocating the joints of their male children, so that once lamed, they did not plot against the women. But he is careful to distance himself,[81] introducing the example

---

[81] As Humphreys points out (1996): ethnographic anecdote replaced by systematic list, she suggests.

with a 'Some tell the story' (Μυθολογοῦσι δέ τινες), and declares that he does not know if this is true. In an expression strikingly reminiscent of Herodotean practice, he ends, nonetheless, 'I do not know if this is true' (Εἰ μὲν οὖν ἀληθέα ταῦτά ἐστιν, ἐγὼ μὲν οὐκ οἶδα). 'But', he continues, 'I do know that the following things would happen if you dislocated the limbs of children' (*On Joints* ch. 53; 4. 232, 7–13 L). The Amazons need careful distancing; the Scythians by contrast needed no such apology, or cautious distancing, or a marked return to true knowledge on physical–medical matters on the author's part. Scythian ethnography was part of scientific knowledge.

Other elements in Herodotus' Scythian *logos* may have a medical orientation. A distinctly medical tinge is imparted to the end of his section on the many Scythian rivers. For he points out that the grass in Scythia is the most productive of bile (ἐπιχολωτάτη) of 'all grasses that we know' (IV 58) – a startling hint of the kind of Herodotean comparison more familiar for human achievements than for grasses. This single appearance of bile (χολή), one of the four humours in *On the Nature of Man*, is given further emphasis by the addition of a very primitive test of the kind found frequently in medical writings. 'It is possible', Herodotus adds, 'to gauge (*stathmosasthai*) that this is the case by opening the bodies of the sheep.'[82] He claims not that he personally opened up any such beasts, but that the biliousness can be tested thus, and this remains one of the few explicit descriptions of some form of empirical test in fifth-century science – along with the optimistically interpreted 'experiment' with water derived from ice in *Airs*, or the tests devised in *Nature of Man*, and a few others.[83] It is also one of the very rare cases where dissection of any kind is actually envisaged; another occurs in *On the Sacred Disease*, where the author suggests in a similarly open-ended way, not committing himself to claiming that he actually did the test, that 'If you cut open the head' of a goat with epilepsy, you will find (εὑρήσεις) the brain to be full of fluid and evil-smelling.[84] Herodotus' claim that it may be gauged (*stathmosasthai*) may also be seen in connection with the fondness to prove, demonstrate (etc.), to which we return later, and which gives his text here an intellectual flavour of a distinct type.

---

[82] IV 58: ἀνοιγομένοισι δὲ τοῖσι κτήνεσι ἔστι σταθμώσασθαι ὅτι τοῦτο οὕτως ἔχει.

[83] These are not, of course, experiments in the modern scientific sense. The *Airs* e.g.: ch. 8, esp. 8.3f. J. See G. E. R. Lloyd (1966), 73–9; and (1979), ch. 3, esp. 146–69 on medicine, 149–50 on *Nat. Man*.

[84] *Sacr. Dis.* ch. 14.11–18 J (= 11.3 G): cited, along with Herodotus' example, by G. E. R. Lloyd (1979), 23–4, and n. 79, both as exceptional for the time; cf. 156 ff. generally for dissection.

Whether the case of Scythian grass was actually part of a specifically medical discussion is impossible to discern, as is whether a doctor was peering over Herodotus' shoulder as he announced this, or whether Herodotus' knowledge about Scythian grass derived from circles who pursued the origin of bile with more tenacity than he did. We recall that he gives a scientific explanation for the Ister's lack of flooding almost as full as his discussion of the Nile's unusual pattern (IV 50). One's suspicion grows that Herodotus' enquiries concerning Scythia were informed far more by – or filtered through – the eyes of someone interested in contemporary physiological and particularly medical theories than merely those of an observer looking for contrasts with Greek customs.

Finally, there is the matter of the beavers. The Boudinoi, autochthonous and nomadic, and not to be confused with the Gelonoi who were originally Greek, catch beavers, along with other 'square-faced animals' in a large lake (IV 108–9). The testicles of the beavers, Herodotus adds, 'are useful for the cure of the womb' (IV 109.2). What is astonishing here is that both product and use as described here correspond exactly with one element of Hippocratic pharmacology. For *kastorion*, or (as it was believed) testicles of beaver, was widely used as an aromatic substance in Hippocratic remedies, and it is invariably used for recipes in the treatises on female health or in the treatment of female patients. Thus the Hippocratic use of *kastorion* for problems of the womb seems to be replicated here in Herodotus' casual description of the Boudinoi. In a further twist, Herodotus is repeating the erroneous Greek belief about its provenance: in fact the substance came from the beavers' scent glands and one would think the Boudinoi, or whoever else collected the stuff to sell to Greek doctors, would know quite well that this was an error. But it was a colourful one, and a description which propels one to appreciate the factor of exoticism in much of this medically oriented ethnography (see further below, pp. 286–8). Herodotus implies that the Boudinoi themselves use the *kastorion* for curing uterine problems, but the conjunction with Greek (Hippocratic) practice is curious and provocative.

The damp and the cold: Scythia and its rivers

Scythia in *Airs, Waters, Places* was very cold and damp, and its inhabitants were also cold and damp. Along with the medical tinge to so much of Herodotus' extensive description of Scythia in Book IV, we may wonder to what extent *his* Scythia is characterized by the cold and the damp – and thus to what extent it forms the opposite of his picture of Libya; and to what extent the human inhabitants themselves are cold and damp, how far their health is affected. We move away here from the question of health itself, though dampness would probably have implications for health. The relation between habitat and inhabitants is a readily familiar question; links with medical theories on climate have been aired repeatedly, but discussion on Scythia has been either unfortunately brief, or somewhat general. Yet, as Lateiner has put it, 'Herodotus' description of Scythian culture shows a nuanced and consequential connection between habitat and habits (IV 16–24)'.[85] There is more still to be said about the intricacy of detail and analysis, and the way Herodotus sees this land as helpful to the Scythians. We find, however, that Scythia is indeed emphatically cold and wet, but that the inhabitants are not actually so deeply affected by this.

Scythia is meticulously described and subdivided by Herodotus, and much of the picture is grim. The furthest north, beset by feathers, is impossible to see or to cross (IV 7.3), and the far northern lands – for example, beyond the Issedones – are quite impossible to know about (16.1). There is desert (*eremos*) beyond the Neuroi (17.2), as one travels, apparently, north of Borysthenes along the river; there is *eremos* beyond the Scythians and above the Androphagoi (18.2) and another, beyond the Melanchlainoi and the *limnai* (20.2).[86] But he is careful to distinguish precise and different types of Scythians, who shade off into non-Scythian areas, or even *eremoi*.[87] We meet the Kallippidai who are 'Greek Scythians', Ἕλληνες Σκύθαι (17.1), and the Alizones who live like Scythians but grow corn, the Scythians who grow corn but sell it (17.2), the Scythian farmers who call themselves Olbiopolitai (18.1), the Scythian nomads (19), well to the east in a land which has no trees, the Royal Scythians who look on other Scythians as slaves (20.1), not to mention tribes like the Melanchlainoi who are carefully described as another non-Scythian

---

[85] Lateiner (1986), 16; also (1989), 155f. Cf. Hartog (1988), 28–30, on importance of Scythian climate in Herodotus. See also Erbse (1992), 160–6, who stresses how ethnography and geographical detail on Scythia provide historical enlightenment, as also for Libya (171–5); cf. Regenbogen (1930). Hartog mentions possible connection with Ionian science: e.g. pp. 356–9. For Lévy (1981), a specifically intellectualizing perspective only enters his discussion for the fourth-century writers. Note the difficulty of pinning down the Scythian *eremie*: this is not necessarily 'empty' or 'desert' for Herodotus or *Airs*: in Herodotus the land is only 'empty' until the Scythians inhabit it (IV 5.2, 8, 11), and there are bits of 'desert' within it. Cf. *Airs* 18.2 on 'the so-called Scythian *eremie*' (ἡ δὲ Σκυθέων ἐρημίη καλευμένη): not however 'desert', but moderately watered, ἔνυδρος μετρίως. Asheri (1990), 165–6 (in discussion) points out that ἔρημος χώρη (V 9.1) is not necessarily a desert but unexplored and inaccessible – with Edelmann (1970).

[86] Note that the *eremoi* are not systematic, nor the furthest part on a radial: you may have human habitation, then *eremia*, then more humans (e.g. IV 22.1). See previous note also.

[87] See Lévy (1981), 64–5 on this: though he stresses the nomadism as 'the true mode of Scythian life' for Herodotus (64); Corcella (1994), Introduction to Commentary, and (1992) on various Scythian types; Erbse (1992), 161–5 on *variety* of tribes.

tribe (20.2), or the Scythians who revolted from the Royal Scythians (22.3), now living well to the north.[88]

As for the land and climate, we are told that 'as far as' the land of the Scythians who had revolted, there is smooth plain with deep soil; and from there on, it is stony and rugged (23.1). But the whole area is diagnosed as very cold, literally 'very harsh in winter', δυσχείμερος (28.1), so cold that if you pour water you will not make mud, and the sea freezes. Indeed the winter is quite different from anywhere else (28.2). This great difference means that it barely rains in winter at all, yet in summer it rains constantly – a more realistic description, incidentally, than the grim one in *Airs* ch. 19. Obviously a Greek perspective – in which it is winter which is characterized by rain – this view seems to mark Scythia as not simply quite different from elsewhere in its winters, but as very cold and very wet (there are also details about thunder in winter and summer, and earthquakes). It is not quite correct to say that 'whatever is in the north happens because it is cold', or that its very severe winter effectively creates 'a confusion between the categories of the dry and the wet and equally between the liquid and the solid',[89] especially since the four categories are indeed here in Herodotus in different combinations. But Herodotus does stress the cold, going on to discuss which animals can bear it (28.4), and his theory about the cause of the hornless oxen of Scythia depends precisely upon the presence of the cold ('I think that it is because of this that the oxen do not have horns', 29). The 'feathers' he thinks, with some emphasis, would be snow falling ('the opinion I have about them', ch. 31.1).

However, the cold is not sufficient to 'explain' Scythia, or even very much of it, as Herodotus indicates quite clearly when he comes to sum up some of the main distinguishing features of the area (IV 46). The Scythian skill in dealing with the Persian invaders, it must be admitted, has nothing to do with the cold. On the contrary it is the nomadic lifestyle combined with presence of the rivers which lead to their greatest discovery.[90] The Scythians, he insists, have discovered one thing which is the greatest of all human achievements (*pragmata*) which we know, for they make it impossible for the invader to escape, 'while they themselves are entirely out of reach unless they wish to engage the invader' (IV 46.2). For, he then

---

[88] Corcella (1994), Introduction xii–xvi, suggests a polemic against Hecataeus' lazy treatment of them all as 'Scythians'. Cf. VII 50.4*, Xerxes' speech with hint about campaigns against pastoral peoples, probably Scythia.

[89] Hartog (1988), 28 and 29, respectively.

[90] He is dismissive about the Black Sea area in general, for the area is the most ignorant (ἀμαθέστατα) of all; they woefully lack any *sophie* or any ἄνδρα λόγιον, with the sole exception of the Scythian *ethnos* and the Scythian Anacharsis (IV 46.1).

goes on, they have neither cities nor walls, but carry their dwellings with them (φερέοικοι) and shoot from horseback, living not from agriculture but from their cattle (not entirely true of all Scythians), their wagons are their only houses; it is impossible to engage them.[91]

This picture seems exaggerated on Herodotus' part as we remember the Scythian farmers, but he links it immediately and very clearly to the geography, particularly the rivers (*not* the climate), 'the nature of the land is suitable for this, and the rivers are themselves allies' (IV 47), for the land is level, grassy and well-watered, and 'the rivers which run through it are almost equal in number to the canals of Egypt'. There follows the long description of all the rivers: we are left in no doubt that the greatest thing that the Scythians have, their security from invaders, is helped by their life-style, mode of agriculture, and lack of cities, and this is helped by this well-watered grassy land and the rivers themselves.[92]

The following description of the Scythian rivers (47–58) serves not simply as a comparison, implicit and explicit, of the Ister with the Nile, but also as an investigation and description of watery details and characteristics over the whole mass of Scythian rivers. The detail is extraordinary, with very many rivers, mostly named, frequently with variant names in both Scythian and Greek (e.g. 48.2, 49), rivers that are 'native' to Scythia, Scythian in origin (48.4: οὗτοι μὲν αὐθιγενέες Σκυθικοὶ ποταμοί), and the great Ister which flows through the whole of Europe. We are given an elaborate and complex comparison between the Nile and the Ister, in which the Ister's regularity through the year makes it far more impressive (50.1), and the explanation for why the Ister remains level through the year (50.1–4) involves the balancing and counterbalancing of the effects of snow, rain and sun in the different seasons, a meteorological balance being maintained.

But the Ister is only the greatest river of them all. There follows a catalogue of other rivers (51 ff.) – including such details as the taste and sweetness of one, the Hypanis (52.2), and the character of the spring (52.3). The 'fourth river', Borysthenes, is the 'greatest' after the Ister (the polis Borysthenes features largely in the story of Scylax and Scythian phobia about foreign customs, 78–9); its relation to the human world is stressed, and in a further comparison with the Nile, it is described (53.1) as not only the greatest, but 'also the most helpful (πολυαρκέστατος) in our opinion, not only of all the Scythian rivers but also of all the other rivers, except for the Egyptian Nile. For this cannot be compared (συμ-

---

[91] Cf. *Eumenides* 700–3, cited above.

[92] This is where a rapid comparison with *Airs*, often regarded as more 'scientific', can only mislead. Hartog points out that Herodotus does not connect this water with Scythians' *physical* condition, and is struck by his emphasis on the northernness/cold as the prime factor of explanation: (1988), 30.

βαλεῖν) with any other river.' This river's epithet is determined by its use
to human inhabitants. We hear more, about its pastures, its fish, its sweet
water, and so on (53.2); even the useful salt which forms at its mouth
'automatically' (αὐτόματοι), and 'many other wonders' (53.3–4). It is
only of the Borysthenes and the Nile that 'I cannot say what the source is,
and nor can any Greek, I think' (53.5). After more description of the
other rivers and whose territory they flow through, he mentions the bile-
producing grass (ch. 58). At the end of the section on Scythian customs,
he concludes that the rivers and their number are the only wonders the
country has (IV 82).

Yet in the whole narrative of the Persian invasion (as well as the section
on customs), there is no trace of an idea that Scythian behaviour in the
face of this threat – or any Scythian behaviour – is related physiologically
to this general dampness, as Hartog points out.[93] Scythians are not
themselves moist, as they are in *Airs*, their behaviour is simply not governed by the terrible disabilities the moist people of *Airs* suffer from. As
human specimens, they seem no different from any others, Greeks or
Egyptians; it is simply their customs which are different. They are, indeed,
brave and resourceful, as the narrative demands, just as Europeans are
supposed to be in *Airs*. There is a separate logic in the narrative of resistance.[94] Their decision to flee is precisely that, a deliberate strategy helped

---

[93] Hartog (1988), 30.
[94] Hartog (1988). The decision not to fight openly is made after a congress of Scythian kings
in which the Scythians fail to persuade others that Darius' aggression is aimed at all the
mainland (IV 118–20). Anticipating later Athenian behaviour (see Saïd (1981), 25 ff., and
bibl. there; Legrand (1932), Hartog (1988)), they fail to inculcate unity, and therefore
decide to make no open fight (120), instead drawing the Persians into the land of those
who refused to fight (120.4). (Chs. 121–2 on the details of the retreat; Erbse (1992), 161–5
on importance of different decisions by the various tribes about resistance, and relation to
the geographic character of each region.) In the ensuing pursuit and retreat across vast
stretches of Scythia, 'the land was bare' and so there was nothing to destroy (123.1). The
nature of the land was not in this narrative the primary cause or excuse for these fleeing
tactics, but once open battle is avoided, the land with its vastness and emptiness, and lack
of cities, make those tactics effective. Their defiant reply to Darius, refusing a pitched
battle, is perhaps surprising after this, for there they declared proudly that they are not
fleeing but simply following their usual way of life in peace (IV 127.2): 'We Scythians have
neither towns nor cultivated lands, which might induce us, through fear of their being
taken or ravaged, to be in any hurry to fight you.' This is the classic statement of Scythian
nomadism: as Herodotus said in his own voice, they managed without cities or agriculture (IV 46). Yet in the surrounding narrative, they were pursuing not exactly their normal
way of life, but a deliberate strategy. Some Scythians did cultivate the land, and had cities
(e.g. the Olbiopolitai, 18.1). Here the symbolic image of Scythians as nomads is eclipsing
the more anomalous details, there is a conflation of their general reliance on pasture and
cattle with the movement of nomadism over a wide area, or the nomadism is deliberately
exaggerated in this speech of defiance to Darius (as much as to say, 'We are not fleeing;
we always behave like this'). Cf. apt remarks on this by Lévy (1981), 64: for Herodotus
the true mode of Scythian life is nomadic, 'son ethnographie se nourrit de la différence'.

by the nature of the land. There is a medical slant and an interest in the nature of the land, but it is not so all-embracing as that of *Airs*.

If the emphasis Herodotus gives the Scythians on their nomadism in their speech to Darius (IV 127.2) does not exactly reflect the image Herodotus gives in his own person, it may emphasize that he is drawing in one part on a simpler, more systematic picture of their nomadic character than his information elsewhere allows. But one cannot mistake the connection of this picture to the important, numerous rivers, the rich pasture they provide, and so on, which he enumerates in such detail, the wonders of the Scythians, and the wastes (*eremos*) beyond, to which several groups flee (e.g. 123, 125.3f.).

The damp and the cold, then, are prominent in the Herodotean description of this land, with its great rivers, its summer rain, and the extreme cold of the winters. In that respect it is consistent with the picture of *Airs*, where Scythia and the Scythians are the example *par excellence* of the effect of cold and wet. So we may regard Herodotus' image as informed by the same preoccupations with geographical climate and nature that appear in *Airs*. It also reflects up to a point the schematic image of Greek doctors and probably *physiologoi* pursuing the schema of the hot, cold, wet and dry. These are the preoccupations of the early Greek enquiry concerning nature. Yet there is a vast gulf in the role of the cold and the wet in *Airs* and the *Histories*. We have here two quite different reflections on the effect of the cold and the wet. It seems unhelpful to see such comparison in terms of intellectual superiority, or a sign that Herodotus is less 'scientific' (because less theoretical) as some scholars claim.[95] The Scythians of *Airs* are very damp like their land, effeminate, weakened. In Herodotus the damp simply does not have a physiological effect: the land, climate and way of life play a part which in historical terms is more indirect and more subtle. We should distinguish sharply between the human inhabitants of the land and the type of circumstances and surroundings with which they interact. The phrase 'environmental determinism' may be appropriate for the damp Scythians of *Airs* where climate and environment have affected the human constitution itself.[96] But it is too harsh for Herodotus who on the contrary insists more upon the effect of land, rivers and climate upon what one can only call Scythian behaviour and their customs or *nomoi*; Herodotus' final emphasis is on the human customs.

---

[95] See e.g. Jouanna (1992), 317–27, who admires the greater sense of 'synthesis' and 'coherence' of *Airs* (320) and its greater originality (325), against Herodotus' 'incoherence'; *Airs* is the first founder of 'une science de l'homme' (319).

[96] Even *Airs*, however, admits to the effects of custom: see next chapter.

Where does this bring us? We have seen something of the role of ethnography in medical discussion. There is a fragmentary but fascinating strand of ethnographical and geographical enquiry which focuses on Libya and Scythia and which pursues an overall interest in *physis*, the physical makeup and character of the human being. There is a strand in the *Histories* which seems to belong closely to this network of discussions and preoccupations, and which may encourage us to take a more imaginative leap in our interpretation of what is going on. Herodotus is clearly familiar with certain quite specialized opinions held by Hippocratic doctors on the question of health (pages 34–42). But, when we come to Herodotus' description of geography and health, there are also signs of interaction with medical ethnography, an interaction which cannot be neatly interpreted as the result of a one-way movement from one set of writers (i.e. medical) to Herodotus, or *vice versa*; nor via any simple correspondence with one single written work that we still possess. Herodotus sometimes seems to be bouncing his data, his opinions, against those of others which may have been better known to his audience than to us: in other words he participates actively in some of the kinds of enquiries also visible in medical circles. The tenor of the remarks we observe here corresponds strikingly to the kind of preoccupations and theories visible in the surviving medical works. We are not always dealing with an exact correspondence of facts or theories, but often suggestive similarities of subject matter or similar approaches to such subject matter. There was at least a two-way process of interaction and interpretation between Herodotus' enquiries and those primarily interested in health. Moreover, these topics sometimes also lie at the intersection where medical writers and some of the later Presocratics or *physiologoi* may meet, though these latter are frustratingly elusive, and Democritus whose ideas might be particularly relevant, is notoriously badly preserved. Against this background, the interaction of Herodotus with this wider milieu seems more dynamic than conventional source criticism allows us to contemplate, and more interesting than is allowed by the familiar recognition that he shares some ideas about the effect of climate and environment that are visible in *Airs*. There is more controversy and debate beneath the written text of Herodotus than our other written sources indicate explicitly.

Herodotus' discoveries about Libya and Scythia are clearly influenced not only by general Greek views about what is normal, but also informed by preoccupations with climate, water, cold, geography, which are also to be found in the more sophisticated views of Greek medical writers – and which thus belong to the 'scientific' world of the latter part of the fifth century (rather than solely the early geographers). Nevertheless these ideas vary over the different authors we have looked at. For Herodotus we can see the grid of the hot, the cold, the wet and the dry, at work in the *Histories*, especially in his stress on Scythia and Libya in contrast; in his occasional comments about the effect of cold and heat upon growth; and in the general discussions of geography and animal or plant growth. This is the polar schematization familiar in Greek thought of the fifth century. The overarching schema, and particularly the way in which Libya is opposed to Scythia, seems to reflect the same view of the world visible in contemporary natural philosophy and medicine. Behind the details, the piling on of information about Libyan animals or Scythian rivers, we glimpse the possibility that Herodotus devotes such space to Libya and Scythia because in current investigations into nature they, rather than Scythia and Egypt, are the natural opposites. As we see, though, Herodotus does not apply the grid of hot/cold/wet/dry rigidly onto all his subject matter, even where it is most appropriate, and as we see further in the next chapters, there is very little environmental determinism in the extreme sense in Herodotus.[97] We may suspect, perhaps, that his methods of enquiry were simply too geared to discovering new information, data, facts, stories, to keep him bound to a highly abstract construct of such a kind.

In the ethnography of the medical writers we glimpse a use of information on other non-Greeks which stands apart from the stereotyping use of ethnography visible in (for example) Greek tragedy or the more acerbic remarks by Athenian politicians and political theorists like Plato and Aristotle. And this gives us an entrée into or at least an alternative perspective from which to view Herodotus' own ethnography. The ethnography of the medical writers, though fragmentary, is suggestive. It forms part of the general enterprise of understanding human health and disease and the general workings of what we may as well call *physis*: Scythian milk-churning can be an analogy for humoural disturbance, Libyan reliance on the goat indicates that goat products cannot possibly be unhealthy; Libya may stand as an example for the effects of heat and dryness on human beings (if we may so use *Regimen*), just as the Scythians illustrated the effects of damp and cold in *Airs*. Here ethnography is being utilized not so much to show difference, to underline a gulf between the Greeks and these other peoples, or to reinforce the rightness of Greek behaviour and character, as to make connections across the whole of the human world – and one suspects occasionally, perhaps the animal world too (how else can a description of Scythian mares parallel so exactly the

---

[97] Cf. Lateiner (1989), 158, 'Herodotus may be considered to some extent to be an "environmental determinist".' But he uses a less deterministic phrase to elaborate: 'he believes that climate affects national character just as climate affects appearance and physiology'.

Hippocratic vision of the human woman?). 'The symptoms would be the same in Libya, Delos and Scythia' (*Prognostic*), was a way of saying that symptoms were universal – the workings of nature affect all indiscriminately. Or the author who wrote 'the *ethnea* of men and *ta phuomena* in these countries are of necessity drier and hotter and stronger than those in the opposite areas' (*Regimen* ch. 37), citing Libya and the Pontic areas, saw all human beings as being affected along with plants by the prevailing climate.

As this latter example shows, there were differences in plenty to be recognized in the various parts of the known world: of course Libyans and the inhabitants of the Pontus were different in many respects. But what is interesting – against the often ethnocentric remarks of other fifth-century authors – is how the differences are part of a larger picture in which it is the climate, the sun, the heat, which are having this effect on these particular groups, and the plants as well as humans. Where is innate character or *physis* here? Plato or Aristotle could declare blankly that Greeks are by nature enemies to barbarians (see chapter 4); non-Greeks could always be paraded simply in order to show how Greeks were superior, barbarian customs mentioned only to highlight the contrast with Greek democracy, or freedom, or bravery. But it is assumed by medical writers that the Libyans are affected by extreme heat, their great health surely the result of such dryness, and the opposite for the Scythians. Similarly in *Airs*, the main argument was that the climate and land had a crucial effect on ethnic character: the ethnographical examples were used to show this (there is, however, some confusion in *Airs*, and the next chapter looks more closely at it). If the Libyans were the example of the effect of the hot and the dry, the Scythians of the cold and the wet, then such ethnography is not being adduced quite so simplistically to reaffirm Greek character and Greek identity as is sometimes implied. True, the touchstone in all this is Greece, or more probably east Greece, taken to have the median and best climate; and the theory being imposed is undoubtedly Greek in character. But of the many ways in which non-Greek peoples to the north and south could have been contrasted with the Greeks, it is along the grid of the hot and dry, wet and cold that one of the contrasts is drawn. A very Greek theory, certainly, but one that is abstract and theoretical, and which effectively seeks to see difference or explain difference through the great variations or alterations of nature – heat, climate, geographical accidents. The lines along which such Hellenocentricity runs seem to be those of the Greek philosophers' and doctors' ideas about *physis*. It is the overarching assumptions and theories about nature, the cosmos, which were being allowed to mould these images of other peoples. These other peoples are different, but they are different in such a way as to reveal some fundamental characteristics of nature. This is ethnography in the service of the study of nature, not simply Hellenism.

But there is a further aspect to all this, more frivolous, perhaps, with which it seems appropriate to end this chapter, and that is the sheer exoticism of much of this medical and ethnographical material. It must be the case that the marvellous, wondrous quality of much of this information from distant parts of the world is what gives it much of its appeal – above and beyond any contribution it might make to the study of nature. But not merely information: in particular, many of the products themselves used by the doctors either have an exotic and distant provenance, or are named as such. The *physiologoi*, in contrast, seem to have used almost no material from non-Greek areas, with the exception of their Nile speculations and Democritus who is associated with Egypt, Libya and Arabia. But the doctors not only show some interest in certain areas which we have discussed; they also make extensive use, in their practical aims of effecting cures, of exotic drugs and spices from precisely those places which feature in this medical ethnography. We encountered *kastorion* from Scythia, as an aromatic product put to use in numerous gynaecological recipes; and *silphium* from Libya. Numerous medical or aromatic substances occur in the Hippocratic recipes with the grandiose epithet 'Egyptian', 'Ethiopian' or 'Indian'. We meet Egyptian acanthus, for instance, Egyptian salt, acorns, saffron, perfume, 'nitron' (i.e. sodium carbonate) and 'stupteria' (i.e. alum).[98] A 'Persian drug' also appears, and Persians occur once as the source of a plant name in a gynaecological recipe.[99] Healing drugs from Egypt are famous to an Aristophanic audience, as they had been to a Homeric one, though the Aristophanic joke seems rather to cut Egyptian medicine down to size.[100] Other products came from afar even if they did not carry the appropriate epithet: we

---

[98] See Index Hippocraticum, s.v. Αἰγύπτιος for refs. and further products; similarly Αἰθιοπικός – far fewer products are 'Ethiopian', cumin being the most common. See von Staden (1989), ch. 1, for Egyptian influence on Greek medicine. Arabia does not feature at all in the Corpus. Byl (1995) collects data on geographical place names in the Corpus: pp. 230f. lists some medical substances and their origins.

[99] For the Μηδικὸν φάρμακον: *Nat. Mul.* VII 364.2 L; *Mul. I* VIII 202. 15 L (alt. reading). Persians as the source of a plant name: *Mul. II* VIII 394.8 L: τὸ ἰνδικὸν ὃ καλέουσι οἱ Πέρσαι πέπερι. Otherwise Persia features in the Corpus only in the late and biographical–rhetorical works (e.g. *Or. Thess.*). See Byl (1995), 231 for other products from Greek areas (and elsewhere). Other refs. in the Corpus to foreigners: beyond *Airs*, Egypt only appears in the late work *On the Seven-months child* (*CMG* I 2,1 Grensemann, p. 122, 11–15) where a parallel is made with Egypt: see ch. 5, p. 152 with n. 54. Otherwise the epithets 'Egyptian' and 'Indian' qualify medical substances (as above). The adjective *barbaros* is used three times, excluding late biographical works: *Airs* (16.5 J, see below), *Anc. Med.* ch. 5.2 J, of those who 'still, even now, do not use medicine, the barbarians and some of the Greeks'; *Epid. V*: v 230. 12 L.

[100] *Peace*, 1253; cf. *Od.* IV 220–32.

may recall the movement of cinnamon, frankincense, cassia, ledanum, supposedly from Arabia, which Herodotus mentions and for which he recounts ever more exotic descriptions of their harvesting (III 107, 110–12). Cinnamon, for instance, he thinks the Arabians get from Ethiopia, and the story goes that the cinnamon sticks have to be extracted, with great cunning and the tempting display of animal carcasses, from the vertiginous and inaccessible nests of giant birds.

Gynaecological recipes are most extravagant in their use of distant and costly products. Expensive combinations of ingredients are prescribed frequently in some form of 'odour therapy' for the mouth of the womb. At one point, for instance, emollients for the uterine mouth are prescribed of 'narcissus, myrrh, cumin, frankincense, wormwood, cypirus';[101] or nitron, resin, myrrh, Ethiopian cumin and perfume, for a woman who has had children and cannot have any more;[102] or a mixture of Ethiopian cumin, hartwort from Marsilia and 'dry leaf of Libya', that is, silphium, should be mixed in wine.[103] In another, Egyptian saffron and Egyptian salt should be mixed in the skull of a sea turtle, boiled and applied.[104] We see here the pharmaceutical reflection of what seems to be a belief in the sentient capacities of the womb, and the ability of the womb to move in response to different forms of odours.[105] These aromatic products from distant parts are probably also meant to be reassuring and hence efficacious – the rarer the substance administered as a cure, the more likely the patient will be impressed, and the higher the status of the doctor who seems to have access to such esoteric knowledge.

Doctors had an interest, then, in certain exotica, those that were part of their healing art. So it is perhaps no coincidence that it is also medicine which looked outwards beyond the Greek world to peoples who shared little common culture with Greeks. Doctors who believed in the effect of climate upon health would have had more reason than most, one would think, to be interested in lands of different climate, and in what went on in the maintenance of health elsewhere – some of the impetus at least, for pursuing enquiries into the habits of these distant lands may have come from those interested in the nature and health of man. One also wonders about what other information and pseudo-information travelled with these exotic products to the doctors of Greece. Did nothing about the

---

[101] *Mul.I*, ch. 74: VIII 154.14–18 L.

[102] *Mul.I*, ch. 75: VIII 164.17–19 L.

[103] *Mul.I*, ch. 78: VIII 182.23–184.2 L.

[104] *Mul.I* ch. 78: VIII 186.15–17 L.

[105] See on this, e.g. Hanson (1991); cf. also her article on 'Paidopoiïa' (1995). The gynaecological treatises are generally regarded as containing a greater depth of traditional practice than the other essays of the Corpus.

possible uses of these exotica travel across to the Greek world along with the products themselves? One can only speculate here. But it is at least worth considering if some of the knowledge in East Greece of other parts of the world and their inhabitants was linked in some way to this luxury trade.

In many respects, then, Herodotus' enquiries into other parts of the known world were not guided merely by a mass of fairly standard Greek preoccupations and prejudices. His ethnographical observations were made through Greek eyes, but the framework through which he described them encompassed some of the preoccupations and specific structures that were common to the enquiries of early Greek medicine and those who were pursuing the meaning of *physis*. In some respects, he was doing much the same thing as those medical writers interested in the ethnography of health, and they could interact with one another. Much of his ethnography slotted very neatly into that milieu, a world of Greek scientific and medical speculation and enquiry, in the latter part of the fifth century.

3   Dividing the world: Europe, Asia, Greeks and barbarians

In two of his more polemical digressions, Herodotus goes out of his way to explain to his audience why the Ionians and Greeks lack understanding when they divide the world into certain continents, Europe, Asia and Libya. Much is at stake, it would seem, in the division between Europe and Asia in particular, and what it signifies in the *Histories*, the Greek–barbarian conflict, the immoveable antagonism between Europe and Asia. Alongside his criticism, Herodotus does, of course, have a certain liking for geographical symmetry in his vision of the world. Both issues, continental division and symmetry, are related in some way to the question of environmental determinism, and to the extent to which Herodotus' geographical and climatic descriptions are meant as explanatory factors on a grand scale in his analysis of the many different peoples in the *Histories*. Does he really see Europe and Asia, Europeans and Asians, as fundamentally and inextricably different, inevitably hostile to each other? And how does Herodotus' scheme relate to earlier or contemporary schemes of world division? His ideas seem both complex and interesting; they also both conflict with and complement the theories of his contemporaries, each set may serve to set into relief the others, and each set has striking contemporary resonances. This chapter pursues Herodotus' manner of dividing the world, symmetrical or not, within a contemporary context; it asks how far such division is meaningful in ethnographic or political terms; and it looks in depth at the treatise on *Airs, Waters, Places* as one crucial example of contemporary discussion of the relation of geography to human life.

In the last chapter we saw that Herodotus' ethnography bore a complex relationship to the ethnography of health visible in writers on medicine and nature, and was informed by what must be contemporary ideas about *physis* and certain parts of the known world. We concentrated upon Libya and Scythia, the two areas which figure largely in both the medical works and Herodotus' *Histories*, and which imply that Herodotus' emphasis on Egypt itself was actually exceptional. His lengthy descriptions of Libya and Scythia seemed in fact to be following – perhaps even enhancing – the preoccupation of the medical writers and other natural philosophers with the grid of hot and cold, dry and wet: Libya and Scythia forming exact opposites. Herodotus' ethnography does not, however, follow the grid slavishly. His Scythian *logos* is clearly moving into a more variegated plan which is not entirely dependent upon climate for causation and motivation. Herodotus' ethnography seems informed but not bound by this grid.

Some interesting questions arise from this. One is the relation of the *Histories* to the difficult work *Airs, Waters, Places*. Another concerns the division into continents, and how far Herodotus or other writers of the time thought in terms of a symmetrical world. Linked to this is the question of whether these larger divisions of geography were thought to have an impact on the peoples inhabiting them. The extreme form of this idea is central to *Airs, Waters, Places*, which claims that the inhabitants of Europe and Asia are fundamentally different from each other insofar as they inhabit different continents and experience separate climates. This shades into the theory of 'environmental determinism', the theory by which human beings and society in general are formed by their physical environment (since the term 'environmental determinism' is ambiguous, I use it strictly as shorthand for the physical environment – as in the title of *Airs, Waters, Places* – rather than social environment).

Since Herodotus offers his audience two polemical attacks on the misleading division of the world into certain continents, Europe, Asia and Libya, he was clearly concerned, at least some of the time, about symmetrical geography, and about the conventional division into continents. I would suggest that we can only make sense of Herodotus' divisions of the world, and his criticisms of others' divisions, as in part a reflection on, in part a response to, contemporary ideas.

Hecataeus had written his *Periodos Ges* in the form of a voyage round the Mediterranean with innumerable notices of places along the edge. This reflected the view of the trader and merchant who sailed around the circumference. What is striking about Herodotus' ethnography is that he concentrates on three large areas of non-Greek peoples, Egypt, where he says he is extending his description because it has more wonders than elsewhere (II 35.1), Scythia, and within the same book (IV), Libya, in third place. Even the very fragmentary remains of Hecataeus indicate that he had devoted space to other areas of the Mediterranean, indeed the whole coastline. In the discussions of natural philosophers and the medical treatises, ethnography or ethnographic climatic observations are clustered, as we saw, around the same three large areas: Egypt, Scythia, Libya – *Airs* discussed Scythia, Libya and Egypt, the latter two sections now virtually lost.[1] In a different matrix, 'Europe' (meaning Greece and Scythia) versus 'Asia', appear in *Airs, Waters, Places*. The Western and NW Mediterranean do not really feature, nor Illyria, the Adriatic or Italy; nor, perhaps more surprisingly, Babylonia, Persia, Phoenicia, the Assyrian empire. Herodotus pursues many other areas of the known, and less-known, world to the furthest reaches of current knowledge (cf. in particular his remarks about the bounds of knowledge beyond the Scythians and to the west of Libya, e.g. IV 24–5; IV 185). But in his main focus upon Scythia, Libya and Egypt, he seems to be mirroring the emphasis also to be found in these contemporary or slightly later medical–physiological discussions. These were the important and interesting areas to pursue in fifth-century enquiries into nature: the tripartite division was not merely a conventional relic of earlier geographical works.[2] Though Heinimann had suggested that the fundamental ordering in terms of Egypt, Libya, Scythia, was taken over from the classification scheme of 'Ionian *historie*', which might have derived from Hecataeus,[3] it is thus rather improbable that this emphasis of Herodotus' was traditional in any meaningful sense of the word. It is also unlikely to have been solely Hecataean, though Hecataeus discussed these three areas.

Nor is it entirely inevitable which symmetry was to be chosen, which geographical antithesis, which axis across the Mediterranean. There were other possibilities. Why not Thrace and Phoenicia, Thrace and Ethiopia, Scythia and Ethiopia, or indeed Ethiopians and Hyperboreans who are so memorable in Homer, if the extremes of north and south within current knowledge were to be used? The Hesiodic *Catalogue of Women* provides evidence for an earlier grouping of the most remote peoples, involving Ethiopians, Libyans and Scythians along with Pygmies and people 'who dwell under the ground'.[4] Pindar mentioned the Nile, the Ister and the Phasis, along with the Hyperboreans, as if they formed the limits of the

---

[1] There is a marginally wider range when one includes exotic medical products: see ch. 2 (end).

[2] Scythia remains an important example: e.g. Aristotle brings in the Scythians in connection with hair (*Gen. Anim.* 782b): moist Scythians have straight hair, Ethiopians (dry) curly. For Ephorus' idealization of Scythians, Lévy (1981).

[3] Heinimann (1945), 22–3. Similarly, A. Lloyd (1975, 168), with Egyptians as classic barbarian people of Asia, Scythians of Europe; Herodotus 'follows tradition even in the choice of peoples to whom he devotes his attention', pp. 167–8 – meaning Scythia and Egypt, as paralleled by *Airs*. Myres (1953), 32–43, thought Herodotus used an 'Ionian map' and another, the 'Persian map', without perceiving their discrepancy (p. 37).

[4] *Cat. Women*, fr.150, vv. 14–18 M–W, with note; and Lévy (1981), 60. This fragment reappears in Strabo 7.3.7; the sudden appearance of Ligurians in the MS is an error.

inhabited world.[5] It is one particular polarity, or more accurately a three-cornered antithesis, which is intellectualized and rationalized.[6]

It also seems probable that it is in some way linked to a peculiarly East Greek, and East Greek intellectual way of viewing the world. Not simply because it corresponds to Ionian science, and the schema of the four qualities, but because Ionian and generally East-Greek commercial interests were predominantly clustered in the Black Sea and in Egypt which notoriously imported numerous Ionian and Carian mercenaries, not to mention the interchange of exotic pharmaceutical products. Practical and commercial factors were pressing upon this Greek image of the world.

Similarly with the symmetry often noted in Herodotus between Scythia and Egypt, the most obvious manifestation of Herodotus' penchant for symmetrical balancing. The Nile is balanced with the Danube (II 33f.), the Egyptians are the oldest of people, the Scythians the youngest; since the Nile is 'opposite' the Ister, we can therefore suppose 'that the course of the Nile as it flows through all Libya is similar to the course of the Ister' (II 34.2).[7] But such symmetry is not strictly bipolar to the exclusion of other symmetries, for as we saw, there is a Scythia–Libya axis alongside the Scythia–Egypt one: for instance when Herodotus discusses the effect of cold and the growth and non-growth of horns of cattle in Scythia and their happier counterparts in Libya (IV 29–30). There is no simple bipolar scheme in Herodotus' geography. Moreover this symmetry has a comfortable place in medical discussion also. The well-known Greek penchant for polarity is not characteristic simply of popular culture, popular or archaic concepts, but also something that lies deep within the intellectual, medical and scientific discussions of the latter part of the fifth century.[8] Nor can we assume that *geographical* symmetry was characteristic merely of the archaic Greek map-makers, or Anaximander. Herodotus himself had criticized symmetrical maps of the known world (IV 36), and one may presume they were still popular, not that he was simply jousting with

---

[5] *Isthm.* VI 23: beyond springs of Nile and through the land of the Hyperboreans; *Ol.* III 14–18: springs of Ister and the Hyperboreans; *Ol.* VIII 47, Ister associated with Amazons; *Isthm.* II 41f.: [hospitality] as far as the Phasis in summer, and to the banks of the Nile in winter. Heidel (1937) over-systematizes.

[6] Note also Herodotus' 'blind spot' about South Italy: Hornblower (1994a), 70.

[7] See Hartog (1988), esp. 14–19; also Levy (1981) on the 'Scythian mirage'; A. Lloyd (1975), 167–8. Immerwahr (1966), 315–17 on the geographical symmetries in Herodotus, alongside his attempts to see a more irregular world (see n. 13 below); Myres (1953), 32–43, with (1896) on Herodotus' maps.

[8] G. E. R. Lloyd (1966); also A. Lloyd (1975), ch. 4, esp. 164–5 on analogy; and 149–53 on antithetical patterning in Herodotus. A. Lloyd (1990) has interesting suggestions about the *Histories* being structured around polarity, of Greeks and barbarians, war and balance, in Heraclitean mode: esp. 243–4, with Dihle's comments, 248.

map-makers long since dead. That Herodotus too is open to some of the same criticisms he levels at these others is only an indication that he also partook of that same mental world. We may compare the way the author of *On the Nature of Man* is not entirely immune from the criticisms he aims so vehemently at his opponents. The symmetrical schema maintained intellectual respectability in late fifth-century science and beyond. Very much later, similar assumptions about symmetry came into play with the discovery of the southern end of South America, for Magellan expected it to terminate with a cape, just as Africa did.[9]

What is particularly interesting is where the tensions lie. Herodotus certainly entertains some ideas of symmetry in geography (Egypt, Scythia), and between geography and human life. But he himself objects to excessive symmetry and indeed the very continental divisions that his contemporaries take for granted. There is a real tension between schema and experience or the evidence of travellers' tales, between the desire for a rational neatness and the apparent evidence of a less balanced more messy world.

We need to look at both Herodotus and *Airs* simultaneously, since the force of comments in one author may illuminate those of the other. Both offer fine examples of late fifth-century discussions of the nature of continental division and whether such continents are linked to human or ethnic character (e.g. Europe and Asia), the role of environmental determinism more generally (in *Airs* in particular), and the Greek–barbarian contrast. *Airs* is both fascinating and puzzling in its own right; it also offers an invaluable comparison with the *Histories*. As will be suggested, Herodotus sees as meaningless the conventional geographical divisions into continents, and criticizes such divisions in terms of *nomos*. We will then return to *Airs*, and see precisely the 'continental determinism' of a kind to which Herodotus could be objecting. I shall argue that *Airs* is not primarily about Greeks and barbarians as such, but primarily and problematically about environmental determinism, and continental divisions, with some influence from *nomoi* thrown in. However complicated this may be, it at least gives one a glimpse of a range of theories, ideas and preoccupations of the time, and perhaps better because they are more enthusiastic than successful. *Airs* cannot be taken as a simple backdrop to Herodotus, as another work on why Greeks and barbarians differ, for it is considerably more complicated. But it does make distinctions which are revealingly centred upon Ionia or Asia, and in terms that were contemporary.

[9] Cited by Thomson (1948), 100.

Continents and Herodotus' dispute about the divisions of the world

While Herodotus is still bound by the attractions of geographical symmetry, he objects to excessive symmetry and declares that the divisions of
the continents are merely conventional. He offers his audience two polemical discussions about the divisions of the world (II 15 ff.; IV 36 ff., esp.
41 ff.). Both involve the fundamental divisions of Europe, Asia and Libya
(not 'Scythia' and 'Libya' as such), and both involve the incorrect views
of 'the Ionians', and in II (ch. 16), both the Greeks and the Ionians, and
the Greeks again (at II 17.2). The unfortunate targets of these criticisms
are usually identified vaguely with 'Ionian geographers', and Jacoby
thought these Ionians referred to Hecataeus. One may guess, though, that
there may be some more contemporary target, perhaps in part the schematization and schematized divisions of the kind we can see so clearly in
the Hippocratic works (and no doubt there were others). Herodotus'
methods of criticism are also interesting; they involve a critique on the
grounds of *nomos*, or convention, and as such, seem to have been neglected in discussions of the development of Greek geography.[10] Let us
look at the details.

Herodotus insists in Book II (15 ff.) that the Ionians are wrong about
Egypt, given his own observations about the Delta. They are wrong to say
that the Delta and the Delta alone is Egypt, the rest of 'Egypt' being, as
they would think, either Libya or Arabia (ch. 15). He carries on to object
to the Ionian idea that the earth has three parts, Europe, Asia and Libya:
at the very least, he insists, they should add a fourth part, the Delta, since
at the moment that would fall neither in Libya nor Asia:

> If we think correctly (ὀρθῶς) about these things, then the Ionians do not think
> sensibly about Egypt; but if the opinion of the Ionians is correct (εἰ δὲ ὀρθή ἐστι ἡ
> γνώμη τῶν Ἰώνων), then I undertake to show (ἀποδείκνυμι) that neither the
> Greeks nor the Ionians know how to count (λογίζεσθαι), who say that there are
> three parts to the earth, Europe, and Asia and Libya. For they ought to add a
> fourth, which is the Delta of Egypt, if it is not part of Asia or Libya. (II 16.1–2)

He ridicules the idea that the Nile should separate Asia from Libya; that
would end up leaving Egypt proper, that is the land inhabited by Egyptians (ch. 17), divided between two continents (ch. 16).

Since he ridicules the Ionian image of the Nile as the boundary between
Asia and Libya, his suggestion that they ought at least to add a fourth
part to the world, the Delta or 'Egypt', can only be ironic: he is saying

---

[10] Downplayed by e.g.: Tozer (1935), 68, and n. 3, 72, 81 (division of 3 continents 'Herodotus accepts with a protest as being sanctioned by custom'); Heidel (1937), 32–3 on
Phasis.

that their system of divisions cannot even account for all the parts of the world. We may guess that the 'Ionian' view that Egypt is equivalent to the Delta is the parochial and popular Greek view, and this would be connected to the fact that the Delta was the section best known to Greek traders and mercenaries, seat of the Greek colony at Naucratis.[11] Thus Herodotus concludes (ch. 17) with the assertion that the only proper boundary line between Libya and Asia is that marked by the Egyptian border:

οὔρισμα δὲ Ἀσίῃ καὶ Λιβύῃ οἴδαμεν οὐδὲν ἐὸν ὀρθῷ λόγῳ εἰ μὴ τοὺς Αἰγυπτίων οὔρους.

We think the boundary between Asia and Libya is nothing, by correct argument, if not the boundaries of the Egyptians. (II 17.1)

Otherwise Egypt would be divided right down the middle. Hecataeus is also said to have held this sensible view.[12]

Herodotus, then, seems to be objecting not merely to the three-fold divisions, as believed by 'the Ionians' (and Hecataeus himself seems to have only two continents), but to the very principle of the division in the first place.[13] Who was he objecting to? Possibly the author of *Airs* or, more likely, others like him. The second half of *Airs* purports to be about the differences between Europe and Asia, which supposes a two-fold division. But *Airs* mentions Libya and Egypt and these seem to come under the umbrella of 'Asia'.[14] If so, then *Airs* was even more schematic than 'the Ionians' Herodotus was criticizing, and its author patently commits what was for Herodotus a serious mistake, that of taking a river as the boundary between Europe and Asia. Herodotus' criticisms were certainly applicable to some of his own contemporaries.

Later in Book IV, he finds quite ridiculous those who have a round earth, 'as if drawn by a compass', and who make Europe and Asia the same size (ch. 36): here we seem to be dealing with the two-continent division. But then he gives us a broader attack (41 ff.), this time not so focused on the discoveries and theories about Egypt he proudly displays.

Libya, he declares, adjoining on Egypt, is an *akte*, a term interpreted

---

[11] Immerwahr (1956), 260, n. 38, cites Jacoby *FGrH* 1, 328–9, on the Delta in early Ionian speculation. See Boardman (1980) for the archaeological evidence.

[12] By Arrian, *FGrH* 1, F 301.

[13] Some think Herodotus accepts the three-fold division: e.g. Jouanna (1992), 320; cf. Immerwahr (1956), 260–1 with n. 38; Immerwahr (1966), 316, points out that Herodotus sees a more irregular world than his predecessors, but Herodotus 'tries to combine the popular two-continent conception (according to which Africa is a part of Asia) with the scientific three-continent theory' – hence the two peninsulas (*aktai*). See further below.

[14] Unless for *Airs*, Egypt was equal to the Delta alone, a view which Herodotus indicates was held by some Greeks at the time.

variously as a 'tract' (Rawlinson's translation), 'tracts of land' (Tozer), or peninsula (Immerwahr (1966) 315f.), and it is very broad. So far, so good, though this description suggests that he really thought it quite modest in size. Then he returns (ch. 42) to the problem of the division of Libya, Asia and Europe:

θωμάζω ὧν τῶν διουρισάντων καὶ διελόντων Λιβύην [τε] καὶ Ἀσίην καὶ Εὐρώπην· οὐ γὰρ σμικρὰ τὰ διαφέροντα αὐτέων ἐστί·

I am astonished that they should ever have divided Libya and Asia and Europe; for the differences between them are great. (IV 42.1)

As he continues, they are really very unequal in size: Europe being the size of the other two together … (ch. 44); Libya is surrounded by sea, so is Asia, but no one knows about Europe (45.1).

So far, his objections sound familiar from Book II (15 ff.): an objection to the three-fold division, this time adding some facts about size and extent, which, one supposes, are to suggest that the divisions certainly did not correspond to size or balance. His criticism of the use of rivers as boundaries to these continents also reappears (45.2). But then he turns to the naming, and this is where his objections become more interesting and also, in Greek rather than modern terms, more intelligible.

For he 'cannot imagine' why three names (ἐπωνυμίας – denoting naming after something else), and women's names, moreover, should have been given to what is in reality one land: 'I cannot imagine (οὐδ᾽ ἔχω συμβαλέσθαι) why three names should have been given to what is one land, and women's names especially' (IV 45.2), or why the Nile and Phasis were fixed on as boundaries, nor who gave them the names, to what is one earth. He then elaborates on several problems about the names (45.3–5): for instance, there are conflicting explanations (and therefore sources) for the name of Asia; no one knows how 'Europe' acquired its name; if Europe was named after the Tyrian Europa, she was definitely Asian and never set foot in Europe; and that also suggests that before the naming, 'Europe' was nameless like all the others. He ends (45.5) with: ταῦτα μέν νυν ἐπὶ τοσοῦτον εἰρήσθω· τοῖσι γὰρ νομιζομένοισι αὐτῶν χρησόμεθα. This seems effectively to mean, 'So much for that. We will have to make do with present conventions' (literally: 'So much on this subject; we will use the current conventions'). The attack, then, seems to extend to the very process by which they acquired their names: this he ridicules, showing how strange these names are and asking rhetorical and ironic questions about where the names came from, who named them.

This preoccupation with names is strikingly reminiscent of Herodotus' theory about the names of the Greek gods in Book II, which has perplexed commentators, and where he seems to say that the Greeks received the names of the gods from the Egyptians. As there, it is, however, important to realize that for Greeks at this period, naming something gave it definition, identity: the name was crucial, the very process of naming was a process of definition, and the name could be assumed to say something about the identity of the person or object so named.[15]

It is peculiarly interesting, then, to see here how Herodotus accompanies his attack on the three-fold division of the world first with objections about points of fact – the extent of Europe, the effect on geographical knowledge of discoveries and so on; and also, with a series of ironic questions about who named these regions and why. Clearly problems about the division itself are seen to go alongside problems with the names of the divisions. As he says, it is just one land, one earth: how did it manage to acquire three names, and names of women? We may note that *Airs* takes for granted precisely those divisions that Herodotus is objecting to here.

The objection to the names may give us a further clue. What Herodotus seems to be doing here is in part using the known, or increasingly known information about the nature of world geography, to undermine or even contradict the big divisions usually made by 'the Ionians': his observation of Egypt and the Nile shows how laughable are their divisions which leave out Egypt, or rather, divide it right down the middle; and the three-fold division leaves extremely unequal, unbalanced units (IV 41 ff., etc.). It is therefore quite misleading to talk of him as 'using' Ionian maps. But he seems also to bring into this connection some elements of a debate about naming and *nomos*, in particular the idea that names are mere convention. There are two further hints of this. Earlier, he was speaking of what in his scheme is one of the two *aktai*, or tracts, in 'Asia', the one which extends from the Persian to the Red Sea, containing Persia, then Assyria, and then Arabia:

λήγει δὲ αὕτη, οὐ λήγουσα εἰ μὴ νόμῳ, ἐς τὸν κόλπον τὸν Ἀράβιον . . .

It ends, that is to say it is considered to end, though it does not really come to a termination, at the Arabian Gulf. (IV 39.1 Rawlinson)

This somewhat cumbersome translation conveys the force of the reference to *nomos*: it only ends by *nomos*: εἰ μὴ νόμῳ indicates that when he talks of termination of a piece of land, Herodotus is concerned only with the conventional view, with *conventional* divisions of the land mass. The second hint is the way Herodotus concluded the whole discussion himself

---

[15] II 3.2; 43–5; 49–58; 143–6. Cf. also his remarks about the invention of the dithyramb, I 23. For works on naming, see ch. 7, p. 230 and n. 39.

(45.5): τοῖσι γὰρ νομιζομένοισι αὐτῶν χρησόμεθα, 'for we will use the current conventions'.[16]

Given that in between these two remarks we have had a long critique of the names of those divisions and some of the problems of these names, it is hard not to suggest that Herodotus is speaking in the terms and language of the *nomos–physis* antithesis. At least he is edging towards contrasting *physis* in the sense of reality, nature, what he knows, and *nomos* in the sense of mere convention, what other people think they know. Heinimann saw the εἰ μὴ νόμῳ sentence in ιν 39 as the one occasion in Herodotus that *nomos* was used in a manner reminiscent of the *nomos–physis* antithesis (that is where the two terms have definitely become antithetical), edging towards the sense of 'false convention'. But Heinimann commented that, 'the sentence is a specially good example of Herodotus as linguistic observer (*Sprachbeobachter*)'.[17] He took *nomos* here as meaning essentially 'Sprache', thus not 'proper usage' any more, but involving the idea of 'linguistic usage' (*Sprachgebrauch*), and thought it striking that this meaning of *nomos* does not need to be explained to Herodotus' audience. We may also add, however, the discussion on boundaries (ιι 17.2), where again Herodotus seems to use the expression νομίζω in a manner reminiscent of these later cases to imply false belief or custom: 'But if we use the beliefs of the Greeks we would take Egypt (τῷ νενομισμένῳ νομιοῦμεν Αἴγυπτον) as divided along the whole length.'

Herodotus is indicating here that we are dealing with 'false' custom, 'false' naming, that is, mere convention that has no support in *physis*. *Nomos* is definitely edging towards the sense of false convention, as Heinimann saw. The current names in use are names only by convention. This seems strikingly reminiscent of the preoccupation fashionable in the late fifth century with the controversy about the correctness of names. Empedocles argued that names were conventional, that they did not actually correspond to reality, but he too admitted to using the conventions (fragments 9 and 10);[18] Democritus also contrasted reality which existed 'by nature', and convention – and names for him existed only by convention;[19] other thinkers were preoccupied with the 'correctness of

---

[16] Sluiter points out that at 39.1 we may, rather, be dealing with a remark about the conventional use of the *word* λήγειν itself: yet the context, the problem of division of continents with which he's dealing, suggests the emphasis lies more on conventional land masses (in fact they are not completely different things): cf. Sluiter (1997), 172.

[17] Heinimann (1945), 82, followed by Corcella (1994), Commentary, on ιν 39; see also Diels (1910), 13 ff.

[18] DK 31, Β 9.5: νόμωι δ' ἐπίφημι καὶ αὐτός; cf. Β 10, of the word *genesis*, 'coming to be'; Β 8; and Anaxagoras, DK 59, Β 17, on Greeks' incorrect belief.

[19] Democritus, DK 68, Β 26: on this, Empedocles and general context, Sluiter (1997), 171–5 – who also cites the highly relevant *On Regimen* ι 4.

names' (see chapter 9 below). Herodotus seems easily familiar with the idea of the conventionality of naming and *nomos*, voicing virtually identical unease. It is interesting that his critique of geographical knowledge is couched in part in terms of *nomos*, used in the derogatory sense familiar in the late fifth century, and in part through ridicule of the system of naming, another, related, intellectual preoccupation of the time.[20] His puzzlement about 'Europe' is the more telling since Europa's seizure appears at the beginning of the *Histories* as part of the series of mythical seizures of women by Greeks and barbarians – these legendary rapes are then set aside quietly in order to progress to the events which are really accessible to true knowledge (I 5.3), a striking juxtaposition of traditional knowledge and more 'modern' ideas which recurs in the *Histories*. Symmetrical views are incorrect, then, the three-fold division – indeed any division – is incorrect, and the naming does not correspond to reality.

Despite this attack, it remains clear that Herodotus himself is still partly bound by these conventional divisions (as mentioned above); the neat, convenient idea of a symmetrical world resurfaces in his analogy between the Ister and the Nile in Book II (ch. 33f.), though the analogy extends to other Scythian rivers in Book IV (IV 50, 53 *bis*), and in the symmetry he sees between Scythia and Egypt, as well as the claims that Egypt is quite the opposite of all other peoples (II 35–6). He also uses the conventional continental names – for instance the Libyan land is compared with that of Europe and Asia (IV 198–9). But this is hardly surprising, given the difficulties of breaking out of a conventional schema. What is interesting is that there is apparently a struggle between the demands and attractions of theory and the less tidy evidence of experience or others' accounts. We may compare the difficulty that the discovery of America created for the conventional belief in three continents, itself built on the ancient continental system, and indeed for much if not all of ancient geographical wisdom.[21] We should not underestimate the importance of Herodotus' criticisms of the standard world divisions; and the extent to which he is critical in exactly the terms of late fifth-century intellectual ideas. Herodotus' concentration on Egypt, Scythia and Libya seemed to reflect the same emphasis found in the medical literature. Yet he can be highly critical of certain geographical ideas which were evidently still widely believed. There is symmetry, schematic division, and anxiety about symmetry, evidence adduced to undermine ideas about

---

[20] Cf. perceptive remarks in Benardete (1969), 111f.: Herodotus stressing 'the arbitrary character of the conventional divisions'; but he sees this laughter as Homeric, comparing *Iliad* I 599 ff.

[21] See Grafton (1992), esp. ch. 3, for a lively account.

such schematic divisions. The strongest undermining principle of all in the late fifth century, that of 'custom' or *nomos* is brought to bear, alongside ever greater detail about the untidy geography of the world as it was increasingly known.

Europe and Asia. *Airs, Waters, Places* and its division of the world

Let us return to the scheme of *Airs, Waters, Places*.[22] Studies of *Airs* have tended to be so preoccupied by the textual, authorial and compositional problems offered by this work, that relatively little attention has been given to the geographical concepts that its author entertains; or else it is loosely read as simply about the difference between Greeks and barbarians.[23] It is also a puzzling work, which often does not say what we think it should, and therefore analysis of what it actually does say will also be useful. Whether or not Herodotus' polemic was aimed at this particular work or not, we cannot know, and its relation to Herodotus may be too rapidly assumed. *Airs* might easily reflect the kind of views under attack, for Herodotus' criticisms apply precisely to the neat plan we find in *Airs*. It is, however, surely more profitable to treat *Airs* as reflecting certain other late fifth-century views, rather than getting buried in debates which seek a one-to-one relationship to the *Histories* – the most recent edition defends their independence from one another.[24] *Airs* offers another perspective on some of Herodotus' more polemical preoccupations, another late fifth-century meditation on the relation of geography, climate and human life.

Airs produces a sophisticated theory of considerable complexity about the effects of climate, the lay of the land, the water, and also the customs or habits of life (*diaita*), upon the human inhabitants. The first part (chs. 1–11) concentrates upon a general discussion of these relationships, with the detailed enumeration of various land and climate types but no specific places mentioned; the second part (chs. 12–24), which includes a lacuna (end of ch. 12), sets the environmental theory to use in a series of concrete examples and in an overarching thesis about the differences between the

---

[22] I use Jouanna's text (Diller's noted if different). The best discussion of the structure of *Airs* is by Heinimann (1945), ch. 1; Grensemann (1979) on the unity of the text and important analysis of the structure of the environmental theory and how it is worked out in detail. Cf. also Backhaus (1976), taking *Airs* to be fundamentally about Greeks v. barbarians; Jouanna (1981), with Heinimann (1945), underestimates the extent in Herodotus of explanations involving geography and *nomoi*.

[23] Cf., however, Lopez Férez (1994), and Nutton's response (1994, 124–30). Some remarks in Hartog (1988), 28–31; cf. also Hartog (1996b).

[24] Jouanna, Budé edition (1996); inclined to follow Heinimann's dating of c. 430, or perhaps a little later (p. 82) – 'at the transition between Herodotus and Thucydides'.

inhabitants of Europe and Asia. There are two crucial theories: (a) the effect of climate, land and environment generally, the 'airs, waters, places' of the title, and (b) the effect of continent, Europe, or Asia.

The inhabitants around the Phasis, for example, suffer the effects of their land and climate which is warm and wet, and what is worse, their river is 'the most stagnant of rivers' (ch. 15), a state which was described in the abstract in the first half (ch. 7 – with Grensemann 1979). The author thus analyses both the local topography and climate and jumps to a far larger thesis involving the two continents. But the continental thesis of the author seems both less detailed and less sophisticated than the first part.[25] While Herodotus very precisely targeted the foolish idea that the earth was truly divided between Libya, Asia and Europe, the author of *Airs* proceeded without a qualm, apparently, to compare 'Europe' and 'Asia', to show 'how they differ in every respect':

I wish to speak about Asia and Europe, how they differ from each other in every respect, and how the peoples of one differ entirely in physique (*morphe*) from those of the other. (ch. 12.1 J)[26]

Europe and Asia here are obviously categories with deep significance in themselves; they are completely different in every respect as the author says, and their inhabitants are also completely different. This fundamental division of the world, which stands over and above the detailed enumeration of local geography, water and climate, gets the author of *Airs* into some difficulties.[27]

For despite the often subtle and detailed distinctions of factors within each section, dealing with localized features, warm stagnant water, winds, and so on, and with a lot of internal coherence, as Grensemann has shown, one of the well-known problems of the work is that many of the detailed case studies involve extreme examples, and examples which do not necessarily illustrate the grand initial statement about the differences between Europe and Asia, and their inhabitants.[28] The Makrokephaloi, for instance, whose elongated heads were originally manufactured by binding babies' heads, but which eventually started occurring naturally,

---

[25] *Pace* Jouanna (1996), who admires the 'scientific' coherence of the Europe–Asia contrast.

[26] βούλομαι δὲ περὶ τῆς Ἀσίης καὶ τῆς Εὐρώπης λέξαι [δέξαι: Diller] ὁκόσον διαφέρουσιν ἀλλήλων ἐς τὰ πάντα, καὶ περὶ τῶν ἐθνέων τῆς μορφῆς, τί διαλλάσσει καὶ μηδὲν ἔοικεν ἀλλήλοισι. (ch. 12.1 J)

[27] Cf. Heinimann (1945, 26–7), pointing out that he does not take North–South as the big division.

[28] Grensemann (1979); also Heinimann (1945), ch. 1 esp. 22, and Backhaus (1976) on inconsistencies of the work; Grensemann, however, shows that it has far more coherence (esp. in general plan, environmental theory, theory and examples) than most attribute to it. Jouanna (1992), 298–329, and his Budé edn, praise its coherence and system.

are a fascinating case of the combination of *nomos* and *physis*, as the writer analyses them, but they seem to get us no further in understanding or even illustrating the supposed differences between Europe and Asia (ch. 14). The Scythians are better case studies, as presented here, of the effect of the cold and wet, than of the characteristics attributed to the inhabitants of Europe to which they belong. But in any case, and this cannot be over-emphasized, the author wishes also to invoke the effects of *diaita*, or way of life, as an important factor, and does so early on (ch. 1.5 J: 'The way of life (*diaitan*) also of the inhabitants which is pleasing to them, whether they like to drink (φιλοπόται), and take lunch and are inactive, or like taking exercise and working (φιλογυμνασταί τε καὶ φιλοπόναι), eating much and drinking little'). *Nomoi* in the crucial sense of political constitution also turn out later to be overriding factors which might even undermine the grand differentiation between Europeans and Asians (ch. 16: see below). Despite all this, the plan of the work, at least the ethnographically oriented section, is still premised on the idea that Europe and Asia are separate and separable entities which engender clear characteristics in Europeans and Asians. However far Herodotus wanted to take the idea that climate and environment affect peoples, he did not, apparently, embrace this degree of schematization.[29]

Let us look more closely at what the author of *Airs* actually makes of the Europe–Asia division. It is useful with this familiar but difficult work, to outline the main lines of argument, concentrating on what the divisions are, which peoples are in them, and what the author does with them. First, who are 'the Europeans'?

The 'Europeans' described in *Airs* are in some ways a surprising collection. Those that get most detailed treatment are those of the very far North, above the Black Sea, the Scythians, definitely classed as Europeans (Lake Maeotis, i.e. Sea of Azov, is the boundary between Europe and Asia).[30] So are the Sauromatae, living around Lake Maeotis, with women who sound like Amazons: 'In Europe there is a Scythian tribe' (ch. 17.1 J). The Scythians, distressed by the cold, receive the longest description (chs. 18–22): the area has many rivers, so moistness and cold are the main characteristics (ch. 19), and as a result of this (along with certain

---

[29] It is therefore also unwise to take this absence to indicate that Herodotus was earlier in date. Jouanna (1992) takes this as indication of Herodotus' work being less original and inferior in conception. The whole debate is bedevilled by a linear scheme of intellectual development.

[30] Cf. Hartog (1988), 30–1: Scythians in *Airs* are definitely in Europe, but 'grounds for hesitation' for other writers: for Herodotus, according to Hartog, 'even if Scythia is in Europe, the Scythians are not necessarily Europeans' (1988, 32) – though they are fixed in Europe by Darius' attack.

customs) they suffer from infertility (chs. 20–2). Otherwise we have to make do with vague generalizations about 'Europeans' and their characteristics (ch. 16, comparison with Asians; ch. 23, and ch. 24, though it is questionable how far this chapter actually describes Europeans as such – see below). The specifically named examples of Europeans are thus an exotic group and, from the Greek perspective, a remote collection, inhabitants of immensely distant areas.

The inhabitants of Asia who receive special ethnographic treatment, on the other hand, include the Egyptians and the Libyans. The descriptions of both are now lost (see ch. 12.6–7 J = ch. 13.1 D), and have been subjected to some extraordinarily tendentious and fascinating reconstructions by modern scholars.[31] The Makrokephaloi are also Asian (ch. 14); their description, as I said, reads more like a set piece on the relative contributions of *nomos* and *physis*, than a full or convincing contribution to the image of Asian character – not surprisingly they were used by Antiphon.[32] The dwellers on the Phasis at the East end of the Black Sea (ch. 15) also seem to belong to Asia, though again their peculiarities are better related to the local conditions, described in full detail, than to the grand characteristics of Asia (cf. the Scythians): their land is 'marshy, hot, wet, and wooded'; they suffer copious rains, and 'the Phasis is the most stagnant and sluggish of all rivers', there are only slight changes in the sea-

---

[31] It is unsound to reconstruct the lost Libyan and Egyptian sections according to certain presuppositions about barbarians: cf. Backhaus' contention that in *Airs* all foreigners are being given an unfavourable image. His reconstruction of the prolific Egyptians and 'promiscuous' Libyans (1976, 174) seems rather to imply his own 'orientalist' leanings, not to mention a hint of misogyny: it is unsound to postulate that the Libyans (women?) in *Airs* were wildly promiscuous by the use of some rather exceptional Libyan tribes in Herodotus who had common ownership of women and 'mated like beasts' (ιν 180.5; also ιν 172.2 (Nasamonians; lots of women and *meixis* 'in common' (ἐπίκοινον), 'just like the Massagetai'); though cf. ιν 176, women seek as many lovers as possible), and with the help of Aristotle's remarks on the way Libyan animals (*not* humans) interbred between species at the water-holes (*Hist. Anim.* vιι (vιιι) ch. 28, 606b). Backhaus seems to assume a link between prolific birth-rates and promiscuity, and neglects the explanations in *Airs* (and elsewhere) of Scythian infertility by means (in part) of their moistness. Besides, high fertility in the Greek world was considered a good: cf. Hesiod *WD* 235, and *Airs* ch. 5. Cf. Lévy (1981), 66: he tends to assume that in *Airs* we see the (older) eulogy of distant places being replaced by 'condemnation' of extremes, the excessive character of South and North; cf. his n. 97. Cf. Thomson (1948), 106 on *Airs*: 'The southern belt, Libya and Egypt and most of Asia, is hot and dry, and it too is generally level; hence it is very productive, has many and large animals, and peoples black, black-haired and feeble. The middle belt has marked diversity of seasons and soil and landscape; the people are tall and fair...'.

[32] DK 87, β 46. Also in Hesiod, fr. 153 M–W. Heinimann (1945), ch. 1, showed that *nomos* is meant in *Airs* to have considerable influence (followed by Lateiner 1986, 16f.); Backhaus (1976, 175f.) on the Makrokephaloi and Phasians contributing little to the section on Asia. Jouanna (1996) on *Airs*, pp. 66f. and 224n., thinks that *Airs* is more nuanced in its use of *nomos–physis* than the sophistic writers.

sons; hence the fruits of the country are stunted and flabby and do not ripen, and the human beings are tall, rather fat, yellowish, 'and neither joint nor vein is visible', an unpleasant and peculiar image[33] – quite different, oddly, from Herodotus' Colchians. Not surprisingly they are disinclined for physical exertion. It is in the next chapter that the grand characteristics of the Asians are elaborated (ch. 16): they lack spirit, they are more gentle and less warlike than the Europeans, and the cause is most especially the uniformity of the seasons, 'for it is changes of all things that rouse the temper (*gnome*) of man and prevent its stagnation'. But also, the author adds, the *nomoi* are a cause, most particularly the fact that most peoples in Asia are ruled by kings (ch. 16.3–5 J).

It is common – and easy – to take the opening declaration about Europe and Asia (ch. 12.1 J) in terms of Greeks and barbarians, if not actually as a covert manifesto about Persians versus Greeks.[34] If this is so, and if modern scholars can see this, presumably fifth-century Greeks could also make this interpretation. But it should be said that it is virtually invisible in the text as it stands. It seems to be the Europe–Asia division which is primarily at issue, which is rather different. For it is remarkable quite how rarely Greeks as such are actually mentioned. The only Greeks named explicitly are those who live in Asia, and they occur in a fascinating context, the exceptions to the general rule of Asians' cowardice:

ὁκόσοι γὰρ ἐν τῇ Ἀσίῃ Ἕλληνες ἢ βάρβαροι μὴ δεσπόζονται, ἀλλ' αὐτόνομοί εἰσι καὶ ἑωυτοῖσι ταλαιπωρεῦσιν, οὗτοι μαχιμώτατοί εἰσι πάντων·

For all those Greeks or barbarians in Asia who are not ruled by tyrants, but who are autonomous, and labouring for themselves, are the most warlike of all men. (ch. 16.5 J)

There may be exceptions, then, to the grand theory, and they are provided by both Greeks and barbarians in Asia who are autonomous and who are accordingly most warlike. Who might be meant by these clearly real examples depends considerably on the view held of the Athenian empire and the date of the work, but it is clear, at any rate, that the Asian Greeks are the only Greeks to be mentioned. The description of the best area of 'Asia' also sounds very much like Ionia (ch. 12.2 ff.), but Ionia is left un-

---

[33] Jouanna (1992), 309 takes the detail and vividness as a sign of first-hand experience by the author; similarly, Backhaus (1976); and Nutton (1994), 127.

[34] Backhaus (1976) takes the Persian defeat as the starting point, and sees *Airs* generally as about Greek superiority: see e.g. 181, indications for the inferiority of foreign behaviour. Contrast Jouanna (1981), esp. 14 – barbarian inferiority in *Airs* entirely a result of difference in nature, but no fundamental opposition inscribed in nature for Herodotus between Greek and barbarian. Cf. Diller (1962).

named.[35] In the second last chapter 'the other people (*genos*) in Europe' (ch. 23.1 J) must include Greece itself, especially when we are told that Europeans differ very greatly in physique, more than Asians, or that Europeans are more warlike, not being governed by kings (ch. 23), or that they are more independent in spirit (*idiognomonas*, ch. 24.9 J). If these generalizations apply to Europeans *minus* Scythians and other Northern tribes, then presumably the author is thinking of the mainland Greeks (the run of the Greek at the start of ch. 23 suggests this for a while). But we may not be able to assume that he is talking so precisely about Europeans without Scythians. In any case it is striking how consistently the author is inclined to generalize about Europe and Asia as such (see most of chs. 23, 24). The categories at issue are continental. We are meeting neither the language of the Greek–barbarian opposition, nor that of Greeks and non-Greeks, except only at ch. 16 (16.5 J).

Thus in ch. 23, 'Europe' is still being characterized by frequent changes in the seasons, and highly dramatic weather conditions (ch. 23.1): it is because of this that 'Europeans' vary in stature (*megethos*) and shape (*morphe*) more than 'Asians', and the author explains this by a theory about the effect of weather patterns on the seed (ch. 23.2). The character is forecast thus:

τό τε ἄγριον καὶ τὸ ἀμείλικτον καὶ τὸ θυμοειδὲς ἐν τῇ τοιαύτῃ φύσει ἐγγίνεται.

Wildness, harshness and spirit are engendered in such a nature. (ch. 23.3 J)

In this harsh process, frequent shocks impart wildness and weaken or diminish tameness and gentleness (ch. 23.3 J). Hence, he believes, 'those living in Europe' are more courageous (εὐψυχοτέρους) than those in Asia. Then he moves to the great counter-cause, the *nomoi* and institutions (ch. 23.4 J). Ch. 24 is devoted to a more general enumeration of how the various tribes (φῦλα διάφορα) in Europe can be distinguished via types of region and climate, again with a proviso about the possible intrusion of custom or *nomos*, ch. 24.3, and again stressing the diversity of Europe.[36]

Finally towards the end, we meet another enumeration of the kind of environment which applies to Europeans and perhaps to Greeks particularly, though it is not specifically said to apply to either (ch. 24.9 J): hard

---

[35] Cf. Hdt. 1 142.1–2 on the Ionian climate: 'The Ionians ... have built their cities in a region where the air and climate are the most beautiful in the whole world: for no other region is equally blessed with Ionia, neither above it nor below it, nor East nor West of it. For in other countries either the climate is over cold and damp, or else the heat and drought are sorely oppressive.'

[36] Heinimann (1945, 20–1) took ch. 24 not to be about Europe, but general; also Grensemann (1979) who rearranged certain sections of ch. 24. For possible Greek poleis being referred to, see also Backhaus (1976), 184–5.

winters and hot summers produce wild rather than tame characters, those who 'hold their own opinion' (ἰδιογνώμονας), good at war, skilled also in *technai*. This would easily apply to mainland Greece, perhaps Athens in particular, and has been so taken,[37] though it sounds very like Herodotus' resourceful Scythians; 'hard winters' are particularly Scythian. However it is couched resolutely in terms of 'Europe', and if we can take this last section (from ch. 24.6 J = 24.7 D) as the ending of the work,[38] it is significant that the author also ends on the biological note. The penultimate sentence emphasizes that 'everything that grows in the earth assimilates itself to the earth'.[39] We are being told explicitly about Europe as a land mass and Asia as a land mass, whatever is being conveyed between the lines.

Elements of 'European' characteristics, then, can certainly be applied to mainland Greeks but the author hardly goes out of his way to do so explicitly, and it is worth wondering why.

Similarly with the Greek–barbarian division. This is only mentioned once in the text,[40] indeed 'barbarian' is not a favourite Hippocratic word, and it appears in connection with the inhabitants of Asia in a context where the author is clearly preoccupied with the Greeks of Asia Minor (ch. 16.5 J). Even so, the sentiment is surprising. Having explained about the feebleness of those living in Asia in terms of climate, he turns to the political factors, the additional importance of the laws (*nomoi*) and the proof that they are important (16.5 J: the passage above):

For all the Greeks or barbarians in Asia who are not ruled by despots but are autonomous, and labouring for themselves, are the most warlike of all men.

It is striking that even here in his great exception to the feeble and enervating effects of the Asian climate, it is both Greeks *and* barbarians who may possibly become courageous so long as they are autonomous. A free constitution could do wonders, one is meant to understand, and 'the great proof' is that all those Greeks or barbarians who are not ruled by despots but who are autonomous, are the most warlike of all. 'Barbarians' can be courageous as well as Greeks if they have the right kind of constitution

---

[37] Heinimann seems to take the 'Europeans' as essentially Greeks (1945), 39f., neglecting Greeks in Asia. On whether *idiognomonas* is a code word for Athens, cf. Thuc. I 70.2*, Athenians are *neoteropoioi*, 'addicted to innovation', and 70.9* unable to rest in peace, according to Corinthians – rather as Persians are characterized by Herodotus in Xerxes' speech urging Persians to war (VII 8α): Saïd (1981), 20. Cf. Thuc. VI 18.7*, Alcibiades' speech.

[38] Note that Grensemann (1979) argued that this whole section belonged earlier.

[39] τὰ ἐν τῇ γῇ φυόμενα πάντα ἀκόλουθα ἐόντα τῇ γῇ: ch. 24.9 J.

[40] Backhaus points this out as surprising (1976, 178); his further point, that in all Asia, it is only the Ionians who have autonomous cities, therefore profit from the climate, depends on a vision of the Athenian empire which is not generally accepted.

(or live in Europe!), just as Greeks (in Asia) can be as lax and unwarlike as barbarians: such is the importance of *nomos* (ch. 16.3 J):

For these reasons, I think, the Asian race (*genos*) is feeble, and in addition, because of their customs (*nomoi*). For most of Asia is ruled by kings.

Unfortunately for the author this admission seems to undermine much of the rest of his thesis, and the dominant image of 'Asians' as lax and soft – the effects of the soft Asian environment can be circumvented completely. But it is hardly expressive of Greek triumphalism or Greek cultural chauvinism. It cuts dramatically across the clichés we hear elsewhere in fifth- and fourth-century sources about barbarians being naturally fitted to slavery, Greeks to freedom. Aristotle states with satisfaction the obvious truth that barbarians were naturally slaves, citing Euripides' dictum that 'It is reasonable that Greeks should rule barbarians'.[41] Later he reproduces a geographical characterization in which the *ethne* in the cold north and Europe have spirit but lack intelligence, therefore are free but without political organization, while those in Asia have intelligence and art (*techne*), but lack spirit, therefore remain enslaved: whereas the Greeks, situated in between, have both:[42]

Those [*ethne*] who live in a cold climate and in [northern] Europe are full of spirit, but wanting in intelligence and skill; and therefore they keep their freedom but have no political organization and are incapable of ruling over others. Whereas the peoples of Asia [i.e. '*ethne*'] are intelligent and inventive, but they are wanting in spirit, and therefore they are always in a state of subjection and slavery. But the Hellenic race (τὸ δὲ τῶν Ἑλλήνων γένος), which is situated between them, is likewise intermediate in character, being high-spirited and also intelligent. (*Pol.* VII 1327b23–31) (Jowett's transl.)

Here it is obvious how all Greeks are grouped together as sharing the same virtues: for while Aristotle is also drawing a geographical distinction, implying that geography is somehow determinant, he is effectively distinguishing by ethnicity, by whether someone is Greek or non-Greek, rather than by whether they, Greek or non-Greek, might live in Asia or not (see n. 48 below). Greeks are conveniently denoted as living between Europe and Asia. By contrast, the author of *Airs, Waters, Places* is markedly less chauvinistic than we are sometimes led to expect, or than we might anticipate from certain other Greek sources.[43]

---

[41] βαρβάρων δ' Ἕλληνας ἄρχειν εἰκός: from *IA* 1400: *Pol.* 1252b5–9; similarly 1255a28–1255b4 – with the proviso that Greeks reserve the name of slave for barbarians, and think barbarians are noble only at home.

[42] Cf. also Isocrates, *Antid.* 293–4; *Panath.* 163.

[43] Cf. Lévy's remark (1981, 67), that in *Airs* the Greeks 'are naturally superior to the Scythians' because of the climate (what is nature here?). Cf. E. Hall (1989), 173. Georges (1994), 38 is inaccurate on *Airs*.

Where, then, does this bring us? It seems that the work *Airs* is a distinctly strange and unusual piece. Even allowing for the lacunae, the remaining text leaves numerous questions.[44] It is odd partly because it is doing something other than what we would like to find, and using material and examples that do not always fit the grand continental division. The work seems to see the world very much from the point of view of Asia Minor and in particular, perhaps, the Greeks of Asia, as often noted.[45] But the precise angle of that perspective is not as Hellenocentric as some believe.[46] The great exception to Asian feebleness focuses on the effect of political autonomy, and in that exception seems happily to include both Greeks and barbarians as possible beneficiaries of its bracing effects. It is a striking exception.

Secondly, it is nevertheless hard not to see some explanation lurking here for the defeat of the Persians by mainland Greece while Asia caved in to the Persian expansion: Asians are characterized in such a way as to contrast with European courage and wildness, and everyone knew that the Persians were defeated when they tried to invade Europe, Scythia and Greece. So the division by continent might help explain why Asia fell, but Europe managed to mount successful resistance. The continental division avoided any explanation which involved Greekness, any innate characteristics of the Greeks – for to the Asian Greeks, that kind of explanation could only fail to account for their own success (it might even include the Scythian resistance, though that is oddly contradicted in the rest of the work). In other words, the explanation for Asian feebleness, with the possible hope of redemption through the boon of political autonomy, is one which applies to Greeks in Asia and to their own advantage, and exactly to barbarians in Asia as well as to Greeks there. This theory perhaps grew out of, or was encouraged by, the East Greek experience under the Persian empire. There is absolutely no hint of innate Greek superiority, superiority by race or ethnicity as such. The scheme – unlike Aristotle's – could apply also to non-Greeks.

But if *Airs* was aiming, in its second half, to explain the Greek–Persian conflicts, or the Greek–barbarian opposition, it was a strange text to do so with, even taking into account the author's environmental theory; and

---

[44] Perhaps earlier preoccupation with composition is in part a reflection of this; Grensemann (1979) shows a more coherent work. Nutton, briefly (1994, 124): 'The Hippocratic *Airs, Waters, Places*, for all its apparent familiarity, is a very puzzling work indeed.'

[45] Recently, Backhaus (1976), 172–3. Nutton suggests (1994, 127–8) that *Airs*, with *Epidemics I and III*, has the perspective of the North Aegean, but this idea works better for the *Epid.* passages than *Airs*; and perhaps begs questions about knowledge of other areas of the Mediterranean world; and in any case a travelling doctor would know of places beyond his home. Byl (1995), briefly, on the whole Corpus.

[46] Nutton (1994), 126–7.

one would have to say it had been accomplished badly.[47] One might even suggest that the author was going out of his way not to attribute characteristics to Greeks and barbarians as such; or to produce a theory that did not expressly distinguish Greeks from the rest, thereby explaining why the Greeks of Asia Minor were as they were. We may contrast the openly Hellenocentric assertion of Aristotle in the *Politics* (above) which, while distinguishing Europeans and Asians, declares that only the Greeks, in the middle, could attain freedom and good government.[48] Or the way Herodotus immediately talks of the conflicts and achievements of Greeks and barbarians in his Proem (though admittedly the context is more complicated there). The wild, warlike qualities the author of *Airs* attributes to 'Europeans' are, as expressed, as apt in theory for Thracians or other barbarian tribes as for the Greeks of mainland Greece.

The oddity is that the Scythians in *Airs* are not in fact presented as warlike, being dominated by the cold and the wet. Scythian character corresponds more exactly to the enervating effect of the coldness and moistness than to the rugged wildness that the author attributes to Europeans as a whole. This anomaly may perhaps be explained in part by the tradition and theory he was working from[49] – or perhaps one should simply admit that the geographical and continental explanation just will not work (note also chs. 18–19: Scythia has little differentiation in season, also significant for its constitution). As for the inhabitants of Asia, the selection of peoples given special mention is on some levels strange if the aim were to draw lessons about the defeat of the Persians: Libyans, Egyptians and apparently Asia Minor feature, but there is nothing about the Persians themselves. Libya, Scythia and Egypt, the author's main examples, may be unsuited for his grand thesis about Europe and Asia (as opposed to the theory of the effect of climate and land), but they are the areas featured consistently as the main sources of ethnographic knowledge in the medical corpus.

This seems to sit far more comfortably in the world of Ionian science and the ethnography of health, than with the ethnographic and anti-barbarian obsessions of Athens and Athenian literature. Indeed the scheme here is potentially applicable not merely to the military struggles

---

[47] Contrast Backhaus' conclusion (1976, 185) that the author places Asia and Europe against each other less effectively than Greeks and barbarians.

[48] Aristotle, *Pol.* 1327b23–34, is discussed by Jouanna (1992), 327–9: Aristotle replacing Europe–Asia division by Europe–Greece–Asia: 'Aristote rétablit ainsi un hellénocentrisme que l'ethnographie ionienne avait essayé d'estomper' (p. 329) ; cf. also Nutton (1994), 126.

[49] As Heinimann suggested (1945), 21–3. Grensemann (1979) shows how exactly the Scythians and Phasians fit the abstract thesis in the first part of the work: but this is the detailed thesis on environment, not the grand scheme concerning Europe and Asia.

of the Persian Wars, but also to the world of the Athenian empire – where indeed, the Athenian sub-group of Europeans were, in many Greek views, still being 'wild' and 'warlike', not to mention 'self-opinionated' (see n. 37). The fundamental theory remains environmental and biological, with considerable input from *nomoi*: it is the nature of the land and of the climate, along with human customs, which determine the nature of the inhabitants. As the author ends in the penultimate sentence, 'Those things which grow in the earth all assimilate themselves to the earth.' If this is an orientalist thesis – and to a large extent it has the potential to be – then it is based on an analogy with plant growth.

This view of Asians may well have been the origin, or at least the predecessor of the later 'orientalizing' view that tended to see all Asians as effeminate, and cowardly.[50] But it does not yet solely involve non-Greeks, 'the other', and the thesis is still geographical. The division of continents which is its basis, is what was scrutinized unfavourably by Herodotus whether or not Herodotus was thinking precisely of this work or its author. The same fundamental division and interpretation – or rather a division between Europe, Asia and Libya – turns up in amusing form in Aristotle, this time on the animal world. Not only are people in Europe braver (as in *Airs*), but in Aristotle's *History of Animals*, so are the wild animals:

In general the wild animals are wilder in Asia, but all those in Europe are braver (ἀνδρειότερα), while those in Libya are the most varied in form (πολυμορφότατα): in fact there is a proverb that Libya ever bears something new. (*Hist. Anim.* VII (VIII) 606b17–20)

Asian animals are wilder than the 'Asian' humans of *Airs* (and Libyan animals seem to be morally neutral) – perhaps the effect of Asia is somehow to intensify their nature.[51] In a section which discusses the variant sizes of animals and explains them by both food and climate (606a–b), even Aristotle, it seems, could not resist the temptation of characteristics measured out by continent.

It is tempting to suggest that the problematic part of the thesis of *Airs*, or at least the one that is least well carried through and least subtle in its application, is precisely the theory of continental difference. The author has a complex theory of environmental effect on human beings – which allows careful differentiation by water, temperature, winds, land; there is also a large input from human *nomoi* of all kinds, from general way of life, to political constitution; and on top of this, there is also the grand

---

[50] See E. Hall (1989) on Aesch. *Persians* in this role; Saïd (1981) and (1984).
[51] Cf. *Airs* ch. 12.7 J, a mutilated reference to animals which are *polymorpha*.

thesis about the fundamental differences – on all levels – between Europeans and Asians because of the land and climate they encounter. The latter element may have been encouraged by the need to explain, essentially, why Asian Greeks had not managed to repel the Persian expansion. But it creates great difficulties for the author since it cuts across the other elements of his analysis. Or perhaps the trouble with *Airs* is precisely that several of the writer's examples are drawn from contexts where they illustrate some other theory – for example the Scythians exemplifying moistness, the Makrokephaloi the relative effects of *nomos* and *physis*. Perhaps it is that he tries to impose a theory of environmental determinism, with a botanical slant, onto the world as divided into two continents, with an inescapably Ionian or East Greek point of view, and an eye on the way the inhabitants of Asia had generally been less successful in war than the inhabitants of Europe. In other words, he has two contradictory agenda: (a) to show that climate is crucial; and (b) to show that continent is crucial (assuming that climate changes with continent, though at the Hellespont, or Phasis, climate is of course much the same). In addition he stresses a third point (c), that *nomoi* are also crucial – which confounds all.

The author of *Airs*, then, has many of the same ingredients that recur in Herodotus – theories about continents and their human inhabitants, theories about physical environment and human (or ethnic) character, the effect of *nomoi* (which we examine in more depth in chapter 4). Perhaps they also share an awareness of the Greeks of Asia Minor. They both share the problem of combining the schematic world geography and the more messy data on the ground. It seems unwise to assume that the climatic explanation of *Airs* is both more advanced and more 'scientific', as well as later. But the ethnography of *Airs* is not primarily and exclusively about Greek superiority over barbarians: on the contrary it is about continents and general physical rules (climate, continents) that should in theory apply to all mankind. So when Herodotus criticizes a schematic world division on the grounds that the divisions misrepresent land masses and, more important, that the divisions between Asia, Europe and Libya are in any case merely conventional, he seems to be in the thick of an issue and controversy of the time. He could even be aiming some of his criticism at the author of *Airs* or others who tried a similar continental explanation – thus *Airs* enables us to see more securely what range of theories about continents and ethnic character might have been in circulation. Not only does Herodotus seem more sophisticated here, in the sense that he confronts the abstract problem of continental division with physical data about geographical expanses, rather than merely extending it; he also couches his objections in terms of convention or custom (*nomos*), and in such a way as to suggest the sophistic awareness of *nomos* as false convention.

Europe and Asia and the *Histories*

When Herodotus expresses so energetically his disbelief in the current division of continents, we may wonder whether elsewhere he really attributes inherent characteristics to any continent, to Europe or Asia and their inhabitants. Or do Europe and Asia remain for him merely conventional names for certain land masses, as his critique in Book IV implied? Put another way, when he declares so clearly that the continents are only a matter of convention, how should we take the force of his narrative of Persian expansion in which so much is made of the division between Europe and Asia? The Persians themselves, as Herodotus says twice, at the very beginning and the very end of the *Histories*, regarded Asia as their rightful province: Protesilaos could be seen as having borne arms against the Persian king, 'for the Persians believe that the whole of Asia belongs to them and to their king' (IX 116.3); and in the opening series of legends, 'for the Persians look on Asia as their own, and the barbarians living in it, and think Europe and the Greeks are separate' (ἥγηνται κεχ-ωρίσθαι) (I 4.4). There is no doubt that the various conquests and attacks involving any crossing into Asia or into Europe are marked, whether they be by Cimmerians, Scythians, Greeks or Persians.[52] Several of the dreams presaging expansion involve Europe and Asia.[53] Boedeker's fascinating discussion of the role of the hero Protesilaos speaks of a 'framework of division and hostility between the two continents', and shows convincingly the symbolic importance of the Artayctes–Protesilaos episode at the boundary between the two continents.[54] Immerwahr used the Persian view (at I 4.4) and the same story to show that for Herodotus, Asia and Europe are meant to be separate, and thought that 'between the *ideas* of Asia and of Europe there exists an ineradicable hostility',[55] the conflict rumbling on from the Trojan Wars down the centuries.

But it is striking that it is to the Persians that Herodotus attributes the idea that they had the right to rule all Asia, and this must imply that Herodotus is at least distancing himself from this view (in any case, on his own theory, 'Asia' is merely a conventional description of a recognizable

---

[52] E.g.: I 104.2 and 106.1, Scythians ruling Asia; II 103.1, Sesostris from Asia to Europe.

[53] I 107.1 (Mandane's dream, Asia); I 108.1 (vine over all Asia); I 209.1 (Cyrus' dream, wings over Asia and Europe); VII 19.1 (olive branches over whole world – Xerxes). See Immerwahr (1956), 271.

[54] Boedeker (1988): at 42.

[55] Immerwahr (1956), 250; quotation at 263.

part of the world). Moreover, while this passage (I 4.4) is the most explicit expression of the separateness of the two continents, all it says is that, while the Greeks are always hostile (*polemion*) since the time of Troy, the Persians think that Europe and the Greek race (*to Hellenikon*) are 'separated' – not inevitably hostile. The series of legendary injustices set out here are precisely that, injustices which can be avenged, rather than indications of inevitable and lasting enmity. When Themistocles declared in his famous speech that the gods were jealous that one man should rule both Asia and Europe, this comment occurred in a deliberately dissembling speech, and is not an indication of wide acceptance that one man should rule Asia.[56] These declarations are presented as opinions in contexts difficult to evaluate, but in any case, Themistocles' comment would expressly exclude the Greeks of Asia Minor. I find it hard to believe that any Greek from Asia Minor was happy to accept the idea that Asia was inevitably and rightfully the province of the Persian king – indeed later Greek history confirms precisely how very shaming such an idea could be. Nowhere else in the *Histories*, so far as one can see, is there anything similarly explicit.

In other words, the idea that the continents as such, as part of their inherent character, are inevitably hostile to one another seems less well borne out by the *Histories* than one might have expected. The theoretical declarations Herodotus made about continental division seem, in fact, to be maintained: he uses the names of the continents as they are habitually used by everyone, while believing that they are so divided purely as a matter of convention. Asia may belong to the Persian domain, *de facto*, but Herodotus does not connect either Europe or Asia with any particular traits of character for their inhabitants as one sees, for instance, so clearly in *Airs*. This would fit with what we have seen elsewhere with the otherwise difficult and anomalous position of the Greeks in Asia.

Yet at the same time it is undeniable, as Boedeker has shown, that the crossing from Asia to Europe and *vice versa* does denote some sort of transgression in the *Histories*. The bridging of the Hellespont 'breaks down the natural division between the continents',[57] itself a monumental act of arrogance; the crossing into Europe or the crossing into Asia are symbolically momentous. Perhaps we can suggest that Herodotus' narrative of the Persian Wars is bound by widespread perceptions of the importance of the Europe–Asia crossing, carried along by its emotional and symbolic importance – not to mention the feat of crossing the Hellespont – while at the same time Herodotus is aware of the intellectual problems with the conventional divisions of the continents, and any overdetermined

---

[56] Herodotus VIII 109.3.   [57] Herodotus VII 33 ff.: Boedeker (1988), 43.

sense of their eternal significance (chapter 4 goes on to examine the importance of *nomos* in human societies). This is one of the most striking examples of the combination of the traditional and the new in Herodotus, in which the narrative has a symbolic logic which Herodotus elsewhere distances himself from. He is perhaps engaged in two different modes here, the more Homeric and poetic tradition, which uses the continental boundaries to show the hybris of the Persian attempts at expansion beyond their proper realms, and the more abstract argument about the arrangement of continents which eschews any idea of continental determinism, indeed objects to the set divisions in the first place as merely conventional.

Conclusion

Dividing the world, then, could be a serious matter in the latter half of the fifth century. Herodotus objects to continental division on the grounds that it is artificial and merely conventional. Continents are criticized in terms which are strikingly reminiscent of the preoccupations with the *nomos–physis* antithesis of the time and of contemporary unease with the relation between names and reality. 'Europe' and 'Asia' are so named purely by convention, he insists, and at no point, in fact, does he imply a real, natural and politically crucial division between Europe and Asia. In any case his conception of the importance of retribution tells against this, and uses a quite different model to explain the relationship.

Airs, however, uses continental division precisely for an overarching theory about the difference between Europe and Asia. I have argued that *Airs* is rather confused – confusing or conflating environmental determinism with continental determinism. However, it has a markedly East Greek outlook. It is at least not a tract on Greeks (i.e. Europe) and barbarians (i.e. Asia). Its divisions and theories bridge over these cultural distinctions, even though (as we saw above), the author of *Airs* is actually rather keen on cultural explanations as well as physical and environmental ones. In that respect it helps clarify by contrast Herodotus' own approach, what he says and what he could have said, and reminds us of the fascination these early writers on nature had for grand theory.

Herodotus' views can perhaps be connected with an East Greek view in his reluctance to see Europe and Asia as implacably opposed. The Europe–Asia division would be particularly difficult for Greeks of Asia Minor to accept if it was thought to justify Persian rule or to have any long-term political consequences which might separate it irrevocably from the other Greek states. This does not make it any easier to see why *Airs* espouses the division, except insofar as it can look like a physical and 'scientific' justification for the defeat of Greeks in Asia, an excuse for the relative weakness of Asian Greeks. But Herodotus was touchy concerning the ignorance of mainland Greeks about the Asia Minor coast if we can go on his wry comment about Greek reactions to the Persians' initial retreat, that the Greeks on the mainland had no idea what lay east of Delos – along the Ionian and Carian coasts – and were afraid it would be overrun with Persian soldiers and full of danger (VIII 132.3).

In that case the distinction that runs through the *Histories* between Greeks and barbarians is all the more significant. The crucial distinction in the end is between Greeks and barbarians, and indeed while Herodotus states in the Proem his intention to tell of 'the great and marvellous achievements of both Greeks and barbarians', it is precisely that distinction with which he begins the *Histories*. This is perhaps a self-conscious choice for cultural distinctions (and explanations) at a time when other alternatives – geography, continents – were being tried out.

Finally, there is a tension in the *Histories* between the traditional desire for symmetry, or the demands of theories such as that of environmental determinism, and the messier realities of world geography which are revealed both by his experience and by others, and which impinge both on the ethnographical sections and upon the main narrative (e.g. the course of Xerxes' invasion in Book VII). Herodotus goes out of his way to enumerate the Scythian rivers, the many different Scythian and non-Scythian tribes in that area, and to clarify where knowledge gives out. He is scornful of the idea that there is Ocean which neatly circles a symmetrical, round earth, but is drawn to supplement areas of murky geographical ignorance with ideas based on a similar symmetry, as he deduces the direction and flow of the Ister from that of the Nile. As he says about Europe, 'But the boundaries of Europe are quite unknown, and there is not a man who can say whether any sea girds it round either on the north or on the east, while in length it undoubtedly extends as far as both the other two [continents]' (IV 45.1). We are perhaps at a point where ideas about knowledge and truth are on the move, different and competing conceptions coexist of how to get at the truth, the unknown, from the poets, from experience and evidence of experience, to schematic or abstract theories, all with their own plausibility, none quite satisfying or sufficient by itself to jettison all the rest.

4 *Nomos* is king: *nomos*, environment and ethnic character in Herodotus

If Herodotus rejects the idea of Europe and Asia as great dividing lines in explaining the characters of their European and Asian inhabitants (chapter 3), we may wonder whether geography and climate actually have much role in the historical explanations of the achievements of the numerous peoples who appear in the *Histories*. Or is it customs, habits and laws, written and unwritten – all covered by the Greek term *nomoi* – which ultimately have the crucial part? If the overarching theme of the *Histories* consists of the encounters and conflicts of the Greeks and the barbarians, are these encounters seen in terms of physical environment rather than other elements such as culture or ethnic character (and I use 'physical environment' strictly in the sense of the title of *Airs*, i.e. climate, land, water etc.)? Can the achievements of Greeks and non-Greeks, Athenians and non-Athenians, Spartans and other Greeks really be set within this model, as part of the grand explanation for the Greek victory? The place of the physical environment seems, in fact, to sit rather uneasily amongst Herodotus' broader interpretations of the conflict. When we look closely at the main actors in the story of the clash between Greeks and non-Greeks, Lydians, Ionians, Greeks and Persians, there is a complex interplay, it is true, between physical environment and *nomoi*, customs or laws, but at every stage *nomos* is crucial (pages 104–14). Even with the Scythians, we saw (chapter 2) how their successful resistance to Persia's onslaught was helped by geography but how essentially it was the Scythian *nomoi* which were the most active agents. The implications of this stress on *nomos*, which can cross ethnic boundaries, deserve more emphasis than they have perhaps had: they have considerable implications for Herodotus' ideas (and assumptions) about politics, political systems and ethnic character. I look at two important areas – democracy and autochthony – where Herodotus seems to wish to draw his audience to a conclusion which was both controversial and involved particular views about human society and *nomos* (pages 114–22). We turn finally to the question of Herodotus' relation to the wider and much discussed sophistic interest in *nomos* (pages 122–33).

Environment, poverty, *nomos* and courage

It is generally clear that Herodotus' *Histories* give great weight to the role of custom, that he was well aware that customs may vary from people to people inexplicably, and that they may have equal validity (e.g. III 38). Yet geography also plays an important part in Herodotus' explanations or interpretations of various peoples. The final chapter of the *Histories* suggests a belief in the central importance of geography, perhaps even 'environmental determinism' in which people are treated as products of the soil and climate they grow up in, to the achievements and future of the Persians and others: what is the relation of this emphasis to the changing *nomoi* and alterations to a people's way of life which Herodotus also describes? The 'highly tangible and mechanistic doctrine of environmental determinism' (to use A. Lloyd's phrase), often used of Herodotus' mode of explanation, does not give due subtlety to the kind of explanations that Herodotus does offer for the achievements or non-achievements of the actors in his *Histories*.[1] In his wider picture, Herodotus does not follow a biological model in which humans can be treated as nourished and formed by their physical environment. Does the environment have merely subsidiary or indirect effects? Such questions encompass Herodotus' grand vision of history, the remarks at the beginning and end of the *Histories*, as well as his general view of Greek victory.

Part of the problem is that 'environmental determinism' can be used rather loosely, eliding too much, glossing over refinements. Besides, if we are right in seeing signs that Herodotus was aware of certain distinct scientific theories, then he may have a more complex relationship to contemporary debates about environment, *nomos* and *physis* than we would otherwise have thought. There is also a danger of over-stressing the environment at the expense of more variable factors in Herodotus' image of ethnic character, and of the conflict of Greeks and non-Greeks.[2]

So far we have come across different varieties of environmental influence, which may be distinguished as follows.

[1] A. Lloyd (1990), 225, suggesting that Herodotus' empiricist position inclined him to 'environmental determinism', and referring in particular to Egypt (and II 35.2); part of his 'scientific commitments' (ibid. p. 226). Cf. also A. Lloyd (1975), 165–6, mainly on II 77 and change of season; Heinimann (1945); and esp. Dihle (1962a). Cf. also Lateiner (1986), 10, which cites I 142.2, III 106.1–2, VII 102.1*, IX 122.3 for the interesting but improbable suggestion that 'Herodotus could even be a source for (rather than a borrower of) the Hippocratic theory of the effect of climate on health.' And at p. 16 (repeated, 1989, 158), 'Herodotus on occasion 'explains' national character by climate and topography', adding I 71.2*, II 35.2. But as he points out (1989, 157–61, and ch. 7, 145 ff.), other factors are in play, '*nomos* and *nomoi* are at the root' of the conflict itself and the Greek victory.
[2] The most recent discussion of Lateiner (1989) is careful not to do this – see n. 1.

Firstly, there is the 'extreme' biological model in which humans are like plants, nourished and formed by the physical environment, and in which their physical make-up is affected. For the Egyptians and Libyans, Herodotus linked their outstanding physical health, in Hippocratic manner, to climate, the absence of change in season in Egypt, and perhaps the dryness in Libya, or according to Herodotus, to the drying process of cauterization. Here Herodotus *is* willing to deduce information about physical well-being from climate to the physical character of the human inhabitants. The first half of *Airs* saw a close relation between the health of individuals, and therefore of whole groups in the same area, as determined by particular elements of the environment, with physiological and physical effects. For Scythia as we saw (chapter 2), Herodotus knows of this idea and uses it, yet in his Scythian *logos*, at least, he leaned more to the idea that the environment manifested itself through human customs and way of life. He saw the cold and wet nature of their land as important but more as a source for their way of life, their *nomoi*, giving the possibilities for their particular mode of existence, rather than affecting their physical character. Either he did not believe, or was not interested in, the deeper physiological impact of the cold and damp that the writer of *Airs* saw as afflicting the Scythians in their very physique, physical character, existence, and reproductive capacities. Herodotus was drawn rather to the indirect effect of *nomoi*, and in the case of the female disease, the idea of divine punishment.

Secondly, there is the continental application, which we see in *Airs*, and by which, as we saw, Herodotus was unimpressed. This is an extended version of environmental determinism. The writer of *Airs* tried to deduce ethnic character from the very continents themselves – Europe and Asia, though he was not spectacularly successful, and as we saw, introduced factors like constitution and *nomoi* into the uneasy equation.

And thirdly, there is the wider application by which the physical nature of a whole people, an *ethnos*, is affected by physical environment, which we examine further here, where a whole people is conditioned by climate (i.e. this is a somewhat more sociological application). *Airs* used this almost entirely, and the effect of the environment (climate, water etc.) reaches to whole peoples (Phasians) as well as individuals; Herodotus knows of it but, as we will see, does not go far with it.

When we turn to some of the most important Herodotean analyses of historical achievement, what emerges is just how little we can find of sheer biological and geographical determinism (i.e. humans like plants). When it comes to the determining forces behind success or failure, the rise and fall of cities and empires, we hear far more about custom, habit, *nomos*, political constitution. We should thus draw a far sharper distinction between the type of environmental determinism of the kind visible in *Airs* and other Hippocratic works, where physiological effects are expected, and the hints of it visible in Herodotus. Herodotus clearly thinks climate is an explanatory element, but most of the places where he mentions climate, and usually cited in this connection, seem to be doing either more or less than claiming that climate is crucial to ethnic character. His preferred explanations for the nature of human societies seem to involve factors which are dynamic and changeable, not static and immoveable: way of life, custom or *nomos*, political constitution. Ethnic character is not a given, a predictable concomitant of physical environment.

Herodotus' view of the forces of history laid emphasis, it is clear, on uncertainty and the predictability only of changing fortune – from the opening of Book I (ch. 5.3) through the story of Croesus right to the end of the *Histories*. But Herodotus expresses this changeability in part in terms of *nomos* versus physical environment (i.e. nature). I would argue that the role of the physical environment as an explanation of ethnicity is rather muted. It is quite overshadowed by other elements in Herodotus' most central sections on nature and culture; the effects of *nomos* are not only paramount but cross ethnic boundaries.

So we first meet the famous and adoring description of Ionia's climate in Book I, as being placed in the most beautiful position in terms of 'climate and seasons' (τοῦ μὲν οὐρανοῦ καὶ τῶν ὡρέων), of all we know, not oppressed by either the cold and the damp, nor by the hot and the dry, as are the areas to the north and south (I 142.1–2). It is interesting that Herodotus explicitly refers to the four qualities, a reference to a division of the world along these lines. The author of *Airs* had also mentioned 'the mixture of seasons' (ἡ κρῆσις τῶν ὡρέων, 12.3 J) and the 'moderate nature of the seasons' (ch. 12.6) of the land of Asia, where the 'blending' of seasons refers to the temperate nature of the climate; and he connected this with the fact that everything in Asia was beautiful and gentle. Whether Herodotus wanted to do exactly that, however, is doubtful. His praise of the climate seems unconnected with his immediate remark that they do not all share the same language, but have four kinds; and Herodotus says nothing here about the effects of such a climate either on health or ethnic character. Though the rest of Book I might suggest that he would want to link this beneficent climate with way of life more generally, his stringent criticism of the Ionians' unwillingness to undergo *ponoi* during the Ionian Revolt is in connection with their miserable attempt at military training (VI 11, esp. 11.2), and that reminds us of the indefatigable Spartan military training enforced by *nomos* (below: VII 102–4). At least there we are told clearly that the Spartans are indomitable because of their training, which is enforced emphatically by *nomos*.

We may contrast the way in which the author of *Airs* (ch. 12) connected lack of hardship (*ponoi* etc.) with the climate of Asia. Herodotus seems to be drawing attention to inadequate *nomoi* rather than enervating climate.

The other famous description of the climate, this time the climate of Greece, contrasts the way 'the furthest parts of the earth', such as India, have the most beautiful things, while Greece has 'the most beautiful mix of seasons' (τὰς ὥρας ... κεκρημένας) (III 106.1). It seems to be going too far to say, with Lateiner, that 'The Hellenes enjoy a variety of seasons and a temperate climate that stimulates rather than enervates them.'[3] Herodotus says nothing here about health or any other related attribute. He draws no explicit conclusions about Greek physique, health or anything else (though it may be implied). It seems mean-spirited to accuse Herodotus of being inconsistent or of not fully understanding the theory, given that he is aware of such ideas; it would be preferable to suggest instead that he simply did not take it to the extreme lengths of *Airs*. In fact Greece and Ionia seem to be given very similar descriptions, and the further meaning of the temperate climate is unclear. The 'mixture' (Ionic: *kresis*) of seasons is here applied by Herodotus to Greece; yet *Airs* saw the significant 'mixture' in Asia, and connected it with the general gentleness and incapacity for hardship (ch. 12). Herodotus' picture of climatic effect seems to be running along different lines.

Yet more, on the other hand, is implied in those various passages throughout the *Histories* where there are lines of connection clearly being made between land, poverty, way of life, *arete* (virtue) and worldly success. This very theme ends the *Histories*, forming the final chapter (IX 122), in such a way as to offer an interpretation of the events within the *Histories* and, as has often been pointed out, to leave the audience with a warning of universal significance. It arches over the *Histories* from the Lydians at the beginning, the Ionians, the Greeks and the Persians in an elaborate piece of ring composition which encompasses Herodotus' initial warning about great and small states (I 5.4), Croesus' fall and the rise of Cyrus.[4] The final chapter takes his audience right back to the days before the Persian empire and to a suggestion made to Cyrus to move from their

---

[3] Lateiner (1989), 159: citing III 106.1; VII 5.3; with I 142.1, VII 10α3*, and *Airs* 12. Nestle (1938), 25–6 sees a straight connection of Hdt. III 106, I 142, IX 122, VII 102 with *Airs*.

[4] For discussion of this ending, now generally thought deliberate, and ring composition, see esp. Lateiner (1989), ch. 1, esp. 44 ff.; Bischoff (1932), 78–83 (= Marg 1962, 670–6); Boedeker (1988); Raaflaub (1987), 244–6; Moles (1996); Dewald (1997); Beck (1971); Herington (1991); Wolff (1964).

sparse land and get some better;[5] Cyrus answered with the advice, which we all know was disregarded, at least by later Persians if not by Cyrus, that they should stay put, on the grounds that 'soft lands give rise to soft men' (μαλακοὺς ἄνδρας); 'for it is never the case that the same land can produce both wonderful produce and men who are good in war' (IX 122.3). When they leave their 'sparse and rugged land' and rule all of Asia, they will cease to be rulers and become ruled (122.1). So the Persians took Cyrus' advice and chose to rule whilst living in a land which was poor (λυπρήν), rather than tilling the plain and being slaves to others.[6]

This sounds at first like a straight biological link, somewhat like the opening of *Airs* ch. 12 (12.2 J: 'I hold that Asia differs very widely from Europe in the nature of everything, both the plants which grow from the soil and the men'). There is a clear biological metaphor of growth, and Herodotus is evidently playing with geographical and biological explanations. But the chapter should not be taken on its own, and in any case the link involves the corrupting effect of good things on a people's warlike spirit.[7] When one looks more closely, a wealthy, fertile environment, a generous beautiful land, is envisaged as enervating, or conducive to luxurious living, but so are the accompanying customs. So the Persians at the time of their defeat by the Greeks are contrasted in their extravagance with the Greeks' poverty and sparse life-style, particularly that of Sparta (IX 82).[8] At the very beginning of the *Histories*, the Persians are still lacking in 'good things', still not in control of all Asia. It is the wise adviser to Croesus who warns against attacking the Persians, for they are poor, they have neither wine nor figs, 'nothing good', so that if the Lydians beat them, the Lydians would acquire nothing good, yet if the

---

[5] The Greek runs as follows: κότε γὰρ δὴ καὶ παρέξει κάλλιον ἢ ὅτε γε ἀνθρώπων τε πολλῶν ἄρχομεν πάσης τε τῆς Ἀσίης (IX 122.2): 'For when will it be better than when we rule over many men and all of Asia.' I regard this as a reference, in a further link of the ring, to the time before Cyrus conquered Lydia and its good things (see further below); as also Erbse (1992), 43. If it refers to the Persians as *already* ruling all of Asia (as taken by e.g. Moles), then there is a further stage of degeneration.

[6] On the theme of hard and soft, good analysis in Lateiner (1989), 49f.; Redfield (1985); Gould (1989), 59–60; Moles (1996), 265–6; Evans (1991), 66–7; cf. Erbse (1992), 42–3 on IX 122 and its 'historicity' (seeing its origin in *Od.* IX 25–36); pp. 89–91 on relation of IX 122 to Masistes story – Xerxes represents the effeminization Cyrus feared.

[7] See esp. Lateiner (1989), 49: though his 'Cyrus ... endorses the sophistic doctrine of environmental determinism' seems to me to elide too much.

[8] For Persian luxury, see for example: I 133.3–4 (food), 135 (luxury); III 20.1–22 (gifts); VII 135 (wealth of satrap); IX 82, the Persian and Spartan banquets; IX 81–3, booty from Plataea cf. VIII 26.3* (Tritantaechmes, the Persian, on Greek indifference to money); comparison with Greek bravery, VII 210–11.

Persians beat the Lydians, then the Lydians would be throwing away enormous benefits (*agatha*): 'once they have a taste of our good things, they won't be driven away' (I 71.2–3*) – a further element of the ring composition bridging the first and last books. Herodotus adds helpfully to his Greek audience who, given the fifth-century reputation of the Persians, might easily misunderstand such a remark, 'For before they conquered the Lydians, the Persians had nothing either luxurious (*habron*) or good (*agathon*)' (71.4) – a timely reminder of the movement up and down of cities and peoples that Herodotus hints at darkly at the very start (I 5.4).[9] Croesus also seems to press this point home in his advice to Cyrus about the plundering of Sardis, reminding Cyrus that this would be unwise since the wealth of Sardis was now his (I 88.3), and that the Persians are poor and such wealth may have dangerous effects – as Croesus says at this point (I 89.2), 'The Persians are poor and proud by nature'.[10] Cyrus prepared a banquet to persuade the Persians to revolt from the Medes, to contrast these and 'many other good things' with the labours under which they suffered at present (I 126). We might also wish to bring in the Persian customs that Herodotus goes out of his way to admire and which may be said to be in decline by the time of Xerxes or at least in the person of Xerxes himself.[11] A process of learning is involved; as Herodotus puts it, Persians 'immediately adopt any luxury they hear of' (καὶ εὐπαθείας τε παντοδαπὰς πυνθανόμενοι ἐπιτηδεύουσι, I 135).

As for the Lydians, we are here presumably meant to understand that the Lydians have these good things from the benign nature of the land, but something more than simple environment is at issue, something more like Lydian *diaita*, way of life and habits, rather than climate alone. For the Persians will get to know such good things (*agatha*) and like them, and therefore change from their hardy habits of life (and not leave Lydia either). The trouble about the Ionians is that they too took on Lydian habits of life. The accent seems to be tilted less towards climate and physical surroundings, the 'biological' model, as having a direct, immediate effect, and more towards way of life and social surroundings, the sorts of things you can 'get to know, get used to' (for example, those famous

---

[9] Cf. Moles on the potential corruption of all imperialism as a theme in Herodotus (1996, esp. 265–6); yet here Herodotus deliberately signals previous lack of anything 'good', so one suspects he's focusing not on general potential, but on specific life-style, the luxury that comes with imperial power.

[10] Πέρσαι φύσιν ἐόντες ὑβρισταὶ εἰσὶ ἀχρήματοι. Cf. Erbse (1992), 24–30 on the Croesus–Cyrus relationship and Croesus as adviser. Cf., perhaps, the hard-working women of Europe, pointed out by Immerwahr (1956), 263: Paionian women, Hdt. v 12–17, and Greek handmaidens for Atossa, III 134.5.

[11] Point made by Erbse (1992), 178–9 – a lucid discussion of the excellence of traditional Persian customs.

Lydian luxuries), though the two are inevitably linked. The Lydians after their defeat are then made even more 'soft' by some precisely targeted advice from Croesus to Cyrus about damaging changes to their way of life which will render them incapable of revolting – they should be forbidden weapons, be made to wear tunics under their cloaks, buskins on their legs, and educate their sons to play the lute and harp, and – anticipating Napoleon's famous criticism of the English – engage in shop-keeping, καπηλεύειν (I 155.4*). Yet before the Persian rise under Cyrus, Herodotus had explained, in the narrative of Croesus' conquests, 'For at this time there was no *ethnos* in Asia more courageous and stronger than the Lydians' (I 79.3). There is, then, a diachronic dimension that forbids over-emphasis on climate as a determinant, and which links Lydian decline precisely to factors that may equally affect other societies. Hence we are told by Xerxes in his address to Demaratus, of the Persians under his rule and therefore long after the great days of Persian hardiness and bravery, that the Persians will fight through fear, fear of the whip, fear of their ruler (VII 103).

Similarly with the various hints of the moral to be drawn about Greek success, which can be combined into the same picture of development. The greatest full-scale analysis of the 'environmental' and circumstantial factors behind the Greek success, occurs in one of the most important sections of the *Histories*, the debate between Demaratus and Xerxes (VII 101–4), and the explicit terms of the debate indicate that Herodotus was indeed thinking in these terms, they are not simply a product of modern imagination.[12] Again, oddly, this is brought out through the words of a wise adviser, for Greek poverty, poverty of the land and the Greeks generally, is brought up in the fascinating first speech by Demaratus to Xerxes (VII 102.1). Xerxes has asked how the Greeks could possibly withstand his onslaught; Demaratus replies that they will, especially the Spartans, however much they are outnumbered:

τῇ Ἑλλάδι πενίη μὲν αἰεί κοτε σύντροφός ἐστι, ἀρετὴ δὲ ἔπακτός ἐστι, ἀπό τε σοφίης κατεργασμένη καὶ νόμου ἰσχυροῦ· τῇ διαχρεωμένη ἡ Ἑλλάς τήν τε πενίην ἀπαμύνεται καὶ τὴν δεσποσύνην.

Poverty is always a habitual companion in Greece, but *arete* (valour or virtue) is acquired, gained from wisdom and from strong law; by her valour, Greece keeps both poverty and tyranny at bay. (VII 102.1)

---

[12] Surprisingly seldom connected with the hard/soft theme of IX 122. On VII 101–4, see esp. Dihle (1962). Boedeker (1987) is suggestive: little, however, on the exchange here (cf. conclusion, p. 201, Herodotus comments 'principally by means of suggestion and juxtaposition rather than explicit analysis').

The initial reference is to the poverty of the land; poverty is always a habitual or indigenous companion (*suntrophos*), probably hinting at the theme of poverty nourishing a people's warlike spirit again. Yet poverty is immediately put in its place for he adds 'But *arete* is acquired' (ἔπακτός), and *arete* is produced from *sophie* and from a 'strong *nomos*'; with that (i.e. *arete*), Greece can drive off poverty and tyranny. It is very clear here that physical environment, which is presumably responsible for the poverty in the first place, is being set alongside and indeed beneath, *arete* and its progenitor *nomos* as the crucial factors which were to be explanations of Greek and in particular Spartan bravery. Poverty is *suntrophos*, literally, something you 'grow up together with', used of growing organically, growing naturally, and it can be used thus of illness by the Hippocratic writers.[13] This suggests, then, that the opposition between poverty and *arete* is that between nature and *nomos*. This is elaborated in Demaratus' second explanation which responds to Xerxes' characteristic incomprehension, and his usual reliance on sheer human numbers as guarantees of success. For Demaratus then explains that, no, each individual by himself is not strong, but what he means is that they have *nomos* which binds them – the *despotes nomos* – so that they can fight very much larger numbers. Xerxes had insisted that Persians would never fight a far larger force unless they were made to by fear: it was fear that would make them 'stronger than their *physis*' (παρὰ τὴν ἑωυτῶν φύσιν ἀμείνονες, VII 103.4) – quite different, we note, from the Persians under Cyrus (I 89.2). Demaratus' answering insistence on the role of *nomos* here for the Spartans seems, then, to be saying that in their case, 'tyrant *nomos*' is what serves to render them 'greater than their nature'. The debate is being drawn up in part along the lines of *nomos* and *physis*. Lateiner's analysis perhaps elides too much too rapidly: 'In sum, barbarian ingenuity and diversity do not obscure Herodotus' reasoned belief in Greek mental and moral superiority, a result of climate, poverty, political institutions and competitiveness.'[14] There is a subtle structure to the debate of Demaratus and Xerxes; the debate is couched partly in terms of nature and culture, the crucial terms used are complex as well as resonant, and the argument is about the relative, not absolute importance of these factors. They do not declare an inherent, unalterable Greek superiority, but involve precisely those qualities which are changeable. Indeed in the case of the all important *nomos* here, we are dealing with qualities which belong rather obviously to the Spartans, and not to the whole body of the Greeks.

---

[13] See Stein, note ad loc.
[14] Lateiner (1989), 160 (and further, ch. 8 for competitiveness). Note that Carians can also be 'better than their nature', V 118.2.

In an elaborate and subtle article, Dihle saw this conversation as an exchange not only between Demaratus and Xerxes, but also between the theories of what he called 'Ionian ethnography' and the more sophistic views with which Herodotus concludes the episode.[15] Thus in Dihle's interpretation, when Demaratus initially says that the Greeks have poverty and *arete*, Xerxes takes this in the sense of Ionian ethnography, that is, as factors which have an effect on individuals separately (and represented by *Airs*). Then Demaratus has to correct him and explain more fully: here we meet the more elaborate description of how *nomos* works its effects, and *nomos* is a force which works on the whole society, it is a societal force which, for Herodotus and the Greeks, contrives to render the group of individuals stronger than they would be as a mere collection of individuals, the whole stronger than its parts (hence ἁλέες at 104.4). For Dihle, this is a sophistic way of looking at human society: we thus have a sophistic theory overcoming the ways of Ionian ethnography, though Dihle unfortunately does not develop this point. This would reveal Herodotus embracing the sophistic theory.[16] The difficulty seems to lie in the definition of what constitutes Ionian ethnography: how can one be so clear about the nature of Ionian ethnography (with its supposed stress on the effect on individuals as part of nature)? Dihle also draws what now seems too rigid a distinction between the polis development of the mainland and the 'apolitical' conditions of Asia Minor after the Persian conquest, which he thinks could therefore not countenance ideas about the development of the whole society – Ionian anthropology, for him, asks only about the nature of the individual man.[17] Yet even *Airs* includes societal *nomoi* in its schemes of explanation; Protagoras who had political theories, was connected with the Ionian colony of Abdera. At any rate, the simple environmental explanation (poverty of land, poverty of spirit) is deliberately put in second place, in this critical exchange, next to the humanly constituted *nomoi* of the Spartan life-style.

Certainly *nomos* and an all embracing influence on the whole polis (society) are here given the clinching argument and analysis which are eventually borne out by events. The implications are similar in the tale of Cyrus' advice at the end of the *Histories* that the Persians should not try and move to a richer land, and the counterpart in the Lydian–Persian exchanges in Book I, where Lydian luxury is contrasted with the endur-

---

[15] Dihle (1962a); cf. also Heinimann (1945), 29–36; Evans (1965) neglects wider intellectual context. Cf. the important discussion of *nomos* here in Humphreys (1987).

[16] Dihle (1981) develops this, tracing the role of ethnography in later arguments about the individual and free will, esp. 59 ff.; points out slight contradiction in v 78 (democracy works via individuals fighting for *themselves*).

[17] Dihle (1962a), 210.

ance (and poverty) of the oncoming Persians. In other words, Herodotus did not fully embrace the idea that climate had a fundamental effect on human society – though human health in Egypt and perhaps Libya could be affected by climate.

The odd exception, often cited to indicate environmental determinism, is the extraordinary description of Egypt as 'opposite' (II 35.2). Here Herodotus makes what is apparently a loose analogy between the way Egyptians have a quite different climate from anyone else and a river quite different in 'nature', and the way their manners and customs are also 'quite the opposite' to those of the rest of mankind ('Not only is the Egyptian climate different from that of the rest of the world, and the river quite unlike other rivers in nature, but the people also in most of their manners and customs (ἤθεά τε καὶ νόμους) seem to have reversed the practices of others') – manifested in their habits of weaving, trading, eating, writing and many other activities. This crude remark, almost more redolent of paradoxography or collections of 'wonders' than anything else, seems either a loose analogy, no more, as Immerwahr has suggested persuasively, or else, if he is really trying to draw exact connections between strange climate and perverse or opposite customs, a somewhat anomalous view compared to those others we have been looking at. Opposites, schematic antitheses, seem to be at issue rather than anything else (we return to this in the last section).[18]

Such passages suggest that institutions, customs, laws, are indeed fully part of the analysis of 'ethnic' character, and a part in historical explanation, and that a much subordinate part belongs to the geographical and climatic factors which must set the scene and create possibilities for certain human customs (as for example the Scythians) but which are not determinants in any absolute sense.[19] The presence of 'environmental determinism' in any pure biological sense in Herodotus seems muted.

It has perhaps been exaggerated by some sort of conscious or unconscious comparison with *Airs*, and a simplified reading of *Airs* at that. But

[18] See Immerwahr (1956), 279 for 'proportional relationship' ('Egyptian customs differ from those of the rest of mankind *not because* Egypt's geographical situation differs from the rest of the world, but *just as* it is different'); 'analogue', Immerwahr (1966), 15. Cf. Lateiner (1986), 16: 'this solitary example may reflect a peculiar debt to other ethnological writers on a popular subject'; and (1989), 158–9 (but I can see nothing in II 35 linking Egypt's climate with its acceptance of despotism, as suggested at p. 159). Could it be a joke? – I have heard (in Galway) a variation on the claim that Egyptians eat outside etc. (35.3) as a joke about the Irishman in America who is amazed by what he finds: for in Ireland people go to the lavatory outside but eat inside, in America, a much richer country, they have lavatories inside but eat outside. See also below, pp. 130–1.

[19] J. Hall (1997) 44–5, on VIII 144.2, suggested that Herodotus' innovation in definitions of ethnicity is to add religion and customs.

as we saw, the author of *Airs* produced a theory that was consistently one of environmental determinism for the particular physiological effects on humans as individuals. Even there he added that way of life, *diaita,* was crucial also. When he came to broad characteristics of ethnic character, while pressing a most improbable 'continental determinism' which is neither environmental nor climatic in any exact and plausible sense, the author admitted that institutions and *nomoi* were very important factors indeed, so important, in fact, that they could counteract the grim effects of climate so vividly described. Greeks and barbarians even in Asia could have the moral courage of Europeans, if they were only autonomous and free of despots (see above, pages 90–3). This implies, in fact, that even *Airs, Waters, Places* could well have added *nomoi* into the title, and that its eventual combination of elements behind the character and behaviour of other peoples was not actually that different from Herodotus'.

If we look in Herodotus for the kind of clichés and stereotypes about barbarians (or Persians) being effeminate and weak, we can indeed find them: in part connected with Xerxes' luxury and arrogance, but also in strikingly rhetorical arguments used by the characters of the narrative. Aristagoras' treacherous and misleading attempt to persuade the Spartans to help the Ionian revolt, was quite differently argued from his address to the Athenians, and traded in all the Greek clichés about 'the barbarians' being fabulously rich, possessing much silver and gold, and also herds (note all the superlatives beginning in *polu-* here); and easy to defeat since they wore trousers and turbans ... (v 49.3). The arguments of Mardonios about the beauty and fertility of Europe are equally misleading (vii 5.3). In both arguments are produced in misleadingly persuasive contexts. They contradict statements made elsewhere in the *Histories* in the author's own person precisely because they belong to the treacherous rhetoric of Aristagoras and Mardonios.

It may also be emphasized that Herodotus' views here imply that ethnic character is very far from immutable (as suggested by the term 'determinism'), indeed ethnic character is dynamic and will change. This can be connected with his stress on changing fortunes of individuals and cities that is built up so forcefully in Book I, and that seems to be linked with the implications of the final chapter, often seen as a warning to the next empire, that of the Athenians. The final anecdote about Cyrus' warning points to a change in the Persians. The Lydians at the start of the *Histories* are brought low by Croesus' ill-advised war, then even lower by their change in life-style (I 155.4*): their weakness is acquired. At the first Persian conquest of Ionia in the sixth century, Herodotus says that the whole Greek *genos* was weak, but by far the weakest was the Ionian (I 143.2); if the Ionians had only listened to Bias' advice to emigrate, they would have been the most fortunate of the Greeks, but staying in Ionia they would never see freedom (i 170). That this impression is quite intentional is shown by Herodotus' grim opening warning that he would treat all cities, great and small, knowing that 'those many cities which were once great, have mostly become small, and those that in my time were great, were in former times small' (i 5.4). This could hardly be more explicit.[20] Ethnic character, then, the qualities of Persians or Lydians, Greeks or non-Greeks, seems to be as changeable as the fortunes of cities great and small.

Democracy

It is in this connection, perhaps, that we can also see Herodotus' remarks about democracy. He went out of his way to point out that Athens was weak until she got rid of her tyrants; and yet once she did that and acquired *isegoria*, she became powerful (ηὔξαντο) and started to defeat her neighbours, in the first instance Chalkis and the Boiotians (v 66.1; and esp. v 78). His explanation of how this can occur (v 78) is one which does not receive much airing in all the current discussions of ancient democracy: if people work for themselves, they fight far better than if they are fighting in wars which bring gain only to someone else; democracies are better in war. There may be several undercurrents here. Firstly one wonders if this remark in connection with Athens and her rise to prominence would not have aroused knowing glances in Herodotus' audience in the time of the Athenian empire and its seemingly inexorable expansion over the Mediterranean at the cost of its allies' autonomy. Secondly, the explicit connection of democracy (here, the Cleisthenic democracy) with success in war, as opposed to anything else, is surprising and may be understood less idealistically than Herodotus' approval elsewhere of the benefits of liberty (cf. *Airs* ch. 12: Asian softness means among other things that they are poor in war). Thirdly, it reminds one of the mutability of such things; Athens must be one of those cities which Herodotus hinted is now great but once was small (i 5.4), an observation which is perhaps deliberately taken up by Thucydides' comparison of Mycenae, once great, Sparta and Athens (i 10.1–3).

---

[20] Note that both alternatives end with 'small', unusually pessimistic in tone (cf. also Thucydides at the start of his history). Hence I cannot agree with Lateiner (1989, 49), on ix 122: 'The *Histories* thus end with Cyrus' prognostic because the defeat of oriental expansion and megalomania, not the growth of Hellenic power, constituted Herodotus' concern and goal' (he goes on to talk about the Greeks being the agents of eternal balance). A warning to Athens: see above all, Boedeker (1988); Moles (1996).

Moreover, Herodotus' causal analysis of the effects of democracy is virtually identical to that voiced by the author of *Airs* for Greeks and barbarians (in Asia) who are autonomous: the same view of human motivation is brought into play, as pointed out by Dihle (1962a). Besides, Herodotus' explanation of the power of democracy can and should be brought into any discussion of the roles of physical environment and *nomoi*. Autonomy in *Airs* is one of the *nomoi* that can alter the ineffectual nature of inhabitants of Asia; so, presumably is the democracy to which Herodotus gives identical explanatory power. Democracy is a *nomos* also.[21]

Herodotus' insistence on the Persians' relation to democracy is surely pertinent here. As often noted with some embarrassment at its historical implausibility, Herodotus allowed the Persian conspirators to debate on three types of constitution, oligarchy, monarchy and democracy (III 80 ff.). They chose monarchy, of course, and Darius became king. Herodotus tells us that 'these words [or arguments: *logoi*] are disbelieved by some of the Greeks, yet they were said' (III 80.1: καὶ ἐλέχθησαν λόγοι ἄπιστοι μὲν ἐνίοισι Ἑλλήνων, ἐλέχθησαν δ' ὦν). Then again, at the time of the Ionian Revolt, the Persian Mardonios removed the tyrants set up by usual Persian practice to rule the Ionian cities, and allowed the cities to have democracy. Herodotus is again insistent on this fact and again brings into the open Greek disbelief that the Persians could have anything to do with democracy (cf. his more usual expressions of tolerant disbelief). For after the Ionian Revolt, Herodotus says (VI 42.1), there was no more strife (*neikos*) from Persians to Ionians but they carried out the following 'useful' measures: common Ionian agreements etc., measurements of land and tribute at nearly the same level as before the revolt. In addition (VI 43.3):

Here I will relate a great marvel (μέγιστον θῶμα ἐρέω) for those of the Greeks who cannot believe that Otanes declared to the seven conspirators that it was necessary to make Persia a democracy (ὡς χρεὸν εἴη δημοκρατέεσθαι Πέρσας); for Mardonios put an end to all the tyrants of the Ionians and established democracies (δημοκρατίας) in the cities.

Wholesale imposition of democracies in Ionia by Persians after the Ionian revolt would indeed be 'a great marvel'. But it is quite clear: Herodotus uses the work *demokratia* (not the weaker '*isonomia*'), which in the mid-fifth century and later could only be understood as democracy. Yet another gesture of defiance towards those Greeks who had not believed in a democratically inclined Otanes, and a 'great marvel' for any Greeks who

---

[21] As Evans, on constitutions generally: (1965), 151.

think the Persians could not possibly have any truck with democracy. This was proof that they were wrong.[22]

Why is Herodotus so dogmatic here? This back reference to the constitutional debate is usually seen only in terms internal to the text, a sign of Herodotus' previous readings perhaps,[23] or of his foolish insistence on his own accuracy on a matter which most modern historians disbelieve – and relevant only to the alleged incident just before Darius' accession.[24] Yet if we ask what Greeks in the mid- to late fifth century thought about the connection between Persia and democracy, most would have said there was none. The overwhelming evidence of Athenian tragedy linked democracy with Greece or still better, Athens. The dominant cliché about the Persians was that they were ruled by tyrants, the antithesis of Greek liberty.[25] Herodotus' insistence seems mischievous.

Athens may have been particularly implicated in this idea; the claim of Athenian propaganda, visible overwhelmingly in the evidence for the Athenian empire and its justifications, was that Athens had done most to save Greece from the Persians, that she freed the cities ruled by Persia and (perhaps more muted) that she gave them democracy. The setting up of such democracies has indeed been seen as one of the major benefits of the empire, and one that effectively counterbalanced any disadvantages in loss of autonomy and self-determination.[26] Against this background, any suggestion that the Persians could countenance democracy in their own state or willingly allow democracies elsewhere, would seem outrageously implausible. The incredulity Herodotus tried to combat may relate not only to the event before Darius' accession, but to any Persians of any period. For Herodotus, Cyrus brought freedom to the Persians, freeing them from the Medes (I 210.2). The discussion of Persian democracy is the only time Herodotus uses the term 'wonder' in this way, for a political message that goes against the tendency of the propaganda and clichés (which Herodotus partly accepts) developing about Persia after the Persian Wars.

---

[22] Note that the Medes were once free before Deioces took over power, and are described as 'autonomous' – αὐτονόμων (I 96.1).

[23] Though that is not exactly what he says.

[24] On the constitutional debate see e.g. Stroheker (1953/4); Morrison (1941); Dihle (1962a); Lasserre (1976); Harvey (1966); Lateiner (1984); Raaflaub (1990), esp. 41–9, puts it in a wider context; Demont (1994b), 81–5.

[25] E. Hall (1989), 191–5 (barbarian tyranny); Konstan (1987); Georges (1994) *passim* for this image (unnuanced). Persian rule in *Histories* is, of course, often linked to slavery; good section on Persians in Lateiner (1989), 152–5 (his list of 'good attributes' of barbarians, p. 152, omits the example of Persian-fostered democracy).

[26] Cf. de Ste. Croix (1954–5). Massive spread of democracy under the Athenian empire is usually accepted as fact: Meiggs (1972) – and cf. suggestive remarks on Herodotus pp. 4f. – though editors of the Athenian Tribute Lists were cautious.

These separate pieces of Herodotean polemic and explicit comment on the forces of his history, enable us to build up the following picture (perhaps speculative, but a coherent picture emerges). Democracy helped Athens grow powerful and it is therefore a most important thing, one of those *nomoi* which helped the Greeks defeat the Persians, for there is greater incentive for people to work or fight for themselves. But it is not a monopoly of the Greeks, or the Asians. The Ionians gained democracies after their revolt (in which Athens played a foolish and fatal part: she's out of it by Book VI), and what is more, the Persian satrap allowed them these democracies. Ionians were weak because they were governed by tyrants and had to fight for the Persians. Indeed we might go further and suggest that the story of the Ionian Revolt, whose detailed narrative is so problematic if one seeks a sociological and political explanation of the uprising, may be meant partly as an indictment of the system of Ionian tyrants. They were also weak because of their easy life (partly learned from the Lydians) and because they were not prepared to bear sufficient hardship at the time of resistance (VI 11–12). But Ionians can have democracy too, and Persians also; it is not a monopoly of mainland Greece, or Athens, or need not be. It is possible for barbarians and perhaps there is a hint also that had the Ionians had democracies they too would have been better at armed resistance.

Given Herodotus' emphasis on the existence of change in the status and character of any people, and on such change as accompanying changes in habits of life, then not only do we have a possible warning to Athens, but the implications are that both Greeks and barbarians can, if they want, have democracy, change their *nomoi*; and that ethnic character, mostly dependent on these customs, is mutable also. Alongside contemporary Athenian images of the barbarians or Persians specifically (and they *are* mainly Athenian), it is hard not to find Herodotus' democratically inclined Persians striking and controversial for his time.

Autochthony and Athens

If we turn from democratically inclined Persians to what Herodotus has to say about the early antecedents of the Athenians, we meet another puzzle of ethnic definition. The Athenian myth of autochthony might have presented a perfect opportunity for someone keen to link ethnic character with the land. Athenian myth and patriotic sentiment, after all, saw in their supposedly indigenous origins and (often linked) birth from the land the origin of Athenian nobility, equality and superiority.

Herodotus is well aware of the Athenian myth of 'autochthony': when he introduces Athenian early history, he says that the Athenians had always lived in their land, unlike the Spartans (I 56–8). He allows the Athenians to argue that they are superior to the Spartans – this for the benefit of Gelon of Syracuse – precisely because they were the oldest people in Greece, the only ones who had never moved (VII 161.3). This further reference was again to autochthony and to a political use of the myth which would have been familiar to audiences in the fifth century. Herodotus is apparently also aware of the way Athenian patriotic tradition (most obvious in the public funeral speech) linked autochthony with the series of mythical exploits in which Athenians had helped others, or repelled barbarian invaders. For he allows the Athenians to use these mythical achievements to assert their superiority over the Arcadians in their speech in Book IX (ch. 27) claiming the left wing in battle. Here they do not mention their autochthony, though it tended to accompany the other myths: but they could not flaunt it, precisely because the Arcadians also claimed they were indigenous; Athenians had no uniqueness here.[27] In the Athenian patriotic tradition autochthony became a many-edged weapon to assert political and cultural superiority. It became linked with several elements of Athenian democratic ideology in the fifth and fourth centuries, not merely superiority in general, loosely linked to being older than other Greek poleis, but also with Athenian claims to have become civilized first (e.g. Isoc. 12.124; Thuc. I 2, on importance of stability, implies a similar idea),[28] while other Greeks were still homeless, and with the more democratic ideas of equality of all the citizens, an equal nobility (*eugeneia*) which embraced them all (e.g. *Menex.* 239a–b).[29] It suggested that the Athenians, born from the earth and always living in Attica, were the most true Greeks. As Parker has put it, 'Athenians were, so to speak, the only authentic citizens of Greece, all other groups being mere immigrants, a motley rabble tainted with foreign blood.'[30]

Yet, while well aware of such traditions, Herodotus seems hardly to endorse them himself. Not only does he leave the patriotic interpretations specifically to Athenian speeches,[31] but he himself expressly linked Athenian military superiority to her democracy (*isonomia*: V 78). What is particularly curious for our purposes is how Herodotus takes the Athenian

---

[27] As Rosivach notes: (1987), 305.

[28] Cf. also: Isoc. IV 25–7; IV 28–9 (Athenians first to cultivate grain); IV 39, IV 63 (autochthony and superiority); VIII 49; *Menex.* 237c–238a, 238b (Athenians first to learn *technai*).

[29] See on this: Rosivach (1987); Loraux (1979), (1987); for specific connection with *epitaphios*, Thomas (1989); Ermatinger (1897). For suggestions on how the myth relates to fifth-century Athenian use of Ionian identity, Connor (1993a); J. Hall (1997) is good on relation of authochthony claims to older and contemporary Athenian links with Ionia.

[30] Parker (1987), at 195. Cf. *Wasps* 1076f. for the connection of true birth and autochthony, and courage.

[31] Parker (1987), 195, in fact cites Herodotus VII 161.3 along with Euripides *Erechtheus* fr. 360.6ff.N² as examples of 'hyperpatriotic interpretations' being first attested in the 420s.

myth in a direction quite different from those taken by patriotic Athenian sources, and in a direction of ethnic definition.[32] Here we need to return to the earliest appearance of Athenians in the *Histories* (I 56–8), at the point where Croesus enquires about them, and we, the audience, are told about Athens' earliest history.

When Croesus enquires about both Spartans and Athenians, Herodotus launches into an explanation of Athenian early history and the Pelasgians, those strange figments of Greek historiography, which throws us immediately into one of the murkier areas of Greek speculation about their remote origins (I 56–8). Croesus learns that of the Spartans and the Athenians, the one *ethnos*, the Spartans, was Dorian, the other, the Athenians, was Ionian; the one (obviously Athenians) were Pelasgian of old, the other (the Dorians) were Greek (*Hellenikon*).[33] The one (Pelasgians) never went anywhere, the other was 'much-wandering' (πολυ-πλάνητον), a reference to the Athenian claim that they had always lived in Attica, and the Dorian invasion, respectively. Then there is the question of what language Pelasgians spoke (I 57), and Herodotus concludes from the indications of present day communities that are Pelasgian remnants, that the Pelasgians spoke a 'barbarian tongue', and:

εἰ τοίνυν ἦν καὶ πᾶν τοιοῦτο τὸ Πελασγικόν, τὸ Ἀττικὸν ἔθνος ἐὸν Πελασγικὸν ἅμα τῇ μεταβολῇ τῇ ἐς Ἕλληνας καὶ τὴν γλῶσσαν μετέμαθε.

If therefore all the Pelasgians were like this, the Attic *ethnos*, being Pelasgian, at the same time as their change to being Greeks, also changed their language. (I 57.3)

He points out that the Krestonians and Plakienians, who he thinks are Pelasgian, speak a quite different language from all their neighbours, yet he insists, 'the Greek *ethnos*' (τὸ δὲ Ἑλληνικόν) – that is, the Dorians – 'had always spoken the same language' (I 58.1).

There have been attempts to interpret Herodotus somewhat differently. The problems are compounded by the notorious obscurity surrounding the Pelasgians and by the fact that Herodotus' view of Pelasgians here is strictly incompatible with his remarks about them elsewhere.[34] But to describe the whole section as 'the fog and quicksand of an antiquarian

---

[32] A possibility neglected by (e.g.) Rosivach (1987); Parker (1987); J. Hall (1997) (who tends to take Herodotus as straight evidence for Ionian ethnicity). Georges (1994) notes the significance (see below, n. 44).

[33] Linguistic commentators have made a meal of this, but the overall result and Herodotus' meaning is clear: see most recently, McNeal (1985); Laird (1933), on meaning of σύνοικοι ἐγένοντο (I 57, II 51).

[34] E.g. the story about the Lemnian women (VI 136–40): Pelasgians are offered land by the Athenians, then expelled to Lemnos, unjustly according to Hecataeus, but the story still sees the Pelasgians as a separate and subordinate group to the Athenians. There are other Pelasgians in Herodotus who have moved, e.g. I 146.1; VI 137. See How and Wells on 56.2, and Appendix xv.

mire' misses the importance of this sort of debate in fifth-century Greece, and in particular what Herodotus is up to here.[35] McNeal argued, for example, that the whole passage (I 56–8) in fact involves a group of Pelasgians who live in Athens alongside the Athenians, more like alien workers who live *with* Athenians but separately; that the Athenians are not (at this early stage) wholly Pelasgian either, but that there is a 'Greek part' of Athenians, that is, an aboriginal part of the Athenian population who speak Pelasgian and a Greek-speaking part.[36] However what we cannot ignore are the remarks about the language (57.2–3) which seem relatively straightforward: the Pelasgians must have spoken a barbarian tongue to judge from Pelasgian remnants, and 'the Attic *ethnos, being* Pelasgian' therefore changed its language when it became Greek. The later remark about 'the Greek *ethnos*' (τὸ δὲ Ἑλληνικόν, 58.1), is most easily understood in the same sense as before (at I 56.2) to mean the original Greeks (i.e. Dorians).[37] We may add the later genealogy of the Athenians given in the Herodotean 'Catalogue of Ships' in Book VIII: 'the Athenians were Pelasgians when the Pelasgians held what is now called Greece, named Kranaoi, when Kekrops was king, they were called Kekropidai, when Erechtheus took power, they changed their name to Athenians, and when Ion son of Xouthos was general, they were called Ionians after him' (VIII 44.2).[38] Thus the Athenians were originally Pelasgians but joined the Greeks later and changed their language appropriately.

What is going on here? Herodotus seems to be taking the autochthony myth literally and rationalizing it into current ethnic definitions. If they had always lived in Attica, unlike the later Greeks, and if the Dorians who came south were original Greeks, then it follows that the Athenians

---

[35] Quotation from McNeal (1985), 11: 'Suddenly the sunlit landscape of the tale of Croesus disappears.' See J. Hall (1997) for the importance of ethnic affiliation within fifth-century Greece.

[36] McNeal (1985), esp. 17–18, taking τὸ Ἑλληνικόν as partitive, as also (he thinks) at I 60.3: so at I 58 Herodotus means 'the Greek speaking part of the Athenians'. This seems hopelessly forced.

[37] Cf. How and Wells on ch. 58 who question the precise implications of ἀποσχισθέν – the 'separation off' of Greeks from Pelasgians (and also 60.3); cf. the long Appendix XV. How and Wells' conclusion (p. 444) is: 'But it is clear that Herodotus only meant by these "Pelasgi" the Greeks in an undeveloped stage' – hence VIII 44. Asheri and Medaglia (1990), Commentary on 56–8, oddly, see τὸ δὲ Ἑλληνικόν of 58.1 as 'the Dorians and the mass of hellenized barbarians'.

[38] McNeal (1985) neglects the arguments put forward here about language. One should admit though that Herodotus' remarks (I 58) about the Hellenic *ethnos* originally being weak, when it 'splits off' from the Pelasgians, but then becoming stronger with the admixture of Pelasgians and other barbarian *ethne*, does seem muddled. Cf. II 51, which mentions the Athenians as *entering* the Hellenic body; but here the Pelasgians are conceived as coming to live with the Athenians.

were not originally Greek and did not speak Greek until they entered the body of the Greeks ('at the same time as their change to being Greeks', 57.3: a vague and ambiguous phrase). For, of course, they were Pelasgians earlier.

Can this bear any relation to Athenian traditions about their origins? It would seem not, or not at least with the particular spin Herodotus gives it.[39] So far as one can see, the Athenian use of the myth, far from spelling out the precise ethnic implications, seems to assume a continuity of culture and ethnicity: at least when Isocrates contrasts Athenians with those who are 'mixed' (μιγάδες, Isoc IV 24), he implies that Athenians are more purely Greek than the rest. Thucydides uses the same idea in his 'Archaiologia', where he declares that Greece in early times had a constantly shifting population in the fertile areas, whereas Athens, being poor in soil, never changed its inhabitants.[40] In Athenian tragedy, the Athenians keenly stressed their own nobility and autochthony in contrast to the barbarian progenitors or founders of Peloponnesians or Thebans; thus with the barbarian influxes or influences suffered by other Greek cities.[41] The manifestations of the myth in Athenian writers serve only to heighten by contrast the point Herodotus makes. The Athenian interpretation appears in the *Histories* voiced by Athenian speakers (VII 161.3, IX 27); in his own person, Herodotus tells his audience that the Athenians were once not Greek, and seems even to wish to emphasize the changes they had undergone (VIII 44.2).[42] While Athenian myth-making used the remote past to explain and define the present in an image of ever enduring stability, Herodotus seems willing to go far in his image of ethnic and polis character as unstable.[43]

---

[39] Cf. Stein's verdict, Commentary ad loc. (57.3).

[40] Isoc. IV. 24, of the Athenians: 'nor did we come together a motley crowd composed from many tribes (οὐδ' ἐκ πολλῶν ἐθνῶν μιγάδες συλλεγέντες), we are thus of a lineage so noble and pure ...'; cf. Isoc. XII.124. Thuc. I 2; cf. Thuc. VI 17.2–4*, for Alcibiades on the Sicilians as 'mixed', 'the cities are teeming with motley rabbles' (ὄχλοις τε γὰρ ξυμμείκτοις πολυανδροῦσιν αἱ πόλεις). Cf. also Eurip. fr. 360.7–10 N² (= Lyc. *Leocr.* 100); *Menex.* 238c; Lyc. *Leocr.* 47.

[41] Tragedy: E. Hall (1989), 168; cf. also Hall (1996) on 'When is a myth not a myth?'.

[42] Cf. also VI 35.1, signalling that Philaios, ancestor of the hero Miltiades, was the first of the family to be Athenian. We may guess that the later story (mentioned n. 34 above) about the expulsion of the Pelasgians by the Athenians, with Athenian disagreement about its justice, would be more suitable for Athenian pride (VI 137).

[43] Not expressed in terms of *nomos*: contrast Plato's *Menexenus* (239a–b) which expressed Athenian identity in terms of *nomos* and *physis*: *isogonia* disposes Athens by *physis* (κατὰ φύσιν), towards *isonomia* by *nomos* (κατὰ νόμον), 239a2–3. The speaker links autochthony (equal birth and *physis*) very closely with democracy (*nomos*): democracy (*nomos*), then, is simply an extension of *physis*. The speaker then claims that Athenians are pure Greeks, antagonistic by nature to barbarians (245c–d), and that unlike other Greeks they, the Athenians, are not *meixobarbaroi*.

We can only guess how his contemporary audience might have received this – this passage was probably not one of those Herodotus delivered in Athens.[44] Perhaps his fifth-century audience could take it as highly ironic, especially when the Athenians are made to lay claim later to a common Hellenism based, among other things, on language (VIII 144.2) – while they had indeed acquired a Hellenism by the time of the Persian Wars, it was not as old as they would like? Or purely provocative? For if the Athenian myth of autochthony developed as an anti-Dorian claim, then Herodotus seems to be developing the contrast between Athenian and Dorian in a way which is at the very least mischievous.[45] Perhaps it is relevant, too, how many strictly non-Greek peoples Herodotus claims are autochthonous: if it is a virtue, Athens is not alone. What is clear, at any rate, is that what Herodotus says in his own person implies that the boundaries between Greek and barbarian are permeable, and Greekness can be acquired (he also goes on to say that the Greeks became stronger also with the addition of several barbarian peoples, I 58). Thucydides opens his *History* with remarks about 'what is now called Greece', which read like a silent correction of either Herodotus' views, or views very like his (I 2.5–3): for there Thucydides discusses at length how before the Trojan War there was no entity called Greece, no group named Hellenes before Hellen son of Deukalion, nor were there barbarians, 'because the Greeks were not yet gathered together under one name'; the first Greeks were those with Achilles from Phthiotis.

Nomos and the barbarians

Herodotus' remarks linking a people's character to the climate and land they inhabit are, then, both muted and ambiguous. By comparison with the climatic explanations of *Airs*, his explanations for ethnic character are far more fluid than those of environmental determinism, just as he had declared that even the current divisions of the continents between Europe, Asia and Libya were only 'conventional'. Indeed there is more going on: the Demaratus–Xerxes exchange indicates a concern with *nomos* as a major explanatory factor, here to explain the Spartans' military courage, and explicitly allows it a superior role to *physis*. With the Ionians, their whole way of life, not merely the climate, indicated why they were en-slaved; as Herodotus lets Bias say, they could have ruled over a great

---

[44] As Georges (1994), 137 remarks.

[45] An anti-Dorian claim suggested by Parker (1987); also Legrand (1932), ad loc. Georges (1994) sees Herodotus as virulently pro-Dorian, noting neglected elements, but his claims are too sweeping, ignore Herodotus' subtlety, and neglect many important sections.

deal, had they only moved to the West – surely not merely pointing to change of climate and geography. Democracy, a central factor in Athenian success for Herodotus, is also a *nomos*. As we saw in his otherwise oddly categorical insistence on the Persians' acceptance of democracy for Ionia, it was a *nomos* that need not be confined to Greeks. Barbarians can benefit from democracy; the *nomos* is not ethnically determined, nor is it necessarily linked to any geographical conditions. One may perhaps suspect here a silent contradiction of Athenian claims or visions of the barbarians in the East. Finally in Herodotus' treatment of the autochthony of Athens, we may see how in fact it is the Athenian elaboration of the myth that sets the land at the centre of Athenian character. Herodotus, on the contrary, uses it to emphasize that the Athenians had acquired the Greek language and Greekness. He is very far from embracing a fundamental and inherent Hellenism here either (contrast Plato).

This puts the explanation for Greek success in the Persian Wars firmly in the realm of Greek *nomoi*, Athenian democracy, Spartan discipline, and factors which are fluid and changeable. Spartan discipline and *nomoi* make them 'greater than their nature' – even if they were the first Greeks, that was certainly not enough by itself. Athenian democracy was acquired, indeed they were not even Greek in early times and spoke a barbarian language. The Persians in the early days had had the qualities that would gain an empire, so had the Lydians.

As often said, prosperity (*eudaimonie*) is transient in Herodotus, an inherently archaic idea.[46] But while the idea persists in any case well into the fifth century,[47] Herodotus seems ready to add explanations in terms of *nomoi*, and it should be added that in his further explanations for Greek success and for earlier Persian success, the operative factors are also transient, flexible and mutable, and that they too involve an emphasis on *nomos* in all its manifestations. While he certainly comes down in agreement with Greek superiority, for all his 'philobarbarism', the grounds on which he does so involve fluid and changeable factors.

This emphasis stands out in especial contrast to Athenian patriotic tradition which stressed land, continuity and indigenous origins. Herodotus stresses change and interaction with barbarians, even borrowings from them. Perhaps this is connected in some way to his East Greek perspective and the recent experiences of Ionia – which were hardly such as to create an automatic confidence in innate Greek superiority.

---

[46] See Moles (1996) for sustained discussion: on the theme of transience, the Solon story is symptomatic of the whole.
[47] Cf. *Troades* 509f.; Hecuba says call no one lucky (εὐτυχεῖν) who is *eudaimon*, until they are dead.

Let us turn more firmly to the question of intellectual affiliation and influence. It is hard not to wonder whether Herodotus' emphasis on the mutability of ethnic character and on changing *nomoi* was informed – or even propelled – by the lively intellectual interest in the relation of *nomos* and *physis* in the latter part of the fifth century; or by other 'spin-offs' from that.

The role of *nomos* and *physis* in the late fifth century, particularly in sophistic thought, is well known; the gradual development of the two concepts, their multiple meanings, implications and the development of antithetical and judgemental interpretations, in which the two become opposed and one superior to the other, have been elegantly and extensively analysed in particular by Heinimann.[48] As Heinimann stresses, we should see a slow, gradual development rather than sudden change. But Herodotus' position here is difficult to discern – and it seems to have puzzled Heinimann – while more recent scholarship pays less attention to the question. While it is easily accepted that *nomoi* (in the sense of customs) are very important to Herodotus' views of human culture, what exactly is the intellectual background to this emphasis, or the differing connotations of the very word (from custom, divine order, laws, mere convention), and specific concrete instances of its implications?[49] Herodotus' remarks about *nomos* are sometimes close to some views associated with certain well-known sophists, as we saw in the case of Demaratus' exchange; and there is a possibility that some of his ethnography is influenced by these new ideas. The problem is how far to go along this route.

So for example we can see no sign in the *Histories* of the extreme antithesis of *nomos* and *physis* in which the writer takes sides, offers moral judgement for one in order to dismiss the other. This 'judgemental, antithetical' approach is visible, for instance, in the extreme espousal of nature as in some way 'true' as against the mere conventions and falsities of *nomos*.[50]

On the other hand there are less extreme cases where Herodotus does pair them suggestively in such a way as to imply that *nomos* and *physis* are not simply complementary but in some way antithetical. We have met most examples already. This was particularly clear in the Demaratus exchange. There, Xerxes at first says fear makes people better than their

---

[48] Heinimann (1945); cf. also Guthrie (1971); Kerferd (1981a); Pohlenz (1953); Gigante (1956), ch. 9 on Herodotus (diffuse); and Dihle (1962a), above.

[49] See esp. Heinimann (1945), passim, esp. 78ff., for different uses of *nomos* (but not democracy). Immerwahr, (1966), 306 ff., thought Herodotus' *nomos* wasn't sophistic, following Stier (1928). Cf. Humphreys (1987) on *nomos* in Herodotus.

[50] E.g. Antiphon and Hippias (further below).

physis; Demaratus retorts that 'tyrant *nomos*' (δεσπότης νόμος) is what is crucial (VII 103.4; 104.4). There is a hidden antagonism: Persian natural instincts, or nature, are counteracted by fear, Spartan nature by *nomos*. Herodotus implied that continents only exist by *nomos* (IV 45.5; IV 39.1); there is an implied antithesis here and a sense that *nomos* is somehow not entirely real, mere convention, not the pure truth. He remarks that Greeks do not understand at all either the *physis* or *nomoi* of the Egyptians (II 45.2). The antithesis between *nomos* and *physis* that Heinimann found in *Airs* is also visible in Herodotus.[51] And in his long discussion about the Nile, he makes a fascinating contrast between the 'right argument' (the ὀρθὸς λόγος) and 'what the Greeks are accustomed to believe' (τῷ ὑπ' Ἑλλήνων νενομισμένῳ ..., νομιοῦμεν ...), where *nomos* is effectively made to denote false belief (II 17.1–2).[52]

Not only are customs in their inclusive sense (religion, political constitution) marked strongly and suggestively throughout the *Histories*, but in Herodotus' scheme of explanation customs do explain almost everything, as we have seen.[53] Yet they offer an explanation which is set against a background of geography and physical environment as part of the historical picture, in which environmental determinism is less important. So when Herodotus says outright in the tale of Darius' experiment with Greeks' and Indians' treatment of their dead (III 38), that all people adhere to their own customs, *nomos* is indeed king, he implies some alternative view – *nomos* as opposed to what? To emphasize *nomos* in this period in this way presupposes some controversy, some debate, some alternative. It may be that his insistence was directed at men who thought human culture was determined by environment rather than at thinkers like Hippias or Antiphon who embraced *physis* in a different sense (nature). But at any rate he is making a stand for *nomos*.

He cites Pindar, it is true, as a conclusion to the tale, which might be taking refuge in traditionalism. However, not only does he use the phrase '*Nomos* is king' in a different sense from Pindar,[54] but the very expression of such a statement about the rule of *nomos* seems to have been a fash-

---

[51] Heinimann (1945), 29–35 on Demaratus, and esp. at 33, draws too rigid a distinction between Herodotus and his political explanation, and *Airs* with its 'rational, scientific' explanations (see ch. 3 above); he thinks Herodotus shares none of the knowledge of the doctors: e.g. p. 32. *Ibid.* pp. 40–1 on Hdt. II 45.

[52] See Heinimann (1945), 83 (with 84–9 on development of *nomos* as a concept opposed to truth).

[53] As Lateiner (1989), ch. 7, 146, *nomoi* are 'at the root' of the conflict and Greek victory. Cf. also Heinimann (1945), 29 ff., 82, for importance of *nomoi*; also Evans (1965) (without wider intellectual context), but oddly he decides that *nomoi* are not the 'moral cause' of the conflict.

[54] See Heinimann (1945), 67f. on Pindar. Callicles also cites it, Plato, *Gorg.* 484b.

ionable one in the latter part of the fifth century, albeit with various nuances. In Plato's *Protagoras*, Hippias says that *nomos* is a tyrant that forces man to do many things contrary to nature (337d1–e2). The first sentence of the Hippocratic *Gen./Nat. Child* opens with '*Nomos* governs all' (Νόμος μὲν πάντα κρατύνει) – though the author appears here to refer to natural law, that is (here) the regular processes of nature. To assume all these writers are simply referring to Pindar seems forced and over-literary given that discussion on *nomos* is so lively in the period. In this quotation, in the reinterpretation of a poet, and in his expression of *nomos*' power, Herodotus seems to be sharing a method and general sentiment (though with differing interpretations) with these other writers.

If we were left in any doubt that the whole section had close links with elements of contemporary ideas usually associated with certain prominent sophists, there remain the details of the Darius experiment which form one of the best concrete illustrations of 'sophistic relativism' that we have.[55] As already suggested (chapter 1), the tale is the best example of ethnographic data used to back up a statement about the relativity of human customs – and this may enable one to move on from the relatively narrow question of whether Herodotus used the *nomos–physis* antithesis. So sophistic is it, in fact, that Heinimann suggested that Herodotus got the whole story, as well as the concluding sentence on everyone preferring their own customs, from a sophist. Yet his explanation for its presence was convoluted and forced, constrained by rigid categorization of disciplines and a need to separate Herodotus quite distinctly from more 'intellectual' writers (the explanation can thus stand as an illustration of the problems of method involved). For he adds that we can take the Darius anecdote 'for a sophistic inference from pre-Herodotean ethnography'.[56] But this conjures up a strange picture of a sophist using pre-Herodotean ethnography (i.e. Hecataeus?) to make interesting relativist inferences, which are then borrowed wholesale – both anecdote and comment – by Herodotus himself; presumably this piece of unadulterated sophistry then lies unabsorbed like a lead weight in the *Histories*. This dodges the question of why it is placed in the *Histories* in the first place and how far it coheres with the rest of the work.

The tale of the Greeks' and Indians' horror at each others' habits could almost stand as an illustration of Protagoras' dictum that anything which is held right and good for a particular state is right and good for it

---

[55] On some problems with talking about sophistic 'relativism', along with generalizing from Protagoras, see Bett (1989).

[56] Heinimann (1945), 81 – and the inference is not by Herodotus but a sophist; but cf. pp. 79–80, and remark about Herodotus advancing in the direction of the 'Relativierung' of the sophists (p. 79). Cf. a similar problem with Dawson (1992), 18–21.

(*Theaet.* 167c, 172b, if this is Protagorean; cf. 170a for the individual's subjectivism). We can never know whether Protagoras actually used such an example in his lectures or writings, though he could have.[57] But even if he did not, we may note the further extrapolation Herodotus makes which is so close to the Protagorean view – 'For if one were to offer men to choose out of all the customs (*nomoi*) in the world those that seemed to them the best, they would examine all and end by choosing their own; so convinced are they that their own customs are by far the best' (III 38.1). Nor can we pinpoint an exact origin for the story. What is clear is that it is too coloured by Greek ideas to have come in unadulterated form from a Persian account; and it so perfectly bears the mark of a particular sophistic *logos*, that we must at least affirm that, rather than inserting it as 'raw material', Herodotus was ready to emphasize its message in a manner suspiciously consistent with contemporary experiments with subjectivism and relativity. A weaker variation, a remark about everyone preferring their own evils to others', appears elsewhere (VII 152.2). We can jettison any idea that Herodotus inserted it unknowingly as 'raw material', or was unaware of its contemporary implications.

There are other reasons for believing that Herodotus' descriptions of other peoples may often have been influenced by ideas associated with 'the sophists' – whether by a specific individual or general ideas in circulation (below). Or perhaps we should speak of a degree of interaction (a deliberately vague word): rather than ask whether any one sophistic writer ever said something similar, something the evidence seldom allows one to answer, it is preferable to suggest, first, that Herodotus' enquiries are sometimes informed or even formed by some of these ideas; and secondly, that his descriptions were couched in terms that could be directly transferred to the more abstract discussions of the time. That is, he seems often to be asking similar questions. In that sense, Herodotus was a sophist too.

It is striking, however, how little evidence there is that any of the sophistic writers had much to say about precise ethnographic examples. Antiphon is attested as having mentioned the Skiapods who sheltered their heads with a single enormous foot (and who appear in Herodotus too). He also mentioned the Makrokephaloi, who appeared in *Airs, Waters, Places* as practitioners of skull-binding, which they did to give their children elongated heads. In *Airs* they formed an example of how

---

[57] Vlastos actually cites Herodotus in his imaginary dialogue in which Protagoras explains his doctrine: (1976), at 280 – making Protagoras generalize from Herodotus' specifics. There is constant tension in Heinimann (1945), esp. ch. 1 and 78 ff., between the passages he discusses in Herodotus and his attempts to separate Herodotus from the medical writers and other intellectuals.

custom could eventually change *physis*, and how acquired physical qualities could become inborn and inheritable physical qualities.[58] This is supposed by conventional chronology to be the oldest example (extant) of the *nomos–physis* antithesis. Perhaps Antiphon used the Long-Headed people for similar reasons. Democritus' attested interest in foreign animals is intriguing but does not get us far in our search for data on human societies; he may, however, have compared the Massagetai, who occur in Herodotus, with camels' mating behaviour (Ael. *NH* VI 60). Hippias is said to have written a piece on the 'Names of Peoples' (*ethne*) (DK 86, B 2). The fullest example we have of concrete ethnographic illustrations, comes from the author of the *Dissoi Logoi*, the only extant sophistic work which shows precisely how very different, even shocking, customs from other peoples, can be used to destroy the idea that there are universal human rules of behaviour (*Dissoi Logoi* 2, esp. 9 ff.). Several, though not all, of his examples are taken from Herodotus or are very close to Herodotus' account: for example, the Thracians who tattoo even girls, the Scythians who scalp enemies they have killed, the Massagetai who cut up their dead parents and eat them, the Lydians who allow their girls to earn money by prostitution, and the Egyptians who 'differ from everyone else on what is good'. The other lurid examples are so extreme, as well as ethnographically incorrect – for instance the claim that the Persians sleep with their daughters, mothers and sisters – that one would imagine they might serve to persuade his audience only that barbarians really were 'barbarous' after all, rather than that they should break down the bounds of an ethnocentric morality![59] However, we can perhaps draw two inferences. First, and more securely, the fact that Herodotus' examples can be so easily taken over in this excessive piece of sophistic relativism may itself indicate that Herodotus made his ethnographic enquiries at least occasionally via an awareness of such issues even if he did not share the extreme moral relativism of the arguments presented by the *Dissoi Logoi*. Secondly, if the dearth of other such evidence is not accidental but expressive of the sophists' preference for abstracts, then Herodotus' use of

---

[58] See ch. 3, pp. 87–8 for further refs. The same practice is attributed to the Huns and Alans many centuries later: Ascherson (1995), 241–3. Jouanna, Commentary on *Airs*, 304–5 for other ancient refs. to 'Long-Heads', or people like them, and for archaeological confirmation.

[59] These examples all from *Dissoi Logoi* 2.9–20: cf. Hdt. V 6.2 for Thracian tattooing; I 216.2 and cf. III 38.3–4 for Massagetai; I 93.4 and 94.1 for Lydian girls; IV 64 for Scythian scalping; and Hdt. II 35, compared with *Dissoi Logoi* 2.17 for the Egyptians. *Dissoi Logoi* 2.15, on Persians, can be compared with the equally unlikely statement that for the Macedonians, it is good for girls to sleep with boys before marriage, but shameful after (2.12). See T. M. Robinson (1979), though Robinson's view of the author as 'clearly well read in recent ethnographic lore' is questionable (p. 73).

concrete examples (as the Darius experiment) might suggest that he was that much more central than we might have thought, in providing both the ethnographic 'data' and the relativist approach for that generation to make use of.

It may be possible to see how some elements of Herodotus' ethnography could have been transformed or translated via his interest in debates about *nomoi* (and here we must move beyond the sphere of ethnographic customs alone). Much of his ethnography may have been influenced by, or filtered through, these preoccupations, which is why they seem to bear the marks of such ideas. Thus throughout the *Histories* he is particularly careful to describe funeral customs of many different kinds. Not only the Greeks' and Indians' mutual disagreeement (III 38), or the long description of Egyptian embalming in Book II: Cambyses' attempt to maltreat Amasis' body is an excuse for an excursus about the Persian and Egyptian ideas about fire, both highly relevant to the corpse here (III 16). Cambyses can therefore be shown to be disregarding both Persian and Egyptian beliefs. We may compare the Androphagoi, or Man-eaters, who have no justice and no *nomoi* at all (IV 106): they are the fiercest of all men, 'they neither observe justice, nor do they have any laws' (οὔτε δίκην νομίζοντες οὔτε νόμῳ οὐδενὶ χρεώμενοι), apparently a society without law or customs of any kind, in a state of nature.[60] Another tribe, the Atarantes in Libya, have no personal names (IV 184.1), and the Garamantes avoid any contact with men, and have no knowledge of war or defence (IV 174). Some of his ethnography may be very closely related to contemporary Greek ideas about ideal societies, or impossible or highly primitive societies (no *nomoi*; no names). The holding of women in common, for instance, occurs quite frequently (e.g. I 216.1, Massagetai). The communistic features of the Babylonian marriage market are also striking. By auctioning the women for marriage in order of beauty, and using the proceeds from the beautiful to provide dowries for the less attractive, the Babylonians succeed at once in levelling wealth and in enabling rich, poor, beautiful, and ugly women to get married (I 196). This extraordinary fantasy (as I believe it) would conform in some respects – though not all – to the suggestions of the political thinker Phaleas of Chalcedon who thought wealth could be equalized through the dowry system.[61] We might also add the numerous examples in the *Histories* of the prospect of humans behaving

---

[60] Heinimann 62–3: in the context *nomoi* here may denote formal or semi-formal 'laws'. For speculations on the origins of human society in this period, see Kahn (1981).

[61] Arist. *Pol.* II 1266a39–65: a point I owe to A. Griffiths (forthcoming). But note that Herodotus' story is cleverer – an auction in which the social and economic balance is altered via beauty, and the aim is for all, rich and poor, beautiful and ugly, to find a mate. McNeal (1988) for the Greek elements. Cf. Dawson (1992), 18–21.

like animals, peoples who mate outside 'like beasts', and the possible resonances of this in a period which saw increasing experimentation with the
idea that what was natural (and therefore 'good') was what was done by
animals: wild Caucasian tribes who live on the fruits of the forest, and an
Indian tribe both mate in the open 'like beasts' (I 203.2; III 101.1; cf. II 64
discussed in the Introduction).

Such fascinating examples do not appear in Hecataeus, so far as we can
tell. And to say that Herodotus might have acquired such examples from
a sophistic thinker, merely transfers the problem. I would prefer to suggest that in the combination of direct research via autopsy and personal
enquiry, and his use of other accounts, Herodotus selects and perhaps
transforms his material through the preoccupations and questions of his
time – just as we saw that some of his ethnography was in some way
related to and partially moulded by ideas which seem to belong to the
medical sphere. To return to his famous section on the paradoxes of
Egypt, the list of Egyptian opposites (II 35), we might even wonder if that
is not part of this too, indeed doing something similar to the *Dissoi Logoi*
when that author lists customs which are 'shameful' for the Ionians but
'good' for the Lacedaimonians, or good for the Ionians but shameful for
the Lacedaimonians (2.9–10), then customs of Thracians, Persians, and so
on, in order to show that there are two arguments on the good and the
shameful (*Dissoi Logoi* 2). The *Dissoi Logoi's* use of examples which
appear in Herodotus has always channelled attention to the fact that it
must be later and to some extent derivative. But if we ask about genre and
aim, it is perhaps conceivable that they belong to a similar mode of argument and perhaps a similar genre. The *Dissoi Logoi* uses the antithesis
'it is good for X but bad for Y'; Herodotus mostly says, 'the Egyptians do
X, but others do Y', implying the same contrast and there is an occasional
mention of overt moral judgement (e.g. II 35.3, they think what is
shameful should be hidden; 36.2). The thumpingly obvious moral relativism of the ethnography of the *Dissoi Logoi* is not brought out in Herodotus, but it is implicit nonetheless, and the form is the same. In other
words, to come full circle, II 35f. has little to do with environmental determinism, perhaps, though it opens with the perverse nature of the river
and climate; but more to do with the oddness of Egyptian *nomoi*, an
exercise in portraying a society which confounds all expectations of how
human beings should behave. It is a clever, amusing piece, contrived and
exaggerated in several cases (as is *Dissoi Logoi*), perhaps a sophistic exercise in antilogy, portraying a society which is exactly opposite to Greek
ways (though as the rest of Book II shows, it is not completely opposite), a
long sophistic joke perhaps – akin to the *Dissoi Logoi* but going less far –

which might have delighted an audience of the latter part of the fifth century.

If we turn to general reflections upon Greeks and barbarians, Herodotus gives us a couple of reflections on the relativity of being a barbarian, which are curiously similar to sentiments offered by Antiphon – though Antiphon uses them as a proponent of the rule of nature. For Herodotus is aware that the barbarians have their own barbarians. He remarks of the Persians that they respect their neighbours but not those further away, and those furthest away are thought to be *kakistoi* (I 134.2–3). More significant, he remarks that 'the Egyptians call all people who do not speak Egyptian *barbaroi*' (βαρβάρους δὲ πάντας οἱ Αἰγύπτιοι καλέουσι τοὺς μὴ σφίσι ὁμογλώσσους, II 158.5). So Herodotus is aware that non-Greeks, too, have a degree of 'barbarizing' – they have their own barbarians.

In the long fragment of *On Truth*, by Antiphon, now supplemented by a new papyrus text, we find sentiments about how 'we make barbarians of each other', which bear some similarity to these Herodotean comments. While in the end they tend towards quite different conclusions about human society, we may be able to use them in comparison as a way of teasing out some of the implications of Herodotus' ethnographic comments and perhaps helping to locate such comments about *nomos* in some sort of wider context. *On Truth*, 44, Fragment B, col. 2 (new text) reads as follows:[62]

ρων ἐπ[ιστάμε-
θά τε κ[αὶ σέβομεν·
τοὺς δὲ [τῶν τη-
λοῦ οἰκ[ούν]των
οὔτε ἐπι[στ]άμε-
θα οὔτε σέβομεν.
ἐν τ[ο]ύτῳ οὖν
πρὸς ἀλλήλους
βεβαρβαρώμε-
θα, ἐπεὶ φύσει γε
πάντα πάντες
ὁμοίως πεφύκ[α-
μεν καὶ βάρβα-
ροι καὶ ἕλλην[ες
εἶναι.

---

[62] New text: *Corpus dei papiri filosofici greci e latini* (Firenze 1989), vol. I, no. 17 Antipho, ed. F. D. Caizzi and G. Bastianini: text and commentary at p. 176 ff. (*P.Oxy* 1364 + 3647 + *P.Oxy* 1797). Cf. also Caizzi (1986), 61–9. Cf. Barnes (1987a): his translation is 'similarly endowed to be foreign or Greek'.

We understand and revere the [? laws] of our neighbours, but those of remote people we don't. Thus in this respect we are made barbarians in respect of each other since we are all by nature (*physis*) alike fully adapted to be either barbarians or Hellenes.[63]

The fragment continues with simple physical reasons why everyone is the same by *physis*. The new fragment makes the restoration of 'laws' more secure;[64] at any rate the earlier restored reference to revering 'those with illustrious fathers' must go. The general tendency is reasonably clear, involving an antithesis between *physis*, by which everyone is the same, and attitudes and *nomoi*, through which certain people are 'barbarized'; between Greeks and barbarians and the conventionality of the distinction. On the further more complex implications of the argument here, there is uncertainty. Much depends on how one reads ἐπεὶ φύσει γε πάντα πάντες ὁμοίως πεφύκ[α]μεν (translated above as 'since we are all by nature alike fully adapted') and what exactly is meant by the use of the rare verb βαρβαρόω: does the author mean that in not respecting the laws of those distant to us, we are simply behaving as barbarians do; or more likely, that we make each other into 'barbarians' by this lack of respect (literally, 'we are made into barbarians in respect of each other'), thus that 'the barbarian' is a product of mutual incomprehension? It is unclear, moreover, where the burden of Antiphon's antithesis lies, except insofar as he affirms that by nature, at birth, we are all equal and the same. He may not, for instance, be accepting that distance simply reaffirms and solidifies different values; but rather, attacking any idea that differences in values, *nomoi* etc. are founded on *physis* in any way.[65]

We probably cannot delve far into the philosophical controversies concerning the relative meanings and values of *nomos* and *physis* in our reading of Herodotus. For our purposes, however, it is intriguing that Antiphon's declaration 'we are made barbarians in relation to one another', is elucidated by the editor of the new papyrus, through the surprising comparison with Herodotus' remark about the Persians, who show ever decreasing respect to other peoples as they live further and

---

[63] For the last clause, I follow the translation of Grenfell and Hunt, followed by Kerferd (1981a) and Caizzi (n. 62).

[64] An alternative supplement, 'the gods', fits poorly with the general tendency of the passage.

[65] As Caizzi and Bastianini (1989), 189, commentary: Antiphon's object is to 'attack any difference of values, religion or of customs, which pretend arbitrarily to be founded on *phusis*'. For Caizzi, Antiphon's polemic goes further against the Greeks' absurd behaviour and the value of *nomos*; an antithesis to the kind of sentiment parodied, for example, in the *Menexenus*, that Athenian superiority lies in their superior *nomoi*, which are inextricably linked to their superior *physis* – i.e. their autochthonous origin: see studies cited in n. 62 above. Cf. also remarks in Furley (1981), 89–90 (with old reading); Dillon (1984).

further away from Persia (I 134, above).[66] We should add the equally relevant remark that Egyptians think all people who do not speak Egyptian are *barbaroi* (above). If this were in any other author, one would see that author as deconstructing the Greek–barbarian antithesis, as has been most plausibly suggested of the tragedies *Andromache, Troades*,[67] and as is clearly the case in Antiphon. Herodotus seems to be implying that 'barbarizing' occurs, just as Antiphon does, and even that the 'barbarian' is a creation, an invention in the eye of the beholder. It would be absurd, of course, to imply a close affinity between Herodotus and the rather later Antiphon in their approach to barbarians as well as to *nomos*. Herodotus respects *nomoi* whatever their provenance, and the emphasis of his Darius anecdote is mainly on the sheer power of *nomoi*.[68] Antiphon, the 'antinomian', on the other hand, sees their variety as a reason to denigrate them, to stress their mere conventionality. Yet if we may compare Herodotus with the later, jingoistic, parody in Plato's *Menexenus*, where the Athenians are declared to be by nature hostile to barbarians (*Menex.* 245c–d), or with the calm statement in the *Republic* that Greeks were enemies of barbarians *by nature* (470c), then Herodotus' cautious playing with the idea of 'the barbarian' is noticeably closer in spirit to these late fifth-century attempts to undermine the antithesis.

It seems hard to believe that Herodotus' ethnography is not on some level informed by certain abstract ideas and speculations about *nomos* and about the Greek–barbarian antithesis which appear in our evidence most clearly in the late fifth century – it is less easy to envisage abstract thinkers simply crystallizing their abstracts from an undifferentiated mass of raw data presented by Herodotus. Certainly Herodotus indicates in his more explicit and rare general statements, that he thinks *nomos/nomoi* are the crucial determining factors in ethnic character, success, decline, and that *nomoi* govern human societies. Alan Lloyd makes the fascinating suggestion that the *Histories* are Heraclitean, in the sense that Greeks and barbarians are warring opposites trying to attain equilibrium.[69] Yet Herodotus' espousal of the dominance of *nomos* suggests at least that his Greek and barbarian 'opposites' are tempered or mediated by more contemporary ideas about *nomoi*, and that his Greek–barbarian antago-

---

[66] Caizzi and Bastianini (1989) 188 (commentary); article (1986), 63–5. Cf. Eurip. *Orestes* 485, βεβαρβάρωσαι, χρόνιος ὢν ἐν βαρβάροις for another use of the verb.

[67] With E. Hall (1989), ch. 5; Saïd (1984).

[68] As Dihle (1981), 60. Cf. also remarks of Kahn (1981, 106) on Protagoras and Herodotus.

[69] A. Lloyd (1990): at 243–4 (*Histories* are partly about 'historical manifestations of the cosmic πόλεμος to maintain order', p. 244); with Dihle's comments, 249–50, stressing a more nuanced appreciation of the meanings of 'barbarian'.

nism is informed by the later fifth-century curiosity about *nomos* and *physis*. His awareness that even the barbarians have their own barbarians (who include the Greeks) indicates willingness to deconstruct the Greek–barbarian antithesis in a manner which is visible in Antiphon's new fragment and in some of the Athenian tragedies by Euripides. His analyses of the deterioration or increasing success of different peoples reveal an emphasis upon the changing, fluid nature of ethnic character, the importance of customs as well as place, which would render any rigid picture of a Greek–barbarian antithesis highly implausible. One cannot believe both that Herodotus thought *nomoi* paramount in ethnic character and historical explanation, and that he thought the Greeks innately superior by nature.

5   'Wonders' and the natural world: natural philosophy and *historie*

This chapter turns from the human world to the world of animals, marvels and the intersection between natural philosophy, medicine and *historie*, or, literally, 'enquiry'. In some parts of the *Histories* the audience is offered information, tales or theories concerning the natural world – animals, geology, biology – which at first glance seem to be very much the preserve of the *physiologoi*, those natural philosophers, at least, who speculated about the animate and visible parts of the natural world. Yet to pin it down so specifically is clearly unwise, since it is virtually impossible to separate subjects dealt with by certain *physiologoi* (Anaxagoras, Democritus, Diogenes of Apollonia) and those treated by writers of the Hippocratic Corpus. There was considerable interaction and sharing of ideas and concepts between them; in terms of methodology, the medical writers can be integrated into a continuous investigation of the development of Greek philosophical and scientific method, though there is debate on the extent to which Greek medicine was based on observation and empirical methods (see pages 153–61). Moreover, not only do we find a community of interests and ideas between *physiologoi* and doctors, but a continuity also between certain Herodotean descriptions and those of writers of the late fifth century and early to mid-fourth century, which is suggestive and exciting. Herodotus' debts to the geographical theories of the early *physiologoi* are well known: for instance his pointed curiosity about the significance of fossils which obviously played a part in earlier attempts to uncover the development of the world,[1] his theory that the northern part of Egypt was once a gulf of the sea, backed by observations about the silting up of river valleys,[2] and his assured and impressive discussion of theories about the flooding of the Nile itself. But it would be implausible to regard these interests simply as intellectual relics of

---

[1] II 12.1, combined with other factors for the example of Egypt; cf. Xenophanes on fossils, DK 21, A 33. A. Lloyd, comm. ad loc. suggests perhaps Anaximander; also Xanthos, *FGrH* 765, F12; cf. Brown (1965) on the geographical theories (68–72 on Hecataeus).

[2] II 10; Hecataeus was interested in sedimentation *FGrH* 1, F301: see A. Lloyd, Commentary ad loc. and 36f.; cf. Thomson (1948), 103 ff.

an older Ionian science, still less as a fossilized preservation of a younger Herodotus who was soon to turn to higher historical questions.[3]

Let us consider for a moment one subject where Herodotus' discussion has close affiliation with other ideas of the time, the section on the Nile flood. The very length of his section on the flooding of the Nile (II 19–27) suggests that the problem attracted a contemporary fascination, and the section is replete with the language of enquiry (e.g. II 19).[4] The longest rebuttal is devoted to the theory of Anaxagoras, a contemporary or near contemporary (II 22), and while Herodotus offers a critique of Thales' solution of probably more than a century earlier,[5] as well as Homer's belief in Ocean adopted by Hecataeus (II 21), his own solution – that the sun is the root cause – has elements which would have been familiar to some earlier Presocratics as well as later fifth-century writers such as Diogenes of Apollonia and Oinopides of Chios (II 24ff.). His stress on evaporation and more especially that the sun 'pulls' (ἕλκει) the water up, recurs in Diogenes' slightly different explanation.[6] And he reverses the question in such a way as to present the problem as one about why the river level should be so low in winter, rather than so high in summer – a trait shared by Oinopides of Chios.[7] Whether contemporaries gave an equal attention to the Ister, as Herodotus himself does, is unknown. Meanwhile the Anaxagorean theory involving melting snow was resurrected in a different context by Democritus who thought melting snow in northern countries created clouds and later rain, which with the help of Etesian winds, then fell in the south.[8] Not only were these still live questions which continued to fascinate, but the manner and ideas with which Herodotus approached them sits easily amongst these other contemporary – and later – theories. Similar suggestions may be made about Herodotus' forays into biology.

---

[3] As Jacoby (1913).

[4] For analysis of the argument itself, ch. 6 below. See detailed commentary ad loc. by A. Lloyd for the whole section, who comments (p. 104), 'H., as usual, shows himself fully aware of contemporary scientific doctrines'; and Bonneau (1964); Foucart (1943). The modern explanation has nothing to do with melting snow.

[5] II 20, Etesian winds: DK 11, A 16.

[6] DK 64, A 18: also involves *ikmas* being 'drawn up' (ἕλκειν is a favourite word of Diogenes, though not in the fragment here). See also ch. 2, p. 52 on Diogenes.

[7] DK 41, A 11 (= *FGrH* 647, F1 (6), Anon. MS). A. Lloyd sees Herodotus as closest to Oinopides – though Oinopides thought the sun passed below the earth in winter, to diminish the Nile water at its source. Herodotus' complex argument about the movement of the sun between summer and winter would have been shared by other *physiologoi*. Cf. also *Breaths*, ch. 3.3 J, which thinks the 'wind is responsible for the movement of the sun, moon and stars'.

[8] DK 68, A 99 (= *FGrH* 647, F1 (4)).

So the argument of the first part of this chapter will have two prongs: firstly it will try to show that, in his treatment of the animal world, Herodotus sometimes works along lines similar to those visible in contemporary and later Greek natural philosophy and medicine, the quest for the nature of the natural world and of man. Secondly, our detailed study will illustrate quite how closely intertwined are the separate disciplines, as they became later, of philosophy, medicine and the enquiry into nature (i.e. of the *physiologoi*). This is not, of course, an unfamiliar notion,[9] but its application and relevance to Herodotus' *Histories* could be explored more fully than it has been. While it is always important to bear in mind that there was no separate discipline such as history when he wrote, it is harder to imagine exactly what that meant in practice in the mid to late fifth century. The interaction of ideas, as well as the rivalry between incipient disciplines (or *technai*) may do something to illuminate the kind of pre-disciplinary world in which Herodotus wrote. Accordingly the second section of this chapter looks more closely at some elements of this interaction and community of ideas. The final section brings the implications to bear upon Herodotus' *Histories* and our interpretation of his description of his work as an *historie*.

Two further points will lie behind much of the discussion and deserve high-lighting here – both related to the nature of early Greek natural philosophy and medicine. As we have seen occasionally in earlier chapters, early Greek natural philosophy and medicine combines empirical and theoretical methods in varying degrees. Observation and observable phenomena are brought into play but often interpreted by means of theoretical or abstract considerations or unvoiced assumptions about what should be the case.[10] One may even suspect that such enquirers into nature often saw what they thought they should see, observations being theory-led (cf. the notorious modern example of theories about race and intelligence linked to skull size, which were clothed in the impeccable language of science and scientific experiment). Herodotus' enquiries are no different. It is hard to credit his 'description' of the hippo, a creature often inconveniently submerged under water, or the phoenix, a mythical bird he admits he has never seen, except as descriptions borrowed from Hecataeus,[11] but in other controversial examples the problem may be

---

[9] See works on relation of philosophy and medicine, n. 57 below.

[10] For the degree of observation and experiment in Greek science, n. 57 below; and for a particularly controversial case of 'autopsy', *Nat. Child.* 13, p. 165 below, with n. 98. Expressed rather differently, Corcella's stress on *gnome* in Herodotus (1984, 63–7) touches upon this general issue.

[11] As Porphyry: *FGrH* 1, f 324a for the accusation of plagiarism.

more complex. The propensity even of early Greek science to combine schematic theory with visible phenomena needs constantly to be borne in mind.

This brings us to Herodotus' 'wonders' or *thaumata* (θώματα in the Ionian dialect), his descriptions of marvels and wondrous things. If we tend to see Herodotus mainly within a lineage of historians, and part of the line of historical development from Hecataeus who begins to 'rationalize' Greek myths (that is, remove some of the more far-fetched elements) to Thucydides who is rigorously rationalistic, the presence of marvels in Herodotus is something that calls for some apology – and possibly mild patronizing. Of course marvels often do take their place in the *Histories* simply because they are marvels, as Herodotus says of his reason of extending his coverage of Egypt (II 35.1), not to mention some of the more fabulous descriptions. But wonders also play an important part in early Greek natural philosophy; they are not simply the tools of the story-teller anxious to keep his audience. Democritus for instance is said to have written about 'the most wondrous and paradoxical things of nature' (τὰ θαυμαστὰ καὶ τὰ παραλογώτατα τῆς φύσεως),[12] and a work appears under the name of Aristotle, which may be genuine, with the title, 'On marvellous things heard'. This forms a list of odd and inexplicable phenomena mostly of the natural world, though it also includes elements from human society, from springs, natural fires, metals, to dangerous animals and multiple births. The unusual, the wondrous, the marvellous might well provide exotic phenomena which need explaining as part of *physis* – the phenomena of silphium, for instance, and of bitumen, brimstone (*theion*), and alum (*stypteria*) were apparently discussed by Democritus (DK 68, A 99a; cf. chapter 2, p. 52 for other connections), just as those medical curiosities, the Scythians with the 'female disease', the Anaries discussed by *Airs*, also demanded to be explained by the laws of natural philosophy. Indeed as with these last people, fantastic 'facts' might be created by *a priori* assumptions – as the author of *Airs* asserts that the Scythians cauterize themselves in several places 'simply because of their moistness and softness'.[13] Or as Aristotle declares, 'males have more teeth than females, not only in men, but also in sheep, goats and pigs' (*HA* II 3, 501b19f.) – there was no need to check. A perusal of early 'scientific' theories and questions about nature leaves one in no doubt

---

[12] DK 68, A 99a.

[13] Ch. 20.2 J. Cf. the statement of *Airs* (ch. 22) that they attempt to cure their condition by cutting a vein behind the ear; *Airs* points out that this would not help, because of the notion that semen starts in the head.

about the role of *a priori* assumption rather than observation in many of these ideas.[14] So the remoter parts of the world may be described because they are remote, exotic, marvellous and therefore fascinating,[15] but not solely for entertainment value and for their quality as *thaumata*. They might also be interesting for the enquiry into nature, in which India is as important as Libya, the Nile as interesting as the Maeander. The Nile constituted a 'marvel', so did its counter-intuitive summer flooding: as Herodotus puts it, its nature (*physis*) is quite different from that of other rivers (II 19.3). Yet Herodotus tries to show at length that there is an explanation which would fit the Nile without contradicting the experience of other rivers – he gives equally full attention to the Ister (IV 50). He is seeking a conformity to what are effectively universal laws of nature, and he reinforces this by explaining how exactly the same would happen to the Ister were the heavens and winds reversed (II 24–7, esp. 26.2).[16] Similarly Democritus mentioned Arabian cattle with good horns as part of a wider discussion of the growth of animal horn, the flowing of humours, *ikmas*, and *phlebes*,[17] Libyan asses (ὄνοι) as part of a discussion of prolific creatures.[18] Later, Aristotle picked up the theme of the 'many-formed' animals of Libya and sought to explain why they were so varied by considering the consequences of an essential practice in Libya, the gatherings of animals at waterholes (*Hist. Anim.* VII (VIII) 606b17–28: cf. chapter 3, p. 96). Marvels were clearly part of the enquiry into the natural world.

Oligogonia and *polygonia*, and the Arabian snakes

Let us turn to the fascinating case of the Arabian snakes and the matter of prolific birth and its opposite that occur in Herodotus' third book.

In Book III, Herodotus moves from the remarkable list of satrapies of the Persian empire (89–97) to an equally remarkable excursus on some of the peoples at the far edges of the Persian kingdom, beginning with the

[14] See Vlastos (1970); Mansfeld (1980a); G. E. R. Lloyd (1979); and works cited below, n. 57.
[15] See Redfield (1985); Romm (1992). Cf. Greenblatt (1991) for a range of responses and interpretative strategies surrounding the 'wonder' of the New World in the Renaissance and early modern period – mostly, however, as a prelude to conquest or destruction.
[16] For the idea, surely right, that he is underlining the uniformity of nature, Corcella (1984), 80–1.
[17] DK 68, A 153–5, from Ael. *Nat. Hist.* XII 18–20.
[18] A 151: from Ael. *NH* XII 16.

Indians – a series of exotic and marvellous tales. The initial excuse is that he will explain how the Indians acquire the gold which goes to the Persian king. 'Of all those we know about in Asia, and about which we can speak truthfully', the Indians lie furthest east (98.2). Finally we reach the notorious tale of how the Indians acquire gold dust in the face of opposition from terrible giant ants (III 102–5), which always intrigues apologists and cynics alike, though Herodotus seems to want to distance himself from it.[19] Then he declares, 'It is the farthest reaches (*eschatiai*) of the earth that have the most beautiful things, while Greece has by far the best mix of seasons' (III 106.1), both summing up what he said about India and anticipating more on Arabia. For, Herodotus continues, India is very far east, 'as I said earlier', the animals are bigger than elsewhere, they have plentiful gold, and the wild trees grow something better and softer than wool. As for Arabia, it has wonderful spices, though the Arabians can only get at them with great difficulty. There follows a detailed description of the Arabian snakes (ὄφιες, chs. 107–9; 110 ff. continues with the extraordinary methods used for gathering the spices). These snakes are winged and guard the frankincense trees. They would overrun the whole world were it not for the fact that they, like the vipers, procreate in such a way that when the male and female come together, the female bites clean through the male's neck. The male dies, but he is avenged by the unborn young who make their entry into the world by eating through the mother's womb. Hence they do not multiply as fast as their nature (*physis*) would allow (III 109.1).

The whole section is a wonderful description of 'marvels', *thaumata* (used of cinnamon at ch. 111.1). The flying snakes themselves have elicited particular scepticism, especially as they have already made their appearance in highly questionable circumstances in Book II.[20] Herodotus'

---

[19] Cf. III 105.1: 'as it is said by the Persians', and finally again, ὡς Πέρσαι φασί. Note that the tale also requires explanations about climatic heat and camel behaviour! See Fehling (1989), 97–8 for a different view. Pritchett (1993), 90 ff., mentions various 'explanations' for the ants; marmots resurrected by Michael Peissel, anthropologist and explorer of Tibet (*Times*, 4 Dec. 1996). Perhaps a mistranslation: the Persian calls these creatures 'mountain ants'.

[20] II 75. Cf. Fehling (1989), 24–7 for scepticism on the snakes (which surely most would share): whether or not Herodotus or his informants believed the tale is, however, quite another matter. There have been many ideas on the presumably garbled origin of these 'snakes': Rawlinson favoured locusts; cf. A. Lloyd, Commentary on Book II, pp. 75f.: he thinks II 75 'may owe something to Hecataeus'; he favours flying lizards and suggests that III 107 was the result of elaboration of tales about them from the East, travellers like Scylax etc.

statement about the *eschatiai* has been seen, surely rightly, as part of his over schematic division of the world, a tendency to see geography in terms of binary opposites, and a schematic apportioning of the world into the extreme and atypical on the margins, and the mixture in the centre.[21] Romm suggested that Herodotus is at times working with two slightly contradictory models of world geography, one in which the furthest places are deserted (*eremoi*), the other, more mythical, in which they contain wonderful or idyllic peoples like Ethiopians and Hyperboreans.[22]

But wonders turn out to be important for an understanding of the natural world. In the remarkable and rather neglected section following the statement about the *eschatiai* on the one hand, and the snakes in Arabia on the other, we are treated to what is almost a lecture on biology in miniature, and an almost Darwinian theory about the survival strategies of different species of animal.[23] We move in other words from one 'theoretical' or schematic framework to another.

The flying snakes guard the trees of frankincense (III 107). 'The Arabians also say this', that the whole land would be filled with them, if they were not checked, as Herodotus adds, 'in the way I know happens with the vipers' (108.1). It is not till later (ch. 109) that we learn precisely how the snakes' and vipers' breeding habits manage to reduce their numbers spectacularly in a horrible example, as Herodotus points out, of animal 'retribution' between male and female.[24] But first, he continues:

---

[21] See particularly Redfield (1985), esp. 110–12 ('We place the fabulous beyond the edges of the known world, he [Herodotus] suggests, not only because they are beyond our knowledge, but because, as we move toward the edges, we encounter more extreme conditions and therefore atypical forms, both natural and cultural', p. 110). Cf. also Romm (1992), 38 ff., 68–70, on the *eschatiai* producing the best, and on the difficulties of getting at these benefits (but see n. 22); also Romm (1989). Heinimann (1945), 22–3, stressing the schematization, talks in terms of the scheme of classification of Ionian *historie*. On Hdt. III 106 see also: Immerwahr (1966), 49f. (antithesis), 102f.; Detienne (1972), 20f., 36f. (ch. 1); Romm (1987) – for the five stories about acquiring the gold etc.; Nesselrath (1995).

[22] Romm (1992), 38; he is over-schematic: he sees Herodotus' account of how Arabians and Indians obtained these valuable products as 'hard primitivism', in which 'a bare living has to be wrested at great cost' (p. 68): the rough distinction ('hard' and 'soft') is often useful (see Redfield 1985), but the point here in Herodotus is that these *fabulously* rich or valuable commodities can only be obtained with difficulty and pertinacity – he is not talking about scraping a living.

[23] Nestle (1908), 16–18, discussed an aspect of this (see below). Note esp. Demont (1994a) – concentrating on Plato's *Prot.*, Herodotus and providence (less on wider context). Romm (1992), 38 ff., 69–70, on 'hard primitivism', and geographical schemata. Falus (1977) has strikingly little to say about content or context.

[24] Cf. Demont (1995) on motif of revenge.

The god's foresight is wise, as is likely (ὥσπερ καὶ οἰκός ἐστι), for it has ensured that those animals which are cowardly and edible are all prolific (πολύγονα), while all those which are savage and troublesome, have few progeny (ὀλιγόγονα). (108.2)[25]

So it is by the 'foresight' of the divine that timid animals are prolific (*polygona*), the others are *oligogona*, they have few offspring. He then gives detailed examples to back up this statement: the hare is the example of the timid creature (to which we return), the lion is the opposite. For the lioness conceives only once in her life and 'the reason is' that the lion cub in the womb has such sharp claws that the womb is ripped to shreds with the one birth (108.4). Vipers (*echidnai*) and the winged snakes have a similarly self-destructive way of procreating (see 109 and above).

There is much in this surprising passage which suggests a serious physiological angle in the midst of what seems to be a typical section of merely exotic wonders. Let us start with the concepts of *oligogonia* and *polygonia*.

Herodotus is the first writer in extant Greek literature to use the word *oligogonos*, the first in which the dual concepts appear together.[26] This in itself is interesting (though the limitations of 'extant' literature should be stressed: both appear in Plato's *Protagoras*: we return to this below). However, *Airs, Waters, Places* has a brief section on the same phenomenon, and in connection with the Scythians. The Scythians are characterized by their moistness, 'their bodies grow relaxed and squat', and various other physical characteristics follow from this moistness (ch. 20). They are characterized as 'least prolific' (ch. 19.1 J), and at ch. 21.1, 'Such a nature cannot be prolific (πολύγονον)' – because of the moistness of their *physis*, the men have no desire to have intercourse; also they indulge constantly in horse-riding. The women have fat and moist flesh, which means the womb cannot absorb the seed: 'Because of these necessary causes (ὑπὸ τούτων τῶν ἀναγκέων), fecundity (πολύγονον) is absent from the Scythian race' (21.3). The author continues with this miserable catalogue of Scythian traits; we then hear about the Scythians suffering from the female disease, the Anaries (ch. 22).

It is interesting that this passage in *Airs* on Scythian lack of *polygonia* was noted and discussed by Heinimann, but Heinimann did not notice the Herodotean interest in the same matter.[27] Heinimann combined *Airs* ch. 21 with a passage in Aristotle, *Gen. Anim.* (IV, 770a34f.), where Egyptian

---

[25] καί κως τοῦ θείου ἡ προνοίη, ὥσπερ καὶ οἰκός ἐστι, ἐοῦσα σοφή, ὅσα μὲν [γὰρ] ψυχήν τε δειλὰ καὶ ἐδώδιμα, ταῦτα μὲν πάντα πολύγονα πεποίηκε, ἵνα μὴ ἐπιλίπῃ κατεσθιόμενα, ὅσα δὲ σχέτλια καὶ ἀνιηρά, ὀλιγόγονα.

[26] On conventional chronology; *polygonos* occurs in Aesch. *Suppl.* 692, of plants.

[27] Heinimann (1945), 22–3, suggesting that Egyptians in *Airs* also were *polygonos*; also briefly pp. 198–9.

women are mentioned as prolific (*polygonos*), and speculated that both derived from Ionian *historie*. The implication that Egypt featured in this way in the lost part of *Airs* is certainly strong. But such a suggestion about Ionian *historie* is impossibly vague: Heinimann seems to imply a long distant source, since he also mentioned the possible derivation of schematic geography from Hecataeus. Indeed he contrasted nearby the doctor's 'scientific' thinking[28] and Herodotus' supposedly archaic idea that the ends of the earth had the most beautful objects (III 106). But the omission of Herodotus in the discussion of *polygonia* in any case undermines his suggestion. What we can see from other Greek discussions enables us to refine the picture and make some suggestions about Herodotus' intellectual affiliations and milieu.

Prolific birth or its opposite was a subject of interest to some of the most serious thinkers on the subject of generation in the second half of the fifth century (contrast the slightly patronizing tone one senses in Heinimann's use of 'Ionian *historie*'). Thus the author of *On the Nature of the Child*, dated by its most recent editor to c. 420, turns in ch. 31 to the cause of multiple births and how twins can result from one act of intercourse (answer: the womb has a number of pockets). Animals who produce large litters are mentioned, both wild and domestic; the dog, pig and 'other animals which produce two or more offspring from one act of intercourse' are produced as evidence that twins are, in fact, born from one act of intercourse (31.2). This was clearly an issue of importance, though we may note that the Hippocratic author concentrates on the physical cause of multiple births, not the significance of this in the wider scheme of animal survival, as does Herodotus.

The antecedents of this view are problematic and complex, but it is clear that the Hippocratic writer was not the first to discuss this. He seems to be using 'an account which is definitely ascribed to Democritus in the tradition', though as a recent commentator admits, the same explanation might have been used by Anaxagoras or by Diogenes, since its elements are pre-Democritean.[29] Thus according to Aelian (DK 68, A 151): 'Democritus says that the sow and the bitch are prolific and he adds the explanation that they have many uteri and places to receive the seed' (then follows more on the seed itself). Empedocles also had an explanation for twins or triplets, again apparently for the biological process itself

---

[28] Heinimann (1945) 22; 'Der naturwissenschaftlichdenkende Arzt', p. 23.
[29] See Lonie (1981), 63 (both quotations); 252–5 for further discussion. Cf. Diller (1934), 45 and esp. n. 78, on Hdt. III 108 (also IV 29) and Democritus to show that the questions asked by Democritus in A 150a–155 were older: concerned with Democritus' *Aitiai*, he seems to see Herodotus as evidence for Ionian origin of aetiological literature.

(DK 31, A 81: superabundance of sperm and its division). Democritus' view lies closest to that of *Nature of the Child*.[30]

Herodotus obviously approaches the question of prolific birth from a different angle: he does not give us a general biological theory for *how* it occurs, the physical, internal mechanism, that is, which would apply to all animals. Indeed he seems rather uninterested in the general mechanics of the process. But two elements of his account are crucial: firstly, he does give lengthy (and gruesome) biological detail for the hare, and the lion, as well as the snakes, so he does not gloss over precise details of animal biology altogether; secondly, he asks, indeed he begins with, the question why some animals have *polygonia*, others have *oligogonia*.

Both are brought together neatly in the Pseudo-Aristotelian *Problemata*, always a fascinating treasure-trove for what are to us wildly improbable questions of a pseudo-scientific nature:

Why are some living creatures prolific, like the sow, the bitch and the hare, but others, like man and the lion not? Is it that the former have many wombs and places which the sperm hastens to fill and into which it is divided, while the latter are the opposite?[31]

What is remarkable is both that this is precisely the question Herodotus asks, or rather, the question to which he offers an answer; and that the author covers some of the same examples: the lion and the hare, Herodotus' main examples apart from the Arabian flying snakes and the vipers, feature here as prime suspects.[32] It would seem then, from this combination of ancient discussions that Herodotus' few paragraphs should also belong in the thick of discussions of late fifth-century speculation about prolific and unprolific animals. But where exactly does his account stand?

Any degree of certainty is, of course, impossible. But there are inter-

---

[30] Democritus' dates: he said himself he was 40 years older than Anaxagoras; he had a long life, born perhaps c. 470 or 460 (see D.L. IX 41); at any rate he will have coincided with several natural philosophers; Jouanna sees him as contemporary with Hippocrates. Cf. also *Regimen*. I 30 on twins; ch. 31 on cause of superfetation in women (here Ἐπίγονα).

[31] *Probl.* 10, 14. 892a38–b3. Cf. also Arist. *Gen. Anim.* IV 4. 771b27 ff. (uterus with different sections), and 771a14 ff. generally for elaborate discussion of whether there is a single cause for 'monotokia', 'polytokia'.

[32] Later, Aristotle is still trying to combat the idea that the lioness gives birth only once: *HA* VI 31, 579b2–4; he declares that the idea about the lioness losing the uterus 'is nonsense' (ληρῶδης), and invented to explain the scarcity of lions (cf. Herodotus VII 126 on lions in Europe?). The vipers' methods reappear in Arist. *On marvellous things heard*, ch. 165, 846b18–22, where it is cited as an example of revenge by the young on the mother (with the Atreids in mind? – cf. Clytemnestra's dream, Aesch. *Choeph.* 523–50). For what it is worth, the long discussion in Arist. *Gen. Anim.* has a rather different range of both examples and categories.

esting respects in which Herodotus stands out. If we can take the question and answer of the *Problemata* and Democritus as the fragment stands, we receive a biological explanation involving the physical character of the womb which has no place in Herodotus. Herodotus' gruesome account of the fate of the lioness explains her single conception by the lion cub's use of his sharp claws in the womb: this explanation involves the behaviour of the unborn rather than the nature of the womb; it is also quite different from the generalist explanation given in *Airs*, which simply invoked moistness. The same can be said of Herodotus' details about the snakes. We can perhaps simply guess that Herodotus was aware of other discussions about animal birth-rates that simply have not survived. For the hare and the lion were certainly classic examples for the question for the later author of the *Problemata*.

In fact it is probably significant that this Herodotean description of the lion's birth pangs seems to correspond neatly with the medical view that the pains of giving birth were produced by the infant struggling to emerge. This description, implying a passive uterus, has been seen as 'the most explicit expression of the notion that a parturient's pains were due to blows from her rambunctious infant as it forced its way out from the maternal womb',[33] though its presence in a complex passage of this kind should make one wary of taking it simply as a reflection of popular misconceptions about lions.

From the presence of the topic in Democritus, *Airs* (however disappointing), as well as *Nat. Child*, one would guess easily that here Herodotus was touching an issue of the latter half of the fifth century and a contemporary one, and certainly not merely harking back to some very much earlier account of 'Ionian *historie*', perhaps Hecataeus.[34] To assume that this kind of detail in Herodotus' *Histories* must go back always to some earlier source implicitly misrepresents the nature of contemporary debates about biology and animal reproduction.

But what makes this even more probable is the presence in his description of the hare as a high producer, of an extraordinarily technical and unusual word: ἐπικυΐσκεται, meaning superfetation, or the capacity of an animal to become pregnant again when it is already pregnant. The hare, a timid animal, is especially *polygonos*, for, 'it alone of all wild animals can be doubly pregnant' (ἐπικυΐσκεται μοῦνον πάντων θηρίων), (108.3). This

---

[33] Hanson (1991), 90; also 94; she mentions Aesop's fable (257 Perry) – though not wider intellectual context, and points out similar ideas about the human baby forcing its way out in *Nature of the Child*.

[34] Pherecydes of Syros, DK 7, A8, is added tentatively by Lonie (1981, 255): 'an early example in mythic form, of the belief that multiple birth is determined by the structure of the uterus': but the fragment in its present form is unhelpful.

verb occurs in Herodotus, in the late Hippocratic treatise *Superfetation* I, where the Greek title is ἐπικύησις, and in the discussion on the subject in Aristotle's *Generation of Animals*.[35] The Hippocratic treatise discusses superfetation in women, and assumes the presence of a two-horned uterus for the purpose. Superfetation is also discussed in *On Regimen* I 31.[36] Herodotus is thus *au fait* with one of the most technical terms in the discussions relating to prolific births (to which superfetation is obviously relevant). One can easily assume that the term so attested in later Hippocratic works was current in medical circles earlier.[37] From the way Herodotus insists that the hare is the only one 'of all wild animals', he may also be aware of ideas that domestic animals, or even humans were capable of this (perhaps also of ideas that multiple births as such were results of superfetation). This might imply that he was on the whole closer here to Hippocratic-related ideas, or at least detailed, quite technical discussion on this issue, possibly in the more medical writing, than to Democritean ideas.[38] Certainly the type of explanation provided by *Airs* was also quite different (though no more 'rational' or scientific than Herodotus'). It is worth contrasting the easy comparison made by Heinimann between *Airs* on *oligogonia* in Scythia and (selectively) Herodotus' declaration that the furthest parts of the world have the most beautiful things, not necessarily the place with the best climate – in which Heinimann says that the doctor attempts a rational solution to the problems of differences, Herodotus stands closer to an archaic way of thinking.[39] This is a fairly conventional view, but untrue, as we have seen, to all of Herodotus' text.

There is yet another strand: the form of the question. The *Problemata* asked the question why some animals were prolific, others not, and answered it narrowly in the physical sense, via the nature of the womb (this

---

[35] *Gen. Anim.* IV 5. 773a33–774b4; cf. Arist. *HA* VI 33 (579b–580a) on hares: accepts superfetation without discussion or much explanation.

[36] Ἐπίγονα; superfetation also occurs in the case at *Epid.* v 11. There is a problem whether multiple birth could be regarded as the result of superfetation: for Lonie (1981), comm. on 31.2 (p. 256), the author of *Nat. Child.* in his insistence that twins are conceived from a single act of copulation, implies that others thought multiple births were result of superfetation; Aristotle 'regarded multiple birth as a kind of "superfetation", whether there was one act of copulation or not' (*Gen. Anim.* IV 5. 773b6–7).

[37] For possibility of earlier material in *Superfetation*, see Thivel (1981), 94–7; and Lienau (1973), 37–42, 66f.; and generally on superfetation, Hanson (1994), 161–2, and Lienau (above). On the general possibility of older practice/knowledge within the gynaecological treatises, Hanson (1991).

[38] Cf. Arist. *Gen. Anim.* IV 5.774 a (c. 32 ff.), for example, for a quite different set of explanations for the hare's prolific nature (physical, e.g. hairiness).

[39] Heinimann (1945), 24: 'Es ist kein Zweifel, daß Herodot mit dieser Auffassung der archaischen Denkweise nähersteht, die jeden Geschöpf seine ἀρετή zuweist, während der Arzt von πάϋτ. [*Airs*] nach einer rationaleren Lösung des Problems der Verschiedenheit sucht.'

sounds rather Democritean).[40] It is significant that Herodotus is effectively addressing the same question: more exactly, he provides an answer to the same question, which is on a quite different level: 'The god's foresight is wise, as is likely, for it has ensured that those animals which are cowardly and edible are all prolific, while all those which are savage and troublesome, have few progeny' (108.2). Herodotus, then, is interested in the grand overall plan of animal survival, though he also goes on to give some biological detail. There is a wider pattern here, by which animals which tend to be a prey for others, and especially the hare, have numerous offspring. The idea that an equilibrium is maintained in nature, in the world of animals, is new (whether it is ultimately Herodotean or Protagorean – for which see below), and is later developed by Aristotle into the idea that nature itself keeps the balance.[41]

Finally, there is a possible and fascinating connection with Protagoras. Characteristically the relevant evidence occurs in a context notoriously hard to evaluate, within the myth told by Protagoras in Plato's *Protagoras*. Here, before we reach Prometheus' and Zeus' gifts for the preservation of humankind, Epimetheus apportions various 'powers' to the animals, strength or speed, size, ability to fly or burrow in the ground, and so on, the wherewithal to survive (320d7 ff.):

καὶ τοῖς μὲν ὀλιγογονίαν προσῆψε, τοῖς δ' ἀναλισκομένοις ὑπὸ τούτων πολυγονίαν, σωτηρίαν τῷ γένει πορίζων.

And some he made have very few young (*oligogonia*), while those who were their prey were very prolific (*polygonia*), and in this way the race was preserved. (321b5–6)

The similarity with Herodotus' opening statement is striking, but it is hardly a verbatim record of the sophist himself. Besides, Protagoras is better known for his theories about human society than the animal kingdom. It is generally assumed that Protagoras was not much interested in 'natural philosophy', though Cicero did remark that Prodicus, Thrasymachus and Protagoras wrote 'even about nature' (*etiam de natura rerum*: *De Orat.* 3.32. 127–8).[42] Protagoras may, then, have had something to say on natural philosophy, but the evidence, inadequate though it is,

---

[40] So does Aristotle, asking whether there is a *single* cause.

[41] See Demont (1994a).

[42] Cf. Guthrie (1971), 46, sceptical, on natural philosophy among sophists: the interest in 'nature' is merely for the further aim of being able to answer all questions. Eupolis ridiculed Protagoras for 'pretending an interest in the heavens but eating what came out of the ground' (DK A11), but Guthrie thinks this has as little value as Aristophanes' calling Socrates and Prodicus 'meteorosophists'; Kerferd (1981a) is more positive. See below for other sophists.

suggests that the intricacies of nature were far from the centre of his vision. This is borne out by Plato's portrayal of his aims – Protagoras is concerned with political and moral questions, not arithmetic, astronomy, geometry and *mousike*, he says, looking at Hippias who was discoursing on just those areas.[43]

The Protagorean link (to use a neutral term) was noticed by Nestle long ago, and he devoted some time to the implications.[44] He thought that the most likely solution was that both Herodotus and Plato derived the idea about *pronoia* from Protagoras' work, Περὶ τῆς ἐν ἀρχῇ καταστάσεως, usually translated as 'On the Original State of Man' (D.L. ix. 55), partly on the grounds that it was improbable that Plato and Protagoras had relied on Herodotus.[45] This is not unlikely, though it is unclear how far that really helps in understanding Herodotus here. For even if the source were certain, one would then like to know what Herodotus had done with the 'source'. But there are other problems here. For on present understanding of Protagoras, and his scepticism about the divine, it seems most improbable that Protagoras had been keen to stress divine *pronoia*, indeed even in the Platonic version of the myth, there is no mention of *pronoia* itself, though the elements of the myth effectively denote it. Surely Herodotus' stress on the god and on foresight was his own and not Protagoras'.[46] Nor can there be a single source. Nestle, for example, did not discuss the full context, the details about snakes, hares and lions; nor the lively controversy about *polygonia* and *oligogonia* visible in Hippocratic texts and Democritus, not to mention the later writers (which underlines the danger of concentrating only upon certain prominent thinkers). It also highlights the fact that whatever ideas Herodotus may have accepted from Protagoras about the general distribution of the animal kingdom, he was absorbed also in some of the biological detail: his main examples recur, after all, in the list in the *Problemata*; he knows a highly technical medical term which was presumably current in medical discussion at the

---

[43] *Protag.* 315c5–7; 318c. For an analysis of the rest of the myth and importance of Protagoras' division between the gifts of Epimetheus, Prometheus and Zeus, see Demont (1994a).

[44] Nestle (1908), 16–18; also Kerferd (1981a), 150: the prolific v. strong animals contrast fits with myth in *Protag.*; Herodotus either drew on Protagoras, or on 'the source used by Protagoras'. Cf. Demont (1994a), undecided, but stresses plausibly the originality and coherence of Herodotus' whole section (pp. 149–50 surveys other views on the relation of Herodotus and Protagoras).

[45] Demont (1994a) stresses intertextuality and Plato's play on Herodotus' text. Stein, commentary on iii 108.2, concentrating on issue of providential divinity, suggested Anaxagoras as a possible source for Herodotus, but did not note Protagoras.

[46] For Protagoras' agnosticism and current consensus that he would not have attributed such matters to the gods: Guthrie (1971); C. W. Müller (1967); *contra*, Morrison (1941), 14–16, who connects Protagoras with Herodotus.

time he was writing, earlier than its first occurrence in our Hippocratic texts.[47]

The simplest solution – given the evidence, it can only be tentative – is that Herodotus was himself not only familiar with the current discussions of the day, but using them in his own way to create something of his own. Hence the Protagorean echo, but no obvious single source. His idea, for instance, that this is the result of divine *pronoia* may be his contribution to the controversy, especially if Protagoras was unlikely to stress this. Equipped with the examples of biology, he yet concentrates upon the grand pattern of existence and survival between species, and sees it as part of a divine ordering. He seems to share certain lines of interest and knowledge with natural philosophers and medical experts, but offers his own slant.

The flying snakes also look like a Herodotean contribution – and it was the behaviour of the flying snakes and vipers which triggered off the whole discussion. After all, the hare and the lion were amongst the examples in the *Problemata*. But there was nothing there so exotic as the Arabian flying snakes who threatened to engulf the country had they not been blessed with such self-destructive tendencies (109.1–2)! Somehow this example did not enter the later technical literature on generation: the viper did, but not the winged snakes (note 32). Herodotus does not emphasize that this is his own theory as he sometimes does, but it looks like a Herodotean contribution to the mélange.

We seem to have here, then, a section which at first glance belongs to the category of Herodotean wonders, originating in or embellished by fantastic travellers' tales or merchants' yarns, but which turns out to be a reflection on the workings of nature and divine providence through the habits of animal procreation. It is a fascinating combination of schematic ordering of the exotic margins, biological knowledge and theory which belongs in the centre of late fifth-century discussion about procreation and prolific animals: an example, also, where 'wonders' obviously form part of a serious enquiry into nature as well as material simply to entrance the audience. The intellectual connections are too complex, too various, to sort out a neat genealogy of knowledge: Protagoras, Democritus or one of his predecessors, Hippocratic doctors all have something to say on this issue. But so does Herodotus, and why should a genealogy of knowledge be neat in any case? He seems well aware of the general issue of animal survival. He is asking the same questions, he seeks a general explanation for these natural phenomena and while his own approach looks more

---

[47] *Regimen* is dated to end of the fifth or early fourth century by Jouanna (1992). Perhaps similar problems hold for Demont's discussion (1994a) of Herodotus and Protagoras.

akin to the medical writers or Protagoras, he was creating a picture and an argument that could not be attributed to anyone but himself.

There are other areas where Herodotus treats subjects we know were dealt with by natural philosophers, subjects which could be classed as wonders, where we can also see this intermeshing of interests between groups who might later be placed in separate disciplines. Even with our fragmentary evidence for the *physiologoi*, there is an interesting cluster of common interests around the topics of growth, reproduction, and the effect of hot and cold upon these animals.

Take, for example, the effect of cold on animals. Herodotus is quite certain that the area beyond the Ister cannot be overrun with bees, as the Thracians think, because bees are intolerant of the cold (v 10) – a question that recurs in later writings on animals.[48] The cold of Scythia affects other animals, and he explains which ones can bear it, which cannot; he points out that there are no asses or mules either (IV 28.4).[49] Having stressed the extreme cold, he offers his own opinion about the hornless cattle:

It seems to me (δοκέει δέ μοι) that it is because of this that the hornless oxen do not grow horns; a verse in Homer's *Odyssey* supports my opinion (μαρτυρέει δέ μοι τῇ γνώμῃ): 'Libya too, where horns grow quickly on the heads of lambs', and it expresses correctly (ὀρθῶς) that horns grow rapidly in warm countries. But in countries with severe cold, either cattle do not grow horns, or they grow them with difficulty. So it is because of the cold that this happens. (IV 29–30.1)

The passage is striking. It is introduced with a personal opinion, a Homeric passage is added in support, though it is not a particularly conclusive one, as a *marturion* of the opposite phenomenon that in warm countries the opposite holds true, again with a hint of personal opinion, then again the importance of the cold is affirmed in restraining horn-growth. Why does this issue arouse such a detailed and personal argument from Herodotus? And where does it come from?

Herodotus' theories about hornless cattle do not stand in a vacuum, for the cause of horn growth was a matter of concern to those thinkers interested in *physis*, linked as it was to the fundamentals of explaining birth and growth. Democritus discussed the growth of horn – with a different explanation involving *ikmas* (humour), the nature of the skull, and the cold outside the skull which hardens the excrescences into horn, Empedocles had views on the related matter of the growth of nails, created

---

[48] Cf. *Gen. Anim.* III 10. 759a8–761a2 on the 'puzzle' of bee-generation. Note Herodotus' language: argument from likelihood, first person, combination of animals and humans.

[49] This absence returns, crucially, in the great Persian invasion where it is a *thauma*, no less, 'because of the cold', IV 129.

when tendons are hardened by cold,[50] and *On the Nature of the Child* tried to explain the growth of hair.[51] *Airs, Waters, Places* also mentioned briefly the hornless cattle, taking the same line as Herodotus, that the lack of horns is caused by the cold (ch. 18.3 J: 'they do not have horns because of the cold').

Perhaps Herodotus' text bears no relation to these other views, and we should simply take Herodotus on his own account.[52] But this does not really explain why he is so insistent on the importance of cold, and it is reminiscent of those other passages where one suspects a controversy not entirely explained in the text: 'It seems to me', he says, 'that the type of hornless oxen do not grow horns because of this... It is because of the cold that this happens'. He seems to be presenting a theory of his own, or contradicting some other view held by others, or both. A clue may be offered by the way he moves immediately, with slight apology, to the different issue of why there should be no mules in Elis (30.1–2): the absence of mules, he insists, is not because of the cold 'or any other clear cause' (30.1). Mules were another topic we know was discussed by *physiologoi*, though admittedly they tried to explain the sterility of the mule. Alcmaeon's explanation had involved the cold (again the cold as a fundamental cause), and also the thinness of the semen (DK 24, B 3), Empedocles had another explanation (DK 31, B 92, A 82). Herodotus is discussing the absence of mules, but the whole section seems to be based on some sort of relationship to issues which were matters of controversy amongst the *physiologoi*. He moves easily from hornless cattle in Scythia to the absence of mules in Elis by a train of association – the cold, animals and animal growth – which is surely made ready by the fact that, in both subjects, he is dealing with problems which are being debated (with singular disagreement) by certain *physiologoi* as well. We seem to be within a circle of interrelated issues which Herodotus enters with his views on Scythian cold.

The growth of horns and related substances recurs suggestively in Herodotus and again in later discussions about animals. A great many horned

---

[50] DK 68, A 153–5, with excellent discussion by Lonie (1981), 198–200; DK 31, A 78.

[51] Ch. 20, through porosity of the outer skin. The author is particularly concerned with baldness and eunuchs. On this, see Lonie (1981), commentary on *Nat. Child.* ad loc., pp. 198–200; also Longrigg (1993), 95; cf. Lonie (1981), 200: 'Taken together, these passages imply precisely the same explanation of the growth of hair as Democritus gave for the growth of horn; this is the explanation which is implied by [*Nat. Child*] ch. 20 and possibly by the account of nails in ch. 19'; but cf. p. 63 against influence of a single philosopher: it could have come from Empedocles via Anaxagoras or Diogenes, or via Democritus.

[52] Pohlenz used this discussion of horn-growth to argue that Hdt. IV 29 was the source of *Airs* ch. 18: see Heinimann (1945), 173.

animals appear in his Libyan *logos* – not surprisingly if horns grow
because of the heat. The preponderance of horned Libyan animals exactly
fits his remarks about hornless cattle in Scythia. We find asses (ὄνοι) with
horns (IV 191.4), and a little later, asses which 'are *not* those with horns'
(192.1), also snakes with horns (192.2), and the strange oxen with horns
turned backwards, the ὀπισθονόμοι βόες (IV 183.2). It seems unlikely to be
a coincidence that Libya can offer so many horned animals. The distinction between Scythia and Libya in terms of horn growth reappears in
Aristotle's *History of Animals*, where rams with horns in Libya contrast
with those without in the Pontus[53] – we are back again to the Libya–
Scythia axis we looked at before (chapter 2). It does not matter whether
there really are more horned animals in Libya, something no ancient
writer was in a position to verify: surely the observer/enquirer noticed
more horns precisely because of the idea that heat generates horn growth.

Perhaps a similar idea is behind the assertion about the hair growth of
human Egyptians in the notorious section on the skulls at the battlefield
of Pelusium, mentioned before (chapter 2). Egyptians, he said, were least
prone to baldness of any men, and the cause of this is that they have
strong skulls, because they shave their heads, and the bone is thickened
(παχύνεται τὸ ὀστέον) by the sun (III 12.2–3) – the sun again with its
prolific effect now on human hair and skulls as well as animal horns. It is
not entirely clear why *thick* skulls help hair growth; in any case the
observer could hardly discern luxuriant hair if heads were shaved. But
perhaps the association of thought is that hair, bone and horns all benefit
from the sun. Of course there is also a wider application to humans: the
same basic theories are applied as much to human procreation as to the
animal world. As we saw, the Libyans themselves were thought to be
prolific, just as Egyptians were, and Egyptian women in one later Hippocratic essay are thought likely to have premature births.[54]

There are also hints that Herodotus knew something about the growth
of plants and ideas about why some plants might grow in one place rather
than another, another area where information about wonders might mesh
with the pursuit of the workings of nature. We recall how the mysterious

---

[53] *Hist. Anim.* VII (VIII), 606a18–21.

[54] See *On the Seven-months child*, a late work (*CMG* I 2,1 Grensemann, 122, 11–15) where a
parallel is made with Egyptian women – because of the 'polyphilia' of the land and the
heat of the περιοχή (enclosure). For modern interpretations of prolificity, see ch. 3, n. 31.
Cf. also David Hume, 'Of the populousness of ancient nations', in *Essays Moral, Political
and Literary*, ed. E. F. Miller (Indianapolis, 1985), 378 n. 1: 'Columella says [*On Agriculture*], lib. iii cap. 8 that in AEGYPT and AFRICA the bearing of twins was frequent, and
even customary; *gemini partus familiares, ac paene solennes sunt.*' He adds that this is not
the case nowadays: 'On the contrary, we are apt to suppose the northern nations more
prolific ...'

substance *ikmas* was invoked by other writers[55] as a way of explaining why silphium could only grow in Libya. Herodotus also occasionally points out that a plant grows 'spontaneously' (*automatos*) in certain places, in such a way as to suggest that he may be partaking in the language of scientific, medical or physiological discussion. Thus he offers this description of 'sillikypria', of a millet-like plant in India, of cannabis, and of roses in the garden of Midas.[56]

The descriptions of the food and diet of Egypt, of the Ister and all those other Scythian rivers, of Arabian spices and Indian exotica, all could be construed as part of an interest in the wonders of nature as well as an appetite for marvels in their own right. And Herodotus will interrupt his main narrative at some of the most crucial junctures to give his audience a short lecture on some such wonder: just after the narrative of the battle of Marathon and before the Spartans arrive belatedly at the scene of devastation, he explains about the bitumen well near Susa (VI 119). At a momentous point in the invasion of Xerxes as Xerxes enters Thessaly, we have the long 'digression' about the nature of early Thessaly, the rivers and the effect of what must have been an earthquake (VII 128–30). In his attention to the wonders of nature, Herodotus seems to partake of a circle of enquiries which are visible also in the *physiologoi* where marvels are a clue in the investigation of nature.

Medicine, natural philosophy and 'science'

So far, then, we can see Herodotus' *Histories* delving into questions of natural science, particularly into natural wonders, questions of growth and procreation, which were matters of interest both to those conventionally known as *physiologoi*, and to the early medical writers. The doctors of course focus on the human species, but the same natural processes as well as the same questions are often applied to man and animals, and the categories are often taken from the more abstract philosophers. In looking at Herodotus' forays into the natural world, particularly into prolific birth, it is extraordinarily difficult to separate rigidly borrowing from *physiologoi* or from medicine, or common interests, to disentangle any one strand entirely from the rest. If this was a period in which these different areas were either not entirely separated or in the process of

---

[55] *Dis. IV* ch. 34: see ch. 2, pp. 49–50.

[56] II 94.1, τὰ σιλλικύπρια ... τὰ ἐν Ἕλλησι αὐτόματα ἄγρια φύεται (castor-oil plant); III 100, millet-like plant; IV 74, cannabis (wild and cultivated); VIII 138.2, roses (an example which occurs in the medical work); also for salt forming spontaneously, IV 53.3; he makes other observations of 'wild' plants (ἄγρια). He knows, like everyone else, of silphium: IV 169.2, 192.3.

attempting to distinguish themselves, it may be useful to outline something of this interaction, and of the attempts to separate or define the
different fields of enquiry, before returning to Herodotus' conception of
his 'enquiry' as a way towards understanding this pre-disciplinary world.

The interaction between doctors, *physiologoi* and 'philosophy' and the
development of Greek science in the latter part of the fifth century, has
been thoroughly studied by scholars of Greek science, the intense interaction of ideas and intellectual debts, and also the incipient rivalry between developing *technai*.[57]

It is particularly in the realm of the problem of the nature of man, what
he consists of, how he comes to be (generation, embryology) that the
community of interests and questions – as well as controversies – between
the theories of certain natural philosophers and the Hippocratic works is
most striking. The problems in disentangling the possible lines of influence or borrowing between the one or other group illustrate the difficulties
in separating them too strictly.

The belief that man is composed of several humours is a particularly
apt example.[58] For the author of *Ancient Medicine*, health is caused by a
'coction of the humours' (e.g. ch. 19); for the author of *On the Nature of
Man*, the humours are blood, yellow bile, black bile, and phlegm, and
these humours cause either health or illness (and one predominates during
each season).[59] The idea of four humours, which eventually became most
popular, bears obvious relation to Empedocles' theories about man which
involved four constituents, and some influence from Empedocles has been
accepted here.[60] Yet the origin and development of this influential idea
seem to have grown out of fundamental ideas and divisions of the world
in earlier thinkers: not simply Empedocles' idea that man is made of four
elements, earth, air, fire and water, but ideas conventional to Presocratic
philosophy like the importance of opposites, the theory (of Alcmaeon's)
that health is the result of equilibrium (*isonomia*), are all involved.[61] The
medical writers may have taken over these ideas and assumptions about
the world and adapted their own (probably very early) recognition of the
existence of humours to a model of four *constituent* humours which could

---

[57] On this interaction and overlap see esp.: G. E. R. Lloyd (1966), (1979), (1987); Jones
(1946), esp. section 1; Jouanna (1992), 366–403 – less inclined than some to see all the
influence coming from 'philosophy'; Edelstein (1952); Longrigg (1963), and (1993)
(though he tends to separate the two rather categorically). On role of concepts and theory
in observation, cf. also Lloyd (as above), Mansfeld (1980a), who stresses the debt of
medicine to theory; Joly (1966); Bourgey (1953); Diller (1932).

[58] See also ch. 2, on 'Libya and the humours'.

[59] Cf. a further variation in *Diseases IV* (e.g. ch. 32: phlegm, blood, bile and water).

[60] See Jouanna's edition of *Nat. Man*, *CMG* (1975), 43 ff.; Longrigg (1993), 85 ff.

[61] See e.g. Lonie (1981), 54 ff.

only have been developed through the lens of earlier philosophical theory. In other words, 'the philosopher provides the categories within which the medical scientist can order his experience'.[62]

Yet of course there was a wide spectrum of theories about man. The author of *On the Nature of Man* opens his work by objecting to what is essentially a position taken by philosophical monists, but probably also by many who regarded themselves as doctors. The atmosphere of intellectual interaction and debate is vividly illustrated here. *On the Nature of Man* begins with a full-scale attack on 'those who talk about the nature of man' (Ὅστις μὲν οὖν εἴωθεν ἀκούειν λεγόντων ἀμφὶ τῆς φύσιος τῆς ἀνθρωπίνης: literally, 'Whoever is used to listening to people who speak about the nature of man'), who go further than that which pertains to medicine, and who talk in terms of a single ingredient, those for instance, who declare that 'man is all air, or fire, or water, or earth' (ch. 1.1 J).[63] This is an obvious attack on the kind of theories used by earlier Greek *physiologoi* who saw a single principle as the basis of the world. But it is not an attack merely on long-past theories, nor simply on 'philosophers' as a separate group: the author could be aiming his polemic at Diogenes of Apollonia, for instance, a contemporary of the latter half of the fifth century who believed in air as the governing principle, declared it to be a god and thought it an agent of thought.[64] Diogenes may well have been a doctor himself,[65] and certainly had an interest in relevant human biology, a reminder, if so, that a doctor in the second half of the fifth century could well look very like an earlier Ionian monist. Or he could be attacking Hippon of Samos who, similarly, revived the idea that water was the first principle. He too was active in the latter part of the fifth century, satirized by Cratinos (DK 38, A 2), and had interests in biology and causes of illness. Or others of whom we know nothing. The debate here seems to be a live one between contemporaries or near contemporaries.[66] After this initial attack, the author turns explicitly to doctors and declares what 'the constituents of man' actually are; not simply phlegm, he insists, nor bile or

---

[62] Lonie (1981), 61; cf. also Mansfeld (1980a).

[63] For the view that *akouein* here and elsewhere may mean 'to read', that is, to read a text oneself, or to listen to a slave read, see Schenkeveld (1992a), 137f.: his suggestion that a live lecture is not necessarily implied by the word is plausible, but there is other evidence for this period for live lectures, and the opening paragraphs of this essay seem most easily understood in terms of live debates: see further, ch. 8 below.

[64] See Jouanna (1965); Longrigg (1993), 86 ff. further on the Melissos, Diogenes, *Nat. Man* relations.

[65] Jouanna (1992), 375–6 for clear presentation of the problem, and Diogenes' biology and medical competence (NB esp. DK 64, A 4 and A 19). Diller assumes this, (1932), 38–9 (from the presence of medical forms in his work); Longrigg (1993), 76 ff., and n. 101 (p. 238) on the evidence.

[66] Cf. G. E. R. Lloyd (1979), 92–5 on background to attack by *Nat. Man*.

any single substance (ch. 2), and presents his idea that man is composed of more than one quality or *dynamis*, developing the famous theory of the four humours which eventually became the one most widely accepted.

It is striking that the only individuals named in these earlier medical texts are thinkers who are not usually considered 'doctors' in any sense. The opening paragraph of *Nature of Man* (ch. 1) makes one of the rare mentions in the Corpus to a specific thinker: these mistaken theories, he declares scornfully, manage only to 'establish the theory (*logos*) of Melissos'. This reference to the Eleatic Melissos, incidentally also a famous Samian general, evidently needed no further explanation.[67] To this audience, listening to a debate about the nature of man from a 'doctor', the theory of Melissos was known and vivid, not a separate sphere of Greek intellectual enquiry – no more separate than the monistic theories also being attacked here.[68]

Similar implications arise from *Ancient Medicine*, sometimes thought to have been by Hippocrates himself.[69] The author opens with an attack on 'those who have assumed a postulate (*hypothesis*) as a basis for their discussion – heat, cold, moisture, dryness, or anything else they might fancy' (ch. 1.1 J). This attack on 'hypotheses' has attracted particular attention because it is the earliest use of the word itself before Plato; there has been much debate on which thinkers could be meant, and who was guilty of basing their theory of disease upon these opposites (below). But on a general level, the type of theory under attack is again reminiscent of philosophical speculation on the first principle and it is sometimes thought that the author is attacking the input of philosophical theory into medicine. It might seem on one level, perhaps, to be a segment of a debate between philosophy, so named, and medicine,[70] or an attack on the

---

[67] General: Plut. *Per.* 26 ff. Other allusions in *Nat. Man* to Melissos: see Jouanna (1965), and Longrigg (1993), 87–8.

[68] It is partly for this reason that *Nat. Man* seems to me to belong easily in the late fifth century; not 400 BC, as is often suggested on the grounds that it is attributed to Polybus, Hippocrates' son-in-law – which is a very conservative use of chronology. (Lonie 1981, 55, accepts c. 400; Jouanna in ed. of *Nat. Man* (pp. 59–61) puts it 410–400.)

[69] Littré and Gomperz attributed it to Hippocrates, largely on the basis of the resemblance of ch. 20 to *Phaedr.* 270c–d (with its tricky use of τοῦ ὅλου (universe or merely 'the whole'?) attributed to Hippocrates' view), but this is much disputed; against, see (e.g.), Jones (1946), 16 ff. (he dated *Anc. Med.* to between 430 and 400); Jouanna, *Hippocrate* 16–19.

[70] See e.g. Longrigg (1963): including discussion on whether Anaxagoras is influenced by *Anc. Med.* or *vice versa*: he believes the former; cf. Longrigg (1993); Jones (1946), 44–7, on connections with other philosophers (incl. Pythagoreanism); Jones, Introduction to Loeb, p. 5 takes it as an attack on philosophical theory. Cf. more nuanced discussion by Jouanna (1992), 366–403, esp. 379 ff.; Jouanna, Budé edn of *Anc. Med.*

growing influence of philosophy. The author mentions Empedocles by name: on the necessity of knowing what the nature of man is, he says,

τείνει δὲ [τε – J] αὐτοῖσιν ὁ λόγος ἐς φιλοσοφίην, καθάπερ Ἐμπεδοκλῆς ἢ ἄλλοι οἳ περὶ φύσιος γεγράφασιν ἐξ ἀρχῆς ὅ τί ἐστιν ἄνθρωπος, καὶ ὅπως ἐγένετο πρῶτον καὶ ὁπόθεν συνεπάγη.

But the question they raise is one for philosophy, it is the province of Empedocles or those others who have written on *physis* (nature), what man is from the beginning, how he came into being at the first, and from what he was constructed. (*Ancient Medicine*, ch. 20.1 J)

Here we glimpse an explicit separation of medicine from 'philosophy', which seems in this context to denote natural philosophy, the province of Empedocles and 'others who write about *physis*', in their attainment of knowledge. But it may be read as an attempt by the author to differentiate himself from others, rather than a statement of clear and widely accepted divisions between thinkers. It is perhaps part of a strategy to separate medicine, to stake out a corner of the intellectual field and guard it from encroachment, and thus to claim that medicine is a *techne* in its own right.[71]

The distinction is not actually that clear cut, even here. For the same chapter had begun with an attack on both doctors and philosophers (actually called 'sophists') for the same kinds of faults. This again implies (as we saw was a plausible background to *On the Nature of Man*) that doctors at this period were sometimes engaged in intellectual enquiry very similar even to self-styled philosophers. Thus *Anc. Med.* ch. 20 begins:

Λέγουσι δέ τινες ἰητροὶ καὶ σοφισταὶ ὡς οὐκ εἴη δυνατὸν ἰητρικὴν εἰδέναι ὅστις μὴ οἶδεν ὅ τι ἐστὶν ἄνθρωπος.

Certain doctors and sophists say that no one can know medicine who does not know what man is. (ch. 20.1 J)

The author totally disagrees. We have his outburst about Empedocles (above), then further mockery:

ἐγὼ δὲ τοῦτο μὲν ὅσα τινὶ εἴρηται ἢ σοφιστῇ ἢ ἰητρῷ ἢ γέγραπται περὶ φύσιος ἧσσον νομίζω τῇ ἰητρικῇ τέχνῃ προσήκειν ἢ τῇ γραφικῇ.

But I think that everything that has been said either by a sophist or a doctor, or that has been written about nature, belongs less to the medical art than to the art of painting. (*Anc. Med.* ch. 20.2 J)

---

[71] See esp. G. E. R. Lloyd (1979) on development of *techne*; Jouanna (1992), 398–403 on insistence on autonomy of medicine.

Here both the *sophistai* and the doctors and anyone who talks about *physis* are dismissed as woefully irrelevant; *sophistes* here seems to denote 'philosopher' in the widest sense (i.e. *sophos*), rather than the narrower group known since Plato as 'sophists'. He adds immediately that knowledge 'about *physis*' can only be obtained through the medical art; then states what the doctor *should* know 'about *physis*' to be a decent doctor.

It has been argued that the main and immediate focus of attack in *Ancient Medicine* is Philolaos of Croton rather than Empedocles.[72] But in the opening chapters the author seems to have a wider target and his opposition is directed to a range of people, 'doctors', as well as *sophistai*, perhaps in fact a large number who laid much emphasis on the 'hypotheses' (heat, cold, dryness, moisture) rather than a single individual.[73] Jouanna points out that the object of scorn is reminiscent of the kind of 'enquiries into nature' conducted by Socrates as he says in the *Phaedo*, in his earliest youth.[74] One has the impression that a large range of thinkers are delving into the question of the nature of man, and Herodotus was among them with his extensive curiosity about the whole of the known world – to its limits. Even the ambiguity of Hippocrates' statement, as reported by Plato, that one cannot understand the human body without a knowledge of 'the nature of the whole' (τῆς τοῦ ὅλου φύσεως) – the whole universe or the whole man? – may be expressive of the range of areas which could be thought relevant to medicine.[75]

On the Sacred Disease created its radical theory about the natural causes of epilepsy with the help of a theory about the centrality of the brain, a belief held by Alcmaeon and by Diogenes,[76] and not universally accepted; and another about the importance of air in the veins. Alcmaeon had a theory about disease. Diogenes, we recall, parodied in the *Clouds*

---

[72] G. E. R. Lloyd (1963). Note that he concentrated on finding specific *medical* theories in medically based writers, which fitted the bill, though admitting that a wider target was possible. Part of the problem is that *Anc. Med.* talks of the 4 opposites while most medical theories are more complex.

[73] Jones (1946), 47–8 points out that such objectionable views may be found in *Generation* and *Diseases IV*, plus *Affectations*, *Diseases I*, and in Dexippus, Philolaos and Petron: 'It is quite likely that the author ... had no single individual in mind, but was combating all thinkers who attached undue weight to the effect of the four traditional opposites on bodily health' (p. 48). Cf. G. E. R. Lloyd (1963). One might also suggest as targets *Breaths* or *Nat. Man*, or the views they represented. Cf. Longrigg (1963), 152, on *Anc. Med.*, who may overstate the clarity of the distinction between medicine and philosophy. Similarly Longrigg (1993): cf. 46, of fifth-century developments, 'for its influence upon philosophy here medicine itself had a very heavy price to pay'.

[74] Jouanna (1992), 366–403; on Socrates' remark, p. 402.

[75] Plato, *Phaedrus*, 270c–d: cf. n. 10 above.

[76] Diogenes, DK 64, A 19 (= Theophr. *De Sensibus* 39 ff.), on Diogenes' theory of health; Longrigg (1963), 153–4; Alcmaeon, DK 24, A5; cf. A 10.

(227 ff.), had re-emphasized the importance of air. He saw air as crucial to intelligence and therefore to thought, declared that air needed to mix with the blood. Birds, who might otherwise be the cleverest of all, had flesh too dense to benefit from the thought-provoking nature of air.[77]

If Diogenes of Apollonia may have been a doctor (n. 65 above), and the confusion on this question may be significant, the Hippocratic work *On Breaths* also laid stress on air, here as one of the causes of disease. Again, this is a work long thought to have been written by a sophist rather than by a doctor, though its medical provenance and milieu is now more readily accepted.[78] But it could be an example of precisely the type of discussion about the nature of man and his health that is attacked *by Ancient Medicine* (that is, a doctor who talks about *physis* without proper attention to the truly important facts the author of *Ancient Medicine* thinks necessary for the art). Anaxagoras had a theory about the cause of acute disease (bile); his speculation about the nature of matter involved as fundamental elements things such as flesh, bone and nails.[79] Empedocles may have been a doctor himself; he believed at any rate that he could heal, though we have to admit that his healing had decided mystical properties.[80]

Democritus seems to have written works on clearly medical subjects, if we can trust the list of titles of his works preserved in Diogenes Laertius: *Prognosis, On Regimen*, and *Medical Opinion* (Πρόγνωσις; Περὶ διαίτης ἢ Διαιτητικόν, Ἰητρικὴ γνώμη).[81] At any rate certain fragments attributed to him overlap significantly with the matters of concern to the Hippocratic texts: for instance the nature of the seed in the womb (B 148), the causes of the senses.[82] Specific Democritean influence has been discerned in certain Hippocratic works, most notably *Generation/Nat. Child*, and closely allied, *Diseases IV*[83] (see previous section, pp. 143–4). It is certainly

---

[77] DK 64, A 19 again; see also n. 7 above for general discussions on Diogenes.

[78] Cf. Longrigg (1963), 153 for a good example of its dismissal; also Jones' ed. (Loeb), vol. II, pp. 221–5 ; *contra*, Jouanna (1992), 109 ff., esp. 116 ff., and (1984b).

[79] DK 59, A 105 (*de Partib. Animal*. D2 677a5): for similarities between Anaxagoras and *Anc. Med*., Vlastos (1955), 67 n. 2; Jones (1946); Longrigg (1963) (cf. n. 70 above); Jouanna (1992), 373–5, generally, on Anaxagoras' biological interests and relation to cosmology.

[80] DK 31, B 112; cf. B 111; Diller (1932), 37; it is often doubted that Empedocles wrote a separate medical work (e.g. Longrigg 1993, 69) but see DK 31, A1 and A2 for work on medicine, with Jouanna (1992), 371–3, and A3 for Galen's classification of Empedocles among 'the doctors from Italy'.

[81] DK 68, B 26 b, c, d. Accepted by (e.g.) Jouanna (1992, 378–9). Other titles attest to his general interest in the nature of man. Cf. Stückelberger (1984).

[82] Theophrastus, *On the Senses* 49–50 (cited by Barnes (1987b), 257–8): DK 68, A 135. Cf. A 143 (Ar. *Gen. An.*) on creation of male and female children.

[83] See esp. Lonie (1981), 62–70, and commentary; Stückelberger (1984); Longrigg (1993).

possible that Hippocrates himself and Democritus were contemporaries.[84] But the difficulties of separating, for instance, the various affiliations, lines of influence, between Presocratic philosophers and the theory of embryology in *Nat. Child* (chs. 12–31), or on the botany of plants (chs. 22–7, 33–4) tends to indicate not a neat and tidy division of specialities, but a community of contemporary interest and debate, theory and counter-theory, in which *physiologos*, 'scientist', 'doctor', *sophistes*, were not always easy to disentangle. Of course our information is often fragmentary. Yet even with the state of our evidence, the complexity of interaction between 'philosophers', *physiologoi*, and medical works is striking and important. In one attempt to isolate various lines of influence in one particular area, Lonie concluded: 'Much of the material of the botanical theory is the common intellectual property of the age: to disentangle its separate elements would be rather like attempting to disentangle the separate influences upon a contemporary writer of the Freudian school. The botanical theory, like the genetic and embryological theory, bears witness to lively and complex contemporary discussion.'[85] Jouanna's recent study puts a strong case for seeing a spectrum of medically inclined philosophers and doctors with more or less philosophical (i.e. cosmological) tendencies and methods even within the Hippocratic Corpus itself.[86]

It would be unwise to deny any differentiation between Hippocratic writers and other *physiologoi*. Some Hippocratic writers are in the process of trying to define and determine the separateness of medicine from the general enquiry into nature – though in part that need for definition may have been the more acute precisely because there often might not seem to be any great difference in theory. The detailed observation of symptoms and discussion of prognosis by the Hippocratic school (e.g. in *Epidemics*) were peculiar to the medical treatment of disease – though even there observations were to some extent formed via certain abstract assumptions (see n. 57 above). But in some areas of enquiry, it is clearer that the very structures, basic concepts and assumptions about *physis* were at work in medical arguments, and these do not always lie so distant from the concerns of the *physiologoi* themselves. Some doctors looked like *physiologoi*, others (*Anc. Med.*) rejected that model or posed as rejecting it, and vice versa. This muddies the water, but offers a plausibly complex picture of intellectual interaction in the second half of the fifth century. The intel-

---

[84] Jouanna (1992), 378–9.
[85] Lonie (1981), 69.
[86] (1992), 379 ff. esp. 386–7, eloquent against attempts to find origin of (all) ideas on embryology and related subjects in philosophy.

lectual circle which knew of certain theories about nature or medicine may have been wider than the immediately obvious practitioners.

Finally we should add that some sophists ('sophists' as designated by modern scholars) were interested in physical problems and there were occasional overlaps with the interests of natural philosophers (as also of sophists and medical writers, as the more rhetorical of the essays clearly imply). Galen was able to list works with the title περὶ φύσεως or 'On Nature', by Melissos, Parmenides, Empedocles, Alcmaeon, Gorgias, Prodicus, 'and all the others' – though they surely treated the topic very differently.[87] Certain sophists did touch on areas of natural philosophy, though our sources tend to dwell on their other theories, and the subject of 'nature' may have been for some merely part of the general knowledge necessary for a polymath. Prodicus, for instance, had a theory about phlegm, and if we can accept any of these titles wrote a work, according to Galen, *On the Nature of Man*,[88] as well as *On Nature*; the *Clouds* even called him a μετεωροσοφιστής, a 'meteoro-sophist' (v. 360). Hippias answers questions on 'nature' and 'meteorology', and knew about astronomy,[89] while Gorgias discussed problems of vision (*Men.* 76cff.); and Antiphon's *Truth* dealt, among other things, with topics of biology and meteorology.[90] We have mentioned the possibility that Protagoras had an interest in the study of nature (above, p. 147), though Plato makes Protagoras set himself aloof from this and from the kinds of subjects that Hippias taught (*Protag.* 318e). Some well-known sophists, then, delved into these areas, but it should be admitted that these forays into nature seem from our evidence to be just that – forays – amidst many more dominant interests in politics, ethics and rhetoric.

Historie and the *Histories*

Where, then, does this leave Herodotus? This chapter has tried to show how some elements in the *Histories* bear unmistakeable similarity to contemporary 'science' of the mid and late fifth century, and that in some cases Herodotus' own discussion should be seen more readily as part of

---

[87] DK 24 (Alkmaion), A 2. (Heinimann (1945), however, seems to take it that the title *Peri Physeos* is a late fifth-century creation).

[88] G. E. R. Lloyd (1979), 87, n. 146 gives refs.; Guthrie (1971), 277 (ambivalent on Prodicus).

[89] *Protag.* 315c5–7, 318e1–5; *Hipp. Mai.* 285c1–d2.

[90] Frags. 22–39. G. E. R. Lloyd (1979), 87, n. 146 collects further evidence for sophists' discussion of physical problems; (1987), 92–5 (with notes) on the 'permeability' of the categories of sophist and natural philosopher; Kerferd (1981a); Guthrie (1971), 46, is more sceptical.

that complex of questions. He is not, of course, interested in or informed about the more abstract philosophical arguments of the Presocratics, in questions about the first principle, for instance, or the nature of the stars, the balancing principles of Empedocles, the nature of being, or the details of the internal workings of matter. He is unmistakeably drawn to the observable world. But he sometimes covers the very subjects that are discussed by *physiologoi* and self-styled doctors. Had we fuller evidence on the *physiologoi* – and most particularly on Democritus – we might be able to say much more; we have concentrated on only a few areas where there is good external evidence, and perhaps to contemporaries many more elements of his ethnography and geographical enquiries would have seemed part of that world – for instance the lengthy description of the fauna and flora of Egypt (e.g. II 65–76, 92–7). To regard his remarks on the natural world as the result of earlier 'sources', implying that he borrowed unquestioningly from another source, does not do justice either to the nature of the language and concepts he uses for it, or to the manner in which he presents these views as his own. He seems to wish to imply that he is contributing to a matter discussed by others. While that is by no means proof that he is being original, we should probably also accept that his own enquiries involving the natural world were influenced by some of these ideas and questions discussed by the *physiologoi* or actually part of the same milieu.

Yet as we have seen, it is hard – indeed unwise – to specify that one particular method was peculiar to the *physiologoi* or to the early medical writers. We may not be doing justice to the fluidity of boundaries and expansiveness in the quest for knowledge, the absence of disciplinary limits, in this period. The interlocking of methods and ideas is striking, sometimes most striking where the medical writer is particularly anxious to distance himself from the *physiologoi* and maintain the distinct identity of medicine (*On the Nature of Man*). Even some of the thinkers conventionally labelled sophists shared an interest in the workings of nature; Socrates also professed to a youthful, but passing enthusiasm, for the 'enquiry into nature'.

This implies that in this period (broadly to the end of the fifth century), certain questions concerning the natural world, from cosmology and astronomy to the intricate observable details of the animal world, were more widely discussed by a wider range of thinkers than study of the *physiologoi* alone might imply; and perhaps that in this period where separate fields of enquiry are either not separated or in the process of defining themselves, that the enquiry into nature seemed to lie in the general realm of the *sophos*, that is, it was to some extent common property to the prominent thinkers of the time. We saw above how contemporary sources fail entirely to use our own (conventional) categories: and how *sophistai* may refer to a vague group who seem to have ideas about nature and talk about medicine and the nature of man. We shall need to return to this (last chapter); let us concentrate here upon the character of this enquiry into the nature of the world, and the resonances of Herodotus' description of his own work as *historie*.

Herodotus' *Histories* might also, in this predisciplinary age, be considered part of this enterprise. His *Histories* do not cover the nature of the Nile because it was an element of the older Ionian *historie*, but because it was a fascinating subject of contemporary Ionian and non-Ionian *historie*, and a topic that everyone who considered himself *sophos* in the area of nature should have an opinion on. Similarly, perhaps, with the widely discussed questions concerning reproduction and growth in the animal world, and the whole mass of world geography, the attempt to find out what he could for the furthest parts of the world until all information gave out completely. As often pointed out, his *historie* encompassed all subjects of enquiry.

The 'wonders of nature' seem to belong here too, though it is probably impossible to draw a line between those wonders which can be discussed as a serious part of scientific enquiry, like the Nile's summer flooding, and wonders which cater to a popular love of the sensational, the fantastic, and might be wheeled out simply to entertain a general credulous audience (compare the Arabian sheep whose fat tails are carried on miniature trolleys, III 113). One would like to know how far Herodotus' 'enquiries' about the remote areas, and marvellous 'facts' and life and nature on the margins, were meant to contribute to an earlier version of the later pseudo-genre of the study of nature represented by the Aristotelian *On Marvellous things heard*. After all, the vipers' horrible birth is mentioned in this latter work, along with the length of time for which the elephant carries her young, the behaviour of camels in Arabia, and the ability of Ligurian women to bear children while they are actually at work.[91] One of the greatest natural wonders and 'paradoxes' of all, the summer flooding of the Nile, could be explained by natural processes – in effect natural laws – which were universally applicable.[92]

What is clear, is that Herodotus calls Hecataeus a *logopoios* along with Aesop (II 143.1; V 36.2; II 134.3) – rather than a sophist or a *sophos* or any other possiblity – and that his use of *historie* of his own work suggests that he wished to present it in a different light. Here we treat an area very

---

[91] All prefaced by λεγέται or similar distancing device. Refs.: vipers, ch. 165 (846b); elephants, ch. 177 (847b); camels, ch. 2 (830b); Ligurians, ch. 91 (837b).

[92] On Herodotus' quest for uniformity in nature, Corcella (1984), 74–84, and p. 139 above.

extensively discussed.[93] The etymological link of *historie* with οἶδα, 'know' and thence seeing, is obviously of some relevance. Another stimulating approach is to connect Herodotus' *historie* with the *histor*, which shares the same root. The figure of the *histor*, who appears in the *Iliad* (e.g. XVIII 501, shield of Achilles), the mediator and arbitrator of the archaic period, would, through the philological link, convey Herodotus as the *histor* who sees, hears, and arbitrates[94] – thus fitting with Herodotus' liking for settling controversies, judging between two stories. Yet while this is suggestive, and the root meaning must retain some force, it tends to interpret Herodotus in the light of a remote archaic world (perhaps up to 300 years before). Etymology can perhaps only take us so far (compare an interpretation of the institution of the British Parliament via the French *parler*) and there is a danger of missing any contemporary resonances. When Herodotus famously opens his work by saying he is giving a demonstration of his enquiries, he is the first extant writer to use the word *historie*,[95] and with this placing one would suppose a deliberate emphasis. In the few other places where it occurs, method is at stake (II 99.1; II 118.1; 119.3; VII 96.1).[96] When he stands aside in Book II (ch. 99) and makes his rather formal statement that 'Up to this point what has been said is the product of my own sight (*opsis*) and judgement (*gnome*) and enquiry' (*historie*), but from now on he is repeating what he has heard of Egyptian traditions, he is not using the language of the archaic mediator. Nor is he using *historie* about his enquiries about the past, which in this case are still to come – *historie* here clearly refers to his enquiries into the

---

[93] Discussions of *historie*: esp. Snell (1924), 59–71; Jacoby (1913), 396; Sauge (1992); Connor (1993b); Immerwahr (1966), 315 (stressing all-embracing conception of *historie* in Herodotus); Weber (1976); cf. Christ (1994); Evans (1968), stressing fairness of the *histor*; Erbse (1956) on Herodotus' first sentence; and further works below.

[94] See most recently, e.g., Connor (1993b), who looks at the *histor* in later Greek sources, but the burden of his interpretation still lies in the archaic *histor*; Sauge (1992), with my review, *CR* 45 (1995b), 456–7; Lateiner (1989), 84. A problem with the archaic '*histor*' is that it has other associations also: cf. *Od.* XXI 26 (compound denoting skill), *Hom. Hymn* 32.2; also *Il.* XVI 695, Bacchyl. 9.44 (all cited by Connor).

[95] Note, however, Heraclitus: B 35 (χρὴ γὰρ εὖ μάλα πολλῶν ἵστορας φιλοσόφους ἄνδρας εἶναι καθ' Ἡράκλειτον). Diels-Kranz lists DK 22, B 129, on Pythagoras' *historie* among fragments of dubious authenticity. Xenophanes (DK 21, B 18) speaks of 'searching/discovering' (cf. ἐξευρήσει, DK 22, B 18); Parmenides' word for enquiry is the related (and older) word δίζησις (DK 28, B 2: B 6, 1–3; B 7, 2; B 8, 6), used also by Heraclitus (B 101), and Herodotus (e.g. I 95.1, ἐπιδίζηται).

[96] VII 96.1 is sometimes seen, unnecessarily, as approaching our word 'history'. For use of the verb: of Herodotus' enquiries: II 19.3 *bis* (Nile), II 29.1 (Nile sources), II 34.1, II 44.5, II 113.1 (Helen), IV 192.3 (Libya); by various tyrants or kings, I 24.7, I 56.1 and 2 (Croesus), III 50.3, 51.1 *bis* (Periander); by others, I 61.2, I 122.1, III 77.2 bis; cf. also VII 195 (Greeks). Almost all of Herodotus' own 'enquiries' (self-styled) concern present geography: but the priests' enquiries (II 118.1, 119.3) and II 113.1 concern the Trojan war, II 44.5 concerns Heracles.

land, river, nature of Egypt and its people, not its history.[97] Rather, he is distinguishing precisely his own enquiries and sources of knowledge in exactly the language that was favoured by the early Hippocratic writers and no doubt other contemporaries – the distinction between what you can deduce from *gnome*, and what you can tell by experience, and via concepts used by the natural philosophers (for which, see next chapter). A revealing comparison can be made with the notorious section in *On the Nature of the Child* (ch. 13) where the author lays great emphasis on the fact that he actually *saw* a six-day embryo – the age is probably provided by the woman's testimony, the embryo by the fact that she terminated a pregnancy – and that he has evidence that what he says is true. Quite what he can have seen, and how far he saw what he thought he ought to see, are moot points: but the intense emphasis on the doctor's own personal autopsy, his experience and his own inferences from that, are most striking, and his argument makes careful distinctions between what he saw, his opinion, and *historion*, evidence which is seen.[98]

If we look carefully at the writers who actually use *historie* of their own activity, it seems to be part of the vocabulary of 'scientific' activity of the latter part of the fifth century and early fourth century (I use 'scientific' here in its weak sense, as denoting the attempt to find out the truth about the world without resorting to divine or supernatural explanations). We may then press this later contemporary milieu far more forcefully than any earlier association.[99] In one of the earliest Hippocratic treatises, *On Ancient Medicine*, which we discussed above, the author declares in characteristically dogmatic fashion that it is quite impossible to understand

---

[97] Indeed most of his refs. to *historie* in Book II are not about sifting stories and traditions, *pace* Connor (1993b). See previous note.

[98] See on this Lonie (1981), Commentary ad loc., 158 ff.; and Lonie (1977), who notes the unusual emphasis on sight; interestingly, he connects this with the term *historion*, meaning 'evidence (which is *seen*)' (commentary p. 163). See also Hanson (1987), esp. 596–9 on the problem of theory and observation here and in other cases (pregnancies). A clearer example of the distinction between experience and *gnome* in *Art*, ch. 11, amidst much play on sight, *gnome*, hearing: where the doctor cannot use *opsis*, or *akoe*, he tries *logismos* – theory (see further below, ch. 6, pp. 200–11).

[99] Gould implies this, but sees the phenomenon more as one which stretches from Herodotus back over a century before: (1989), 11, 'Perhaps, by using the word *historie* Herodotus aligns himself, perhaps deliberately, with a tradition of positivist thinking and rational analysis of available data which had been created in Ionia over the past century.' For *historie* as expression of rational enquiry, natural science: Gould 10–11, who presses implications of rational analysis etc. (I would reinforce even more the contemporary and late fifth-century relevance); A. Lloyd (1990), 215–16 ('as a scientific enquiry with a clear awareness of problems of evidence and a determination, where possible, to solve them'); Cf. A. Lloyd (1975), *Introduction*, esp. 81–4 on *historie* (stressing *historie* as usually oral enquiry, and scientific overtones). On *historie* and its later development into 'history', Hornblower (1987), 8–12.

the nature of man by any other means than by medicine – 'impossible, I say, to understand this *historie* (enquiry), what man is, by what causes he is made, and similar matters, accurately' (λέγω δὲ ταύτην τὴν ἱστορίην εἰδέναι, ἄνθρωπος τί ἐστι καὶ δι' οἵας αἰτίας γίνεται καὶ τἆλλα ἀκριβέως: ch. 20.2 J). Even more striking is the opening of *Art* (ch. 1.1 J), for which there is an interesting ambiguity about whether the author was a doctor or a sophist (or both): he opens by objecting to 'those who make an art (*techne*) of criticizing the arts, who consider that they are making a display of their own *historie*' – their own enquiry, their own knowledge.[100] Socrates' reminiscence about his early interests in nature refers to that subject as 'that branch of knowledge (*sophia*) which they call enquiry about nature' (ταύτης τῆς σοφίας ἣν δὴ καλοῦσι περὶ φύσεως ἱστορίαν, *Phaedo* 96a7–8). Despite his hints at Anaxagoras in the following paragraphs, he seems also to refer more widely to the whole 'branch' of philosophical enquiry belonging clearly to the *physiologoi* but not confined to them. A fragment of Euripides also refers to the happiness of life devoted to 'historia' into 'the ageless order of nature' (fr. 910 N²). Moreover, none of these remarks imply an intimate or necessary relationship between *historie* and a resort to visual evidence.[101]

These descriptions are clearly not all absolutely contemporary with Herodotus and scholars have expressed doubts as to their relevance,[102] but this is the evidence we have, and as our only contemporary evidence, it suggests unequivocally that *historie* was a term which in Herodotus' time and even later, was intimately paired with the enquiry into nature, the nature of man. In all our fifth-century (and also early fourth-century) evidence apart from Herodotus, it is a term used to express the enquiry of the natural philosopher, the doctor, those seeking after the truth about the nature of the world in whatever manner they pursued this. Thus even if we believed that natural science took its cue from Herodotus, as the earlier writer, we would then have to explain why this could occur. These methods might range from highly theoretical speculation to the use of

---

[100] For further comparison with Herodotus' opening sentence, see ch. 7 below.

[101] A link stressed e.g. by Hartog (1988), 265; or Lonie (1981), 163 on '*historion*'. For what it is worth, Proclus speaks of Hippias' discovery of the quadratrix curve in terms of enquiry (ἱστόρησεν): *Commentary on the First Book of Euclid's Elements*, p. 356, cited, Kerferd (1981a), 48.

[102] Connor (1993b) sees the Presocratics as problematic because of our dependence on later sources; and *Anc. Med.* and *Art* as too late to be relevant (see esp. p. 4 n. 3). Sauge (1992) astonishingly omits the late fifth-century instances: see e.g. p. 306. Democritus perhaps discussed *historie* among his many lost works: D. L. has a title Περὶ ἱστορίης in the list of his works (DK 68, A 33; cf. B 299, but doubted by DK); stressing lack of disciplinary divisions, Gould (1989, 10) mentioned Democritus, but treating Democritus simply as Herodotus' successor, did not press the implications.

visual evidence, experience, empirical evidence, or logical proof: *historie* here is clearly not confined to the process of using personal experience, visible evidence; it can equally involve theoretical argument; nor is it necessarily related to enquiry about the past.[103] And as we shall see (chapter 6) Herodotus himself shares some of the methods and vocabulary of certain natural philosophers and doctors. Moreover, while Connor makes an interesting connection between the *histor* and Herodotus' penchant for controversy, conflicting views and competing stories, and links the latter with the model of the mediating arbitrator,[104] controversy is as central to the conflicting and antithetical arguments of intellectual debate in the late fifth century as it was in the archaic world of early dispute settlement – and probably considerably more refined. This would tend to confirm the idea that when Herodotus talked of his work as *historie* he was deliberately setting it within the milieu of the philosophical and proto-scientific enquiries of his time: a signal to his audience, perhaps, that he was not merely a *logopoios*.[105] The concept of an 'early Ionian *historie*', of the sixth and early fifth century, and which called itself *historie*, is, I would suggest, an entirely modern one. For Herodotus' audience, the word *historie* would have contemporary resonances; it made contemporary claims that his work belonged in the world of scientific enquiry, whether it be into nature, or the nature of man, or as in Herodotus, the nature of the conflict between Greeks and barbarians in the widest possible interpretation of that conflict.

---

[103] Not just personal experience or witnessing, as von Fritz took it (1936, 315), building on the meaning of *histor* (*historie* 'meant knowledge of all sorts which was not based on speculation, demonstration, intuition, practice or the like but on personal experience. It meant all that a man could tell, because he had been a ἵστωρ, a personal witness', or had knowledge from other witnesses). Cf. Lateiner (1989), 225, who perhaps assumes *historie* is enquiry into past actions; pp. 83–4: '*Apodexis histories*,... for Herodotus means serving as a *histor*: to see, report, compare and arbitrate among contending claims of truthfulness'; Lateiner (1986), on the other hand, stresses *historie* as empirical research of the type visible in the medical writers keen to use visual evidence (e.g. pp. 5, 10, 17).

[104] Connor (1993b).

[105] If it is significant that *historie* becomes less frequent in the *Histories*, as Connor (1993b) stresses, then that would reinforce this suggestion.

6   Argument and the language of proof

Herodotus' *Histories* are so universally admired for their narrative skill and what has sometimes been called the art of the oral narrator, that it may seem perverse to turn to them for any illumination of the use of logical, deductive argument and the language of proof. This would also upset the conveniently neat contrast so often made between Thucydides and Herodotus – Thucydides as the rigorous scientific and analytical historian, Herodotus as the more casual enquirer and entertainer. Yet one of the fascinating characteristics of the *Histories* is that the author is able to operate in several modes or styles, and that he can, and does, turn occasionally to the methods and language of argumentation that are more readily associated with early Greek science, natural philosophy and Thucydides. When he does, this is in a quite different vein from the image of an Herodotus who is anxious to please, to entertain, and merely to repeat what he has heard, as he says at one point (VII 152.3).

Methods of argument which evince praise for the development of rational argument in more philosophical writers often lie unnoticed in Herodotus.[1] He is familiar with many of the terms of philosophy and science in the latter half of the fifth century. He is, for instance, one of the earliest writers to use the term *elenchos* (ἔλεγχος) in the context of an abstract debate about the possibility of knowledge.[2] Thucydides' dismissal of the stories of the logographers as 'incapable of being tested' (ἀνεξέλεγκτα) (I 21.1), is exactly the same point Herodotus is making.[3] Herodotus is

---

[1] Examples below. The argument from what is likely (*eikos*/Ionic *oikos*) need hardly be archaic in Herodotus (*pace* Cole (1967), 145, on Hdt. IV 110) – his argument that Helen never reached Troy (II 120) is effectively based on likelihood: cf. D. Müller (1981), 307 for stress on *eikos* in Herodotus; sensible remarks in Dihle (1962a), esp. 218; A. Lloyd (1975), 162–3 (*eikos* a feature of forensic oratory of the period); Lateiner (1989), 193 (Herodotus has 'an historian's distrust' of arguments from probability); Hornblower's remark, (1987), 106f., that ὡς εἰκός is 'quasi-legal' seems somewhat misleading. Cf. Goebel (1989); and O'Sullivan (1992), 28 more widely. See also n. 51 below.

[2] II 23–4; also II 22.4: see further, page 208, n. 94 below on *elenchos*.

[3] Both cited by G. E. R. Lloyd (1979), 253 for parallelisms between political/legal debate and philosophical; see now, Fowler (1996), 81.

quite familiar with the use of *tekmeria* ('proof' or 'decisive evidence' –
below), often in the context of sophisticated theories, *marturia* ('evidence',
'testimony'), and *ananke* to denote logical necessity; he also uses the language of the *apodeixis* and even *epideixis* in a manner which is reminiscent of later rather than earlier writers. The problems of deducing what is
'invisible' from what is 'visible' are expressed in ways exactly parallel to
the early medical writers when they confront similar doubts (below, pages
200–11). Other expressions relating to knowledge recur both in Herodotus and certain other writers: for instance the accusation of ignorance,
insufficient knowledge, which Herodotus levels at 'the most ignorant
opinion' (γνώμη ἀνεπιστημονεστέρη) at ΙΙ 21, is the same as that levelled
by the author of *On the Art* against the layman when he says that even an
'ignorant layman' (ἰδιώτης ἀνεπιστήμων) would not think such a thing (*Art*
ch. 6.2 J).[4] Herodotus seems, at least superficially, to share much of the
early medical and philosophical discourse about the sources of knowledge.

When Thucydides opens his *History* by declaring that he has engaged
in the most rigorous testing of evidence, that he has left no testimony
unchecked, we would assume that he was pointedly distinguishing himself
from his most famous historical predecessor Herodotus. Indeed the very
language in which he chooses to do so has itself been seen as significant,
indicative of the new rigour, the new emphasis upon proof and evidence,
which set his historical research, as well as his generation, apart from
Herodotus'. Thus he opens by declaring that he started his work at the
very beginning of the war, 'expecting that it would be great and the most
worthy of record of any that had gone before', and:

inferring this (*tekmairomenos*) from the fact that they were both at the height
of preparation for it (τεκμαιρόμενος ὅτι ἀκμάζοντές τε ἦσαν ἐς αὐτὸν ἀμφότεροι
παρασκευῇ τῇ πάσῃ). (Ι 1.1)[5]

He adds that despite the difficulties, 'he thinks' that earlier wars 'were
not great, in so far as it was possible in my examination to trust from
evidence' (ἐκ δὲ τεκμηρίων ὧν ἐπὶ μακρότατον σκοποῦντί μοι πιστεῦσαι
ξυμβαίνει οὐ μεγάλα νομίζω γενέσθαι) (Ι.1.3).

This opening reads like a statement of intent, and an attempt to make
clear to his readers by the most rigorous and up-to-date language of proof
that his methods were superior to those of his predecessors – and so it
has often been taken.[6] Yet while this is clearly Thucydides' intention, it

---

[4] Cf. also ΙΙ 45.1, λέγουσι δὲ πολλὰ καὶ ἄλλα ἀνεπισκέπτεως οἱ Ἕλληνες.

[5] τεκμαιρόμενος: we may understand 'being assured of this from evidence' or 'inferring this
from evidence'. Gomme's note (Comm.) on Ι 1.3 and Ι 20.1 (*tekmerion*) is over rigid.

[6] See (e.g.) Hornblower, *Commentary on Thucydides*, ad loc. Cf. also similar remarks on
method at Ι 20.1, 21.1.

cannot necessarily be taken as a straightforward indication of his relation to Herodotus – rather, it may be in part a strategy, part of Thucydides' attempt to separate his work from that of his predecessor, rather than a simple and unassailable declaration of the truth. As we shall see, Herodotus shares much of this language, and the relationship between the two historians must in fact be very much more intricate. As we observe elsewhere, a more plausible and rounded sense of Herodotus' achievement can sometimes be gained from an appreciation of the context beyond the historians who immediately succeeded or preceded him. In some respects Herodotus delights in using the language of proof and open argumentation considerably more than Thucydides does – and one must wonder why. To investigate this is a complex task, involving as it does, at least potentially, much of fifth-century Greek natural philosophy, philosophy and medicine, most of which has been lost. In order to reduce this huge area to manageable proportions, we concentrate on some of the areas where our evidence allows reasonably clear conclusions, (i) argumentation; (ii) the language of proof; (iii) the problem of the invisible. All are united, as will be seen, by a kinship to a particular intellectual method and intellectual milieu.

This 'kinship' has occasionally been noticed of Herodotus' *Histories,* often by scholars whose primary interests lie in the development of philosophy and science rather than historiography. In his use of analogy, for instance, he can be compared with Hippocratic writers.[7] The close comparison of the language and mode of argument was almost totally neglected by the earlier scholars who linked Herodotus to the philosophers and thinkers of his day,[8] but more recent work on the development of Greek philosophy opens up interesting opportunities in this area. Gould has remarked justly on Herodotus' 'astonishing breadth of imagination and open-mindedness and remarkable powers of analytical thought', a point which he illustrated with Herodotus' description of the geography of the Nile valley (II 5.1–2), which showed a 'combination of observation and analytical reasoning at its most impressive'; he added that Herodotus' ability to envisage historical change on a massive temporal scale (20,000 years) in the opening chapters of Book II (11–12) displays 'a relaxed open-mindedness' surpassed only by his remarks made on the conventional

---

[7] G. E. R. Lloyd (1966), 341 ff.; but see Lateiner (1989), 191–6 and Corcella (1984), and further below (pp. 200–11) on analogy. Corcella (1984) sees Herodotus more in terms of Presocratic attempts (i.e. from Milesians down to Empedocles, Democritus) to ascertain knowledge about the invisible from the visible: note however, that Corcella is talking about analogy in the widest sense and that he sees this quest as generally part of an 'Ionian *historie*' which includes the early Presocratics.

[8] E.g. Nestle (1908); Pohlenz (1937) and (1953).

Greek opinions about the boundary between Asia and Libya (II 15–17).[9] Herodotus extrapolates well into the future also (II 13–14). Yet since some of the occasions where Herodotus engages his audience in sustained and elaborate argument have involved conclusions which have embarrassed modern scholars keen to defend Herodotus' veracity, attention tends sometimes to be deflected towards the truth value of his final conclusions rather than the manner in which he reached them.

Book II confronts the reader with some of these features with particular acuteness; in the fullest discussion of this subject, Alan Lloyd's commentary discusses some aspects of Herodotus' construction of his theories.[10] For instance Lloyd shows the important role in Herodotus' theorizing of the idea, in fact strictly fallacious, that if something occurs after something else, it was *caused* by the earlier factor, the so-called *post hoc ergo propter hoc* fallacy.[11] He also points to some types of argumentation in Book II where Herodotus shows a 'mastery of contemporary science' and a skill in argument that was rational and characteristic of the sophistic period.[12] Lloyd singles out the following types of argument: 'elaborate inductive arguments showing a mastery of scientific method', argument from *eikos*, empirical argument, archaeological proof, *reductio ad absurdum*, argument from *logoi* (i.e. tradition), argument from chronology.[13] Lloyd links these types of argument loosely with 'Presocratic speculation'; he points to inductive arguments specifically linked to scientific method, by which he means theories about the nature of the earth, about the sun's behaviour, about geology, but unfortunately he does not develop these observations any further.[14] Moreover his remark that the *post hoc propter hoc* fallacy and the preference for 'schematization' show we are dealing with what he calls universal propensities of 'the Greek mind' tends to draw the explanation away from the specific historical and cultural context, the specific types of construction of argument peculiar to a particular period.[15]

An important recent study by Lateiner on the other hand offers a more specific and detailed comparison of the language and concepts which

---

[9] Gould (1989), 86–7.

[10] A. Lloyd (1975), *Introduction*, ch. 4: p. 141, what he calls 'the mind of Herodotus'.

[11] P. 147 – i.e. assumption that if A occurs after B, then A was caused by B.

[12] P. 160, citing Nestle (1908), 35.

[13] Pp. 160 ff. Note also some important remarks on formal proof in Corcella (1984), 74 ff., and Darbo-Peschanski's discussion (1987, esp. part 2.2) (less on contemporary context).

[14] He cites: II 5, 10–14 (Egypt built up from silt); II 22 (Nile flood created by snow); II 24–7 (flood connected to sun's behaviour); II 104 (Colchians are Egyptians by origin).

[15] A. Lloyd (1975), 150, 151 (there are also difficulties in talking about 'Herodotus' mind' when dealing with a literary work). Cf. also Lateiner (1989), 193 on 'the Hellenic impulse towards symmetry'.

touch upon method used by the early Hippocratic writers and Herodotus, in particular the terms used for proof, evidence and sight and about the pursuit of knowledge. This study, which forms the basis for any future work, concluded that they shared a 'common epistemological response' (the title of the article), a common empirical method, basing their researches upon secure observable evidence, autopsy of memorials, for example, the evidence of experience, rather than untestable theory.[16] While there may be doubts as to precisely how empirical Herodotus really was, Herodotus' emphasis on autopsy, and reliable witnesses whether human or inanimate (monuments), is undeniable, and Lateiner's discussion supersedes any study which confined itself to a comparison of Herodotus solely with the Presocratic philosophers.[17]

Yet these discussions do not seem to have had as much impact on general perceptions of the *Histories* as they should have, perhaps partly because Lloyd's study at least was comparatively undeveloped; and perhaps because they seemed to offer an image of Herodotus which was too rigid, either too rigidly empiricist, or too positivist, too scientific, too 'serious'?[18] Besides, these methods are more obvious and more overt in the sections treating geography, customs, ethnography (and throughout Book II), rather than the narratives of past events. As for the historical narrative itself, it is unclear how far these methods are really applicable to the past, especially the past of archaic and legendary Greece. Many historians, in any case, would be uneasy about seeing the study of the past as based on strictly empirical methods in the full scientific sense – that is, on evidence that is observable and testable, susceptible to experiment. If one means by empirical methods, reliance on evidence of the senses, and of experience, observable evidence (the kind of evidence *Ancient Medicine* stresses), then there is difficulty in seeing any enquiry into the Greek past, reliant as it was on tradition and hearsay, as 'empirical'. As Corcella treats it in his book the stuff of history would be as much part of the realm of the 'invisible' for Herodotus as the wastes of northern Scythia. If one sees empirical methods to involve the use of evidence of any kind, as opposed to abstract theory, then Herodotus certainly poses as one who uses

[16] (1986). Note, however, G. E. R. Lloyd (1966) who compared Hippocratics and Herodotus.

[17] D. Müller (1981) thought Herodotus was the first empiricist by comparing the general Presocratic disdain for visible, empirical evidence, the evidence of the senses: but he ignored the Hippocratic writings; cf. also Weber (1976) on Herodotus' empiricism; with Corcella's criticism, (1984), 63–4.

[18] For reservations on Lateiner's interpretation of the significance of Herodotus' remarks about evidence and proof, see Thomas (1997a).

evidence. But then he also speculates and, as we shall see, tries to infer, about the unknown, in areas where there is very little evidence of any kind.

Let us look in more depth into the intellectual world to which these methods, arguments, proofs, belonged. This can be done best by looking closely not only at the vocabulary used, but at the structure of the arguments, the building blocks as it were, and above all, the contexts or theories, for which Herodotus makes use of these methods of argument. For they can be shown repeatedly to be the kind of arguments visible in the examples of 'logical deduction' of our best evidence, the early medical writers; they are also by no means allied indissolubly to questions which involved empirical evidence (experience, visible or tangible evidence), rather than theoretical and abstract considerations. We will start by looking at deductive reasoning. What emerges is that Herodotus resorts to elaborate argument often precisely where empirical evidence is lacking, and the contexts where he makes use of the current terminology of proof and argument are sometimes those where his theories are most ambitious and most sophisticated. This raises the question of the 'rhetoric' of his use of this type of language and argument – what it was meant to imply to his audience – which is discussed in this and the next chapter.

Two further points. Firstly, it deserves considerable emphasis that Herodotus stands aside anywhere in his *Histories* to take his audience through the evidence for a particular statement; or the proof that what he says is the truth; or perhaps more surprising, fairly long argument with each move or step set out in order to demolish some rival theory. Thucydides does not tend to do this (though there are exceptions), and there is no reason, and in any case no evidence, to think that Herodotus' prose predecessors who treated the past did so either.[19] But it is an increasingly common habit of the natural philosophers and medical writers of the latter half of the fifth century and with increasing sophistication beyond. The development of the habit of giving explicit argumentation, that is, setting out the evidence, or the proof, or marking the steps of argument made, in these other areas has been seen as a precise stage in the development of Greek philosophy and natural philosophy or 'science' (in its infant sense): Xenophanes and Heraclitus declared what was (in their eyes) the truth, Heraclitus in deliberately mantic and enigmatic style, though Xenophanes hints at the process of discovery (DK 21, B 18; cf. A 33, implied reason-

---

[19] Studies of Hecataeus which credit him with many of the attributes of Herodotus' techniques of *historie*, drawing on Jacoby (1912) – e.g. Corcella (1984) – seem to be taking for granted what they need to prove.

ing). But Parmenides is the first extant natural philosopher who presents sustained abstract, logical argument to prove his thesis, and he mentions 'signs' once (*semata*, B 8, line 2);[20] his followers, Zeno and Melissos, continued the method, producing strong connected series of arguments. Anaxagoras tends simply and baldly to tell his audience what they must think – so far as we can tell from the meagre fragments ('as I have said', B 12.23; B 4.5, what 'it is necessary to think' (χρὴ δοκεῖν) seems to be the conclusion to certain statements, so there is some overt argument, but slight). The development of argument, and therefore, closely linked, of persuasion, can be traced in some detail in the later *physiologoi* and with most wealth of evidence, the early medical works. Should we not see Herodotus' deductive proofs as part of this wider development, part of this change in the way in which philosophers or *sophoi* tried to convince, part of an intellectual *koine* of the time attested from Parmenides to the early Hippocratics?[21]

Secondly, if there is unease about presenting a Herodotus who is too adept at logical argument, a skill which would seem to contrast too sharply with his charm as a narrator and his love of fabulous tales, it can perhaps be suggested how little we really understand about the so-called 'sophistic period' of the mid to late fifth century.[22] There is an unexpected and unexplored bridge between Herodotus as story-teller and the way at least some of the sophists presented their ideas at least some of the time. For as Aly pointed out long ago, several of the major sophists clothed their teachings in myth and fable.[23] One thinks of Protagoras' famous myth in Plato's *Protagoras*, which forms a metaphor for his theory about the origins of human society and the forces which keep it together; or more authentically attested as a separate work, Prodicus' *epideixis* on the choice of Heracles.[24] A story in Antiphon's *On Concord* which Aly also mentions, begins, 'there is a story, that . . .' (ἔστι δέ τις λόγος, ὡς ἄρα . . .);[25] a habit of which presumably Plato's myths are the successors. Aly saw the sophists as successors to an East Greek tradition of story-telling. It is unclear how far one can take this, especially without more evidence for the

---

[20] Note, however, that the 'signs' of Parmenides are in fact connected to his road imagery (I owe this point to Michael Trapp).

[21] For the development of logical argumentation, see above all, G. E. R. Lloyd (1979), (1987).

[22] Cf. interesting recent work on sophists' cultural position: O'Sullivan (1996).

[23] Aly (1929), esp. 70–6 (on Die Kunstformen der frühen Sophistik).

[24] Note esp. *Protag.* 320c2–4, 324d2–7, where Protagoras makes it clear that the *logos* and *mythos* support each other closely. Prodicus: DK 84, B 2 = Xen. *Mem.* II 1, 21–34.

[25] Antiphon DK 87, B 54, with Aly's discussion (1929).

sophists themselves,[26] though they did after all regard themselves as in some way successors to Homer. For the time being, it at least serves to suggest that a combination and continuation of story-telling with inductive argument was not entirely alien to the world of the *sophoi* and *sophistai* in the mid to late fifth century. If we throw into the picture of this extraordinary period the figure of the fifth-century Homeric rhapsode and the way that the fifth-century sophists seem to have seen themselves as successors of Homer, then the dizzy combination of narrative, story-telling and the use of deductive proof may not be so jarring.

Argument

Let us look at instances of deductive argument in Herodotus. This type of reasoning lies alongside his more readily recognized use of analogy, and it is in some respects considerably more prominent. We will look at the basic structure of the arguments, the way in which the building blocks are actually arranged, the steps by which the argument is spelt out, rather than the content of the theories or any truth value they might hold. What we need to do here is to examine a few examples in detail and alongside other remarkably similar arguments in some medical writers. Our aim is not to examine the deductive arguments available or used from a philosophical point of view, which would be inappropriate and unnecessary for Herodotus; nor to cover the whole range of ways in which Herodotus tries to persuade his audience of what he says;[27] but to examine quite how similar his methods are, in some places, to those of certain medical writers, who provide our fullest evidence for this type of argumentation, and then to consider what this implies. These passages of reasoning tend to be long. Recurrent methods and features of argument are: argument of the type known as *Modus Tollens*, that is: If A, then B; but not B; therefore not A – a type of deductive argument not formally expressed in general terms until Aristotle but used well before; the enthymeme; argument from likelihood (*eikos*); listing of arguments; explicit citation of evidence or 'proof' as part of this; *reductio*; argument from analogy; *a fortiori* reasoning.

---

[26] It may be objected that the sophists' stories had clear philosophical and didactic aims which would distinguish them from Herodotus; but then so do some of Herodotus' (e.g. the tale of Solon's visit to Croesus). This raises interesting questions: e.g. about how far a 'story' has truth value which does not consist in it having happened: Aly (1929) also mentions the tale about Darius (Hdt. III 38) as a tale which looks like a folk-tale but is clearly a sophistic 'fable'. See also Calame (1996) for the interchangeability of *mythos* and *logos*.

[27] E.g. through citing witnesses, his own experience, Egyptian priests, etc. or even by juxtaposition of tales.

Herodotus is unmistakeably showing himself to be cognizant of, or actually part of, a particular kind of intellectual style here. These attempts to persuade are amusingly distant from the author who says, apparently quite blandly, that his practice is simply to repeat what he has heard.

In his famous polemical argument about the nature of Egypt (II 15–18) we have a series of balancing, antithetical claims and counterclaims. The initial problem is that 'the Ionians' think that Egypt consists only of the Delta, a wild misconception as Herodotus is keen to prove. The demolition of their mistake is highly effective and to see it mainly in terms of criticism of Hecataeus deflects attention from its contemporary style. These are the main blocks of argument, isolated and partly paraphrased for clarity:

15.1: 'If we wish to follow the opinions of the Ionians [who think the Delta alone is Egypt ... long description] ... then we would show, using that argument (*logos*), that the Egyptians previously had no country'.[28]

This is a good example of *reductio ad absurdum*.

15.2: 'For, as the Egyptians themselves say, and as I think, the Delta is quite recent ...'
'If no country existed, how could they waste time thinking they were the first men?' Nor would they have needed to make the experiment with the children.

Here the steps of reasoning are not totally spelled out, and put in the form of a rhetorical question, what in later rhetorical theory would be classed as an enthymeme. The implied steps are: if A then B; but not B; therefore not A: if no country existed, then they would not think they were the first; but they do think that, and therefore the first premise is false.

15.3: 'But I do not think (δοκέω) the Egyptians came into being at the same time as the Delta, as it is called by the Ionians ... but that as the land went on increasing [i.e. by silt], they moved down ... [i.e. into the Delta].'

16.1: 'If we think correctly about these things, then the Ionians do not think sensibly about Egypt;
but if the opinion of the Ionians is correct, then I undertake to show that neither the Greeks nor the Ionians know how to count, who say that there are three parts to the earth, Europe, and Asia and Libya.'

---

[28] Εἰ ὦν βουλόμεθα γνώμῃσι τῇσι Ἰώνων χρᾶσθαι ... ἀποδεικνύοιμεν ἂν τούτῳ τῷ λόγῳ χρεώμενοι Αἰγυπτίοισι οὐκ ἐοῦσαν πρότερον χώρην.

(εἰ ὧν ἡμεῖς ὀρθῶς ... γινώσκομεν, Ἴωνες οὐκ εὖ φρονέουσι περὶ
Αἴγυπτον· εἰ δὲ ὀρθή ἐστι ἡ γνώμη τῶν Ἰώνων, ... ἀποδείκνυμι οὐκ
ἐπισταμένους λογίζεσθαι, ...).

The options, then, are that either we are right or they are wrong: the
method is the eristic one of detecting an inconsistency in the opponents'
arguments.

16.2: For it is necessary for them to add the Delta, if it is not part of Asia
        or of Libya. 'For the Nile is not, according to this *logos*, the boundary
        between Asia and Libya.' For the Nile flows round the Delta, making it
        between Asia and Libya.
17.1: 'We leave the opinion (γνώμην) of the Ionians, but we say about
        this (ἡμεῖς ... λέγομεν), that Egypt is the whole country inhabited by the
        Egyptians',
        and, 'we think the boundary between Asia and Libya is nothing, by
        correct argument, if not the boundaries of the Egyptians' (οἴδαμεν οὐδὲν
        ἐὸν ὀρθῷ λόγῳ εἰ μὴ τοὺς Αἰγυπτίων οὔρους).
17.2: 'But if we follow the conventions of the Greeks (τῷ ὑπ' Ἑλλήνων
        νενομισμένῳ), then we would consider Egypt ... as divided into two
        parts [i.e. down its middle] ... for one side would be Asia, the other
        Libya'; and he continues with more about the dividing of the Nile, and
        the Delta branches.

This is another *reductio*, and a *Modus Tollens* argument (if A, Greeks are
right about the boundary to Asia and Libya, then B, Egypt is divided
down the middle; but B is clearly ridiculous, therefore not A).

The argument is long, sustained, and highly polemical. Particularly
striking are the repeated balancing and antithetical if-clauses: if A, then B;
but not-B, therefore not-A, or variations, sometimes completed with a
rhetorical question; *reductio ad absurdum*; repeated attacks on certain
(generalized) opponents, the first person plural combined also with first
person singular assertion, the repeated stress on demonstration or proof in
the form of the verb ἀποδείκνυμι. The demonstration that your opponents' arguments are inconsistent at ch. 16.1, so familiar both from Socrates and rhetorical arguments, has a neat parallel, for instance, in the
argument of *On the Sacred Disease* (chs. 3–4), that those who try to cure
the Sacred Disease by purifications show impiety rather than piety, since
they thereby imply that the disease is not in fact divine.

If the Ionians are right about Egypt equalling the Delta, *then* Egypt was
formerly non-existent; *if* no country existed, *then* how could the Egyptians
think they were the oldest? At ch. 16, *if* we are right, *then* Ionians are
wrong about Egypt; but (and here is the rub), *if* the Ionians are right

(Egypt = Delta), *then*, it can be proved, they cannot count, for they have left out the Delta in their image of the three parts of the world. *If* the Delta is not part of either Asia or Libya, *then* they should add it, to make four parts. *If* we follow Greek beliefs (about the boundary line), *then* Egypt is divided down its whole length (ch. 17.2). Triumphantly, he ends with the witness, in the unimpeachable form of the oracle of Ammon, that Egypt is 'as I prove by my argument' (ἐγὼ ἀποδείκνυμι τῷ λόγῳ) (18.1) – the final witness of the god is brought in, presumably in case there could any longer be any doubt about the matter, but as Herodotus is careful to mention, in a curious anticipation of modern scholarly disclaimers, he only learned later of this *after* forming his own opinion (*gnome*).[29]

The divine evidence only confirms: if Egypt is the Delta, either Egypt was non-existent in previous times or the Ionians cannot count. And it is clearly ridiculous to divide Egypt down the middle – so much for the conventions of 'the Greeks'. The if ... then ... argument thus catches the Ionians either way. Herodotus' observation about the Delta being built up from silt means that the Ionians' views about Egypt are doubly questionable. They do not recognize four parts to the world (to include the Delta), so even on their own reckoning – guilty of internal inconsistency – there is something deeply inadequate about their attitude to Egypt.

A similar type of argument appears in *Airs, Waters, Places*, in the well-known passage in which the author shows that the Scythian Anaries did not derive their disease from a god, as the Scythians themselves think (ch. 22). First the author declares his hand: 'I think that these diseases are divine and so are all others, and none are more divine than any other, but each disease has its nature (*physis*)' (ch. 22.3 J: ἐμοὶ δὲ καὶ αὐτῷ δοκεῖ ...); 'and I will explain how, in my opinion, this disease arises': καὶ τοῦτο τὸ πάθος ὥς μοι δοκεῖ γίνεσθαι, φράσω (22.4 J). And he launches into first the explanation (22.4–7 J): their habit of riding, which causes swelling and pain, which they try to cure by cutting the vein behind the ear, which (in the author's view) is what makes them impotent. Then we have the clinching proof:

22.8 J: 'This disease affects the rich Scythians, not the *kakistoi* ... etc.', for the latter, the poor, do not ride horses.

22.9. 'Yet if this disease was more divine than the others (καίτοι ἐχρῆν, εἴ γε θειότερον τοῦτο τὸ νόσευμα τῶν λοιπῶν ἐστιν), it would not fall only

---

[29] Corcella makes the point (1984, 64–5) that Herodotus' *gnome* often does not add to his observation, the results of *akoe* and *historie*, but precedes them: as at II 12.1, here at II 18.1, and II 104.1. Certainly that is what Herodotus wishes to imply!

on the richest classes,... but all equally,... or rather on the poor especially'.[30]

This is a *Modus Tollens* argument: if the disease was more divine than others, it would affect all; but it does not, therefore it is not especially divine.

But he adds at the very end the crucial addition (above), 'but rather, it would fall on the poor', in a further extension of the *Modus Tollens* argument, and he launches into a further explanation and an important proviso: further deductions are based on certain premises about divine behaviour and likelihood:

22.9 that is true, *if* the gods ... repay worship with favours (... εἰ χαίρουσιν οἱ θεοὶ ... ἀντὶ τούτων χάριτας ἀποδιδοῦσιν).[31]

This is a crucial proviso, which makes it even more likely that the rich should be the ones spared the disease if it were really particularly divine.

22.10 (= 22.9 D) 'For it is likely (εἰκὸς γάρ) that the rich give numerous sacrifices ...' etc., and the poor fewer [an argument from likelihood]; and so, he implies, the rich will suffer less (as put above, if the gods reward the rich accordingly);

'and also (ἔπειτα καί ... J) the poor anyway blame the gods for not giving them money', so that they are are more likely to pay the penalties for sins than the rich.

22.11. 'For, as I said before ...' (ἀλλὰ γάρ, ὥσπερ καὶ πρότερον ἔλεξα), these are neither more nor less divine than the others. (22.10 D) There follows further self-assertion for the explanation (*prophasis*) 'which I have expressed' (οἵην εἴρηκα).

22.12. (22.10 D) 'And it happens in a similar way with other men' ...

– and he adds a few more explanations for the unfortunate condition, including the wearing of trousers (22.12–13).

Particularly curious here is the conditional clause concerning the behaviour of the disease: if the disease were really more divine than any other, then it would fall on all equally (an argument used by *On the Sacred Disease* ch. 5: below): but, as he shows, it does not fall upon all, but only on the rich Scythians: therefore, it is implied, it is not any more divine than other diseases, and there is a physical cause. Along with the *Modus Tollens* argument here, we have a further, interesting twist: at first the writer thinks to carry his case by the assumption that a divine illness

---

[30] Diller reads: εἴ τι, not εἴ γε (22.9 D).
[31] Diller's text is somewhat different, but the essential argument remains the same.

would affect all; then by bringing in a premise about the gods (backed up by likelihood), he creates an *a fortiori* argument which furthers his case: given this likelihood, a divine illness would not actually affect all, but would actually be more likely to fall on the poor, who can appease the deities less ably, but that is not the case: this sociology is backed up by an *eikos* argument, that it is likely the rich give more to the gods. The author is advancing an argument for the physical, rather than divine, cause of illness, while at the same time assuming that the gods can in fact affect human lives, and therefore the workings of nature: all this by carefully reasoned argument.[32]

We also encounter here the first person insistence, and clear authorial presence ('as I have said' etc.) but no first person plural or rhetorical questions. The interrelation of the argument and continuing assertion in the first person, of the author's view, is perhaps also reminiscent of Herodotus on the Delta (above, II 15 ff.).

The author of *On the Sacred Disease* used similar arguments to convince his readers about the nature of the Sacred Disease, in the famous chapter where he argues that the disease is hereditary, 'like other diseases' (ch. 5). Having stated what is in his opinion the case, that the disease is not more divine than any other disease, and can be cured, he claims that it is hereditary:

(1) 'For if a phlegmatic parent has a phlegmatic child, a bilious parent a bilious child, a consumptive parent a consumptive child, and a splenetic parent a splenetic child, what is there to prevent some of the children suffering from this disease [epilepsy] when one or other of the parents suffered from it?' (εἰ γὰρ ἐκ φλεγματώδεος φλεγματώδης, . . . τί κωλύει ὅτῳ πατὴρ ἢ μήτηρ εἴχετο νοσήματι, τούτῳ καὶ τῶν ἐκγονον ἔχεσθαί τινα;)

This was proof 1, in the form of : if A, then B, which creates a pattern, and a rhetorical question involving a supposed analogy. But it is assuming that epilepsy will be passed on by heredity just as these other physical qualities. After further explanation about the seed coming from every part of the body, we move to argument two:

(2) 'Another strong proof that this disease is no more divine than any other is this' (ἕτερον δὲ μέγα τεκμήριον ὅτι οὐδὲν θειότερόν ἐστι τῶν λοιπῶν νοσημάτων·):

---

[32] See van de Eijk (1990) and (1991), on the divine in the Hippocratic Corpus. Herodotus prefers divine punishment for the female disease in I 105.4; cf. also IV 67.2.

'For it affects the naturally phlegmatic, but does not attack the bilious; yet, if it were more divine than others (καίτοι εἰ θειότερόν ἐστι τῶν ἄλλων), this disease ought to have attacked all equally, without making any distinction (καὶ μὴ διακρίνειν) between bilious and phlegmatic.'

This is another *Modus Tollens* argument (not-B, therefore not-A implied).

This is an argument reminiscent of that in *Airs* involving the propensity only of the rich among the Scythians to suffer the female disease. If the disease were divine, it would affect all equally; but it only affects the naturally phlegmatic, so it cannot be divine: again, the *Modus Tollens* argument. In fact it assumes that the divine would attack all equally, something that *Airs* had modified considerably, whereas if a disease were natural and caused merely by physical causes, it assumes that it would with equal uniformity attack only a subsection of the population, a section defined by a particular quality (here, those who are naturally phlegmatic).

We may compare Herodotus' attempt to argue that the Greeks got the name of Heracles from the Egyptians and not the other way round (II 43). This is the first case so far where such types of argument are applied to the past, and it is interesting that his whole argument, scattered in Book II, that the Greeks learned about most of their gods from Egypt, is couched in highly argumentative style. In this part of his larger claim about the relation of the Greek and Egyptian gods, he has, he claims, 'many proofs (*tekmeria*)', of which one was the following:

'Besides, if they [the Egyptians] had taken the name of any *daimon* from the Greeks, they would in particular have kept a memory of these [Poseidon and the Dioscuri], if indeed they were using ships even then and some of the Greeks were sailors, as I am convinced was the case' (ὡς ἔλπομαί τε καὶ ἐμὴ γνώμη αἱρέει) (II 43.3).

He then describes his visit to Tyre to ascertain the truth about Heracles.

The argument is elaborate, based on a pattern of the transference of divine knowledge from one people to another in the remote past. The argument is that *if* the Egyptians were to have borrowed any gods, they would have borrowed the names of Poseidon and the Dioscuri; but they did not take over these deities, therefore they could not have borrowed the name of Heracles (an *a fortiori* argument again). And as with *Airs* above (*if* the gods reward those who give them sacrifices), Herodotus carefully adds the proviso – stating his premises – that this would be the case, that is, if the Egyptians were using ships that long ago, and if the Greeks were already sailors – the sociological proviso again ... all of which he is inclined to believe. To us this may not be the most crucial premise, but it was a possibility presumably very easy to accept for a Greek in the fifth century – not to mention a nice glimpse at fifth-century Greek assumptions about Greco-Egyptian contact in the very distant past. *If* the gods reward those who sacrifice to them, if the Egyptians needed ships and *if* the Greeks were sailors that long ago ... Case proved.

While the *Modus Tollens* type of argument (*tekmerion*) was not theorized and formalized until Aristotle, the particular passage of *Sacred Disease* cited above, for instance, has been singled out in one study of semiotic argument as an interesting and seemingly surprising anticipation of this later formalized definition of the *tekmerion*: 'It is nonetheless interesting to note that the Hippocratic author is already linking the expression *tekmerion* (which from Aristotle onwards takes on the definite meaning of "irrefutable sign") with the inferential scheme of the *Modus Tollens*.'[33] The same mode of argument occurs in Melissos and again, would naturally be seen in that philosopher as an early case of the development of the formal and explicit – i.e. fully expressed – type of argument.[34]

If this type of logical argument is hailed as an important anticipation in a philosophical or medical context, if it should be a surprising find in *On the Sacred Disease*, what should we make of the occurrence of the same kind of argument in Herodotus, especially when in at least one case (II 43.2) it occurs in conjunction with the word *tekmerion*? The argument itself is used before – for instance, it is used, apparently, by Xenophanes in his argument about water coming from the sea; and Heraclitus effectively uses it in his scornful dismissal of other philosophers ('Much learning (*polymathia*) does not teach sense; for it would have taught Hesiod, Xenophanes, Hecataeus and Pythagoras'[35]). Yet it is in these later writers (Hippocratics, Melissos, Herodotus) that the process and whole argument is spelled out. Moreover, the author of *On the Sacred Disease*, and similarly Herodotus, tell their audience outright that they have proof, or that they have evidence. The strands of the argument are unwoven and laid out, and the audience is alerted to the fact.

Finally, I would like to look at three more examples of sustained logical reasoning, examples which have features we have already encountered, including argument from likelihood, but which also show sustained argument given in list form.

Herodotus' discussion of the various theories on the cause of the inundation of the Nile (II 20 ff.) is probably the single most sustained piece of

[33] Manetti (1993), 41.
[34] Cf. G. E. R. Lloyd on Melissos: (1979), 77; Darbo-Peschanski noted its occurrence in Herodotus (1987, 154).
[35] DK 22, B 40.

argumentative proof in the *Histories*. It is a superb sample of Herodotus' argumentative and polemical style.[36]

20.1: 'Some of the Greeks, however, wishing to acquire a reputation for wisdom (*sophie*), have offered explanations for the river, for which they have accounted in three different ways – two of these I do not think it worthwhile to speak of, other than to mention what they are' (τῶν τὰς μὲν δύο οὐδ' ἀξιῶ μνησθῆναι εἰ μὴ ὅσον σημῆναι βουλόμενος μοῦνον)

In fact he does more than merely 'mention' them (σημῆναι), but this superbly dismissive put-down may remind one generally of a few medical examples.[37]

20.2. One of them says that the Etesian winds are the cause of the rise of the river, by preventing the Nile running into the sea:
'But it has often happened (πολλάκις δέ), when the Etesian winds do not blow, that the Nile has risen as usual.'

(This is a potentially invalid argument, which would only hold if the theory goes, 'If and only if the Etesian winds blow, then the Nile rises.' However, it still has persuasive force.)

'In addition, if the Etesian winds were the cause (Πρὸς δέ, εἰ ἐτησίαι αἴτιοι ἦσαν), the other rivers which flow in a direction opposite to those winds, ought (χρῆν) to present the same phenomena as the Nile, and the more so as they are all smaller streams, and have a weaker current.'
'But', he continues, 'there are many rivers both in Syria and Libya, which behave entirely unlike the Nile in this respect.'

A clear argument of the *Modus Tollens* type: if the Etesian winds are the cause A, then other rivers would behave in the same way B; but not-B, therefore not-A. The Syrian and Libyan rivers are counter-examples which destroy this theory. The general assumption is that the workings of nature should be uniformly susceptible to the same physical laws.[38]

Ch. 21: The most ignorant theory involves Ocean: it is ἀνεπιστημονεσ-τέρη, and even θωμασιωτέρη (most extraordinary), and is not to be deemed even worth a detailed refutation (he returns later to it, ch. 23). This vocabulary of intellectual disapproval was commented on above.

---

[36] Good discussion to be found in Corcella (1984), 77–81, for Herodotus' *gnome*.

[37] Cf. *Nat. Man* 1.1 J: ἀλλὰ τοῖσι βουλομένοισι ταῦτα λέγειν παρίημι. Cf. pseudo-apology below.

[38] As Corcella points out (1984, 78), this implies that you cannot use *ad hoc* hypotheses; strengthened by his later 'thought experiment' in 26.2.

22.1. 'The third is most plausible, but also most false.' (ἡ δὲ τρίτη τῶν ὁδῶν πολλὸν ἐπιεικεστάτη ἐοῦσα μάλιστα ἔψευσται.) This receives the lengthiest refutation, as hinted before (20.1): the view that the Nile flooding is caused by the melting of snows literally 'says nothing in its claim that the Nile flows from melted snow which runs out of Libya, through the middle of Egypt and comes out of Egypt.'

22.2: 'How is it possible that it flows from snow, flowing as it does from the warmest lands to the cooler?' (κῶς ὢν δῆτα ῥέοι ἂν ἀπὸ χιόνος, ἀπὸ τῶν θερμοτάτων [τόπων] ῥέων ἐς τῶν [τὰ] ψυχρότερα τὰ πολλά ἐστι;) Many are the reasons why 'anyone capable of reasoning on the subject must be convinced that it is most unlikely that it should flow from snow' (ἀνδρί γε λογίζεσθαι τοιούτων πέρι οἵῳ τε ἐόντι, ὡς οὐδὲ οἰκὸς ἀπὸ χιόνος μιν ῥέειν),

(i) of which the first and strongest *marturion* (πρῶτον μὲν καὶ μέγιστον μαρτύριον) is furnished by the winds, which always blow hot from these regions.

22.3 (ii) 'Secondly' (δεύτερον δέ), the land is always without rain and frost, and if it does snow it must of necessity (ἀνάγκη) rain there within five days, so that if it snowed, there would also be rain.

(iii) 'Thirdly' (τρίτα δέ), the inhabitants are black from the heat. Also the kites and swallows don't leave, and cranes flee Scythia to spend the winter there.

So he backs up his refutation with three pieces of evidence (*marturia*), listed as such, and the 'necessity' of what seems to be equivalent to natural law.

22.4. Finally: 'Then, if it snowed (εἰ τοίνυν ἐχιόνιζε) at all in the country through which the Nile flows and from which it begins, none of these things would occur, as necessity proves (ὡς ἡ ἀνάγκη ἐλέγχει)'. We find a similar use of 'necessity' to denote something very close to 'logical necessity' in the argument in *On the Nature of Man* examined below.[39]

23. 'The person who speaks about Ocean refers the matter to the invisible, which therefore does not have any means of refutation.' This is an important remark about method in dealing with 'the invisible' (see pages 200–7 below).

24. He gives his own solution, in brief (ὡς μέν νυν ἐν ἐλαχίστῳ δηλῶσαι ...) and then in full, ch. 25 (ἐν πλέονι λόγῳ δηλῶσαι ...); with

---

[39] Stein, Commentary, glosses the last phrase as 'logical necessity'; other translations avoid any hint of philosophical language or argument. E.g. new Penguin edn: 'for they are contrary to reason'.

numerous appeals to likelihood for the physical workings of the phenomena involved.

26.2. 'But if the position of the seasons and the heavens were reversed'
(i.e. so that the position of the north wind and south winds are reversed
etc.) . . . the sun would go to the upper parts of Europe instead of Libya,
'and I believe (ἔλπομαι) his passage across Europe would affect the
Ister exactly as the Nile is affected now.'

A curious but internally logical argument given the premises about
the nature of earth and heavens. This 'analogical hypothesis' creates a
reverse picture from the same building blocks of the theory, which
have also been reversed, and is effectively an appeal to the plausibility of
his theory on the grounds that it is consistent and based on universally
valid rules – thus the Ister would behave like the Nile if the climatic
conditions of the southern part of the world and the northern could be
reversed.[40]

Herodotus, then, uses a large battery of arguments here, formal and
informal: logical arguments appear again. We have a rhetorical question
resting upon common sense, a nice rhetorical ploy; an appeal to the man
who uses rational calculation (λογίζεσθαι) to which an argument from
likelihood is appended, backed up by three pieces of evidence that what
he says is true; with the conclusion that if there was any snow, none of
these (i.e. the three proofs) would occur. The appeal to 'necessity' is in the
context an appeal to logical inference, an appeal which recurs a lot in, for
instance, *On the Nature of Man*.

The listing of 'proofs' or pieces of evidence is particularly striking: it
recurs in the next two examples, subtly in *Nature of Man*, more crudely in
Diseases IV.

In a section of the essay on the *Nature of Man*, we find a singularly
striking (and insistent) list of 'if . . . then . . .' clauses and rhetorical questions, though the subject matter is far from Herodotean. The style of
argument is in many ways remarkably similar to what we have seen in
Herodotus – a range of 'if . . . then' clauses, rhetorical questions, and an
overt and explicit listing of arguments. The author has just declared that
he 'will prove, and present *tekmeria*, and reveal proofs', for why each
constituent increases or decreases in the body (ch. 2.5 J) (ἐγὼ μὲν γὰρ
ἀποδείξω . . . τεκμήρια παρέξω . . . καὶ ἀνάγκας ἀποφανῶ . . .). The main
attack proceeds from here, first against those who think that man is
composed of one thing (e.g. phlegm, or bile), that is, that man is a unity:

---

[40] See Corcella (whose phrase this is), (1984), 80–1.

he argues that a unity cannot have offspring – generation would be quite impossible (ch. 3). And we have a list of reasons (ch. 3):[41]

Ch. 3: (i) 'First, of necessity, generation cannot take place from a unity' (Πρῶτον μὲν οὖν ἀνάγκη τὴν γένεσιν γενέσθαι μὴ ἀφ' ἑνός). 'For how could a unity generate, if it did not copulate with something?' (πῶς γὰρ ἂν ἕν γ' ἐόν τι γεννήσειεν, εἰ μή τινι μιχθείη;). (ch. 3.1 J)
(ii) 'Again, if the copulating partners are not of the same kind (εἶτ' οὐδὲ ἦν μὴ ὁμόφυλα ἐόντα μίσγηται) and do not possess the same qualities, there will be no generation.' (ch. 3.1 J)[42]

If A (partners not of same kind), then B (no generation); but (implied), not-A, therefore not-B: this sounds plausible, but it is in fact an invalid form of argument.

> (iii) 'And again, if the combination of hot with cold and of dry with moist is not moderate and equal, but one is much in excess of the other ... then generation would not occur' (καὶ πάλιν, εἰ μὴ τὸ θερμὸν τῷ ψυχρῷ ... μετρίως πρὸς ἄλληλα ἕξει καὶ ἴσως ... ἡ γένεσις οὐκ ἂν γένοιτο). (ch. 3.1 J)

We are given the conditions for generation: but these conditions would not be present if man were a unity (if not-A, not-B).

> 'So how is it likely (ὥστε πῶς εἰκὸς) for a thing to be generated from one, when generation does not take place from more than one unless they happen (ἢν μὴ τύχῃ) to be mutually well-tempered?' (Jones' transl. adapted): (ch. 3.1 J)

If A, then B (generation will not occur): the retort is dealt by a rhetorical question.

> 'Therefore (ἀνάγκη τοίνυν...), since such is the nature both of all other things and of man, man is of *necessity* not one, but each of the components contributing to generation has in the body the power it contributed.' (ch. 3.2 J)
> (iv) 'Again, each component *must* return to its own nature ... (καὶ πάλιν γε ἀνάγκη ἀναχωρεῖν...)'. (ch. 3.3 J)

In this very different range of questions and problems, we can still see the technique clearly, a range of listed arguments (πρῶτον μὲν,... εἶτ' οὐδὲ..., καὶ πάλιν...), with conditional clauses and rhetorical questions

---

[41] See Jouanna, *CMG* Commentary, 251 ff.
[42] Note that the text is problematic; this translation understands a comma after οὐδὲ, and corresponds to Jouanna's interpretation in the commentary (p. 251).

('For how is it likely . . . ?'). The rhetorical question above, 'Then how is it likely . . . ?' is reminiscent of Hdt. II 22 (above), where he uses an argument from *eikos*; so is the general appeal to 'necessity'. If A is the case, then B would follow, but A is not the case, therefore not-B (i.e. generation will not occur). This is not in fact a strictly valid argument: but a range of conditions which the author thinks are necessary for generation are given; he goes through each one showing that these conditions would not be present if man were a unity. Case proved. In his full commentary on this text, Jouanna sees the influence of Melissos in the form and style of the argument here;[43] yet what is most striking is that almost all the characteristics he sees as due to Melissos' influence are features we have noted in Herodotus. It does not involve the ridicule that Herodotus brings in to his arguments against opponents, but the insistent listed set of arguments to prove his point is certainly similar.

The author of *Diseases IV* offers us another parallel, much less sophisticated. In the remarkable section attempting to counter the idea that drink goes into the lung (ch. 56), the author gives his audience a somewhat relentless series of 'proofs', or 'evidences', for which he uses the word *historion*, listed and numbered. They amount to seven, with a further one at the end (56.7). It is simplest to quote the opening section to give a taste of the tone of argument:

56.2 Now I shall counter (ἐναντιώσομαι) the opinion of those men who say that drink goes into the lung. The fact is that drink goes into the stomach, and the rest of the body draws it from the stomach. You must give note to what I am about to say, for I shall give the following proofs that drink does not go into the lung but into the stomach. (i) If drink goes into the lung, when the lung became full, a man could not easily breathe, nor could he give voice, because there would be nothing to resonate in the lung if it were full. That is my first proof. (ii) Secondly, if drink went into the lung, our food, being dry, would not be digested to the same extent. That makes two proofs. (iii) Moreover, when we drink purgative medicines, it is the stomach that is evacuated. (iv) Furthermore . . . .

and so on, until we reach the seventh:

---

[43] Commentary, *CMG* 252 (also cf., 230 ff. on ch. 1): Jouanna singles out as points of similarity: 'emploi dogmatique de ἀνάγκη dans des formules lapidaires'; 'cascades de preuves accumulées'; 'emploi dans l'argumentation de l'interrogative introduite par πῶς ἄν'; 'fréquence de conditionnelles'; 'même façon de souligner les articulations du raisonnement par des particules logiques un peu lourdes'; and finally, 'emploi de ὅτε pour reprendre les conclusions acquises dans les arguments précédents' (a feature not to be found in Herodotus).

56.7: That makes seven proofs (ἱστόρια). Moreover, how could milk feed babies, if it went to the lung? I give this as an additional proof – indeed I would not have advanced any of these proofs in support of my argument, were it not for the fact that it is a very generally held opinion that drink goes into the lung, and against an opinion strongly held one is obliged to advance many proofs, if one is going to turn the hearer from his former opinion (*gnome*) and persuade him by what one says.[44]

We are left in no doubt about the abundance of 'evidences' or 'proofs' (ἱστόρια); and then finally we come to the last, and then an extra 'evidence', along with a rather naively phrased excuse for the piling on of proofs – the need to bring to bear many 'proofs' if one is to persuade the hearer to change his former opinion.

The most recent editor comments upon the somewhat naive repetition of this author's style, especially in his formulaic way of bringing sections to an end, and in his first-person insistence.[45] We see here perhaps the more excessive manifestation of the contemporary desire to give proofs, evidence, if possible in a series, that was accomplished more elegantly and with more stylistic variation by the author of *On the Nature of Man* (above); similarly the first-person intervention in the text, though not the rhetorical questions.[46]

What I hope emerges is firstly that Herodotus occasionally indulges in deductive reasoning and sustained argument in a manner definitely not appropriate for merely repeating what he has been told. This is a phrase he uses (VII 152.3) but in the context, it occurs at a point where a serious accusation of Medism is at issue, not merely some harmless traditional tale. The statement might appear innocent but it may in fact be barbed.[47] He enjoys tackling a problem with an extended argument from deduction. Secondly he uses certain types of deductive proof which are more usually discussed as part of the development of logical argument in the world of philosophy and 'science'. Despite the gulf in subject matter and varieties

[44] Lonie's translation. Note repetition: λέγω δὲ ἱστόρια ... τάδε ... καὶ ἓν μὲν τοῦτο ἱστόριον ἐστιν (56.2). Ἔπειτα ... δύο δὲ ἱστόρια ταῦτά ἐστι. (56.3) ... Ταῦτα δὲ πάντα ἱστόριά ἐστι, ... Ταῦτα μὲν τὰ ἱστόρια· (56.5).

[45] Lonie (1981), 71. On 56.8, Lonie points out (p. 366) the similar structure in the overall argument to that seen in *Sacred Disease*: first the evidence against the view, then the physical cause is given (56.8).

[46] See Lonie (1981), esp. 71 for dating and criteria for such dating.

[47] See further below (ch. 7, pp. 213–14); ἐγὼ δὲ ὀφείλω λέγειν τὰ λεγόμενα, πείθεσθαί γε μὲν οὐ παντάπασιν ὀφείλω, καί μοι τοῦτο τὸ ἔπος ἐχέτω ἐς πάντα λόγον. Corcella makes the apposite point, p. 64, that on the contrary the remark is to forestall criticism: it shows precisely his awareness of the need to judge and criticize. Equally we may read the general statement not so much as affirming a need to repeat all he's heard, but as emphasizing that Herodotus does *not always believe* what he has been told.

in sophistication, we see striking parallels in the presentation of these sustained arguments between Herodotus and some of the earlier medical texts. Even though there are so few long fragments from other Presocratics or sophists of this period, at least the similarities with medical texts suggest interesting implications about an intellectual milieu that they shared.[48] The coincidences of method that we have looked at: logical deductive proof, combined with rhetorical questions, arguments about physical causes involving an appeal to *eikos* and analogy, and a certain relentless quality to the listing of points, urge us to consider the implications seriously.

To his contemporary audience, these passages of sustained reasoning would probably have sounded in method very like those offered by certain medical writers, and Melissos, and perhaps (despite our fragmentary evidence) those others who occupied common ground between these natural philosophers and 'doctors'. Since the disciplinary divisions are not particularly distinct in this period (ch. 5), it is very possible that the logical reasoning we see in the Hippocratic texts is not a style particular to them, as was the close listing of symptoms, but their own expression of a more widely diffused style of argument. These methods belong, in other words, to the world of serious, logical enquiry into those difficult questions which were not immediately accessible to the empirical evidence of sight and experience, where opinion and judgement (*gnome*) must be exercised as well as the interpretation of visible evidence. These are indeed matters invisible to normal straightforward observation – causes of observable phenomena, the possible causes of the Sacred Disease, of the Female Disease of the Scythians, or of the Nile flood; the very nature of Egypt and whether it could be considered coextensive merely with the Delta, and the nature of continental division; the nature of Greek learning from Egyptians about gods in the very remote past;[49] how man cannot be a unity – via the highly theoretical causes of generation; the nature of the internal organs – whether or not drink goes to the stomach. In all these cases the author seeks by logical argument to attain knowledge about a matter which is not immediately susceptible to being solved by observation – but which could in some cases be backed up by visible signs.[50] In fact Herodotus uses a similar mode of argument at the crucial moment

---

[48] Among the natural philosophers, the more immediate similarity is with Melissos. This kind of sustained deductive argument seems absent from much of Gorgias except B 3.

[49] One of the very few examples where deductive reasoning of this kind is used for the past.

[50] Though one, possibly two, of these could in theory be helped by observation and dissection – the difficulty is that you still need to have some idea of what to look for. For a notorious and problematic case where the author is desperate to convey that he has seen a human embryo: *Nat. Child* ch. 13, with Lonie (1977): ch. 5 above.

where he attempts to justify his unpopular view that the Athenians did most to defeat the Persians (vII 138–9). Appeals to likelihood are important: they sometimes appeal to common sense and everyday experience, but also to general ideas of how nature works.[51] It may also be stressed how in several cases the premises are carefully spelled out: this would be the case if the Greeks were already sailors; or if the gods reward devotion. Similarly, he thought the tradition that the gorge of the River Peneus was created by Poseidon, 'a likely idea', but with a proviso: 'for whoever believes that it is Poseidon who shakes the earth and who creates chasms caused by earthquake, would, seeing it, definitely say it was Poseidon' (vII 129.4). All these issues are effectively invisible in some way or other – either because they lie in the past, or because they are just not susceptible to the eye. All are examples of the exercise of *gnome*: not merely opinion, but informed opinion. All are examples of the exercise of *historie* and indeed of wisdom, *sophie*; whether or not they also belong to the arts of persuasion is another matter.[52]

The language of proof

With this in mind we turn to another aspect of Herodotus' presentation of proof, the way in which he asserts openly and explicitly to his audience that he has proof. Here too he seems to share something of the technical or increasingly technical language of proof of the latter part of the fifth century. Again, what concern us are the comments that he makes explicitly, where we can see Herodotus deliberately choosing to express his method in a particular way. His declarations that he has seen such and such a thing are very familiar; as is his famous declaration in the middle of his Egyptian account that he has so far relied upon his 'sight' (*opsis*), his 'judgement' (*gnome*) and his 'enquiry' or *historie* – but that from now on he relies on what he has heard from the Egyptian priests, with a slight addition also of his own observation (II 99.1). He is also keen to tell his audience that he has 'proofs' and evidence; the way in which he does so, and the contexts in which he does, are extremely interesting.[53] Such claims might seem to be the monopoly, as well as the innovation, perhaps,

---

[51] *Eikos* (Ionic *oikos*) we met above in *Airs* 22.10; *Nat. Man* 3.1 J. In Herodotus, cf. II 22.1 and esp. 22.2 – appeal for his case which is about to be backed up by *marturia*; II 25.2 and 5, οἰκότως of winds, part of the argument about the flood, in which likelihood rests upon general suppositions about the workings of nature. οἰκός occurs forty times in the *Histories*. See n. 1, above.

[52] Some of these elements have an overlap with elements of style belonging to writers more interested in 'mere' persuasion and early rhetoric: e.g. Gorgias, *Helen* 13 lists and numbers arguments, in an argument about persuasion and truth.

[53] For what follows, more detail and full references may be found in Thomas (1997a).

of Thucydides. But as we said before, Thucydides' opening claims about his far-sighted inferences about the war, and his careful checking from evidence (*tekmeria*), are paralleled in the *Histories* and in fascinating contexts. Herodotus is keen to use the language of proof, to claim that he has proofs and evidence (*tekmeria, marturia*). What is going on?

It will help to clarify immediately some points about the range of meanings involved in these terms, especially since they are not used with water-tight precision in any fifth-century writer. What is clear is that when Herodotus speaks of *marturia*, he means evidence to back up his statement, and the root sense of 'witness' is in play; they tend to be the kinds of evidence that are tangible, visible or the kind of evidence that might be presented in law-courts. For instance, Melissa returns to the tyrant Periander after her death and gives him 'a *marturion*' that what she says is true (v 92 η 2), or the oracle of Ammon acts as a witness (μαρτυρέει) for Herodotus' views about the nature of Egypt (II 18.1). *Tekmeria*, on the other hand, one may wish to translate as 'proof' in the sense of decisive evidence which, given the limits of the evidence, can lead to a conclusion. For Aristotle later, it denoted conclusive proof that is formally valid,[54] a philosophically rigorous formulation which would be inappropriate and anachronistic at this earlier stage. Sometimes in Herodotus (as well as other fifth-century writers) we would prefer to translate it as 'evidence' – and a similar blurring is visible in English usage, when one says 'I have evidence' in such a way as to mean 'I have proof, I have evidence which is decisive'.[55] But it usually implies in the *Histories* more than simply evidence, something closer to probative evidence (or even 'argument'). Similarly, Herodotus occasionally claims to have *tekmeria* where the *tekmeria* are pieces of evidence which he regards as decisive proof.[56] There are other means by which Herodotus indicates that he had decisive proof or at least some kind of demonstration: *ananke* we met above with the sense of 'logical necessity' (II 22.4); also *apodeixis*, 'demonstration', which we examine in more depth in the next chapter.[57] Another common word for

---

[54] For later formulation of *tekmerion* as conclusive proof that is formally valid: Arist. *Prior Analytics* B 27, and cf. *Rhet.*, 1357b7–10. For reasons that will become clear, I disagree with Darbo-Peschanski (1987, 140) who sees Herodotus' practice in this respect as simply 'intuitive'.

[55] Cf. Thucydides: Hornblower shows that for Thucydides there is not always a neat distinction between *marturion* and *tekmerion*, as Gomme thought, nor is there in the orators (1987, 100 ff. on 'vocabulary of evidence'). A similar blurredness is visible at times in Herodotus.

[56] There is a clear break from earlier usage: see Corcella (1984), 42f. for use of *tekmairomai* in Pindar (and root in Homer) for the 'inductive' process of soothsaying and for access to divine knowledge; for distinction and continuity between this and the inferring of 'science' from Alcmaion onwards: G. E. R. Lloyd (1966); Corcella (1984), 42 ff.

[57] Note also *eikos, eikazein,* and *sumballein*.

evidence, or signs from which you can infer, is *semeion*, which takes on the technical meaning of 'symptom' in medical works. But Herodotus retains its primary meaning of 'mark, sign'.[58] He is keen to use the language of demonstration as part of an argument: for instance phrases such as 'as I will show' (ὧδε δηλώσω, IV 81.4), or expressions such as 'it is clear that' (δῆλον ... μοι, VII 137.2) recur repeatedly. But perhaps the most interesting implications surround the *tekmerion*, which along with the related verb, he used twelve times, and the *marturion* which occurs, with its related verb, ten times. The following section will concentrate upon these.

If Herodotus uses the language of proof that appears in Thucydides and in certain of the writers of early science, what are the implications? Is Herodotus therefore grounding his *Histories* on scientific principles or upon a proper regard for empirical evidence – or at least trying to signal that he is?[59] The picture seems somewhat more complicated, and when we look at the contexts more closely we move rapidly away from any impression that these are straightforward citations of decisive evidence. Rather, they seem to point to inference of a rather elaborate kind.

His famous declaration, for example, that he believes that the gods do in fact intervene in human affairs, is prompted by the miracle of the rumour of the Plataea victory reaching Mycale across the Aegean, and it is couched in the language of proof:

It is clear from many *tekmeria* that the gods take part in the affairs of men (δῆλα δὴ πολλοῖσι τεκμηρίοισί ἐστι τὰ θεῖα τῶν πρηγμάτων), if indeed it is the case that, when the battles of Mycale and Plataea were about to happen on the same day, such a rumour should have reached the Greeks in that region. (IX 100.2)

We note the careful proviso, that this is so if the rumour is true, a proviso we met in the previous section a few times (we may well wonder what the other proofs are!). We also saw above the careful reasoning used to convince his audience that the Greeks borrowed Heracles from the Egyptians rather than the other way round. He introduced this with:

And I have many other arguments (*tekmeria*) for this, amongst which is the following ... (πολλά μοι καὶ ἄλλα τεκμήριά ἐστι τοῦτο οὕτω ἔχειν, ἐν δὲ καὶ τόδε ...) (II 43.2)

---

[58] Signs used in Herodotus of inference from the divine: e.g. II 41.4; VI 27.1 (portent); for σημαίνω used of foretelling: I 34.2; I 78.2; I 108.2; and of 'meaning': II 57.2, V 35.3, VII 142.2 (wooden wall oracle), VII 173.3 (a sign to revolt).

[59] As Lateiner argues (1986) – that Herodotus' use of this language, which he shares with Hippocratic writers, indicates a shared preference for empirical evidence; cf. also Weber (1976); and D. Müller (1981) on *tekmerion* (in Herodotus alone), seeing it as part of empiricist scaffolding.

We recall that the logical argument was backed up with the presumption that the Greeks had been sailors in the distant past, and made contact with the Egyptians (43.3). His further investigations at Tyre then continue to pursue the theory. *Tekmeria* may therefore involve complex inferential arguments.

The other strand to his overarching theory about the Greeks' acquisition of religious practices from Egypt invites a similar introduction: 'My proof (*tekmerion*) for this is the following: for the Egyptian practices have clearly been established from a long time back, but the Greek ones have only recently been known' (II 58). Here his *tekmerion* consists not so much of evidence, as of a decisive, or supposedly decisive, inference from the relative periods at which the Greeks and Egyptians knew of these religious practices.

It rapidly becomes clear that for Herodotus, the claim to have 'proofs' often signals some of his most complex or most controversial ideas. So far none of the proofs have involved straightforward evidence: rather, a tradition of a tale of a rumour reaching Mycale, an argument about the logic of cultural interaction between Greeks and Egyptians (for Heracles) based also on a suggestion about early trading interaction, or about the (very uncertain) dates from which religious customs have been in use. *Tekmeria* certainly do not involve empirical evidence, if by 'empirical' one means evidence from experience, or from sight, or evidence that can be tested, though they do involve evidence of some kind. Similarly the nature and extent of Egypt is backed up by a 'strong proof' from the Egyptian priests, information that the Nile had flooded all Egypt below Memphis in the long distant reign of Moeris (II 13.1: ἔλεγον δὲ καὶ τόδε μοι μέγα τεκμήριον ...). But for once this is a proof that relies on a precise piece of testimony, a tale from the past which Herodotus perhaps may reckon as strong proof because of his high respect for the Egyptian habit of keeping records. It serves as important backing for his enquiries about the gradual build up of Egypt from the silt of the Nile.

The Colchians are really Egyptians by origin – despite the fact that they inhabit the far end of the Black Sea, a fact which almost elevates the 'discovery' to the level of a marvel: 'and I have strong proof for this' (II 104.4: μέγα μοι καὶ τόδε τεκμήριον γίνεται). There follows the wonderful passage of intense and highly questionable personal observation and personal argument. Herodotus had already remarked on this possibility and his enquiries confirmed it, he says in an amusing anticipation of similar modern scholarly remarks, though the Colchians had better memory of the Egyptians than the Egyptians had of them. Herodotus 'guessed' (αὐτὸς δὲ εἴκασα τῇδε: 104.2) in particular from their black skin and woolly hair ('though others are the same'), and most especially from

the practice of circumcision they both share, 'for alone of all men, the
Colchians and the Egyptians and the Ethiopians have practised circumcision from the beginning'. The Phoenicians and Syrians of Palestine say
they learnt it from the Egyptians, other Syrians from the Colchians, and it
is harder to be sure about the Ethiopians; 'but a strong proof' that the
others learnt it from the Egyptians is this: 'All those Phoenicians who mix
with the Greeks no longer imitate the Egyptians and do not circumcise
their children' (104.4).[60] So, a combination of observable, or supposedly
observable, facts, even if modern scholars are sceptical, and an inference
from the changing habits of circumcision among other peoples when they
start consorting with Greeks. Herodotus presents this as strong evidence
for his Colchian/Egyptian theory, but in fact it involves indirect and cir-
cuitous inference from Phoenician behaviour. Effectively the argument is
as follows: Phoenicians cease to circumcise children when they mix less
with Egyptians, therefore they learnt it from Egyptians, therefore the
Colchians must also have learnt it from Egypt.

Another context where inference from customs is in play, concerns
Xerxes' brutal treatment of Leonidas' corpse. Xerxes impaled Leonidas'
head, showing that he was more angry with Leonidas than with any other
mortal, as 'It is clear to me from many other *tekmeria*', and particularly
this, Herodotus says (VII 238.2). The *tekmeria* are not the banal fact of the
brutality but an argument from Persian customs: 'he would not otherwise
have treated the corpse in this way against the usual custom (παρενόμησε),
for the Persians are most accustomed (νομίζουσι) of all men I know, to
honour men who are brave in war'. In a surprisingly similar case of a
Persian king who is acting in excess, Herodotus affirms, famously, in the
narrative of his outrages, that Cambyses clearly was mad, for he deliberately overturned the customs and sacred rituals of other peoples. 'That
everyone thinks their own customs are the best, can be established by
many other proofs (*tekmeria*) and among them the following'; and the
proof that follows is the tale of Darius' questioning of Greeks and Indians
about their feelings about exchanging each others' funeral customs for
their parents (III 38). The proof, then, is inference from a tale of an 'experiment' which points towards a certain conclusion.

It is curious that in two cases of Persian kings acting cruelly and bru-
tally, Herodotus is moved to offer a 'proof' which depends upon understanding of other peoples' customs – in one case the usual Persian respect
for the brave, in the other, all peoples' love of their own customs – in
order to highlight an explanation of the king's behaviour. 'Inference' also

---

[60] One further point concerns the linen (ch. 105): φέρε νυν καὶ ἄλλο εἴπω περὶ τῶν Κόλχων
... Fehling's discussion at (1989), 17–21.

makes its appearance for two intriguing but controversial theories which involve a considerable amount of speculation, however informed – one about the Nile and Ister to which we return below;[61] and one about the Pelasgians and Athenians (discussed in chapter 4) where Herodotus goes to considerable trouble to argue, with all the language of proof, that the Athenians, being Pelasgians, cannot originally have spoken Greek (I 57).

Where, then, does this get us? It is clear that Herodotus is familiar with a language of proof more usually associated with – and discussed of – other philosophical and more rigorous writers of the latter part of the fifth century. But can we be more precise about the associations and connotations of this kind of appeal to proofs and evidence?

It is certainly striking that this kind of direct and explicit appeal to 'proof', a claim that proofs are going to come, is most spectacular in the early Hippocratic essays, some of which are almost tediously full of assertions that they will provide proofs, and evidence for their own theories. A few examples will illustrate. The author of *Airs*, for instance, offers 'strong proof' for Scythian moistness (μέγα δὲ τεκμήριον ... παρέξομαι: ch. 20.1 J): this proof is the fact that the Scythians cauterize themselves – and the author assumes that this can only be intended to dry themselves out. Earlier, his surprising admission that *nomoi* as well as climate may be contributing factors in ethnic character had a 'strong proof' (*tekmerion*): this is that the inhabitants of Asia 'who are autonomous and not ruled by despots are indeed the most warlike' (ch. 16.5 J) – a statement that could hardly be easily verified, but which was perhaps fervently held by the author and his audience. *On Ancient Medicine* frequently appeals to evidence or proofs: 'These are all proofs (*tekmeria*) that the art of medicine, if research is continued on the same lines, can all be discovered' (ch. 8.3 J). Or as the author imagines an objection, 'but I consider that this is my strongest evidence (μέγιστον τεκμήριον ἡγεῦμαι εἶναι) that men are not feverish only through heat' (ch. 17.2 J). For the all important argument that the so-called Sacred Disease is no more divine than any other, the author of *On the Sacred Disease* says that he has 'another strong *tekmerion*': that the disease affects the phlegmatic and not the bilious. This occurs in the midst of the inductive proof that we looked at in the previous section.

In *On the Art*, we get a hint of arguments less rooted in medical knowledge or medical theory, and closer perhaps to the antics of sophistic argument, one of the reasons why this is often regarded as a sophistic

---

[61] Of inference: II 33.2, inferring the unknown (below, pp. 201, 209 on the visible); and twice in speeches – VII 16 γ 2, for interpreting a dream, and VII 234.1 (Xerxes on Demaratus' character). Note also ἀτέκμαρτον, of an oracle (V 92 γ 1).

piece. So, for instance, the author declares that 'it is surely strong proof of the existence of the art, that it both exists and is powerful', that even people who do not believe that such an art exists still recover by means of its help (ch. 5.3 J). Even mistakes are evidence (μαρτύρια) that the art exists (ch. 5.5 J). And medicine can infer conditions of the patient by means of certain symptoms (τεκμαίρεται, ὧν τε σημεῖα ταῦτα) (ch. 12.2 J).[62]

There are also hints of this explicit marking of evidence in certain Presocratics. Melissos asserts several times even in our meagre fragments that he will provide signs, though these signs (*semeia*) are deductive arguments (DK 30, B 8.1: 'This logos is a great sign that there is only one; but there are other signs'); so does Diogenes of Apollonia (DK 64, B 4); whereas as we saw above, Anaxagoras tends simply to tell his audience what they should think. Parmenides also mentioned *semata* once (B 8.2). But the habit of appealing to the fact that you have proofs, evidence, does seem from this evidence to be part of a trend of the latter part of the fifth century, as with the development of deductive proof. More precisely it occurs in some writers more than others, writers with leanings towards the questions of natural philosophy, and it is in the medical works that this style becomes overwhelming. If we consider not merely the vocabulary itself, but the style in which Herodotus tells his audience that he can provide 'many other proofs', it would seem that his affinity is with the early Hippocratic writers or the methods they represented. These methods were probably diffused over a wider range of writers, but they are certainly well illustrated in the early Hippocratic essays.

But the presence of similar language and similar appeals in the medical writers cannot really be interpreted as indicating simply that we are dealing with an empirical method in any straightforward way.[63] The picture needs further refinement, and some further interesting distinctions emerge. For even in the examples above, some make appeal to empirical evidence of some kind, where that 'evidence' itself is actually formed and interpreted through the mediation of theory. This is a point which we have encountered before, but one that has considerable ramifications for the *Histories* – not least that some of Herodotus' 'facts' and evidence have been formed through the mediation of pre-existing theory or assumptions: at least we should be cautious about assuming that what he 'saw' was exactly what *we* would see if transported suddenly to the same spot.

For instance, *On the Sacred Disease* appeals to the 'fact' that the disease affects the phlegmatic, but it assumes, of course, that people may be

---

[62] For more detail and references, see Thomas (1997a).
[63] See n. 59 above.

divided up into such types, and that it is these types which affect their susceptibility. Similarly with *Airs* for which Scythian cauterization is in itself proof that they are moist (why else, after all, would they cauterize themselves?); or the airy declaration in *On the Art* that even mistakes are evidence for the existence of an art of medicine; and that even people who don't believe it is an art still recover by its good graces. This is not to undermine the importance of the Hippocratic attempts to rely on evidence – physical external signs or visible evidence of symptoms, minutely illustrated above all in *Epidemics I and III*'s listing of symptoms and the progress of an illness. But it is curious that it is the *Epidemics* which do least to flaunt verbally their presentation of 'evidences', symptoms, proofs. The sober essays and accompanying 'constitutions' of the *Epidemics* do not claim that they have 'many more proofs' that their theory is correct;[64] the authors of *On the Art*, and *On Ancient Medicine* do; so does *Airs* to a lesser extent. These first two are just those treatises which seem to read most like lectures, most like vivid, persuasive and lively talks to an avid audience.

Most telling perhaps, are the opening remarks of *On the Nature of Man*, where the author castigates his opponents who adduce evidence and proofs which 'amount to nothing', while adding that he, on the contrary, will provide evidence and proofs which will be utterly convincing: thus of his opponents, he says,

καὶ ἐπιλέγει ἕκαστος τῷ ἑωυτοῦ λόγῳ μαρτύρια τε καὶ τεκμήρια ἅ ἐστιν οὐδέν.

each appends to his own account *marturia* and *tekmeria* which amount to nothing. (ch. 1.2 J)

Of himself,

ἐγὼ μὲν γὰρ ἀποδείξω, ἃ ἂν φήσω τὸν ἄνθρωπον εἶναι, καὶ κατὰ [τὸν] νόμον καὶ κατὰ [τὴν] φύσιν, . . . καὶ τεκμήρια παρέξω, καὶ ἀνάγκας ἀποφανέω, δι᾿ ἃς ἕκαστον αὔξεταί τε καὶ φθίνει ἐν τῷ σώματι.

For I will prove that what I say the constituents of man are, both by convention and by nature [are always the same] ... and I will provide proofs, and I will set forth the necessary causes, why each constituent grows or decreases in the body. (*Nat. Man* ch. 2.5 J)

Are we not edging gradually towards the more rhetorical, more persuasive end of the spectrum of the claims to provide proof, the need to show that you have proof and your opponents' arguments are mistaken? In reading *On the Nature of Man* one begins to sense that the author is

---

[64] For *semeia* ('signs') in *Epid. I and III*: e.g. *Epid. I*, ch. 10, lines 6–8 (Jones); *Epid. III* ch. 10, line 5 (Jones).

indeed using a rhetoric of proof: that is, that the author's lively and vigorous promises to give evidence, proofs and *anankai* that are so much more convincing than his opponents' which 'amount to nothing', belong to an intellectual fashion and style which demanded that you adduce evidence, proofs and bring home the fact to your audience by underlining your intentions. This is a style which flaunted the presence of evidence and proofs for the theory in question, and which begins to have an overtly rhetorical edge: such claims have become the necessary claims to make, whatever the nature of your evidence. We may contrast Parmenides who persuaded primarily through long inductive argument but who also used the goddess, and the trappings of poetic fantasy to elevate and enhance his 'Way of Truth'; or the mantic persona of Empedocles who invoked the Muse (DK 31, B 3, B 4, B 131) in his exposition of the Truth.

It is striking if we return to Herodotus, that he tends to use the language of proof not for relatively straightforward cases where (for example) a monument or inscription attests to a particular statement, but as we have seen, for far more complex arguments where, on the contrary, he deals with either obscure cosmological problems or controversial arguments about the gods (in the present and remote past) or inferences drawn from *nomoi* in which understanding of other peoples' customs allow one to draw certain inferences. In other words, it seems to be precisely where Herodotus offers a difficult, uncertain, or controversial idea that he resorts to the language of proof (cf. the theory about the Pelasgians). We may be reminded too of other methods to dismiss one's opponents. *On the Nature of Man* declares (ch. 1, cited p. 197, above) that his opponents' 'proofs' amount to nothing (literally 'are nothing'), Herodotus dismissed the theory of melting snow which, he says, literally, 'says nothing' (II 22.1, λέγει ... οὐδέν).

There is obviously a difficult and delicate balance to be held between regarding some feature as part of the art of rhetoric – that is, part of the formalization of argument to be used in law-court and assembly speeches – and between regarding the same feature as more generally part of an intention to persuade in a wider sense.[65] And to speak of 'persuasion' seems to raise the spectre of rhetorical manipulation at the expense of any interest in the 'truth', to suggest the excesses of Gorgianic rhetoric, the strictures of Plato. The trumpeting of 'proofs' itself has been seen as a

---

[65] Note however that it is very difficult to ascertain what early rhetorical theory consisted of. Some discussion on proof and argumentation in rhetoric: Radermacher (1951), 209, 214–15; Due (1980); Schupp (1926), esp. 26 for rhetorical use of remarks about proof; cf. also Kennedy (1963), and (1994). Butti di Lima (1996) emphasizes the law-court origin of Herodotus' use of proof, but this seems to suppose a more strictly Athens oriented Herodotus than I would.

feature of rhetoric, a development to be attached to men like Protagoras, who is credited with a theory of *tekmeria*, and the sophist Antiphon.[66] Certainly *tekmeria* as such appear in Diels–Kranz only for a rather significant group of writers: Protagoras and Antiphon,[67] though we may note that Alcmaeon also talks of inference (τεκμαίρεσθαι, B 1). And while Thucydides refers to his own historical methods in such terms, he actually tends to do so in an austere manner, and leaves to the speeches the more flamboyant claims; this suggests he thought such claims appropriate to speeches.[68] The earliest orators attested do indeed make use of similar language to further their case.[69] In an obvious parody of such methods, in the *Knights* Paphlagon declares that he will test his opponent by proofs.[70]

But for this period it seems unwise to erect watertight barriers between the development of the arts of persuasion, and the development of methods of argument in philosophy, natural science, and medicine. It is likely that the two went hand in hand, as Geoffrey Lloyd in particular has argued, and for reasons we will look at in the next chapter, 'scientists' needed the arts of persuasion as much as politicians or defendants. Talk of having proof and evidence is increasingly common, even insistent, within the expositions of some of the medical works, and there are perhaps similar, though slighter, parallels in some of the later natural philosophers, especially Melissos.[71] Protagoras, as we have seen, is connected with ideas about *tekmeria*, as well as how to strengthen the weaker argument. But on the fuller evidence we have, Herodotus' method of asserting not only that he has evidence, but that he has 'many other proofs', seems to belong most clearly to the style visible in the rather more osten-

---

[66] Cf. Finley (1967), 74 showed (against Aly) that use of *tekmeria* was not merely a Gorgianic or Sicilian device, occurring in Antiphon's *On Truth*, as well as Euripides' *Phoenix* (fr. 811N²). Solmsen (1975) discussed proof in rhetoric, philosophy and tragedy, but deliberately omitted Hippocratic evidence. For the evidence of tragedy, see Thomas (1997a).

[67] Protagoras, DK 80, A 26 (from *Phaedrus* 266d ff.); Antiphon, *On Truth*: DK 87, fr. 44 B col.1, line 10 (the possibility of inference, τεκμαίρεσθαι).

[68] Thomas (1997a), 145: see Thuc. I 1.1, 1.3; I 20.1; I 21.1; II 15.4 (acropolis); II 50.2 (for effect of plague on birds) – all of his own methods. Homer provides evidence (τεκμηριοῖ) at: I 3.3; I 9.4; III 104.6. In speeches: I 34.4*; I 73.5*; I 39.2*; II 87.1* (*tekmarsis*); III 66.1*; also VI 28.2 for indirect accusations against Alcibiades; and I 132.4; IV 123.2 where there are hints of the forensic.

[69] For an orator's exploitation of the language of proof, e.g.: Antiphon, *Tetral.* A δ 8, 10; VI 30–1; Andoc. III 2, χρὴ γὰρ, ὦ Ἀθηναῖοι, τεκμηρίοις χρῆσθαι τοῖς πρότερον γενομένοις περὶ τῶν μελλόντων ἔσεσθαι. Antiphon, frag. 72 (Blass) claimed that *tekmeria* were for the future, *semeia* for the past, in what was surely meant to be a persuasive definition! Cf. also, Antiphon, *In Defence of Myrrhus* frag. 35 (Blass): οἱ γὰρ ἄνθρωποι ἅττα ἂν ὁρῶσι τῇ ὄψει πιστότερα ἡγοῦνται ἢ οἷς εἰς ἀφανὲς ἥκει ὁ ἔλεγχος τῆς ἀληθείας.

[70] *Knights* v. 1232 (cf. v. 33): καὶ μήν σ' ἐλέγξαι βούλομαι τεκμηρίῳ.

[71] Probably really only Melissos (DK 30, B 8.1), and Diogenes (DK 64, B 4: τάδε μεγάλα σημεῖα).

tatious and polemical medical essays, where the language of proof is used conspicuously to draw attention to the author's argument, his superiority to all others, and not always in contexts where his arguments are unassailable. Similarly in Herodotus, it is for some of his most complex or most daring theories that he feels the need for the language of proof. It is the language which belongs clearly to the developing arts of philosophy and medicine; but there is a distinctly ostentatious, argumentative edge to it.

However, before we turn to this more ostentatious side (chapter 7), let us look at that other awkward element which invites explicit comment about method, the search for the 'invisible'. In fact a later definition of *tekmerion*/proof is precisely 'demonstration of the unseen (or non-evident)', ἀπόδειξις ἀφανοῦς (Ps. Plat. *Definitions* 414e1).[72]

The visible and the invisible: analogy to the unseen

Another aspect of Herodotus' language and usage is closely linked to those declarations of proof: analogy to the invisible, which forms part of his wider use of evidence.

Herodotus' striking emphasis upon the 'visible' and the 'invisible', and his claims to have seen himself, are very familiar, indeed they have acquired some notoriety. His claims to autopsy may be models of empirical research; other scholars think they deserve only the utmost suspicion.[73] Whatever we eventually think of their veracity, the very openness and explicitness with which he marks out these methods does look very similar to the insistent stress on the importance of the senses in early medical work, as Lateiner (1986) shows, and unlike anything earlier. His related use of analogy is also well known: for instance, his optimism about a symmetrical world in which one can analogize from the course of the Nile to that of the Ister (II 33) seems safely reminiscent of an earlier world of crude and schematic map-making of the early Ionians.[74] We concentrate here, not on the controversy about autopsy, nor on analogy in general,

---

[72] Also Eurip. frag. 811N[2].

[73] On his autopsy: D. Müller (1981), Schepens (1980), Lateiner (1986) and Marincola (1987); critics: Fehling (1989), Armayor (1978), (1980), (1985): but they in turn have been criticized as too positivist in their attitudes to research, which skews their interpretation of Herodotus and his 'source citations': see most especially Cobet (1974); also Corcella (1984), 65–6; Marincola (1987), 126; Dewald and Marincola (1987), 26–32; most recently, N. Luraghi (forthcoming).

[74] Corcella (1984) on analogy, particularly good on the need for judgement (*gnome*) (pp. 63–7), which for Corcella is essentially analogical; also Lateiner (1989), 191–6 – who sees the analogical method in Herodotus as explaining in part 'the omnivorous, even cannibalistic instincts of Herodotean historiography' (p. 192).

but a different and narrower aspect of 'the visible' and the 'invisible', one which had an important bearing upon Herodotus' use of experience and 'sight', but which belongs primarily, it seems, to a more sophisticated range of questions – that is, how he actually articulates the method or problem of speculating about what is 'invisible' (τὸ ἀφανές). We may note immediately here that the word *aphanes* (and cognates) usually denotes, in the texts we will be using, what is 'invisible to the eyes' – and much play is made of this; but it does also merge occasionally with a wider sense of the 'non-evident', 'non-manifest', that is, where sight is not the sole criterion; to signify that there is nothing out there at all, nothing susceptible to any sense-perception of any kind.

On the notorious question of whether or not Ocean exists, for instance, Herodotus declares, in a passage much used to illuminate his methods of research, (II 23), that

he who talks about Ocean refers the question into the realm of the invisible (ἐς ἀφανές), which therefore does not admit of refutation (οὐκ ἔχει ἔλεγχον). For my part, I know of no river called Ocean. (ὁ δὲ περὶ τοῦ Ὠκεανοῦ λέξας ἐς ἀφανὲς τὸν μῦθον ἀνενείκας οὐκ ἔχει ἔλεγχον. οὐ γάρ τινα ἔγωγε οἶδα ποταμὸν Ὠκεανὸν ἐόντα).

He thinks 'Homer or some other of the earlier poets found the name and put it into his poetry' (II 23), then adds,

But if it is necessary when one has criticized current views (γνώμας) to show something oneself about the unseen (περὶ τῶν ἀφανέων), then I will say why I think the Nile floods in summer. (II 24.1)

What kind of language or style is this couched in? It is interesting in itself that he expresses doubt explicitly at all. But why does he express it in this way rather than the many others available? He uses similar language in connection with the Nile–Ister analogy (II 33.2), trying to deduce the source of the Nile from that of the Ister:

καὶ ὡς ἐγὼ συμβάλλομαι τοῖσι ἐμφανέσι τὰ μὴ γινωσκόμενα τεκμαιρόμενος

as I conjecture, adducing evidence/inferring (τεκμαιρόμενος) for the unknown by the clear (ἐμφανέσι). (II 33.2)

Herodotus' articulation of doubt or inference by mention of the 'invisible' has extraordinarily close affinity with that of the 'scientific' medical writers. That is, while Herodotus' liking for analogy and symmetry in his vision of the world may well have roots in a more traditional world view, the manner in which he introduces, explains and defends his use of such analogy, belongs to this particular mode of discourse. It is for problems of natural phenomena that this method is articulated.

There are various ways to approach this apparition of the invisible in a statement about method. The self-conscious use of 'the visible' to get to 'the invisible' or the unclear, can be found explicitly voiced in philosophical and medical thinkers of the second half of the fifth century and beyond, and it has been approached mainly in the broader context of the Greeks' use of analogy in philosophy and theoretical argument, from Diller's article which began with Anaxagoras (below), to G. E. R. Lloyd's *Polarity and Analogy*, which looked also at the roots of analogy in popular Greek culture and religious practice. Corcella built on the latter particularly, examining Herodotus' quest for the invisible in the widest sense (to include the past), and seeing it as part of the general development of Presocratic and early Ionian speculation, but with popular and religious roots, into what could not readily be seen.[75] There are perhaps wider implications for Herodotus' methods in these remarks couched in terms of 'the visible' and 'the invisible'. While it is significant that Herodotus can be brought into the wider development of the use of analogy in science and natural philosophy, the implications of this have, understandably, been left unclear. Herodotus is not, after all, a primary philosophical text; besides, he tends to be situated in a more archaic context or thought-world. Diller, for instance, took the comparison of the Nile and Danube (II 33) to be simply a paraphrase of Anaxagoras, and seemed to see it as akin in more significant ways to Hecataeus.[76] Herodotus' analogy from the Nile to the Ister may, however, be quite rooted in the habits and assumptions of natural philosophy and medicine of the later fifth century.

It is also related to the degree to which Herodotus relies – and stresses his reliance – upon empirical evidence. The very way he marks the problem of analogizing to the invisible seems at least to be a sign of his firm commitment to empirical evidence, especially that of experience and sight – hence his dismissal of Ocean (above), as Corcella thought.[77] Similarly Lateiner thought that Herodotus shows 'a reluctance to set data in unproveable schemata',[78] though he also added that both Herodotus and the medical writers did produce schemata and theories and that they did not always live up to the rigour of the methods they professed. But 'analogy to the invisible' is not just a statement of empirical method.

---

[75] Corcella (1984).

[76] Diller (1932), 16. See also pp. 21–2 on the historians: a rapid discussion of 'proof' in Herodotus and Thucydides, mainly in terms of their use of the present as analogy for the past, not, as is frequent in Herodotus, on the present to illuminate other aspects of the present.

[77] Corcella (1984), 57, 78–9.

[78] Lateiner (1986), 13. See also Lateiner (1989), 189–96 on analogy (and concentrating mostly on *tisis*, retribution, and equalization).

Herodotus is in fact happy to discuss subjects and produce theories for which there is little adequate evidence: he treats what one might call 'prehistory' at some length, remote origins, geographical determinism, he even presents us with a theory on the origin of the Greek knowledge of the gods (e.g. II 43–5). He also comments explicitly on the use of what we would call schemata, and his phraseology occasionally echoes the language of the early medical writers, who discuss precisely these problems.[79] This is where other remarks about 'the visible' and 'the invisible' come in.

Certain Hippocratic works were immensely preoccupied by the problems of appeal to the visible or invisible. As we saw, despite their awareness of empirical evidence, and polemical attacks on the abstracts of philosophers, they were hardly entirely independent of theory or theoretical construction. One schematic theory is attacked by the author of *On the Nature of Man* only to be replaced by his own equally theoretical one. So little was known about the internal organs of the body, let alone the workings of disease, that the doctor simply had to employ analogy – or sometimes, perhaps more precisely, speculation by means of analogy. The author of *On the Sacred Disease*, for example, made an analogy between the effect of the south wind on wine stored underground, and the effect of this wind on the brain (flabbiness) and the veins (enlargement) (ch. 16 = 13 G). Another doctor made an analogy between a chicken's egg and a human embryo (below). As the doctors put it, they had to reason from the known to the unknown, the visible to the invisible. The early Hippocratic texts are rather preoccupied with the extent to which one could get beyond the immediate evidence of the senses.[80]

The preoccupation is often expressed precisely in terms of the visible and invisible. For instance *On Ancient Medicine* offers a rather bizarre argument about the effects of structures (i.e. hollows) in the body that might be conducive to disease, and with enviable confidence the author asserts at one point that, 'I take it that the best adapted structure [for drawing in liquid] is the broad hollow that tapers: one should learn this from visible things outside' (ἔξωθεν ἐκ τῶν φανερῶν) (ch. 22.2–3 J). Since he then talks about the different effect of protruding and contracting the mouth and inserting a tube, he obviously refers to analogy from visible, external objects (i.e. outside the body).[81] Similarly he cannot resist talking about the 'more visible' or possibly 'more manifest' (τὰ φανερώτερα)

---

[79] Cf. Lateiner (1989), 193: 'Herodotus wisely refrains where he can from relying on analogy to determine facts.'

[80] See, e.g., Bourgey (1953); Joly (1966); G. E. R. Lloyd (1979); Mansfeld (1980a).

[81] Cf. Jones' translation (Loeb), 'from unenclosed objects' loses the directness of the Greek. Cf. also *Anc. Med.* ch. 24 for further comparisons.

signs (*semeia*) of the contribution of heat and proceeds to talk about the external signs of a cold, the effect on nose and nostrils (ch. 14).

The early doctors were much more interested in the value of empirical evidence, far more trusting of the evidence of the senses, than their philosophical contemporaries. *On the Nature of Man*, for instance, objects strongly to the creation of theories about the nature of man which bear little relation to what you can actually experience or see. But they still desperately needed to understand the internal organs from the visible. So while analogy was used by other philosophers, the element of sight is given particular emphasis in the medical works, and the main antithesis is between what you can see and what you cannot, as a further, mannered and elaborate discussion brings out in the *On the Art*. Thus the author describes diseases which are hidden (τὰ ἧσσον φανερά; also τὰ φανερὰ τῶν νοσημάτων, ch. 10.1), and then launches into an extended piece upon knowing and opinion, sight and lack of sight, reasoning, *gnome* and *logismos* (ch. 11), ending with a confident declaration that the 'obscure' (ἄδηλα) can yet be known: 'For everything that evades the sight of the eyes can be mastered by the sight of the mind' (ch. 11.2 J).[82] And the elaborate play on this theme continues: 'the doctor, as he can neither see the trouble by sight (*opsis*), nor learn it by hearing (*akoe*), must try to use reasoning (*logismos*)';[83] indeed, even the reports of their illnesses made to their attendants by people suffering from 'invisible diseases' (οἱ τὰ ἀφανέα νοσέοντες), are the result of opinion rather than of knowledge (ch. 11.4 J).

The whole paragraph, riddled with antitheses between knowledge and opinion, sight and hearing, seen and unseen (even 'the sight of the mind'), brings out very clearly the fundamental quality of the unseen (τὰ ἀφανέα), and the difficulties of understanding it.[84] It is also striking that the self-conscious emphasis here on 'sight', 'hearing' and 'reasoning' (ch. 11.3), though expressed more elaborately, is very reminiscent of Herodotus' equally self-conscious distinction in the middle of the Egyptian book, of his use of 'sight', 'hearing' and *historie*: 'Thus far I have relied on my own sight, opinion, and *historie*, but from now on I give Egyptian accounts as I heard them' (ii 99.1). Moreover, 'invisible diseases' also recur in Herodotus. They seem to be a semi-technical category. We meet them again

---

[82] ὅσα γὰρ τὴν τῶν ὀμμάτων ὄψιν ἐκφεύγει, ταῦτα τῇ τῆς γνώμης ὄψει κεκράτηται.

[83] Ch. 11.3 J: Ὁ μὲν γὰρ ἐπεὶ οὐκ ἦν αὐτῷ ὄψει ἰδεῖν τὸ μοχθέον οὐδ' ἀκοῇ πυθέσθαι, λογισμῷ μετῄει.

[84] Similarly *Art* ch. 9.2 J, where he explains that 'Those who know sufficiently about this art realized that some, but only a few, diseases are visible (οὐκ ἐν δυσόπτῳ κείμενα) but many are not visible' (οὐκ ἐν εὐδήλῳ). Also in *Art* ch. 11.7 J (ch. 12), τῶν τὰ ἄδηλα νοσεύντων. Cf. Diller (1932), 20–1, for discussion of these passages in *Art*; cf. *Art* ch. 12.2 J (ch. 13) on inferring (τεκμαίρεται) from visible 'signs'; also 12.4. On *adelos* possibly as a technical term, n. 102 below.

in *Breaths*, where 'the most invisible and most difficult diseases, are judged more often by opinion than by *techne*' (ch. 1.3 J). And in Herodotus, they crop up when he mentions the odd fact that Egyptians have only specialist doctors: 'each doctor is responsible for one disease'; there are doctors for eyes, for the head, the teeth, the bowels, and some for 'the invisible diseases' (οἱ δὲ τῶν ἀφανέων νούσων, II 84). It is hard not to see a specifically Hippocratic concept of disease here, and one which categorizes via the 'visible' and 'invisible'.[85]

This general preoccupation with the relation of the visible, invisible, and knowledge is so popular that it is even forced into unlikely remarks on knowledge. *Breaths* could see the power of air in the body as visible to calculation (*logismos*): 'invisible to sight, visible to rational deduction', τῇ μὲν ὄψει ἀφανής, τῷ δὲ λογισμῷ φανερός.[86]

The visible, the invisible, *phaneros*, *aphanes*, seem, then, to be central to the language of early Hippocratic medicine, both in its categorization of diseases, and in its attempts to define method. It is for this reason that the earlier fragment of Alcmaeon of Croton may be related but seems ultimately to be concerned with a somewhat different set of issues. Alcmaeon referred to the necessity of conjecturing about things both 'unseen and mortal' at the start of his work (DK 24, B 1):

περὶ τῶν ἀφανέων, περὶ τῶν θνητῶν σαφήνειαν μὲν θεοὶ ἔχοντι, ὡς δὲ ἀνθρώποις τεκμαίρεσθαι καὶ τὰ ἑξῆς.

(Concerning things both unseen and mortal, the gods have sure knowledge but man can only conjecture etc.)

Again we meet *ta aphanea*,[87] and the idea of inference, but here the 'invisible' seems contrasted with 'human matters', perhaps to imply the

---

[85] *Pace* A. Lloyd's note on Hdt. II 84 (Commentary, ad loc.), who finds an Egyptian title denoting 'He who knows (?) of the Mysterious things'; he does, however, think Herodotus exaggerates Egyptian medical specialization. *Breaths*, ch. 1.3 J: περὶ δὲ τῶν ἀφανεστάτων ... νοσημάτων.

[86] *Breaths* ch. 3.3 J; cf. also *On Regimen I*: ch. 11.1 J (VI 486,12f. L), οἱ δὲ ἄνθρωποι ἐκ τῶν φανερῶν τὰ ἀφανέα σκέπτεσθαι οὐκ ἐπίστανται, 'But men do not know how to perceive things which are invisible from things which are visible'; on which, Diller (1932), 40. There is also an extended passage in ch. 12, with a comparison between the arts and the techniques of seers, in their ability to get knowledge of the invisible from the visible. The treatise has been variously dated, though often to c. 400 (Jones; Jouanna – end of fifth, early fourth century), not one of the earlier ones. Stückelberger (1984), 77–9, discusses the possible links between this passage and Democritus, but is sceptical of direct Democritean influence.

[87] Cf. for stress on the visible/clear – but not connected with method for inferring the 'unseen', Herakleitos, DK 22, B 54: ἁρμονίη ἀφανὴς φανερῆς κρείττων; and B 56: note also Philolaos, mid to late fifth century, DK 44, B 11: ἄνευ δὲ τούτας πάντ' ἄπειρα καὶ ἄδηλα καὶ ἀφανῆ.

divine, and the knowledge of the gods is more certainly contrasted with human attempts to conjecture. Conjecturing from the visible to the invisible is a different process. Anaxagoras may also be relevant, with his famous dictum, approved by Democritus, on reaching the 'unknown': ὄψις τῶν ἀδήλων τὰ φαινόμενα: 'things that are apparent are the vision of things that are unclear' (DK 59, B 21a). The fundamental sentiment about obtaining knowledge about what is not 'visible' is similar to that of Herodotus, and it has been suggested by Lloyd that Herodotus' explicit use of analogy in II 33.2 was inspired by Anaxagoras.[88] It is possible that Herodotus' remarks on analogy to the unseen are indeed indebted to Anaxagoras. They do differ, however, in vocabulary and conception (*ta phainomena* for instance, is not a Herodotean phrase), whereas Herodotus' emphasis on the clear and visible is very close to the Hippocratic antitheses. Besides, as we will see, the way Herodotus talks openly about his analogizing methods, is highly reminiscent of the medical writers.[89]

Herodotus is utterly familiar with and aware of the problem of reaching the invisible from the visible, and with criticizing theories on those grounds. When he discussed the Nile's flooding (II 23–4), he used the language of 'the invisible' for a scornful dismissal of a theory known to have been held by, among others, Hecataeus – bringing in Ocean, 'refers the question into the realm of the invisible, which therefore does not admit of refutation' (II 23). His very dismissal of the 'invisible' on these grounds is reminiscent of a tirade in *On the Nature of Man* against people who think that man consists entirely of air, or of fire, or water, or earth, 'or anything else that is not visible/manifest (*phaneros*) in man'.[90] Similarly the opening of *On Ancient Medicine* (ch. 1.3 J) declares that empty (or 'new') postulates or hypotheses are unnecessary for medicine, as one might need them for 'those things which are *aphanea* and unspoken' (τὰ ἀφανέα τε καὶ ἀπορεόμενα). These 'invisible things', insoluble mysteries, he implies, include 'things in the sky or beneath the earth', an interesting

---

[88] G. E. R. Lloyd cites Hdt. II 10 (σμικρὰ … μεγάλοισι συμβαλεῖν), and II 33.2 (ὡς ἐγὼ συμβάλλομαι): (1966), 341 ff.; see also pp. 342–3 for interesting discussion of συμβάλλομαι, 'infer' or 'compare'; also Lloyd (1979), 134 n. 47. See (1966), 338–9 for discussion of what Anaxagoras refers to here, probably natural phenomena. Lateiner briefly on analogy in Ionian philosophers and doctors: (1989), 193; Diller (1932), 14–42; also Wenskus (1983).

[89] As G. E. R. Lloyd points out (1966, 344): on the Nile analogy (Hdt. II 10), Herodotus is 'both more explicit in his formulation of his argument, and more reserved in the claims he makes for his conclusions' than Empedocles or other Presocratics.

[90] οὔτε ἄλλο οὐδὲν ὅ τι μὴ φανερόν ἐστιν ἐνεὸν ἐν τῷ ἀνθρώπῳ (ch. 1.1 J). On φανερόν, see Jouanna, *La Nature de l'homme*, *CMG* I 1,3 (1973), Commentary p. 229. Cf. also G. E. R. Lloyd (1966), 353–5.

reference to what appears to be the subject matter of the *physiologoi*.[91] When Herodotus produces his own theory, he refers to the central problem, the Nile flood, as 'the unseen' (or perhaps 'non-evident') ('But if it is necessary when one has criticized current views to show something oneself about the unseen (περὶ τῶν ἀφανέων) ...' (II 24.1).). The whole passage uses exactly the same language of the 'invisible' that we encounter in the early Hippocratic texts. Herodotus is using an abstract term quite deliberately in the methodological sense in which it is used to refer to the problem of 'the invisible' in early medical works. Translators have tied themselves in knots unnecessarily over its interpretation:[92] we are dealing here simply and precisely with the 'unseen', and – effectively – what is not susceptible to argument because it does not exist.

Herodotus seems here to express hesitation about the desirability of presenting theories about the unknown,[93] but if that is so, it does not last long, for he proceeds to an excursus of some length on precisely this matter (to ch. 27). He is very happy to present his own views on the explanation for the Nile's flooding.

This may be precisely the point. He quibbles about theories involving the 'invisible' (Ocean), but it does not prevent him expressing his own views on a similar unsolvable matter (the Nile flood). While the two problems are on different levels, the one quite beyond reality, the other at least open to rational explanation, and while he can tolerate a problem which is *aphanes*, but not a solution (i.e. Ocean), his use of the same phrase (*aphanes*) in quick succession implies close association between the two problems. We may suspect, then, that when he seems to offer a semi-apology for criticizing all the current views on this subject, we are to understand this rather as a *captatio benevolentiae*. It is a technique of the style he is using, and that style seems to belong to the semi-technical discourse of early medicine – and perhaps related enquiries – which was deeply concerned with matters that could not be observed, and which slides around similarly on the possibility or improbability of knowledge about medicine.

[91] See Jouanna, Commentary, on *Anc. Med.* 1 (p. 158), on the meteorological or cosmological reference here. Also *Anc. Med.* chs. 17–18 on *semeia*, and the 'clearest (φανερώτερα) symptoms'.

[92] Contrast translations: e.g. Rawlinson: 'his account is involved in such obscurity that it is impossible to disprove it by argument'; and de Sélincourt (rev. edn Penguin, 1996), 'his account is a mere fairytale depending on an unknown quantity and cannot therefore be disproved by argument'. Romm takes it in II 23 to mean simply unseen territory: (1989), 100; (1992), 35, 37.

[93] Lateiner (1986), 13 stresses anxiety; cf. p. 9, overestimating doctors' reluctance to discuss matters not grounded in physical data.

Other features support this. The language in this whole section is that of philosophical and medical discourse: we meet *gnome*, *ta aphanea*, as well as expressions of knowing (οἶδα in II 23), and all of these were juxtaposed in *Art* (above, ch. 11). Herodotus' use of *elenchos* here is part of the language of proof: when he says that this question 'does not admit of refutation (*elenchos*)', this occurrence of the term *elenchos* is one of the very earliest cases of its use in the context of any abstract debate about knowledge; it also occurs in Parmenides (B 7). Thucydides was certainly not the first historian to entertain the idea.[94] So he seems to be behaving in a way not dissimilar to the author of *Nature of Man*, for instance, who objects to those who attribute to man qualities which are 'not manifest' (μὴ φανερόν), but who then proceeds to create his own schematized and dubiously proveable view. Perhaps Herodotus is even being more open and ironic about his deductions about the invisible, despite their dangers. It is also particularly interesting that such a barrage of contemporary 'scientific' language, language connected with the enquiry into man and nature, should be used to defeat a view that can be securely attributed to Hecataeus. Herodotus seems to be signalling something to his audience.

Another fascinating example of 'pseudo-apology', as we may call it, concerning method, implies forcefully that Herodotus is indeed on the same methodological level. *On The Nature of the Child*, mentioned before (chapter 5, p. 165) uses a notorious analogy to supplement where direct observable evidence gives out. This is the famous case where the human embryo is compared to a chicken's egg (ch. 29); earlier a human embryo was described, supposedly from direct observation.[95] The chicken's egg and its 'membrane' have been essential to the analogy, and the author certainly does not deny himself its use, even if the analogy may not entirely convince. For the author concludes his discussion with the remark that, 'you will find, on examination, that everything is as I have said, so far as it is legitimate to compare the nature and growth of a bird to that of a man' (*Nat. Child.* 29.2).[96] Analogy, the language of comparison and

---

[94] Parmenides, DK 28, B 7.5, is the closest in tone to Herodotus: κρῖναι δὲ λόγωι πολύδηριν ἔλεγχον / ἐξ ἐμέθεν ῥηθέντα ('Judge by reason the battle-hardened proof which I have spoken', Barnes' transl.), though ἔλεγχος appears in other fifth-century writers: Thucydides, I 21 – Hornblower's note (ad loc.) remarks the novelty of such a self-conscious assertion that statements should be tested; also Sophocles, Euripides; twice in Pindar – *Ol.* 4.22 ('Trial is the test of men'), *Nem.* 8.21 (on the danger of new themes). On Parmenides, see Lesher (1984); note also the arrogance of Parmenides' expression, 'the *elenchos* which he has spoken'.

[95] Ch. 13, for which see Lonie (1977), 123–35; also his commentary (1981), ad loc., 158 ff. – seeing here an unusually systematic and deliberate stress on observation for the Hippocratic Corpus.

[96] Lonie's translation: σκοπέων εὑρήσει ἔχοντα πάντα κατὰ τὸν ἐμὸν λόγον, ὡς χρὴ ὄρνιθος φύσιν συμβάλλειν ἀνθρώπου φύσει.

knowledge, and a semi-apology ('so far as it is legitimate'), or at least an indication that this rests upon an analogy which not all may accept: if this is an example of methodological self-consciousness at a difficult juncture, and a verbal attempt to excuse it, then it suggests that Herodotus' self-conscious 'apology' for continuing to discuss the obscure and invisible matter of the causes of the Nile flood may belong to this same intellectual mode of operation.[97]

A similar conjunction of vocabulary, method and the self-conscious verbal description occurred in Herodotus' later speculation about the sources of the Nile (II 33.2, above), which by now needs little discussion. 'The visible' reappears, as do analogy and the language of proof. The analogy is noted in philosophical studies as a characteristic of Greek philosophy and science.[98] We may add that this symmetrical analogy is noted explicitly by Herodotus: he is hardly embarking upon this analogy unselfconsciously. It is justified in terms now familiar to us in medical discussion ('as I conjecture, adducing evidence/inferring (τεκμαιρόμενος) for the unknown by the clear'). The antithesis here is between the unknown and the 'clear' or 'manifest', not, as before, the visible and the invisible. But the main lines of the problem are recognizable and betray the same consciousness about visible phenomena and their relation to invisible as we saw with the Nile flooding. 'The unknown' (τὰ μὴ γινωσκόμενα) is perhaps used here instead of 'the invisible' because the source of the Nile is not strictly invisible in the same way that the causes for its flooding are: it is potentially visible, and susceptible to enquiry. After his lengthy comparison between the well-known course of the Ister (ch. 34), and the unknown course of the Nile, he concludes, 'An account has been given insofar as it is possible to find out by enquiry' (ἱστορεῦντα: 34.1). The whole passage is marked by a concentration of words which belong to the language of proof and enquiry – including *tekmairomenos*. We note again that these crucial words of intellectual enquiry are occurring in clusters as if certain subjects and problems lay claim to a certain treatment on Herodotus' part.[99]

Other remarks in Herodotus are perhaps related. For instance, he remarks how 'It is not clearly (*phanere*) known to anyone whether

---

[97] Another 'apology' about the possibility of comparison: II 10, 'if, at least, one may compare small with large'; cf. his theory about Pelasgian language (I 57), introduced with elaborate stress on the possibility of inference ('If we may infer ... then').

[98] G. E. R. Lloyd (1966), 341–4, making analogy rather with Hippocratic practice than Presocratic.

[99] Cf. *Gener.* 7.1 J: Συμβάλλεσθαι δὲ παρέχει ὅτι ... τοῖσι ἐμφανέσι γινομένοισι – (for argument that both male and female have male and female seed); the reasons are enumerated.

Europe is bounded by sea either to the west or to the north' (IV 45.1).[100]
There is also a cluster of the familiar words for the process of intellectual
enquiry, knowing, inference: 'I cannot infer' (οὐκ ἔχω συμβαλέσθαι) how
the three areas came to have three names of women. There is also an odd
use of 'the visible' (τῶν φανερῶν) in his description of the marvels of the
Temple of Leto and the island of Chemmis (II 155.3; II 156.1). In both he
seems to be distinguishing the marvels that are visible, clear to see, and
those that possibly (if they exist at all) are not.[101] He is as interested in
what he cannot see, as modern studies are in what he *has* seen, and that
leads us back to Herodotus' famous claims to autopsy.

These expressions seem self-conscious: they make deliberate use of a
range of vocabulary that belonged to a specific milieu, one that is certainly visible in the early medical works, whether or not it is confined to
them. Herodotus seems to go out of his way to point out certain issues
arising out of the search for 'the invisible'. He does not discuss these in
depth; the point is, rather, that he uses terms which have a certain contemporary resonance. Is that resonance that of a medical context or more
generally an east Greek or Ionian scientific milieu? The Hippocratics were
certainly confronting the same problems of sense-perception as Anaxagoras, but stylistically, Herodotus' manner of marking the problem
seems closer to the gusto of the medical writers: the explicit, self-conscious
formulation of the problem and analogy in terms of the unseen, the
pseudo-apology, the use of *sumballein*, all imply that his methods and
style were simply more akin to those of the early Hippocratics, less to
most natural philosophers.[102] Herodotus' methods of using analogy are
comparable to those found in Anaxagoras, Democritus and the authors of
Breaths and *Ancient Medicine*.[103] The language with which he articulated
these comparisons, and the explicit nature of such comparisons, bears a
strong similarity both in actual form and resonances, to that of the early

---

[100] ἡ δὲ Εὐρώπη πρὸς οὐδαμῶν φανερή ἐστι γινωσκομένη, οὔτε τὰ πρὸς ἥλιον ἀνατέλλοντα
οὔτε τὰ πρὸς βορέην, εἰ περίρρυτός ἐστι.

[101] Cf. perhaps the absence of 'any other clear cause' for the fact that no mules can be bred
in Elis – οὔτε ἄλλου φανεροῦ αἰτίου οὐδενος (IV 30.1). Further uses of *aphanes* in geographical contexts: VI 76.1, river Erasinos disappearing; III 104.1, ants; VII 37.2, sun
becomes ἀφανής. Corcella (1984), 57–9 discusses the *aphanes* in space, the limits of visi-
bility and need for *gnome* and conjecture. Note that ἄδηλα (etc.) is not a Herodotean
word.

[102] It may be relevant that ἄδηλος itself may have been becoming a technical term itself in
the latter half of the fifth century: it is a term which appears in, amongst others, Philolaos (DK 44, B 11), Protagoras (DK 80, B 4: ἀδηλότης), *Art* (ch. 11.1 J), but not Herodotus himself: see Mejer (1976).

[103] As G. E. R. Lloyd (1966), 359.

Hippocratics. Such explicit articulation seems absent from Thucydides.[104] This does not imply in any straightforward way that Herodotus is bound to the utmost care in using only empirical – observable, testable – evidence. On the contrary, while he is keen elsewhere to stress what he has seen or heard as evidence, this awareness of the analogy to the unseen implies that he was acutely aware of the possibilities as well as problems of speculating about matters which were not visible. Nor does this prevent him proceeding to speculate at length about these 'invisible' subjects. There is therefore an element of *captatio*; or at the least, an attempt to show his audience that he is embarking on these speculations with the proper up-to-date awareness that they are not easily accessible to human understanding.

The implications are interesting. If Herodotus is clearly aware of this theoretical problem, does it alter our interpretation of other parts of his work? We may wonder about other elements in the *Histories* which are in some sense 'invisible': explanations for Greek success against Persia, for instance, knowledge about the gods and *ta theia*? (II 3.2). It also obviously implies that when he describes or alludes to his methods of research – whether autopsy or *historie* – he was doing so with an eye to the self-conscious markers or method in other enquiries into nature and, the closer parallel, into the nature of man.

This chapter has looked at certain types of argumentation, the way Herodotus marks certain features of his method, and the manner in which he alludes to these proofs and inferences. In each section we found a close affinity to similar markings in medical works in particular, but also some surprising common ground, though less striking, with a few natural philosophers (Melissos, Anaxagoras). This suggests immediately that the very language and methods of argument in parts of the *Histories* were those of contemporary natural philosophers and especially – from our surviving evidence – of doctors. It is tempting to suggest that Herodotus was influenced by them, but that implies a hierarchy of 'borrowing', a one-way movement of ideas and methods from one group to another that is probably inappropriate. Perhaps it is more plausible to suggest that Herodotus at these points uses the language of proof, the language of method, which was common to a new, exciting, form of *historie* of the

---

[104] Though cf. a recent comparison of Thucydides' approach to human nature and the Hippocratic use of external signs to uncover hidden forces: Swain (1994), esp. 316 – but he gives no evidence for *explicit* formulation by Thucydides. Cf. however, the hidden and open causes of the war: I 23.6.

time, one notably inclined towards the visible world rather than a world of (invisible) abstracts of the kind beloved by most natural philosophers. It is interesting that it can be combined smoothly with views that would usually be regarded as more traditional – the oracle of Ammon backs up logical reasoning (above pages 176–8), just as Poseidon appears tentatively within a geographical discussion of the effect of earthquakes in Thessaly (VII 129.4). It is also this language that does much to impart immediacy and vitality to many of Herodotus' arguments and theories. One cannot help wondering how Hecataeus' dull listing of facts could have gone down with an audience. Herodotus engages his audience in his methods and therefore in the very processes of his enquiry.

It may also be seen that the kind of argumentation and language of proof that we have been examining tends to accompany a certain subject matter. Certain topics seem to attract this particular type of discourse. Simple borrowing is unlikely: for as we saw (chapter 5) genres have not clearly separated, but there is some attempt by various writers to distinguish their work and methods from others'. Perhaps what we are seeing in the *Histories* too is that while the 'genre' of *historie* is still exceptionally wide, indeed not really a genre at all, certain subjects are indeed beginning to attract particular methods and language.

We have also seen that this language of proof is by no means a sign that he was happy to rely only on matters accessible through evidence (hence his use of deductive reasoning), still less, on reliable and particularly visible, tangible, evidence of the senses. It is often where his theory is most elaborate and intangible, or where he is on least stable ground, that he resorts to the language of proof. The very fact that he raises the problem of referring a question to 'the invisible' is not so much a sign of honest awareness that such reference would be unfounded speculation; but rather, a more sophisticated awareness that his enquiry is moving towards the invisible and that he should therefore signal to his audience that he is aware of this and in the sophisticated language of proof and analogy that was favoured by contemporary 'enquiries' of the day. This brings us to the theme of the next chapter, where we look more closely at polemic and controversy.

7   Persuasion and polemic

In the last chapter we looked at elements in the *Histories* where Herodotus made use of deductive arguments and the language of proof and of the unseen which are more familiar as part of the history of the development of Greek philosophy and the techniques of logical argument. We also saw that these techniques were often called forth for topics where Herodotus needed to persuade. In this chapter we pursue the subject of polemic and controversy, taking further the implications of the last. This chapter will argue that there is much in the *Histories* which is controversial or polemical – sometimes the polemic is hidden, but one may guess that Herodotus' stance is controversial from what we know of other Greek views, often it is more overt. If we read Herodotus too literally we are in danger of missing much of this; there is a certain style which goes along with this controversial stance, marked by certain expressions which are seen in other writers to belong to a particular intellectual milieu, that which corresponds roughly to the display performance and some of the early sophistic writers. It will be suggested that this is in fact the style of the *epideixis* (or *apodeixis*, for the two can be quite close), the display or demonstration piece which was suited to performance to an audience.

One prevalent and popular image of Herodotus is that of the curious traveller, ready to listen to whatever he is told, anxious like the modern anthropologist to record traditions as they were told to him; tolerant and open-minded. Herodotus is not averse to encouraging this impression. He tells us, after all, at one point, that his method is to repeat what was said (λέγειν τὰ λεγόμενα, VII 152.3; cf. III 9.2, 'but the less plausible version should, since it was given, be declared'; II 123.1), and his declared intention in the Proem includes the recording of 'what has happened'. This might perhaps be seen as a declaration on a par with his open and engaging admission that his policy is to seek 'digressions', though in fact even there, the Greek words usually so translated are considerably more positive than this implies, for he says literally 'my account (*logos*) goes searching from the start for extra material' (προσθήκας γὰρ δή μοι ὁ λόγος ἐξ ἀρχῆς ἐδίζητο, IV 30.1)

Yet whatever one may think about his claims about digressions,[1] it is clear that the principle of 'saying what has been said' is very far from all that Herodotus is interested in, when it comes to other people's views. As has been pointed out often, usually as part of a defence of his powers as a critical historian, he is equally capable of criticizing and judging the *logoi* he repeats, and does so sometimes at length. He is equally clear that he will deal with topics which others have not treated – the camel is too familiar to need description (III 103); the question of how Egyptians managed to take control of the Dorian kingdoms, he says, fascinatingly, has been dealt with by others, and he will leave the subject (VI 55). The moment at which he declares that his principle is to repeat what has been said (VII 152.3), so often quoted in isolation, is one where one of the most controversial subjects of all is at stake, the terrible question of who medized in the period of the Persian Wars – hence the importance of his claim not to believe everything either. In the context, his remark is not so much a gentle declaration that he merely repeats tradition; more an excuse or pseudo-apology that it is important to repeat claims and counterclaims in this most painful and damaging of subjects, even if he does not believe them: 'I am bound to repeat what has been said, but I am not bound to believe everything, and this principle holds for every tale (*logos*).' This was preceded by the observation that, if given the choice, all people would in fact prefer to keep their own evils than take on those of others instead (152.2). The story in question surrounds a much later embassy of the Athenians to the Great king, led by Callias the Athenian, at which some Argives apparently arrived and asked if they were still on terms of friendship with the king. Whether this all actually happened, Herodotus says, 'I cannot truly say, nor can I reveal any other opinion than what the Argives themselves say' (152.1). Many of his audience, at the height of the Athenian empire, would have liked to know very much indeed whether this whole story of the Argives, the previous treaty and the later embassy to Susa at the very same time as an Athenian embassy, was true.

Polemic and controversy

Herodotus is frequently critical, dogmatic, even dismissive of certain views, and can be as insistent on that as on the incredible nature of some tale he has been told. There is a strong and recurrent strand in the *Histories* of either reasoned or dogmatic argument, in which he takes up an

---

[1] For digressions see Cobet (1971), especially; cf. Darbo-Peschanski (1987), pt. 2 on the open-endedness of Herodotus' voice of enquiry.

opponent, usually plural, and demolishes the view held by that individual or group. One of the most striking, for instance, is that in which he attacks the idea of a round world and – it would seem – the existence of the Hyperboreans in the process (IV 36.1–2):

εἰ δέ εἰσι ὑπερβόρεοί τινες ἄνθρωποι, εἰσὶ καὶ ὑπερνότιοι ἄλλοι. γελῶ δὲ ὁρῶν γῆς περιόδους γράψαντας πολλοὺς ἤδη καὶ οὐδένα νόον ἐχόντως ἐξηγησάμενον. οἳ Ὠκεανόν τε ῥέοντα γράφουσι πέριξ τὴν γῆν, ἐοῦσαν κυκλοτερέα ὡς ἀπὸ τόρνου, καὶ τὴν Ἀσίην τῇ Εὐρώπῃ ποιεύντων ἴσην. ἐν ὀλίγοισι γὰρ ἐγὼ δηλώσω μέγαθός τε ἑκάστης αὐτέων καὶ οἵη τίς ἐστι ἐς γραφὴν ἑκάστη.

But if there are Hyperboreans, there must also be Hypernotians. For my part, I cannot but laugh when I see many people drawing maps of the world and no one explaining sensibly. They draw Ocean flowing round the earth, the earth is as round as if drawn by a turning lathe, and Asia and Europe are made equal. For I will show briefly the size of each of them, and how each should be drawn.

There are several interesting features about this passage. It attacks a view Hecataeus is known to have held, in other words it is a covert criticism of a kind we should probably expect more of in Herodotus. Secondly, the complaint he makes is echoed in very similar words later by Aristotle in his criticisms of a round earth (*Meteor.* 362b11ff.):

Διὸ καὶ γελοίως γράφουσι νῦν τὰς περιόδους τῆς γῆς· γράφουσι γὰρ κυκλοτερῆ τὴν οἰκουμένην, τοῦτο δ᾽ ἐστὶν ἀδύνατον κατά τε τὰ φαινόμενα καὶ κατὰ τὸν λόγον. ὅ τε γὰρ λόγος δείκνυσιν ὅτι ἐπὶ πλάτος μὲν ὥρισται.

The way in which they draw maps of the world at present is therefore absurd. For they represent the inhabited earth as circular, but this is impossible both on factual grounds and according to theory (*logos*). For theory (*logos*) shows that it is limited in breadth ...

This underlines the fact that both the substance of the attack and some of its wording were worth repeating by one of the most critical of later philosophers; thus that Herodotus' complaint was in the vanguard of geographical knowledge at the time, and in the fourth century also. Democritus also is known to have championed an elongated world, rather than a round one, so again, we should not see Herodotus' complaint solely against a Hecataean background.[2] Thirdly, we may ponder the language Herodotus uses, which is far from traditional, certainly not tolerant, and couched in language which translators feel compelled to tone down: 'I laugh when I see many people drawing maps and no one explaining sensibly.' Later (IV 42.1), he expresses total amazement: θωμάζω – 'I am astonished'. ἐξηγησάμενον ('explaining') is an intriguing word to

---

[2] Democr. DK 68, B 15; here Damastes of Sigeum is said also to have followed Hecataeus.

find here, with its connotations of 'interpretation' and even 'explanation'; we may perhaps see a faint echo in νόον ἐχόντως of the stringent criticism Heraclitus had made of some contemporaries lacking sense (DK 22, B 40) who had included Hecataeus himself. Herodotus also claims that he will show (ἐγὼ δηλώσω) the real size of each part: this is not simply criticism, but explicit affirmation that he will effectively prove otherwise and he does (IV 37–50).

There is much controversy in Herodotus, some explicit, recently listed most usefully by Lateiner,[3] some less explicit, and much is couched in terms similar to those we have just observed. He takes a stand not simply on Ocean and the Hyperboreans, but on which peoples are Greek, which are not, on the nature of Egypt, on the flooding of the Nile, to name some of the most obvious. Sometimes the controversial nature of what he is arguing is only apparent through the theory itself. So his extraordinary and lengthily crafted thesis that the Athenians did not originally speak Greek at all, discussed earlier in another context (chapter 4) is couched in the most impeccable and circumspect language of proof, and in such a way as to suggest that the language of careful deduction is particularly necessary for this theory:[4]

What language the Pelasgians spoke, I cannot exactly say; but if it is necessary to suggest by inference (εἰ δὲ χρεόν ἐστι τεκμαιρόμενον λέγειν) from those Pelasgians who still live in the city of Kreston ... [etc.], if one must state by inference from these (εἰ τούτοισι τεκμαιρόμενον δεῖ λέγειν), then the Pelasgians spoke a barbarian tongue. If therefore this was the case for the whole Pelasgian race (ethnos), then the Attic ethnos, being Pelasgian, must have changed its language at the time of its entry into the Hellenic body. (I 57.1–3)

He goes on, of course, to speculate how the Athenians learnt Greek. It is hard to believe that this theory was anything but mischievous in a period when Athens was doing so much to create the image of a city which stood at the centre of Hellenic values and civilization.

Or take his theories that Greece acquired many of her central religious customs from Egypt, indeed that they learned of the very names of the gods from Egypt, a theory expounded in several sections of Book II (II 4, 43 ff., 48–58, 143–6). For instance, he expounds what is very definitely his own view about the role of Homer and Hesiod in the development of the Twelve Gods, declaring that the Greeks knew very little of the gods, their origins and forms until very recently:

---

[3] Lateiner (1989), 104–8 for inventory; ch. 4 on 'disputation' and written sources generally.
[4] See Thomas (1997a), 146–7.

For Homer and Hesiod lived, so I think, four hundred years before my time and not more. It is they who were the first to compose a theogony for the Greeks, giving the gods their epithets, allotting them their offices and skills (*technai*), and describing their forms. Those poets said to have lived before these men, lived later, I believe. These first statements are on the authority of the priestesses of Dodona, but the later remarks about Homer and Hesiod, I say myself (ἐγὼ λέγω). (II.53.2–3)

The first person is emphatic, the more so when it is meticulously contrasted (as here) with another authority. Earlier he produced his own theory about Melampous, who, he thinks, was the one who revealed the worship of Dionysus to the Greeks – including the phallic procession – again with emphatic personal statements: 'I now say that Melampous, being a wise man, and acquainted with divination, learned of the rites from Egypt and introduced them into Greece, including the rites for Dionysus, changing a little' (49.2). The rites in Greece cannot coincide with the Egyptian by chance, he continues, for they would then be more Greek and also less recent in origin: 'I will not allow (οὐ μὲν οὐδὲ φήσω ὅκως ...) that the Egyptians took either this custom or any other from the Greeks' (49.2–3). And he continues to describe what he himself discovered, 'I discover from enquiries I have made' (πυνθανόμενος οὕτω εὑρίσκω ... 50.1). The whole theory is expounded with emphatic first-person statements of belief and certainty. Again, it is hard to conceive that he was producing a theory that was already widely accepted by many Greeks, partly from the way he has to argue his case, but also from the fact that there is no evidence that such a view was held by anyone else in the fifth century. Plutarch later singled out this theory as a sign of Herodotus' outrageous disregard for the most sacred elements of Greek culture.[5]

Controversial argument forms a major strand in Herodotus' style; if we can include the even more frequent expressions of his own personal view, then personal opinion and controversy are still more prominent. Yet it has had amazingly little attention. Perhaps such outbursts may seem to correspond to the engaging naivety of Herodotus in other areas, though even under that umbrella they have had little notice. Yet the very existence of such polemical criticism should have some bearing on one's understanding of the nature of the *Histories*. It bears, for instance, on what we think about Herodotus' relation with his audience – whether

---

[5] Plut. *de Malig.* 857d–e. Cf. Aristophanes' *Horai* (frags. 577–89 K–A), which envisages several barbarian gods being imported to Athens, tried on a charge of *xenia*, and expelled. There is little discussion of Herodotus' theories about the Egyptian gods: see A. Lloyd, Commentary ad loc.; Burkert (1990) and (1985a).

he might be telling them what they wished to accept uncritically, going over traditional tales which his audience already knew, somewhat like the Homeric bard, or creating a relationship that was somewhat less comfortable. The image of Herodotus as storyteller does not confront the problem, for despite (or perhaps because of) his narrative skill,[6] the idea that Herodotus was in some ways a traditional storyteller, even a *logios*, can only conjure up a figure who is relatively uncontroversial, who repeats the traditions of his society, who preserves the past for the future, as if this were a relatively unproblematic process. That would imply that preserving the past was fairly straightforward, a process untroubled by the burden of competing traditions, rival views about the past. It is hard to believe that preserving the past in Greece was ever uncontroversial, at least for any segments of the past thought worth preserving. Yet the image of Herodotus as the *logios* or Ionian storyteller creates a fundamentally cosy picture.[7] In his Proem, he expresses his aim of preserving 'the great and wonderful deeds of Greeks and barbarians' from decay, a fine Homeric idea, reminiscent of the Homeric poet's consciousness that he in fact could create fame (*kleos*). But which deeds to preserve? Which were the true tales of the past? The Persian Wars themselves provided a fraught subject in which competing and contradictory claims were made by rival Greek states. The Homeric analogy is rather problematic when we come to the untidy business of Greek achievement in the recent past. Moreover, to pursue the implied analogy with epic, Homer does not step aside and 'lecture' his readers. The poet is, to be sure, the preserver of the truth (*Od.* VIII. 491) but for that truth he appeals to the Muses who know all and are its guarantors (*Iliad* I 1ff., II 484–93).[8] Homer does not tell his audience what to believe and what to dismiss. Herodotus does precisely this, something not easily accommodated by the image of the storyteller or epic imitator.

There is also a wider perspective. The tradition of polemic, outspoken criticism (or for that matter unspoken criticism, unexplained correction) was hardly new. One thinks most immediately of Heraclitus' stringent criticism of some of his contemporaries ('Much learning does not teach sense, otherwise it would have taught Hesiod, Pythagoras, and Xenophanes, and Hecataeus', DK 22, B 40); or of Xenophanes' criticism of Homer and Hesiod (DK 21, B 11; cf. B 12). Hecataeus' opening to his genealogical work stated that 'The stories of the Greeks are many and

---

[6] For narrative technique in Herodotus: Lang (1984); Immerwahr (1966).
[7] Cf. Evans (1991); Murray (1987) allows for more explicitly moralizing patterns.
[8] See Redfield (1975), 32–5, 38; Segal (1983); and Goldhill (1991), 69–108, for irony in *Odyssey* surrounding the poet's claim to speak the truth. Cf. also n. 73 below.

ridiculous, as it seems to me' (*FGrH* 1, F1). The idea that the poets deceived was also fairly commonplace.[9] But such criticism of your opponents or predecessors is far from a monopoly of the sixth-century 'Ionian Enlightenment'. An ever more elaborate method of criticism and detailed argument develops in the fifth century, and this is usually seen as a particular development of the latter half of that century. It is also important and intriguing that such criticism as there is, is more securely testified for philosophical writers or *physiologoi*, than for poets – despite Pindar's unusual but outright rejection of a myth (*Ol.* I 52). The habit of giving explicit argumentation in which full reasons, sources and attributions are given is the preserve of the prose writers.

Polemic is sometimes discussed by historians as if it were primarily a character trait of other ancient historians.[10] Yet in the intellectual world of the fifth century, especially, the latter half, outright polemic and explicit criticism and explosion of your opponent's opinions was raised to levels of vitality that make Thucydides' own restraint seem, rather, to be the element that needs explaining. The latter half of the fifth century saw rapid development in the methods and habits of polemical or rhetorical argument, the refinement of techniques suitable for the law-courts or Athenian assembly, but techniques which were also part of the atmosphere of restless controversy and polemic that lay behind this intellectual revolution, in which opponents' theories are taken up and demolished.[11]

I would like to draw Herodotus into this milieu, to see a large part of his methods and style in the *Histories* as part of this intellectual world. He seems to enjoy criticizing, even to go out of his way to criticize or to contradict individuals, Hecataeus, 'the Ionians', other traditions. As we saw (chapter 6), he also deals explicitly, sometimes at length, with his reasons for rejecting a particular theory. There is no evidence of this kind of procedure in Herodotus' so-called prose-predecessors, the genealogists, mythographers, geographers, despite Hecataeus' opening (frag.1). While one might object that the fragments of those writers are too sparse to be adequate evidence, what is most significant is that Herodotus uses a language in such polemical and argumentative sections that bears a close

[9] Cf. Pind. *Nem.* VII 20–4; Solon, fr. 29W; Xenophanes B 11 and 12 again; see also Verdenius (1981) on Gorgias.

[10] See e.g., Walbank (1962): discussing Polybius' polemic, he notes (p. 2) merely Herodotus, Thucydides, Xenophon and Hecataeus, Hellanicus and then later historians, even though he points out that Polybius himself mentions many other writers than historians. His claim that 'Herodotus contains no open polemic' (p. 2) is a tribute to the strength of the myth of Herodotus' tolerant easy nature. Lateiner's list of Herodotus' criticisms (1989, 104–8) sets this to rest.

[11] See G. E. R. Lloyd on controversy, development of argument: (1966) and esp. (1979), ch. 2 on dialectic and demonstration.

similarity to the polemic and open criticism of philosophical and medical writers of the latter half of the fifth century. Thus if we look initially at matters of language, and ask how such language might have been taken by his audience, his expressions of argument and dissent can be seen to be far closer stylistically to those of later fifth-century thinkers than to earlier. This affinity is borne out further by an examination of where and when he uses such techniques. Such features place the *Histories* in the midst of later fifth-century intellectual life in very interesting ways; and would seem to do so with a security and depth that is sometimes lacking if we try to look purely for correspondences of theory or doctrine. The implications are profound.

I should point out immediately that there may be some overlap in his polemical style with techniques which may be regarded as more technically rhetorical, belonging to the increasingly formal art of rhetoric as it was developing in the late fifth century. It is not easy, or even always desirable, to distinguish the language of persuasion as visible at least in later orators, from that of philosophical argument. This is slippery ground, for philosophical and medical writers, most obviously the latter, used the arts of persuasion in some form. The latter half of the fifth century was a period in which the arts of persuasion were of intense use to certain thinkers, as well as to orators (as indeed they still are). As we saw with Herodotus' vocabulary of proof, that vocabulary corresponds to that of Thucydides and the early Hippocratics, but of course it is also part – or came to be part – of the developing art of argument as it came to be used in rhetoric as well as medicine. τεκμήρια in natural science and medicine stand alongside τεκμήρια in early oratory. Where does Herodotus stand? Are we dealing with one milieu or the other, or are the particular expressions in question part of a wider milieu and circulation that became fashionable in both early rhetorical style and scientific or philosophical argument? Probably the latter. Evidence for the early development of rhetoric is notoriously skimpy, and discussions of early rhetoric tend in any case to confine themselves to a narrow range of genres.[12] Let us look at further cases of Herodotean persuasion under certain stylistic headings, concentrating on those elements which seem to belong to his sense of polemic. The last chapter looked at clearly deliberate attempts to persuade at particularly difficult or complex junctures. We move on, then, from the declarations of 'evidence' and 'proof' examined in the last chapter, to some aspects which are more reminiscent or expressive of a more energetic form of persuasion. In other words, we can perhaps see in

---

[12] For early rhetoric: Finley (1967), Cole (1991), Kennedy (1963); and ch. 6 above, n. 65. Note also Butti di Lima (1996) for an approach to historiography via judicial proof.

Herodotus' more argumentative sections points of style and vocabulary that have connotations not simply of proof but more flamboyant rhetorical persuasion of the kind which might be more expected in speeches and display performances. These elements often come together in clusters, implying strongly that we are indeed dealing with a particular style of argument, display and demonstration.

Display and demonstration

Herodotus' Proem introduces his work with the word *apodexis* (demonstration, display – using the Ionic form for *apodeixis*). An expression which plays a surprisingly large part in Herodotus' *Histories* is *apodeiknumi* and its cognates, which denote a range of meanings in the latter half of the fifth century, from 'show', to 'display', to 'prove'. *Apodeixis* is later the standard expression for proof in philosophy, but it seems also to have rather specific connotations of display in this period. Precise Homeric associations are hard to discern; contemporary or near contemporary connotations should at least tentatively be brought to bear upon our interpretation here (and we recall the discussions of the language of proof in chapter 6).[13]

We have already come across one or two such cases. The declaration in the most outspoken and insistently polemical of the early Hippocratic texts, *Nature of Man*, went as follows (ch. 2.5 J): 'For I will demonstrate ... and provide evidence (or proofs), and reveal necessary causes ...' that this view of the human body is the correct one (ἐγὼ μὲν γὰρ ἀποδείξω, ... καὶ τεκμήρια παρέξω, καὶ ἀνάγκας ἀποφανέω ...). It is natural here to translate *apodeixo* as 'I will demonstrate', 'I will show in a decisive manner', and it is paired with the claim to have proofs.[14] We meet a little later in the same work a final flourish to a long passage on the different elements of man, a final statement that man has all these elements, 'and he is nursed in a human being having them all, all those elements which I declare and demonstrate' – ὅσα ἐγὼ φημί τε καὶ ἀποδείκνυμι (ch. 5.4 J). Demonstration with a strong sense of definite proof is involved.[15] The author proceeds to demolish the supposed reasoning of 'those who say that man is composed of one element' (ch. 6).

---

[13] Nagy (1987) stresses Homeric connotations of the *apodeixis*, but neglects more contemporary use of *apodeixis*; so does Drexler (1972), 11–29, esp. 11–14 (not a complete list; the cases we look at here do not appear in his discussion of use of *apodeiknusthai*).

[14] As one may equally interpret ἀνάγκας. Cf. Plato *Theaet.* 162e4–5 where *apodeixis* and *ananke* are paired.

[15] Jones translates 'I mean those elements I have mentioned with proofs', also conveying the sense that proofs are involved; Jouanna: 'je veux dire tous ces éléments qui sont l'objet de ma thèse et de ma démonstration' (*CMG*, 179).

In the very first paragraph of *On the Sacred Disease*, another highly argumentative work, the author declares his view, and some initial points about the faults of those who think 'the Sacred Disease' is any more sacred than any other. 'For, if the wonderful is thought sacred, ... I will show (ἐγὼ ἀποδείξω) that other diseases are no less wonderful and portentous (θαυμάσια οὐδὲ τερατώδεα), and no one considers them sacred'. Here the meaning is clearly that of proof (though not formal proof), demonstration, of his point.[16] In the rhetorical *Breaths*, *epideiknumi* is used in a similar way: compare the author's claim, 'After that, I will show, by the same reasoning, proceeding to the facts, that diseases are all the offspring of air' (ch. 5.2 J: μετὰ δὲ ταῦτα πρὸς αὐτὰ τὰ ἔργα τῷ αὐτῷ λόγῳ πορευθεὶς ἐπιδείξω τὰ νοσήματα τούτου ἀπόγονά τε καὶ ἔκγονα πάντα ἐόντα). And he concludes, 'This I have shown (ἐπιδέδεικταί μοι) to be the cause of disease...'; 'I promised to declare the causes of diseases, and I have shown (ἐπέδειξα) how wind (*pneuma*) is master, not only in things as wholes, but also in the bodies of animals.'[17]

Apodeiknumi and its cognates play an unexpectedly large part in Herodotus' *Histories*. Herodotus is inordinately fond of it, for the verb occurs no fewer than 137 times (against Thucydides' more sober count of sixteen). Many of the occasions on which Herodotus uses this expression refer to the performance of great achievements, or to the presentation of an opinion (*gnome*). This in itself is interesting, and Nagy has stressed the possible Homeric connotations.[18] But frequently also, in Herodotus, we find its context to be exactly similar to that of the medical writers, connoting demonstration on his part in the sense of 'proof' (again, nearer to the sense of 'show decisively', not formal proof). It is also particularly striking that it often crops up in Herodotus' most polemical, or most outspoken moments. Let us concentrate for the moment on the matter of 'proof'.[19]

In his discussion of the nature and extent of Egypt, for instance, which we analysed in chapter 6, Herodotus engages in a particularly long refutation of other mistaken views, which involves the hypothetical suggestion that if one 'should wish to use the views of the Ionians about Egypt, who

---

[16] Ch. 1. 10ff. J: following Littré's text (Grensemann has δείξω). At *Sacr. Dis.* ch. 4.56 J (= 1.46 G) the verb has the wider sense of 'show' or 'indicate', since fixing boundaries to temples is at issue. On the informal nature of this 'proof' in the Hippocratic writers, however, see G. E. R. Lloyd (1979), 86 ff., 102–3 with n. 244.

[17] Ch. 15.1–2 J; cf. the flatter translations of Jones, e.g., 'I have expounded' and 'I have set forth'.

[18] Nagy (1987); and Drexler (1972) – see above n. 13.

[19] Lateiner (1986), 17 mentions *apodeiknumi* in passing along with *tekmerion* and *marturion*, as indications of inference from evidence and analysis. I would see further overtones (below).

think that the Delta alone is Egypt', then 'we would show by that argument that the Egyptians formerly had no country at all' (ἀποδεικνύοιμεν ἂν τούτῳ τῷ λόγῳ χρεώμενοι Αἰγυπτίοισι οὐκ ἐοῦσαν πρότερον χώρην: II 15.1). A little later on the same controversial issue, we return again to the mistaken views of the Ionians (16.1), 'If the opinion of the Ionians is correct (*orthe*), then I undertake to show (*apodeiknumi*) that the Greeks and the Ionians themselves do not know how to count.' Or again within the same controversy, when Herodotus claims that the oracle of Ammon backs up his contention (II 18.1): 'a witness to my opinion that Egypt is as great as I have demonstrated by my argument (*logos*)' (μαρτυρέει δέ μοι τῇ γνώμῃ, ὅτι τοσαύτη ἐστὶ Αἴγυπτος ὅσην τινὰ ἐγὼ ἀποδείκνυμι τῷ λόγῳ). In this last statement too, we seem to be dealing with a clear sense of demonstration, in the sense of 'proof', certain demonstration, rather than 'display'. This language is being used in contexts where there are opposing views and an argument and demonstration is being presented, just as in *On the Nature of Man*, which is determined to persuade the audience that Herodotus' view is correct.

Another tricky issue, the problem of whether the Macedonian king Perdiccas and his descendants are Greeks, is clothed in the same language of demonstration (v 22):

Now, that these are Greeks, sprung from Perdiccas, as they themselves say, I can affirm of my own knowledge, and indeed, I will demonstrate this later on, that they are Greeks (... αὐτός τε οὕτω τυγχάνω ἐπιστάμενος καὶ δὴ καὶ ἐν τοῖσι ὄπισθε λόγοισι ἀποδέξω ὡς εἰσὶ Ἕλληνες).

This question was clearly controversial; it was something that Herodotus felt compelled to utter a statement on, and he marks his argument with a declaration that he is going to demonstrate that what he says is the truth (he does so also at VIII 137). It is interesting that the same problem of being, or not being Greek, elicits similar language when it comes to the Spartan kings, who are Greeks, according to the rest of the Greeks, up to Perseus (VI 53.1). Here it is the Greeks who are doing the demonstrating, not Herodotus; he adds that if you trace them from Danaë, they would be Egyptians. The whole passage is full of expressions of certainty: 'they are traced back correctly by the Greeks and demonstrated to be Greeks' (καταλεγομένους ὀρθῶς ὑπ᾽ Ἑλλήνων καὶ ἀποδεικνυμένους ὡς εἰσὶ Ἕλληνες). There is no doubt that some form of decisive demonstration, or proof, is being presented.[20]

---

[20] Cf. Georges' discussion of Spartan kings (1994, 152–7), rather one-sided. Curiously he omits discussion of Herodotus' insistence that the Macedonians are Greeks (see pp. 134–5 on Macedonia), perhaps because he argues that for Herodotus only Dorians were Greeks.

Perhaps the most telling of all is Herodotus' opposition to the notion of Ocean, which is expressly based on the lack of proper proof, and which shows, perhaps, how alongside the language of *tekmeria*, *apodeiknumi* is an equal:

τὸν δὲ Ὠκεανὸν λόγῳ μὲν λέγουσι ἀπὸ ἡλίου ἀνατολέων ἀρξάμενον γῆν περὶ πᾶσαν ῥέειν, ἔργῳ δὲ οὐκ ἀποδεικνῦσι. (IV 8.2)

They say (λόγῳ) that the Ocean begins from the rising sun and runs around the whole earth, but they do not demonstrate this in actuality (ἔργῳ).

Here is the clearest distinction between merely saying something and proving or showing it in reality, and in a passage of close argument. Elsewhere too the verb *apodeiknumi* occurs in contexts where showing or demonstrating in the sense of proving is at issue: for instance the Egyptian priests are said to do this in a passage where much is made of demonstration, the section about the length of Egyptian history and the number of their kings.[21] It also occurs in several contexts with the connotation of demonstration (but with less implication of *argumentative* demonstration), or where there is an element of legal proof or controversy: for instance in the story of Glaukos (VI 86 β 1: showing the tokens of a debt); or the demonstration of some fact or feature as a witness, as the Carians do to show that they are autochthonous (I 171.6), or the Sybarites and Crotonians in their dispute (V 45.1: 'each show these items of evidence': μαρτύρια ... ἑκάτεροι ἀποδεικνύουσι τάδε). Perhaps we can also bring in the 'demonstration of his opinion' which Herodotus offers on the reason for the Nile's flooding, where he demolishes other explanations, and admits that perhaps he would then offer one of his own (II 24.1): 'If it is necessary ... to give an opinion about matters which are invisible, I will say' ... (εἰ δεῖ ... περὶ τῶν ἀφανέων γνώμην ἀποδέξασθαι, φράσω ...) what the reasons are, in his view, for the Nile flooding in summer.[22] It is also worth noting here how *gnomai*, theories, demonstration and argument are all occurring together in first-person discussion.

The sense of wider demonstration comes out more strongly in the very numerous cases where, in Herodotus, an opinion is expressed – the phrase is γνώμην ἀποδείκνυσθαι; or where the verb is used in the sense of displaying or performing deeds, showing *arete*, or displaying wisdom.[23] It is

---

[21] II 142.1; 143; 144.1. Cf. also II 133.5, Mycerinus and the oracle; VII 17.1 (Artabanus); VII 118 (Antipatros); V 94.2 (of Athenian claims to Sigeum).

[22] Cf. also II 136.2, showing corpse as security; II 177.2, Amasis' 'excellent' law on those not gainfully employed, where *apodeiknumi* may have the force of 'prove'.

[23] E.g.: deeds, VIII 17, VIII 91; showing *arete*, I 176.1; wisdom, VII 23.3 (Phoenicians).

interesting where he uses these expressions: for example his notoriously difficult judgement, which he says he knows will be unpopular, about the Athenian contribution to the Persian Wars, is expressed thus (VII 139.1). There may still be an element of 'demonstration', but there is also an element of display: *apodeiknumi* wavers between the idea of demonstrating and of displaying.[24] What is important here is the extent to which Herodotus is keen to declare that he can show something to be the case; his language need not always be that of the 'evidence' and 'proof' of the Thucydidean form we have already looked at. But it is a form of expression which has definite connotations of display and persuasion as well – and with a sophistic tinge.

This suggests that the *apodexis* of the very opening sentence of the *Histories* bears the connotations of display and demonstration also. That is certainly the sense of *apodexis* in the other occasions in the *Histories* where the word occurs. *Apodexis* appears four more times, in each case with the connotation of display/demonstration in the sense of informal 'proof'. Xerxes, for instance, often given rather sophistic language, tells Artemisia that Mardonios says the Persians will gladly give him proof (*apodexis*), that they are not to blame for the disasters so far (VIII 101.2); the Egyptian priests gave no *apodexis* (demonstration) of the deeds of any of the other kings.[25] Given a similar use of the verb, it seems likely that the *apodexis* of the opening has a similar implication: demonstration with a hint of display and of proof. The further implications of this, and the wider evidence for the display piece, will be examined in the next chapter.

This seems to be another area, then, where Herodotus' language is unmistakeably related to that visible in the early Hippocratics and certain prose writers of the latter part of the fifth century: the declarations of proof, demonstration, often in the first person, seem close to the usage of the early medical works, and rather distant from anything we can glimpse in the arguments of Presocratic writers, or earlier prose writers. *Apodeiknumi* occurs in Diels–Kranz only in some highly suggestive, epideictic

---

[24] Note also that he uses the verb *epideiknumi*, more clearly in the sense of 'display': see Powell s.v.; there are three occasions in the MSS where *apodeiknumi* and *epideiknumi* are variants (II 42.4; VII 223.4; VIII 108.2; but VIII 108 is the only possible case in Herodotus where *epideiknumi* might denote 'proof' – all the rest concern 'display' of material things).

[25] II 101.1; the following sentence is full of verbs for showing, including ἀποδέξασθαι. Also II 148.2 on the Labyrinth, 'For if anyone were to add together (συλλογίσαιτο) the walls and ἔργων ἀπόδεξιν (lit. display of achievements) of the Greeks, they would not equal the Labyrinth in effort or expense': here *apodexis* = display. And I 207.7, Croesus advises Cyrus that if they set out a great feast for the Massagetae, there will be left for the Persians an ἀπόδεξις ἔργων μεγάλων (proof/display of great deeds). Note also *epideixis*, II 46.4.

contexts: a piece of epideictic rhetoric by Thrasymachus, and an obviously epideictic piece by Gorgias, the *Palamedes*.[26] Presocratic philosophers occasionally talk of showing or proving something to their audience – though Xenophanes' B 7 is figurative: 'I will show you the way' (δείξω δὲ κέλευθον) – but are more likely simply to declare what is the case or speak *ex cathedra*, as does Anaxagoras.[27] Thus Empedocles declares, 'Come and I will tell you' (εἰ δ᾽ ἄγε τοι λέξω, B 38).[28] But as we saw in the last chapter, the intention of persuading the audience by proof is seldom marked explicitly.

Similarly, it would seem, with Thucydides. He declares his careful attention to using and checking evidence, as we saw, but he does not frequently insist that he is seeking to show, to persuade, to demonstrate. He tends not to declare, 'I will show you with the following evidence', he does not buttonhole the reader or audience with claim to have proof, as Herodotus does, and as the more ostentatious of the medical writers do. Why not? We can perhaps isolate the connotations of this type of claim. For it is in the speeches that Thucydides' characters are happy to demonstrate that such and such is the case (the verb is ἀποδείκνυμι): for instance, from many examples, Pericles' speech of encouragement in the depression of the war (II 62.1), where he says 'I have often on other occasions demonstrated why you were not right to be apprehensive' (ἐν οἷς ἄλλοτε πολλάκις γε δὴ ἀπέδειξα οὐκ ὀρθῶς αὐτὸν ὑποπτευόμενον); or the Corcyreans, determined to 'demonstrate' the advantages to Athens of siding with them (I 35.5).[29] This implies that for Thucydides such expressions had a rhetorical tinge suitable to speeches. People also demonstrate or prove that something is the case, often in a semi-legal context.[30] But Thucydides in his own authorial person tends not to.

Thucydides may be casting a side glance, perhaps a lofty one, at a type of research exemplified by Herodotus, when he says, apparently as an

---

[26] Thrasymachus, DK 85, B 1: p. 323. 13: ἀποδείξω; Gorgias, DK 82, B 11a, *Palamedes* ch. 36 (p. 303): φανερὰν οὐδεμίαν ἀδικίαν οὐδὲ πιστὴν αἰτίαν ἀποδείξαντες. Similarly for ἀπόδειξις which occurs in Democritus, Gorgias (*Palamedes*), Archytas and *Dissoi Logoi*: see ch. 8 below, nn. 37–40.

[27] Cf. Anaxagoras' 'these things I have said' (ταῦτα μὲν οὖν μοι λέλεκται, DK 59, B 4); or similarly B 12 (ὥσπερ ... μοι λέλεκται); cf. Empedocles, DK 31, B 17. Cf. Heraclitus, DK 22, B 53: *Polemos* showed (ἔδειξε) both men and gods.

[28] Cf. Parmenides DK 28, B 2. 1: εἰ δ᾽ ἄγ᾽ ἐγὼν ἐρέω, of the ways of enquiry. But the goddess is speaking: the claim to have knowledge is maintained by putting the way of Truth in the mouth of a goddess.

[29] Other cases in *direct* speech: II 72.3*; IV 85.6*; VII 48.1 (indirect report of Nicias' deliberations to council of generals); VII 64.2* (Nicias' speech); cf. I 77.6* (ὑπεδείξετε).

[30] I 25.2 (Epidamnus' appeal); I 26.3; VIII 89.2 showing the 5,000 really existed. The two cases of *apodeixis* in Thucydides are: I 97.2, *apodeixis* of the empire's development; II 13.9, Pericles speaking ἐς ἀπόδειξιν.

ending to the subject, how one *might* (quite indirectly) further demonstrate that ancient Greek life resembled barbarian life now (I 6.6):

πολλὰ δ' ἂν καὶ ἄλλα τις ἀποδείξειε τὸ παλαιὸν Ἑλληνικὸν ὁμοιότροπα τῷ νῦν βαρβαρικῷ διαιτώμενον.

There are many other ways in which one might show how the ancient Greek way of life was similar to that of the barbarians now.

But he does not tend to claim that he will show this or that, or prove his point in quite the same way as Herodotus. His most extended piece of explicitly argumentative historical reconstruction probably occurs in his section on the tyrannicides, where he shows that the Athenians are wrong, that the tyrannicides killed not the tyrant, but the brother, and that the motive was merely a love feud (VI 54–9). Much argument and proof is actually given, and there is plenty of antagonistic rhetoric, claims for superior knowledge, argument from likelihood, but technique and wording are different. His claims for greater accuracy (*akribeia*), and the rare personal expressions of intention are couched in rather different form: for instance, of his argument that Hippias was the eldest, 'I know and am confirmed by accounts (*akoe*) more accurately than others' (εἰδὼς μὲν καὶ ἀκοῇ ἀκριβέστερον ἄλλων ἰσχυρίζομαι, 55.1); and he 'will reveal' (ἀποφανῶ) that no one is accurate (54.1). No promises that he (in the first-person) 'will demonstrate' or display his superiority occur even in his demonstration of Greek historical inaccuracy in Book I 20. Oddly enough it is his exposition on the Plague that invites rare promises to demonstrate his knowledge (II 48.3, ἐγὼ δὲ ... λέξω ... δηλώσω – 'I will say ... I will show'). Is it the subject matter that invites this treatment?

Given that expressions such as ἀποδείξω are regular in the speeches of Antiphon,[31] easily visible in Gorgias,[32] the implication seems inescapable that such expressions had strong overtones of rhetorical persuasion, overtones that Thucydides wanted to avoid: part of the language of proof and demonstration in a world which included early scientific (medical) enquiry, Herodotus, epideictic oratory, and therefore presumably earlier oratory in general. Given its prominence in oratory, it either had, or rapidly took on, somewhat flashy overtones, those of the performance, the

[31] Examples in later oratory: see note 91 for Antiphon – all with ἀποδείξω; *Tetral.* A δ 10, a passage replete with words of proof and demonstration. Cf. also *Medea* 548, Jason to Medea – δείξω – in the great verbal contest between the two (analysed, Solmsen 1975, 26f.).

[32] Cf. Gorgias, *Palam.* ch. 5 (conditional clauses + ἐπιδείξω); *Helen* chs. 8–9, lines 19–21 DK (bis): ταῦτα δὲ ὡς οὕτως ἔχει δείξω, etc. ('I will show that this is the case'). Cf. also, *Protag.* 323c7, 'I will attempt to demonstrate' (πειράσομαι ἀποδεῖξαι); 324c8, ἀποδέδεικταί σοι ... ἱκανῶς, and so on.

epideictic display. That need not be all, for what is so interesting in this period is how the development of proof seems to occur simultaneously in both medicine and philosophy, and in the art of persuasion.

Jouanna singled out as characteristics of the epideictic style 'la volonté de démontrer une thèse' along with the first person and rhetorical questions; the first two are very familiar from Herodotus.[33] We should surely see overtones in Herodotus and in treatises such as *On the Nature of Man*, of more than merely logical proof: there is a glint of the rhetorical, of the art of persuasion, even of the epideictic.

Correctness and certainty

Another strand of what we may begin to see as Herodotus' argumentative style involves his references to truth, certainty, and correct knowledge. Herodotus has plenty of ways, of course, of telling his audience that he has access to the truth (note the plethora of words for truth, ἀληθείη, ἀτρεκείη, etc., and how often ἀτρεκέως in Herodotus qualifies verbs of understanding and 'diagnosis').[34] Here we shall concentrate on perhaps the most interesting claim, the claim to 'correctness', which may encapsulate several of the issues raised by the other declarations about 'truth'. This seems to have rhetorical connotations, but also close associations to the claims of the developing 'arts' or *technai* to be able to attain correctness and truth.

In the remarkable passage in which Herodotus discusses whether the Spartan kings were Greek (VI 53.1–2), we find an interesting combination of features. Herodotus has related the Spartan tradition about their double kingship, which they alone of all the Greeks believe (VI 52–53.1):

But from now on I write according to what is said by the Greeks. The kings of the Dorians, they say – up to Perseus, son of Danaë, omitting the god, are rightly listed by the Greeks (καταλεγομένους ὀρθῶς ὑπ᾽ Ἑλλήνων) and shown (ἀποδεικνυ-μένους) to be Greeks. I said up to Perseus, but I did not take it further, because of this, that Perseus has no mortal father by whose name he is called, as Heracles has Amphitryon. So I said quite correctly [or more literally, 'using a correct argument'] 'up to Perseus' (ἤδη ὦν ὀρθῷ λόγῳ χρεωμένῳ μέχρι Περσέος [ὀρθῶς] εἴρηταί μοι).

As with the issue of the Greekness of the Macedonians, this is, one should presume, an awkward question, and it is interesting to see that Herodotus feels the need to make this statement. The whole section is highly polemical; when he adds a little later, that he'll move on to what has not been treated by others (VI 55) he may imply (unless it refers only to the invasion

---

[33] Jouanna's edition of *Art*, 169–73. See below on the first person.
[34] E.g. (from many): I 140.1, 2; II 28.2; II 54.2; II 119.3; II 145.3; I 172.1 (τοῦτο γὰρ οὐκ ἔχω ἀτρεκέως διακρῖναι); II 167.1 (κρῖναι), etc.

itself) that the whole general question of Spartan kingly origins was much discussed. It is then interesting to see how Herodotus is concerned to stress certainty, the correctness of what he (and other Greeks) have to say: his own view is ὀρθῷ λόγῳ.

Herodotus has a penchant for such ideas of 'correctness', and one may ask whether this would not have certain connotations in this period. We have already discussed the polemical passage about the erroneous Ionian views about Egypt, where the reader or audience was treated to the two stark alternatives: 'If we are correct to think ...; but if the Ionian opinion is correct' (εἰ ὦν ἡμεῖς ὀρθῶς ... γινώσκομεν ... εἰ δὲ ὀρθή ἐστι ἡ γνώμη τῶν Ἰώνων ..., II 16.1). Here we are dealing with correct opinion (*gnome*), not merely correct accounts or traditions.[35] We also find correct measurement on the Royal Road, as part of a discussion of the distance to Susa (v 53: 'If the Royal Road has been correctly (ὀρθῶς) measured' – cf. v 54.1 also). The *chresmologoi* do not interpret an oracle correctly according to Themistocles (VII 143.1: indirect speech), the rumour about the battle of Plataea was 'correct' (IX 101.2, ὀρθῶς). Accounts are correct or not correct. The Egyptian view of Greek reliance on rain is 'correctly said' (ὀρθῶς εἴρηται, II 14.1), the Greek idea that one of the Pyramids was erected by Rhodopis is not (οὐκ ὀρθῶς λέγοντες, II 134.1), and Herodotus proceeds to explain that they misunderstood the character of Rhodopis, the nature of building a pyramid, and the chronology of the relevant individuals and monuments. The Egyptians on the other hand are wrong about the lineage of Cambyses (λέγοντες δὲ ταῦτα οὐκ ὀρθῶς λέγουσι, 'those who say this are not correct', III 2.2), for they have insufficient knowledge of Persian customs (*nomima*). The Greeks are right who honour two Heracles (II 44.5); Pindar is right to say '*nomos* is king' (III 38.4). Homer was 'correct' in what he says about cattle growing horns in Libya (IV 29); but other accounts on various matters – Croesus' dedications, the defeat of Polycrates – are incorrect.[36] Darius uses 'correctness' both in his speech about the Scythians (IV 134.2*), and in the crucial debate on the constitutions, where it occurs twice alone in his contribution (III 82.1*): Megabyzos spoke 'correctly', according to Darius, on 'the masses' but not correctly on oligarchy.[37]

---

[35] Powell's listing (1966) of such passages under the category οὐκ ὀρθῶς λέγοντες over-simplifies. Cf. also Herodotus' approval of the Athenian belief that if they quarrel over leadership, Greece will be lost, ὀρθὰ νοεῦντες (VIII 3.1).

[36] I 51.3, οὐκ ὀρθῶς λέγοντες ('speaking incorrectly') on a claim and inscription to a gift of Croesus; and III 45.3, Polycrates; cf. also ὀρθῷ λόγῳ, an expression also found in Gorgias: Hdt. II 17.1, polemic on Asia/Libya division; VI 53.2 polemic on Spartan kings; VI 68.1*, Demaratus' question who was his father ὀρθῷ λόγῳ.

[37] Also in direct speech: I 91.4* (Pythia to Croesus); II 173.2* (Friends of Amasis on his lack of dignity); V 91.2* (Spartans about expelling tyrant); VI 86. β 2* (Glaukos story). See also n. 58 below.

Corrrect naming is also singled out. For instance in his Scythian section, Herodotus can declare that the third of the great Scythian rivers 'is correctly called mother Hypanios' (IV 52.1: καλέεται ... ὀρθῶς μήτηρ Ὑπάνιος). A little later, on the matter of Scythian religious worship, 'Zeus is, in my opinion, most correctly called Papaios' (IV 59.2: Ζεὺς δὲ ὀρθότατα κατὰ γνώμην γε τὴν ἐμὴν καλεόμενος Παπαῖος); the Greek nicknames for the three Persian kings are also correct.[38] It is interesting in what sense he means this: in all these cases the name he praises as being correct signifies something important and accurate about the essence or the object or individual so named.

This is not, of course, Herodotus' only means of letting his audience know that he has the truth, but this particular mode has interesting connotations in the intellectual life of the latter part of the fifth century. As is well known, 'correct naming' was an important and fashionable interest in that period. Protagoras was interested in *orthoepeia*, correctness of names (Plato, *Phaedrus* 267c, = DK 80, A 26), Democritus wrote a work with this as its title (DK 68, B 20a), and the most famous discussion on the problem of correctness of names remains the *Cratylus*.[39] The issue of 'correctness' seems to have had something of a vogue generally in the period: criticisms involving not thinking correctly, not 'speaking correctly', were not uncommon. Earlier, by contrast, Heraclitus, not known for his restraint in dismissing other men, has quite different verbal ways of expressing that disagreement: for example, 'men are witless' (ἀξύνετοι γίνονται ἄνθρωποι ... DK 22, B 1),[40] or his famous dismissal of learned sages with 'Much learning does not teach sense' (B 40). Parmenides talked about truth and mere opinion, Empedocles had various dismissive adjectives at his disposal (DK 31, B 39 ματαίως (in vain); B 62 ἀπόσκοπος (missing the mark), ἀδαήμων (ignorant)). But the assertion of 'correctness' in these terms does not yet occur.

For it is with Anaxagoras that we meet the kind of objection we encounter in Herodotus: for example, on the matter of coming to be, 'the Greeks' beliefs are incorrect, for ... they do not name anything correctly' (οὐκ ὀρθῶς νομίζουσιν οἱ Ἕλληνες· οὐδὲν γὰρ ... ἂν ὀρθῶς καλοῖεν ..., DK 59, B 17); or with Melissos who even in the few fragments remaining is

---

[38] Also: IV 109.1 (incorrect nomenclature of Boudinoi by Greeks); V 76 (Stoa of Codrus in Athens: correct naming); VI 98.3, on the nicknames given by the Greeks to Darius (ἑρξίης), Xerxes (ἀρήιος) and Artaxerxes (μέγας ἀρήιος), thus signalling his strong approval.

[39] For correctness of names, see Classen (1976b); most recently, Sluiter (1997), esp. 168–88, with further bibl. on the *Cratylus* there and Sedley (1998), on the etymologies in the *Crat.*; Kerferd (1981a), 70–5; Guthrie (1971), 205 ff.

[40] Also B 34; or B 17.

very fond of talking about seeing, hearing and understanding correctly.[41] Indeed, if one excepts the strictly mathematical meaning of *orthos* (e.g. Pythagoras DK 58, B 19), the range of writers who favour the expression of 'correctness' is an interesting one: Democritus, for whom we should add to his interest in correct usage, an expression denoting 'those who think correctly', and 'uprightness' (B 40, ὀρθοσύνη);[42] Protagoras, inevitably in indirect testimony;[43] the expression occurs in Antiphon the sophist – ὀρθῷ λόγῳ, 'by correct argument';[44] Thrasymachus, of running the city correctly;[45] Gorgias, who mentions speaking correctly (*Helen*, DK 82, B 11.2), and correctness of speech, λόγων ὀρθότητα (B 6.17, the Epitaphios);[46] the *Dissoi Logoi* (ch. 8, of speaking and judging, six times), and of course Prodikos.[47] Then correctness occurs with overwhelming frequency in the early medical writers, where 'knowing correctly', 'speaking correctly', and the medical variation, 'caring correctly', form standard terms of affirmation.

'Correctness', then, is a term and idea which was popular and fashionable in a range of philosophical writers, indeed several usually characterized as sophistic, of the later part of the fifth century.

The implications of the Hippocratic stress on correctness may be complex, and involve questions about intellectual communication and intellectual categorization. Jouanna has argued that when *On the Nature of Man* (ch. 1.2 J) declares, δοκέουσι μέντοι μοι οὐκ ὀρθῶς γινώσκειν οἱ ταῦτα λέγοντες ('those who say this do not have correct knowledge, it seems to me'), the term ὀρθῶς is a term from the philosophy of knowledge.[48] Citing Anaxagoras and Melissos, he suggests that ὀρθῶς *here* is

---

[41] E.g. DK 30, B 8.2, καὶ ἡμεῖς ὀρθῶς ὁρῶμεν καὶ ἀκούομεν ... etc. ('we see and hear correctly'); cf. also B 8.5.

[42] DK 68, B 58, thinking correctly, ὀρθὰ φρονεόντων. Also Democritus DK 68, B 5.2: vol.II, 137, line 22 (from Hermippus). Also, somewhat later, Archytas DK 47, A 14 (geometry), and B 1 (ὀρθῶς φρονέειν) (DK I, 432, line 1).

[43] For Protagoras (DK 80), *Protag.* 339a (= A 25, II 261, 21), understanding what has been done correctly; DL IX 55, title (= A 1, B 8e); A 10, κατὰ τὸν ὀρθότατον λόγον (the discussion between Pericles and Protagoras on the javelin accident seeks the 'orthos logos'); *Cratylus* 391 b–c (= DK 80, A 24), for correctness of names (ὀρθότης ὀνομάτων). Cf. also *Clouds* 659, and 679, ὀρθῶς λέγεις, which DK sees as imitation of Protagoras (= DK 80, c3!).

[44] DK 87, B 44, frag. A, col. 4, 10 (DK II p. 349); also ὀρθότερον (of judgement), B 58; B 13, letters (γραμμαί), and B 60.

[45] DK 85, B 1: p. 322, 6.

[46] Cf. *Gorgias* 450c2 (= DK, A 27), λέγων.

[47] On the choice of Heracles according to Xenophon, *Mem.* II 1, 22 (= DK 84, B 2), ὀρθοτέραν τῆς φύσεως; cf. also A 11, where Socrates is teasing him on his one-drachma and fifty-drachma lecture on the correctness of names; and A 16. Cf. also Hippias DK 86, A 12, ὀρθότης γραμμάτων.

[48] *CMG.* I, 1, 3: commentary p. 231.

the result of the direct influence of Melissos, and rejects Heinimann's view that it appeared in the philosophy of knowledge through the intermediary of sophistic.[49]

But perhaps this is expecting too strict a line of intellectual debt. Herodotus' equal keenness to signify correctness must complicate the issue, and we should not underestimate the extent to which 'correctness' appears as apparently a catch term in very obviously sophistic contexts. This raises questions about intellectual milieux and intercommunication in the period. For Heinimann did indeed see ὀρθῶς as part of an 'Erkenntnistheorie' in Anaxagoras and Melissos, which was diffused via 'sophistic' ('since sophistic it was current'), and from there it entered Herodotus, and the Hippocratic works which were sophistically influenced.[50] Heinimann mentioned Herodotus only fleetingly but reveals a problem there, for he does not usually think of Herodotus as specifically influenced by 'sophistic'. Moreover, given its occurrence in such a wide range of other thinkers, from Protagoras to the *Dissoi Logoi*, there is little hope (or use) of working out any mode of diffusion from chronological sequence alone. As we have seen (chapter 5), the early Hippocratic works imply both close interaction with other philosophers, as well as conscious distancing from them. In Melissos' expression, 'and we see and hear correctly' (DK 30, B 8.2), Melissos obviously intends to refer us to the truth as he saw it, but this seems to represent no special theory of knowledge. It seems hard to be so sure of the presence of sophistic thought as a mediator and 'diffuser' of terminology in this case, where we have a group of thinkers who overlapped in time and who were often interested in similar problems. The insertion of Herodotus into this picture only highlights and focuses the problem.

Most reminiscent of Herodotus' style of criticism are the similar castigations of opponents by various medical writers. The expression cited above from *Nat. Hom.* 1, δοκέουσι μέντοι μοι οὐκ ὀρθῶς γινώσκειν οἱ ταῦτα λέγοντες,[51] or the very similar statement of *Diseases IV*, ἐμοὶ δοκέουσι λέγειν οὐκ ὀρθῶς οἱ τὰ τοιαῦτα λέγοντες, ('those who say this are not correct in my opinion'),[52] could have come straight from Herodotus.[53] If we look to style alone, Herodotus' expressions are indistin-

---

[49] Heinimann (1945), 155 n. 22.
[50] See Heinimann (1945), 155 n. 22; also pp. 201–2.
[51] *Nat. Man* ch. 1.2 J.
[52] *Dis. IV* ch. 54.3 J.
[53] Cf. Herodotus: II 44.5 (on Heracles, hero and the god) καὶ δοκέουσι δέ μοι οὗτοι ὀρθότατα Ἑλλήνων ποιέειν: 'I think those Greeks act most correctly', who have a double cult to Heracles; II 16.1, εἰ ὦν ἡμεῖς ὀρθῶς περὶ αὐτῶν γινώσκομεν ('If we judge correctly about this'); VI 53.1–2; or III 2.2 cited above.

guishable. They also share an expressive disapproval of other opinions and stories, and are couched in the first person. Or we may compare the dogmatic certainty of the very opening line from *Airs* (ch. 1.1 J): 'Whoever wishes to pursue medicine correctly must do this'; not to mention the criticism of 'those who have not correctly worked out causes', of *The Art* (ch. 7.5 J: οἱ μὴ ὀρθῶς λογιζόμενοι τὰς αἰτίας). From many other cases, the opening chapters of *Nat. Man* are especially keen on talking of correctness, and *Ancient Medicine* on 'correct' doctoring, which is connected with correct knowledge.[54] Not all of these can be said to be particularly sophistic, or particularly rhetorical in their aims.[55]

The implications for Herodotus seem confused. Herodotus points out several times what he sees as 'correct naming' and in any other writer the presence both of the idea and the 'proper' vocabulary would be seized upon as a sign that they were familiar with the sophistic debate about correctness of names.[56] We have also seen several Herodotean expressions involving correctness which are virtually identical to those found in writers such as Antiphon the sophist (e.g. ὀρθῷ λόγῳ) and which in other circumstances would be assumed to be sophistic. Talk of 'correct opinion' (etc.) implied an idea of the certainty of knowledge (Melissos) and for Protagoras, Democritus, and Prodicus, the correct use of language. Perhaps the most plausible solution is to see this emphasis on 'correctness' as an expression which was the catch-phrase of a generation, overused as catch-phrases are, and a generation of prose writers who belonged mainly, perhaps, to the intellectual world of East Greece, arching over the *physiologoi* like Melissos, doctors and 'sophists'. It is, then, no coincidence that Aristophanes' *Clouds* uses the expression 'correctly' eight times in a philosophical context in its parody of the sophistic style.[57]

Enlisting the idea of correctness is also a powerful way of dismissing the untruthfulness of your opponents in contexts which might not necessarily involve an elaborate theory of knowledge, as we have seen (Anaxagoras,

---

[54] *Nat. Man* ch. 1.3 J: understanding correctly (ὀρθῶς γινώσκειν) and ὀρθῶς ἀποφαίνεται. *Anc. Med.* ch. 13.1; ch. 20.1, 2; ch. 21.3; ch. 23. Also *Art* ch. 5.5 bis, 5.6 J (incl. correctness and the art/*techne*); note also similar examples in *Progn.*, *Acut.*, *Epid. III*.

[55] Heinimann (ibid.) mentioned in this context *Nat. Man*, *Art*, *Regimen*, as pieces influenced by sophistic style. But the range of pieces using such phrases is wider.

[56] Cf. Kerferd, for instance, on *orthe doxa* in the *Meno* 96d (1981a, 137): 'the very expression *orthe* for right in the case of opinion suggests at least a consciousness of the sophistic doctrine of the *orthos logos*, an expression also used by Plato himself on occasion' (and he cites *Phaedo* 73a10, *Laws* 890a7, *Critias* 109b2); cf. also p. 102.

[57] Used of the correct understanding of nature (228, 251, 742), of *nomos* (v. 1186) and of naming (vv. 659, 679). In five of these, Socrates is speaking, in the other (1186), it is Pheidippides *after* he has been educated in the *phrontisterion*. I am grateful to M. Trapp for drawing these to my attention.

Melissos, the Hippocratic Corpus), a successor to the polemical language of distaste found in Heraclitus and others. It seems to be a feature of a brand of polemic belonging to a certain kind of intellectual discourse. Herodotus fits very comfortably here. Moreover he enlists correctness overwhelmingly in statements in his own person of what he thinks of others' opinions, traditions told by others, false beliefs. That is, expressions of correctness are heavily connected with his expressions of method and his pursuit of what he sees as the truth. Here it is tempting to connect the arguments in *On the Art* which declare that there could be no *techne* if there is not a concept of 'correct' and 'incorrect' (ch. 5.5, 5.6 J). Perhaps Herodotus is expressing what we might rephrase as the credentials of his seriousness?

But if Herodotus emphasizes correct opinion in connection with method, there is a striking contrast with Thucydides, for the more restrained Thucydides seems to regard assertions of correctness as more appropriate to the speeches in his *History*.[58] That raises the question whether *orthotes* has specifically rhetorical connotations. Certainly appeals to 'correct judgement' and understanding occur quite frequently in Antiphon the orator,[59] as in the more rhetorical Hippocratic essays (not *Airs* particularly). Dismissal of your opponents, arguments against counter-suggestions by others, belonged as much to the polemical writers (and speakers) behind the early Hippocratic essays as to the development of rhetorical presentations in court, and part of the development of the technique of polemical argument against opponents in general. Herodotus' primarily methodological remarks seem to belong comfortably within this more polemical, dismissive and more rhetorical end of the spectrum. As we are reminded by the debate on correctness of language, correctness is part of the language of certainty, of philosophical proof, of theories of language, in the milieu which seems to have included the early Hippocratic essays, the later prose writers of the fifth century (all from East Greece), certain sophists for rhetorical or display purposes (Gor-

---

58   Thucydides uses ὀρθῶς twice in discussion of method or judgement of his own (I 20.3 – below, V 26.2), 17 times in speeches (this includes one in indirect speech of Themistocles, I 91,7), 29 times in all; it is prominent. for example in the speeches of Pericles (II 40.2*; II 60.1*, 62.1*, 64.5*), of Cleon (III 40.4*), of the Plataeans (III 55.4*, 56.2*, 58.4*), and of Alcibiades (VI 89.3*, 92.4*). Herodotus uses it overwhelmingly to express his own opinion, but only 8 times in direct speech (including ὀρθῷ λογῳ; denotes 'justly' in I 91.4*, II 173.2*, V 91.2*, VI 86 β 2*). Thuc. I 20.3: καὶ οἱ ἄλλοι Ἕλληνες οὐκ ὀρθῶς οἴονται ('the rest of the Greeks do not think correctly') concerns mistaken beliefs about the Spartan kings (voting).

59   Some examples almost at random: Antiphon, *Murder of Herodes*, chs. 88–91 (ὀρθῶς γιγνώσκεσθαι etc.); *Tetral*. II 4.8, 4.9–10 (εἰ . . . ἐκ τῶν λεγομένων ἐπιδείκνυται . . . ὀρθῶς δὲ τῶν ἐλέγχων ἐλεγχόντων . . .); *Tetral*.III 1.1; and in his defence, frag. B 1, col. IV (εἴ γε ὀρθῶς . . . σκοπεῖσθε).

gias), as well as for more obviously philosophical discussion (Prodicus, Protagoras). It could also be exploited to give a persuasive weight to assertions, polemic, to more elaborate sophistic display. As such, it appears in Herodotus almost as a badge of respectability, both as the language of proof, and part of his polemical stance, and they are not unconnected. As we saw, Herodous told his audience the real length of the Royal Road, 'if one measures it correctly', and went into considerable detail on the matter (v 52–4). The context was Aristagoras' attempt to persuade Cleomenes to invade Asia, which failed the moment Aristagoras admitted that it would be three months journey to Susa (v 50). While Aristagoras turns out to be substantially correct, the way Herodotus launches into his exact description implies some kind of 'capping', for he adds, 'If one wants to be more accurate, I will indicate this too', and he calculates that three months and three days would be more precise (v 53, 54). If the sophistic essay *On the Art* can argue that there could be no *techne* if there was not a concept of 'correct' and 'not correct' (ch. 5.5–6 J), could Herodotus be claiming that his enquiry counts as a *techne*? Perhaps this is going too far. But Herodotus in this respect sits comfortably alongside the polemical and methodological assertions of the writers on *physis* of East Greece, doctors and Ionian intellectuals: not only comfortably, but he seems to be asserting his membership of this group.

Polemic and the art of persuasion were hardly absent from this milieu. Both were also expressed with energetic and dogmatic use of the first person.

The first person

One of the most prominent traits of Herodotus' style is his authorial presence. We are continually reminded in the text of the presence of the author, his views, his enquiries, through his penchant for the first person – 'I saw', 'I enquired', 'it seems to me' – a preference which Thucydides conspicuously did not share. It is this style which does much to give the *Histories* their lively form of presentation, and which bring Herodotus' personal enquiries vividly to the attention of his audience. As Gould remarked, Herodotus' authorial presence, which includes his speculations and doubts in his enquiry, is quite different from the style of the folk-tale narrative and highlights both his originality and also the difficulties in reading him.[60] This style can be seen, at least in some of its guises, as part of the style of persuasion, controversy and engagement, and one of the latter part of the fifth century.

[60] Gould (1989), 110–12; note also the important study by Dewald (1987).

Let us first consider the possibility that this might simply be a traditional feature of earlier prose, perhaps Ionian. It might be supposed that
the Herodotean first-person style was simply a standard archaic feature of
a wider literary milieu, that of (archaic) Ionian *historie*. This was assumed,
for instance, in a particularly clear example, by Regenbogen's brief section on the 'Ich-Stil' in a range of Hippocratic treatises (by Ionian *historie*, he meant old (archaic) Ionian proto-history as represented by Hecataeus and Herodotus): the first person is after all extremely common in
Herodotus, especially in Book II. Since Herodotus is to be taken as representative of Ionian *historie* in the archaizing sense, it therefore followed
that this first-person style was an old Ionian one, in fact also Hecataean.[61]
Yet the main textual evidence that we have for Hecataeus using the first-
person style is in the very first fragment (*FGrH* 1, F1); this is an impressive opening, but an archaic writer is more likely to be personal and
dogmatic at the beginning of his work. In other words this seems to rest
more on an assumption about Herodotus' relation to Hecataeus than any
firm evidence. It does not matter then if one finds very similar style in
later, more contemporary writers. As Regenbogen points out, the first-
person style predominates in the Hippocratic works. But 'Ionian *historie*',
that is Herodotus and Hecataeus, have by this time been set apart, and
Herodotus set back into an older stratum of prose style. It is, of course,
problematic that Hecataeus is preserved in a way that may have elimi-
nated these features.[62] But the question exemplifies the wider problem of
how far Herodotus should habitually be assumed to belong to an older
stratum, even where contemporary and near contemporary evidence is
comparable.

This facet of Herodotus' style has, of course, received considerable attention in recent years, most particularly the active side to the first person,
that is, his claims to have seen certain things, to have gone to particular
places, enquired, questioned, in other words first-person claims in the
guise of autopsy and enquiry and as part of his claims to have attained the

---

[61] (1961), 171; on Hecataeus, Regenbogen says that it could be 'no different' in Hecataeus.
The *Odyssey* opens with a first person, but via the appeal to the Muse: see below n. 73.

[62] If we distinguish the use of the first person (i) to express opinion, and (ii) as part of a
narrative on the behalf of the narrator or researcher ('I went' etc.), we then have two
separate questions about Hecataeus: (a) did he habitually express his opinion as Herodotus did (fr. 1; *dokeo* in fr. 234; first person also in fr. 19 and fr. 27b (addenda)); and (b)
was his geographical work couched in terms of his own personal experience? For this,
most of the relevant testimony is derived from Herodotus! We may note incidentally, that
Thucydides was careful to separate the two: he occasionally expresses opinions and talks
about method in the first person, but his part in the historical narrative is in the third
person, except for the plague (II 48.3).

truth.[63] They tend either to be taken literally or regarded as untruths, though there has been little attempt, so far as I know, to examine them as part of any wider intellectual discourse (except under the guise of empiricism). Yet there is a range of other first-person comments which raise rather separate questions. What about the mass of personal opinions, comments, asides which are in fact far more common than the claims to precise personal experience, expressions such as 'so it seems to me' (ὡς ἐμοὶ δοκεῖ), or comments on the methods of his *Histories*? They are extraordinarily common. In an important article on the Herodotean authorial persona, Caroline Dewald has counted 1,087 first persons in the *Histories*.[64]

Many involve comments on the plausibility of the tales Herodotus gives us, which, as Dewald points out, is distinctly odd. As she says, 'what kind of historian expressly rejects his own data, without going on to put something better in its place? What kind of historian warns us that much of what we read in his history is simply untrue?';[65] she goes on to a subtle and plausible reading of Herodotus' first person as in part a rhetorical strategy to remind the readers of the difficulties of his task, to heighten the sense of his own achievement, and to retain a distance from his material. 'Hence he has not tried, as historians after him were to do, to make the narrative surface of the *Histories* a smooth one, or to use his own voice as author to confirm the authority of the third person narrative. He has rather presented the "I" of the authorial persona as an alternative voice, one that goes to some lengths to distinguish itself from the *logoi* it recounts.'[66]

This analysis forces one's attention onto the oddness of Herodotus' authorial persona, and in particular to the way in which the first person can serve to distance Herodotus from his stories, his *logoi* and point to the limitations of the data.[67] I would like to approach this first person from a

---

[63] On autopsy in Herodotus, Schepens (1980); also D. Müller (1981); Verdin (1971); good discussion by Marincola (1987), of Herodotus' autobiographical statements; Fornara (1971a), 19–23, on Herodotus' authorial voice. Cf. scepticism of Fehling (1989), Armayor (1978), (1980), (1985).

[64] Dewald (1987), 150 n. 10; 159–63 on first person as 'the critic'; Marincola (1987) concentrated on the 'autobiographical' claims, but many of the insights may be extended to the rest. Cf. also Lateiner (1989), esp. 25, 92, 240 n. 78; Darbo-Peschanski (1987), pt. 2, esp. 107–12, 164–89 (internal to the text).

[65] Dewald (1987), 150–1; quotation p. 151: she tends to concentrate on the historical narrative and first person within third-person narrative (where the contrast with Thucydides is most striking): see esp. 148, 150 and n. 11.

[66] Dewald (1987), 153; cf. also Darbo-Peschanski (1987), 107–12.

[67] This perhaps applies better to the treatment of the narrative, stories of the past, than to the controversies where Herodotus uses the first person to declare openly what he thinks is correct.

rather different – though I think complementary – perspective. It is unclear, for instance, that the distancing role of the first person always conveys the full force of the first person as it would have struck Herodotus'
fifth-century audiences. Other fifth-century prose texts offer a somewhat
different dimension (though one which would in some ways be complementary), and while there is a clear contrast with Thucydides and his later
authoritative third-person narrative, the points of comparison for Herodotus' contemporary audience might not be with historical narrative at
all, and could hardly be with Thucydides' mode of narrative. And while
the image of Herodotus Dewald presents as a 'heroic warrior' battling
with the *logoi*[68] underlines strikingly the emphatic presence of Herodotus'
persona in the text and the boastful display of his own achievements,
often in problematic cases, we should perhaps also consider more closely
the dogmatic expression of his personal opinion through the first person.
Certainly he was battling to get the information, to get at the truth as he
presents it.[69] But what of the first-person claims to have proved something, opinions about other men's theories, examples where he seems to
express certainty? To what extent do we – or Herodotus' contemporary
audiences – take these as expressions of distancing, of the difficulty of the
material? Or are they simply boastful? The phrase 'it seems to me' is not
necessarily a sign of modesty, as it has been interpreted for Thucydides.[70]
But in any case it may be misleading to compare Herodotus' practice here
primarily with Thucydides': Thucydides may, after all, have been reacting
to Herodotus, or to the style of the milieu to which Herodotus may have
belonged.[71] Nor is it clear that the model of the archaic mediator or Homeric *histor* is necessarily relevant to the first person – and in any case we
lack any evidence.[72] There are interesting parallels with the Homeric poet

---

[68] Dewald (1987), 147.

[69] As Dewald argues (1987), he does want to stress the efforts to attain the truth. Note also
Marincola's point that many of the autobiographical statements seem polemical, or concern far from straightforward matters, using his experience to contradict others (1987,
esp. 128–31); Darbo-Peschanski (1987), 112. Cf. Hartog (1988, 289–94) – first person
demonstrating his credibility.

[70] Hornblower, Commentary, I, p. 16, on Thuc. I 3.2, δοκεῖ δέ μοι as 'I am inclined to think':
'This unconfident and subjective formula', for the uncertain subject matter of early history.

[71] See useful comments by Brock (1991), 101 on Thucydides' use of the third person as an
attempt to be convincing, reviewing Woodman (1988), 4, 23, on third person as part of
rhetoric of authority. Hornblower (1994b), 149 on second person. First persons in Thucydides: most common in Archaiologia, significantly (e.g. I 3.1, 3.2, 3.3, 9.1 + 3, 10.2 (οἴ-
μαι), 10.4, amidst many marks of uncertainty); I 20.1, 21.1, 22 on his methods; cf. also I
97.2 (on his digression); II 48.3 (plague); III 89.5 (αἴτιον δ' ἔγωγε νομίζω); III 90.1 (limiting
subject); v 68.2 (uncertainty about Sparta); VIII 87.4 (*his* opinion after others').

[72] Cf. Connor (1993b) who seems to imply that Herodotus' first-person opinions belong to
the role of the archaic *histor*.

where both Homer and Herodotus declare in the first person that they will (or will not) record certain facts – where both seem to allude to the role of preserving the past and allotting or creating fame – though Homer's appeal to the Muses gives this a different force.[73] But these are not the most prominent of Herodotus' authorial interventions. Is the first person as a sign of modesty, then, or intellectual authority, to indicate the authority of the mediator, or a distancing from the traditions, for emphasis or ambivalence – and no doubt implications change also with context?

Some contemporary or roughly contemporary comparison is instructive. The fragments of the Presocratic philosophers imply that first-person statements were not meant to give impressions of modesty.[74] Such statements are overwhelmingly confident, declarations of strong personalities, even egocentrism. Diogenes, whose interests overlap with Herodotus', and Melissos, express their opinion in the first person. Most spectacular and revealing, partly because they are preserved in their entirety, are the Hippocratic writers. Here we find *in extenso* the kind of expressions of first-person views, opinions, arguments in the first person, that can be read only as dogmatically opinionated, declarations of certain argument, of true and accurate belief. The *Epidemics I* and *III* are somewhat unusual in having very little use of first-person statements, though even they have numerous interpolations stating personal knowledge on the part of the author;[75] *Airs* is also comparatively free of the first person. In the other early texts, personal views, declarations and arguments are ubiquitous: in *On the Nature of Man*, *Ancient Medicine*, *On the Sacred Disease*, *Breaths*, *Art*, and *Gener./Nat. Child/Dis. IV*. First-person statements sometimes accompany outright polemic against others' views, sometimes the context may be less controversial, or (as in *Epidemics*) stands as a straight statement of knowledge. The author of *Nature of the Child* even gives a brief narrative of his experience to back up his thesis. Recent work sees this

---

[73] Erbse (1992), 125–7: he cites the Homeric remarks prefacing the Catalogue of Ships, *Iliad* II 488, 493, with Hdt. VII 96.1, ... τῶν ἐγώ (οὐ γὰρ ἀναγκαίη ἐξέργομαι ἐς ἱστορίης λόγον) οὐ παραμέμνημαι; and other places where 'he cannot exactly say': e.g. VII 54.3; VII 133.2; VII 152.1 ('I cannot truly say', οὐκ ἔχω ἀτρεκέως εἰπεῖν ...); VII 187.1 (*no one* can say); VIII 85.2 (he will only mention two names); VIII 87.1 and 3; IX 18.2. The Homeric poet seems to use the first person at points where he expresses subordination to the Muses, who tell him the Truth (as in opening of *Iliad*): *Od.*I.1 (Ἄνδρα μοι ἔννεπε, Μοῦσα), I.10; *Iliad* II 484–93 differs strikingly from Herodotus, for the poet appeals to the Muses to tell him; he knows nothing without their help.

[74] Cf. Xenophanes, B 7, B 34; Heraclitus, e.g. B 1, B 55, B 108; Anaxagoras slightly, B 4, B 12; Diogenes is fond of δοκεῖ μοι (B 1, B 2; also B 5, B 8); Empedocles uses it pretty constantly: e.g. B 8, B 38 'I will tell you', B 35, B 115 etc.; Melissos, B 8.2; less in Democritus – B 259. Cf. G. E. R. Lloyd (1987), 56 ff. on the 'egocentrism' in these philosophers.

[75] For *Epidemics*, see n. 99 below.

medical first-person style in this sphere as connected with a controversial and rhetorical, even epideictic, style.

So, for instance, On the *Nature of Man* opens:

῞Οστις μὲν οὖν εἴωθεν ἀκούειν λεγόντων ἀμφὶ τῆς φύσιος τῆς ἀνθρωπίνης προσωτέρω ἢ ὅσον αὐτῆς ἐς ἰητρικὴν ἀφήκει, τούτῳ μὲν οὐκ ἐπιτήδειος ὅδε ὁ λόγος ἀκούειν· οὔτε γὰρ τὸ πάμπαν ἠέρα λέγω τὸν ἄνθρωπον εἶναι, οὔτε πῦρ, ... ἀλλὰ τοῖσι βουλομένοισι ταῦτα λέγειν παρίημι. δοκέουσι μέντοι μοι οὐκ ὀρθῶς γινώσκειν οἱ ταῦτα λέγοντες· (ch. 1.1–2 J)

Whoever is accustomed to hear speakers talk about the nature of man beyond its relations to medicine will not find this account of any interest; for I do not say man consists entirely of air, or of fire [... or anything else that is not a constituent of a man]. Such accounts I leave to those who choose to give them. However, those who say these things do not in my opinion have correct knowledge.[76]

He goes on to assert that these people 'give proofs or evidence which amount to nothing'; the clearest sign that none of them have correct knowledge is if one goes to one of their debates ('one may recognize'), and finally, 'But such men seem to me to overthrow themselves in the words (?terms) of their arguments',[77] finishing off with 'About this I have said enough' (ch. 2.1 J).

The equally dogmatic, exuberantly argumentative *Ancient Medicine* opens with similar polemical style ('All those who, in attempting to speak or write about medicine, have assumed a postulate ... are open to censure', ch. 1.1 J). After some more criticism, 'Therefore I have deemed that there is no need for a new postulate, as is the case with unseen and insoluble mysteries' (διὸ οὐκ ἠξίουν αὐτὴν ἔγωγε καινῆς ὑποθέσιος δεῖσθαι, ...: ch. 1.3 J). Again, there is no way of testing for the speaker or the audience whether those statements were true. 'But medicine has long had all its means to hand' (ch. 2.1 J): 'I will try to expound the causes of the impossibility, by a statement and exposition of what the art is' (Δι᾽ ἃς ἀνάγκας ἀδύνατον, ἐγὼ πειρήσομαι ἐπιδεῖξαι λέγων καὶ ἐπιδεικνύων τὴν τέχνην ὅτι ἐστίν, ch. 2.2 J). First persons continue throughout – 'I want to return to the theory ...' (ch. 13.1 J), 'Of course I know' (ch. 14.1 J), and with a further flourish,

I am at a loss (Ἀπορέω δ᾽ ἔγωγε) to understand how those who maintain the other view and abandon the old methods to rest the art on a postulate, treat their patients on the lines of their postulate. (15.1 J)

---

[76] I am aware of Schenkeveld's warning against taking literally all uses of *akouein* (1992a): here, however, *Nat. Man* continues (rest of ch. 1) to talk in terms of contests, debates and 'hearers', which imply strongly the public debate. See also ch. 8, below.

[77] Ch. 1.4 J: ἀλλ᾽ ἔμοιγε δοκέουσιν οἱ τοιοῦτοι ἄνθρωποι αὐτοὶ ἑωυτοὺς καταβάλλειν ἐν τοῖσιν ὀνόμασι τῶν λόγων.

And later, 'About this subject I think I have demonstrated (ἐπιδεδεῖχθαι) sufficiently. Certain doctors and philosophers assert that no one can know medicine who is ignorant what a man is' (ch. 20.1 J), 'But my view is' (ἐγὼ δὲ ... νομίζω), 'I think', 'it seems to me', 'I mean this enquiry' (λέγω δὲ ταύτην τὴν ἱστορίην) (ch. 20.2 J). And perhaps most arrogant, 'I think I have non-plussed my opponents'.[78]

We may note the highly critical, forthright tone about others, about whole groups, *sophistai*, other doctors, philosophers such as Empedocles, and the language of display and demonstration. The author claims a superior and special status for medicine, and he does so with a dogmatic and personal tone in which his personal opinion is constantly being thrust before us and in what is hardly a modest manner ('I am at a loss ...!').[79] As for the treatise *On the Art*, the first-person presence is so constant that its author has been accused of 'obsessive self-advertizing'.[80] From examples on every page, I need quote only one: 'About medicine – our subject – I will give a demonstration. First I will say what I think medicine is'.[81]

The dogmatic and dramatic certainties of the Hippocratic writers even in the face of what seem to us the most obvious inadequacies of the evidence, are continually striking. At one extreme *On the Art* has been called 'an example of authorial egotism', its 'breathtaking self-confidence'[82] part of this. Indeed such 'egotism' has been connected by Lloyd, stressing the dogmatism of the argument, with the need for and delight in innovations in Greek philosophy and science generally; the stress on originality with the presence of a public, often general, audience, which had to be attracted, alerted and stimulated by the speaker or author.[83] This egotism and self-promotion must, then, be connected to the needs of persuasion and performance. Jouanna has looked at these stylistic tricks of the medical writers – including the use of the first person – in more detail from a related perspective, and seeks to distinguish the various works partly by

[78] Ch. 13.3 J: οἶμαι γὰρ ἔγωγε πολλὴν ἀπορίην ἐρωτηθέντι παρασχεῖν; Jones' translation.
[79] G. E. R. Lloyd (1987), 67, counts 30 first-person pronouns, and first-person verbs without an added ἐγώ/ἔγωγε another 22 times.
[80] G. E. R. Lloyd (1987), 61.
[81] περὶ δὲ ἰητρικῆς – ἐς ταύτην γὰρ ὁ λόγος – ταύτης οὖν τὴν ἀπόδειξιν ποιήσομαι. Καὶ πρῶτόν γε διοριεῦμαι ὃ νομίζω ἰητρικὴν εἶναι (ch. 3.1–2 J). *Breaths* is replete with first-person assertions: 'I will try to delare what this is in the following logos' (ch. 2.1 J: πειρήσομαι); 'First, I will begin with ...' (ch. 6.1 J); or on the perennial issue of the 'so-called' Sacred Disease (Δοκεῖ δέ μοι ...) (ch. 14.1 J); or the ending (15.1 J); though note also the hypothetical objection ('but someone might say'), which does not occur in Herodotus, so far as I know.
[82] G. E. R. Lloyd (1987), 114, 116. Cf. also (1979).
[83] (1987), 56 ff.; he makes much of the stress on innovation, originality, and atmosphere of performance with apparently less emphasis as in *Magic* on rhetorical aims. P. van der Eijk (1997) 115–19, examines some less demonstrative uses of the first person.

the nature of performance and audience. Thus there are, he suggests, a spectrum of treatises, from those intended to be referred to purely as written texts (such as *Epid. I, III*), to the didactic lectures ('l'exposé oral didactique ou "cours"'), which would include *Sacred Disease*, *Airs*, and *Generation/Nature of the Child*, to those at the other end, which represented the public lecture, the epideictic or display performance, of which *The Art* and *Breaths* are the extreme and only clear examples.[84] *Ancient Medicine* and *Nature of Man*, particularly the latter, he thought were ambiguous since they displayed both technical and rhetorical elements.[85] His criteria included the emphasis on persuasion, repeated statements such as 'I have shown', 'I will show', and a concentration of terms for demonstration; the use of words denoting 'to say' (though as he admitted that is highly ambiguous), the general periodic style; and the use of the first person.

The 'egocentric' style seems, then, most plausibly to belong to the style of the display performance, and to be encouraged by the needs of the live performance. But that rhetorical aim must also be combined with the image of stunning self-confidence and certainty which has been remarked on – the two existing side by side.

This may offer us a refreshing perspective from which to view Herodotus' expression of personal opinion and personal argument. Moreover the first-person presence in both Herodotus and the Hippocratic writers does, in effect, bring together many of the expressions of proof, evidence and truth that we have been looking at, and which are so often expressed in the first person. At the very least, the expressions of first-person knowledge and certainty in both natural philosophers and medical writers may make us pause before seeing Herodotus' own first-person style as one of naivety alone, or of modest humility and detachment – or simply *sui generis*. Moreover, in both the natural philosophers and medical writers and in Herodotus we are dealing with writers who purported to convey the truth,[86] and with some of the same baggage of proof, evidence and argument. Polemic and a certain rhetorical flair and persuasiveness may be part of this.

The first-person polemic of *Nature of Man* or *Ancient Medicine* was not that distant from Herodotus' polemical manner of dealing with the idea

---

[84] Jouanna (1984b); note also the important analysis of *Anc. Med.* as a 'discourse épidictique' in his Budé edition (1990), 9–22, and of *Breaths* similarly (Budé ed. 1988, 10–24); and of *Art* (1988), 167–74 – which Jouanna believes is by a doctor using sophistic technique (ibid. 179–83). Some doubts about these categories expressed by van der Eijk (1997: – e.g. 79, but cf. 95–6), but he pays little attention to the more flamboyant works.

[85] For *Ancient Medicine*, see also Jouanna's edn (1990) 10–12 on first person, and 9–22 generally.

[86] First-person expressions in lyric poetry raise rather different sets of questions and problems, e.g. persona of poet; nature of choral 'I' in Pindar.

of a round earth – 'I cannot but laugh' (ιν 36); or 'If the opinion of the Ionians is correct, then I undertake to show (ἀποδείκνυμι) that neither the Greeks nor the Ionians know how to count' (ιι 16.1); or a little further on in the same controversy (the whole discussion of the nature of Egypt is peppered with first persons):

μαρτυρέει δέ μοι τῇ γνώμῃ, ὅτι τοσαύτη ἐστὶ Αἴγυπτος ὅσην τινὰ ἐγὼ ἀποδείκνυμι τῷ λόγῳ, καὶ τὸ Ἄμμωνος χρηστήριον γενόμενον, τὸ ἐγὼ τῆς ἐμεωυτοῦ γνώμης ὕστερον περὶ Αἴγυπτον ἐπυθόμην.

A witness to my view that Egypt is as I show by my argument (*logos*), is the oracle of Ammon, of which I learned after I had come to my own opinion about Egypt. (ιι 18.1)

Assertions of proof are expressed strikingly in the first person. We have already encountered his remarks about the foolish ideas concerning Ocean in the discussion about the Nile flooding, which take the issue into 'the invisible, which therefore admits of no refutation' (ιι 23): 'For I know (ἔγωγε οἶδα) of no river called Ocean, and I think (δοκέω) that Homer or one of the earlier poets found the name and inserted it into his poetry.' In his polemical discussion of the myths about Heracles and the wholly mistaken views the Greeks hold about him, we have again a sweeping criticism of a whole group: not only are many of their tales 'quite unconsidered', but their story about Heracles is also simple-minded (εὐήθης) (ιι 45.1).[87] The whole critique is capped with a first-person elucidation of the woeful inexperience of the Greeks when it comes to Egypt (ιι 45.2):

The Greeks who say this are, I think (ἐμοὶ μέν νυν δοκέουσι), totally inexperienced in the matter of the nature (*physis*) and the customs (*nomoi*) of the Egyptians.

Again, clear and uncompromising criticism of others is couched in the first person, in a manner reminiscent of the polemical first-person style of some of the early medical works. It does indeed look as if polemic and controversy are frequently expressed in the first person. The first person is also associated with the demonstration of the processes of his enquiry and including remarks about the progress of the work,[88] his polemic, the ex-

---

[87] Cf. ιι 21; and *Art* ch. 6.2 J: ch. 6 p. 169.

[88] For the progress of the work, cf. Hdt. ιν 30.1, on his principle of digression; or νιι 137.3 ('I return to my earlier *logos*', ἐπάνειμι ἐπὶ τὸν πρότερον λόγον); comparable also with similar markings in some medical essays: *Gener./Nat. Child* ch. 20.6 J, ἐλεύσομαι δὲ αὖτις ἐς τὸ ἐπιλειπὲς τοῦ λόγου, 'I will return to the rest of my *logos*'; or *Anc. Med.* ch. 13.1 J (on wishing to return to a previous subject). For false modesty about the length of explanation, Hdt. ιν 36, 'I will show briefly' (ἐν ὀλίγοισι . . . δηλώσω); perhaps cf. *Dis. IV* 56.7, his reasons for adducing so many items of evidence. For the decision to omit what people know, or what has been discussed, cf. Hdt. ιιι 103 on the camel (οὐ συγγράφω . . . τοῦτο φράσω); or νι 55 on Spartan kings (ἐάσομεν αὐτά· τὰ δὲ . . . ποιήσομαι . . .); with *Acut.* ch. 7.1 Joly, the matters worth writing down, he thinks, are ἀκαταμάθητα, 'unknown'.

pression of his opinion, the dogmatic criticism of others.[89] We recall his remarks about the Hyperboreans and the idea of the round world: 'I cannot but laugh when I see many people drawing maps of the world and no one explains sensibly ... I will show briefly the size of each of them [the continents]' (IV 36, above). The quieter but equally dismissive shelving of his opponents at the end of this section, 'But that is enough on this subject (ταῦτα μέν νυν ἐπὶ τοσοῦτον εἰρήσθω); we will use current conventions' (IV 45.5), is closely parallel to the way the author of *On the Nature of Man* turns dismissively from the mistakes of laymen to doctors, 'About these I have said enough' (ch. 2.1 J: Περὶ μὲν οὖν τούτων ἀρκεῖ μοι τὰ εἰρημένα).[90]

We seem to be seeing a style here which belonged to the manner – or discourse – of the early medical writers, particularly those inclining to the rhetorical: a polemical, dogmatic, first-person style. But rigid distinctions are difficult, and the medical works themselves are varied and complex in style. We seem to have several elements here.

Firstly, there is the outspoken polemic, the tone of demonstration, equipped with sometimes irritatingly frequent first-person assertions. That belongs to the more rhetorical of the medical works (*Art*, *Breaths*, and to a lesser extent, *Nature of Man* and *Ancient Medicine*), and we seem to see traces of it in Herodotus' own more outspoken criticism of certain controversies. Surely Herodotus was here slipping deliberately into the language of proof and demonstration of the more spirited kind, the style that could be associated with the more rhetorical performances of doctors, sophists, and perhaps others – though our evidence is simply fullest for the more rhetorical end of the spectrum in the medical sphere. This was the style with which to capture your audience, present spectacularly opinionated views, challenge all previous opinions. It was both self-promoting, and a style suitable for a rhetorical performance. There is an element of this in Herodotus, and if we may be hesitant of seeing the extremes of, say, the style of *The Art*, we need to bear in mind at least that the first person is ubiquitous in oratory from the earliest stages and often paired with statements that the speaker has demonstrated or will demon-

---

[89] Dewald hints (1987, 156–7) that eyewitness first persons often introduce argument and controversy; also Marincola (1987: n. 69 above); Lateiner (1989), 92 (polemic and superiority). Cf. also (from many examples) II 15.1, where polemical argument is couched in the first-person plural; II 20 (... οὐκ ἀξιῶ).

[90] Note also the close similarity between some of Herodotus' concluding 'formulae' and those found in early medical works: e.g. Hdt. IV 31.2 (ταῦτα μέν νυν τὰ λέγεται μακρότατα εἴρηται) and *Nat.Child* ch. 13.4 J (καὶ ταῦτα μὲν ἐς τοῦτό μοι εἴρηται); or Hdt. IV 82 (... ἀναβήσομαι δὲ ἐς τὸν κατ' ἀρχὰς ἦια λέξων λόγον) and *Gen.* ch. 11 (end: ἀναβήσομαι ...); cf. comments in Joly (1977), 146–7.

strate a matter: to be found in Antiphon's speeches,[91] the speeches in Thucycides, throughout Gorgias' works.[92] Herodotus' expressions of ridicule, 'I laugh', 'I am astonished' are tricks of rhetoric to be found in the speeches of Thucydides.[93]

Secondly, however, the first-person remarks expressing 'tolerance' or distancing from a piece of information, which are relatively common in Herodotus, are virtually invisible in any of the *physiologoi* or medical essays. The tenor of such remarks is not entirely clear, and I would prefer to call them indications of 'suspended disbelief': for instance the opening mythical tales of retribution, with which the *Histories* start, are wrapped up with, 'I cannot say whether these events may have happened like this or otherwise, but I do know (οἶδα) who was the first to inflict injustice upon the Greeks, and having shown this, I will continue further into my account ...' (προβήσομαι) (I 5.3). This emphasizes by contrast the reliability of what is to come. A sign of uncertainty is overlaid with an assertion of knowledge; or else Herodotus expresses suspended disbelief or indifference – 'this I do not believe, but others may', or 'I do not disbelieve or entirely believe ... the story of the underground chamber, but I do think that many years earlier, Salmoxis lived long before Pythagoras' (IV 96.1). Such suspensions of judgement would accord well with Dewald's suggestions.[94] They imply judiciousness and enhance the truth of the rest of his narrative. In contrast the early medical writers very rarely suspend judgement. One rare example of this actually involves a story about the Amazons' treatment of their children, and contrasts the tale with the medical knowledge of which the author is sure. 'If this is true, I do not know (ἐγὼ μὲν οὐκ οἶδα); but I do know that the following would happen if you dislocate the limbs ...', and this he then describes (*On Joints*. ch. 53, IV 232.7–13 L). It is tempting to suggest not only that Herodotus uses this

---

[91] In Antiphon, for instance, we find: 'But first I will demonstrate to you' (πρῶτον μὲν οὖν ἀποδείξω ὑμῖν) (VI 15); or 'so that you understand even better, I will say more and will demonstrate to you (τούτου ἕνεκα πλείω λέξω, καὶ ἀποδείξω ὑμῖν) (VI 33); or Δέομαι δ' ὑμῶν, ὦ ἄνδρες, ἐὰν ἀποδείξω ... (I 3, 'Gentlemen, I have one request. If I can prove [that my opponent's mother murdered our father] ...').

[92] E.g. *Palam*. ch. 5, ἐπιδείξω; cf. also Plato's imitation of Hippias, in DK 86, section C for simple first person; and indeed the "Old Oligarch" of Ps.-Xenophon. On Gorgias and Herodotus, note also Pellicia (1992), comparing *other* stylistic devices, and n. 95 below.

[93] E.g. Cleon, Thuc. III 38.1, 'I am amazed' (θαυμάζω ...). Cf. Immerwahr (1966), 65 where γελῶ and θωμάζω of IV 36.2 and 42.1 are picked out as indicating 'proemial statements' which 'recall the proem of Hecataeus' *Genealogies*'.

[94] Suspended disbelief: e.g. 'others may believe this, but I don't': IV 42.4, ἐμοὶ ... οὐ πιστά, ἀλλῷ δέ τεῳ (sun to the right); cf. V 86.2; V 9.3; IV 105.2; VI 82.1 ('I cannot exactly say whether he spoke the truth ... but he certainly said this'). Thucydides does the same, interestingly, for his account of the plague (II 48.3): 'Let each person, doctor or layman, give their own account of how it arose ... but I will describe its nature ... etc'.

distancing device to include tales he does not necessarily believe, but feels he should include; but that in doing so, in contrast to his other expressions of utter certainty, he is signalling that these tales concerning the past are sometimes beyond certainty, are not accessible to full knowledge, and that these are made to contrast with the rest of his narrative, his arguments and theories. Unlike the theories for which he or medical writers can claim 'correctness', these tales mostly about the past are not susceptible to clear knowledge.[95]

Finally, what is particularly interesting for our purposes about the early medical treatises is that they function within a technical or semi-technical subject: the persuasive style is not a characteristic solely of the more obviously epideictic *Art*, or *Breaths*. In addition, they are trying to convey medical, philosophical or scientific theories, they try to convince their audience of their value, and use the rhetorical or epideictic style for this. Thus in the work *On the Sacred Disease*, which is argumentative but not particularly 'sophistic' in its rhetorical style, the author is always present, his opinion constantly being signalled by such phrases as μοι δοκεῖ, ἔμοιγε δοκέουσιν, ἐγὼ δὲ δοκέω;[96] the first chapter is absolutely full of first persons in a way particularly reminiscent – if we can look beyond the subject-matter – of Herodotus: 'This is about the disease called the sacred; I do not think it is any more divine than any other diseases ... I will show (ὡς ἐγὼ ἀποδείξω) that other diseases are no less wonderful ... I see men who are mad and delirious from no obvious cause ... while in their sleep, as I know, many groan and shriek' (ch. 1 passim).[97] The work *On Generation/ Nature of the Child/Diseases IV* is also replete with first-person opinion,[98] so is *Regimen in Acute Diseases*.[99] So the first-person style is not connected merely with an openly rhetorical style for the law-courts, and is

---

[95] Note the comparison by Pellicia (1992) of Herodotus' preface and Gorgias' *Helen*, focusing on the formal 'false start recusatio'. I prefer to see a wider intellectual milieu here, one including the pursuit of knowledge, and more connection with speculation about the possibility of true knowledge. See Lateiner (1989), 38 with n. 74, 40–3, on the preface as a parody, surely rightly.

[96] E.g. opening words of ch. 2 (2.1 Jones: ἐμοὶ δὲ δοκέουσιν οἱ πρῶτοι), ch. 3 (3.1 J), ch. 5 (5.1 J).

[97] Jones' translation in fact tones down this directness. Cf. also ch. 20.1 J (second word), φημί; ch. 19.1 J (*nomizo*).

[98] E.g. *Gen.* 3.1, 4.1 and 10.1 ('I say'); *Dis. IV* 33.1 (ἐθέλω δὲ ἀποφῆναι ...); *Nat. Child* ch. 13 for the first-person narrative (see ch. 6 n. 95 above).

[99] Cf. *Regimen in Acute Diseases* ch. 23.2 Joly, 'these are the best [evacuants] I know' (κράτιστα δὲ ταῦτα ὧν ἐγὼ οἶδα ἐστίν); or ch. 25.1 Joly, 'I recommend the same rule' (ὡὑτὸς δέ μοι λόγος ἐστίν); ch. 59.2 Joly, 'This is the only bad effect of oxymel I know.' Cf. the frequent certainty in (e.g.) *Epidemics I* where one often meets declarations of personal knowledge: 'I know of not a single case ... which proved fatal when proper bleeding occurred' (ch. 14, l. 14), 'I know of no woman who died if ...' (ch. 16, l. 12); 'all I know recovered if ...' (ch. 20, l. 29–30).

associated with the quest for some sort of knowledge, an engagement in 'scientific' enquiry. Herodotus' polemical argumentation seems to lie closer to that of, say, *Sacred Disease*, or even *On the Art, Nature of Man*: and there the first person gives the authority of personal knowledge, stresses the remarkable originality of the author, and also seems to be a fundamental element of the liveliness of the atmosphere of debate for which those works were originally produced, the style of engagement and controversy. It seems to be this element too that imports to Herodotus much of his liveliness of style in his interaction with his audience. The language of proof, the claims to have demonstrated that such and such is the case, the claims for the display of the truth, the language of correctness, all lie alongside this first-person dogmatism. The first person was above all in this period, perhaps, the mark of persuasion and performance.

We have been looking at the language and expression of display and demonstration, the claims to correctness and truth, the confident, rather egocentric expressions in the first person, and trying to set them within – or see them against – a historical and intellectual context. In all these three areas we find significant similarities between Herodotus' style, and that visible in certain of the later natural philosophers and most particularly the more rhetorical of the early medical essays. His narrative style is rather different – with the important exception of the speeches. This demonstrative, even pugnacious, style is the style he enters when he is being polemical and controversial, and it begs us to take more notice of the extent of controversy in the *Histories*. His language of proof, and his use of inductive proof, which we discussed in the previous chapter, was also couched in the first person, and it will have been noticed that all these features which I separated for clarity, often occur together. They also tend to be concentrated in the first five books, particularly in discussions concerning ethnography, geography, customs, or controversies of various kinds, whether of Greekness or the shape of the world, or any other of the many topics on which Herodotus takes issue with his contemporaries. Our usual comparison with Thucydides can mislead, for there was no 'norm' for this kind of enquiry when Herodotus wrote, and Thucydides may have deliberately avoided certain of Herodotus' characteristics, or characteristics of the milieu he belonged to. Nor is the analogy with the storyteller, the teller of folk-tales, entirely helpful. What is suggested is that these particular features in Herodotus belong most plausibly to the lively style of performance and debate which shared common features with the emerging art of persuasion and, more certainly, shared features with the lectures and performances on serious subjects offered by practitioners of certain of the developing *technai*, most particularly those which discussed nature and the nature of man. That is, when his audience listened to (or read?) his attack on certain theories about Egypt or the Hyperboreans, or heard him giving his personal opinions and demonstrations of such and such a correct view, they would recognize the methods and style of other contemporary lectures and performances on subjects which ranged widely from medical knowledge to discussions of Homer. If elements of persuasion and display, even a few tricks of rhetoric, are to be discerned in the *Histories*, then we need to be particularly wary of reading Herodotus literally, or seeking to find in the *Histories* the anachronistic features of later historiography.

The following chapter will accordingly look more closely at our wider evidence for the display performance and the *epideixis*, the display piece.

8   Performance, competitive display and *apodeixis*

We have seen that separate areas of study were not necessarily clearly mapped out in this period, and that *historie* was a term which applied generally to enquiries pertaining to the pursuit of natural philosophy, the enquiry into nature and into the nature of man in an extended sense (chapter 5). There were strong hints that Herodotus' enquiries made him a *sophos*. We should also consider that the genres of prose writing were beginning to be differentiated in the late fifth century, and that the 'rhetoric' of genre might be used to differentiate one man's work from others', to set his work apart, even, or perhaps especially, when the methods were not so very different. In this chapter we try to draw out some further implications of the arguments of chapter 7. Again we find ourselves dealing with a set of features and a type of persuasive activity which were later to become crystallized into a firm and very specific genre but which at this point seem to leave considerable blurring around the edges.

Our most expressive evidence for persuasion and the persuasive performance in a non-political context in the fifth and early fourth century appears in the medical corpus. The spectacle of a doctor standing up before a fifth-century assembly and attempting to persuade the citizen body of his skill may be surprising. Yet it is clear that not even doctors were exempt from the overwhelming presence of oral performance and persuasion in the latter part of the fifth century and early fourth, not to mention beyond. Indeed the very image of doctors attempting to persuade the demos to take them on alerts one to the ubiquity of oral performance and the needs for persuasion in Greek culture of the period. In one of Xenophon's Socratic anecdotes, Socrates produces a parody of such a doctor's speech delivered to the assembly to urge them to take him on as public doctor: 'I have never yet studied medicine', the speech begins, 'but do give me the job of doctor; for I'll learn by experimenting on you'.[1] Though Socrates' point was the need for training, he could express it by

---

[1] *Mem.* IV 2.5: Παρ' οὐδενὸς μὲν πώποτε, ... τὴν ἰατρικὴν τέχνην ἔμαθον ... ὅμως δέ μοι τὸ ἰατρικὸν ἔργον δότε· πειράσομαι γὰρ ἐν ὑμῖν ἀποκινδυνεύων μανθάνειν.

parodying what we hope was an unsuccessful application; everyone laughed.[2] In such a system doctors might well have to give lectures to lay audiences, as Lloyd and Jouanna have stressed so effectively.[3] We may be reminded of Plato's criticism of the Athenians for being both spectators and judges of so much in Athens (*Republic* 492b5–c8), or Cleon's sarcastic criticism of the Athenian assembly for being 'spectators of words' (Thuc. III 38.4). Addressing a mass assembly needed a range of skills somewhat different from those needed to persuade an individual patient to accept your version of treatment. Nevertheless, 'persuasion' in the rhetorical sense is mentioned even for individual patients and Plato's Gorgias, whose brother was a doctor, mentioned caustically that he (Gorgias) was better able to persuade the sick patient to take the treatment than the more technically skilled doctor himself: even the doctor, he insisted, needed the arts of persuasion (*Gorg.* 456b).[4]

Persuasion, then, but in what form? We mentioned the display performance and the 'apodeixis', in the last chapter. Let us focus more precisely upon the *epideixis* which is the more usual term for the 'display piece', but which seems to merge occasionally with the *apodeixis*; and upon an area of the oral performance, the *antilogiai*, or semi-formal debates, where the antagonistic patterning of *epideixeis* is to be found. It is surprisingly difficult to discern what the *epideixis* was actually like, for it seems in this period, as Demont shows,[5] to be by no means confined to the rhetorical display piece it came to describe later, and more often we seem to find the display piece in an interstitial position between the presentation of formal demonstration and the rhetorical display of skill in words. That is, it sometimes seems to denote 'display', sometimes a 'display piece' in the sense of a definite genre, and quite often something in-between (there is a similar situation with *apodeixis*).

The *epideixis* or display piece is most often associated with the sophists,

---

[2] For earliest mention of a state doctor see Arist. *Acharnians*, 1030–2; we hear of earlier doctors being taken on by a city – Herodotus' Democedes, and Coln-Haft (1956) puts their origin in the archaic period. For public doctors, see further *Gorg.* 455b, 514d–e; Plat. *Polit.* 259a. For education of doctors, *Meno* 90c–d, *Protag.* 311b2–c2.

[3] G. E. R. Lloyd (1979), and (1987); also Jouanna (1992), 109–59, and Jouanna's Budé edition of *Art* and *Breaths* (1988). The range of this evidence (below) indicates that Johnson's useful article (1994) is too rigid in its view that attested performances are confined to sophists and (therefore) to large scale public self-promotion. For other experts, *Protag.* 319b–c.

[4] As he puts it, the power of persuasion might be useful for meteorology, assemblies, and philosophy (in that order) (*Helen* 13). The difficulties of understanding the early development of rhetoric are notorious: see Kennedy (1963), (1994); Cole (1991), for an idiosyncratic view, with review by Schenkeveld (1992b). I concentrate here upon the *epideixis* in the wider sense and on the context of performance rather than the technicalities of rhetorical theory (ancient testimony for *epideixis* has little to say about the oral/written issue).

[5] Demont (1993); cf. Pernot (1993), vol. I, 25–8.

and perhaps in particular with the firework display of a rhetorical mock-
defence such as Gorgias' *Helen* or *Palamedes*.[6] That does not really do
justice to the breadth or the variety of what seem to count as 'display
pieces' in the late fifth century or later, and certain of the earlier medical
texts disrupt the usual neat categorization here, as so often. The epideictic
or display element of early medical texts is now more readily accommodated by historians of medicine in the current picture of the early development of medicine as a science.[7] *On Breaths* and *On the Art* are both
highly sophistic pieces which fit easily into what we might envisage as the
style of the sophistic display piece. While earlier scholarship tended to
ignore them on the grounds that they were merely sophistic pieces, it no
longer seems so clear that they are therefore works by 'sophists' pertaining to medicine, and nothing to do with medical circles in any real sense,
rather than epideictic pieces by doctors. The more rhetorical elements of
some of these early essays might well show that they are display pieces by
men who considered they had mastered the medical craft. But in any case,
they offer us valuable evidence for this kind of epideictic and persuasive
style which is remarkably lacking for those conventionally named sophists
– and it has even been suggested that they should be more widely used to
understand rhetorical style of the time.[8] We have of course encountered
some of these epideictic elements – the excessive emphasis on proving,
displaying, or demonstrating, the theories of the author; the first-person
presence; the elements of style which seem appropriate to oratory; the
appeal to an audience. We also saw that it may be possible to distinguish
degrees of performance, from the rhetorical, highly demonstrative epideictic speech for a lay audience, to the didactic lecture to specialists (see
n. 8). *On the Art* and *Breaths* lie at the extreme end of the spectrum.

  But we do not need to rely on stylistic interpretations alone. For some
of these essays refer to themselves or others as '*epideixeis*' and also to
competitive or antithetical 'debates' which take place on the subject of the
nature of man. The essay *On the Art*, for instance, mentions *epideixeis* of
medical knowledge, that is, display performances which involved knowl-

---

[6] As e.g. Dodds' note on *Gorgias* 447a5 – 'the term ἐπίδειξις seems to have been introduced
by the sophists (cf. *Hipp. Mai.* 282 bc) to describe a public demonstration of oratorical
skill'; Thucydides seems to share the view – III 42.3, where *epideixis* is used in an un-
complimentary manner (*contra*, Cole 1991, 89). See however, Demont (1993), persuasive
against seeing the *epideixis* only in terms of the later rhetorical category, the *genos epi-
deiktikon* (below).

[7] See Jouanna (1984b), esp. for *Anc. Med.*, *Breaths* and *Art*; and his comm. on *Breaths* and
Art (1988); cf. also *Diseases I*, chs. 1–10: against sophistic composition, see Wittern (1974).
Demont (1993), as above (n. 5).

[8] Jouanna (1984b). It should be added that Alcidamas' *On Those Who Write Written
Speeches* shares many of the same features.

edge of the *techne*, the medical art. The author seems to call his piece an *apodeixis* (ch. 3.1 J: 'But as for medicine ... I will make a demonstration of this' – περὶ δὲ ἰητρικῆς ταύτης οὖν τὴν ἀπόδειξιν ποιήσομαι): it is the *apodeixis* of a particular theory, but it seems, like the English 'display' and *epideixis*, to be shading off into 'demonstration piece'. He also refers in the opening sentence and very last chapter to other *epideixeis* by people who understand the art, including those with whom he disagrees[9] – clear evidence for 'displays' by those who saw themselves as experts in the medical art. Other Hippocratic essays refer to 'demonstrations'.[10]

We also encounter the fascinating spectacle of competitive debates between men who appear to be presenting mutually incompatible theories about the nature of man. At the beginning of *On the Nature of Man*, the author emphatically criticizes the debates or *antilogiai* (ἀντιλέγουσι ... ἀντιλέγοντες) in which different speakers all propound quite different theories, with one speaker winning one time, another with a quite incompatible theory winning the next time – all showing, our speaker declares, how it is merely the glibbest tongue (ἡ γλῶσσα ἐπιρρυεῖσα) which wins (ch. 1.3–4 J: partially quoted in chapter 7, p. 240). These are the objectionable imposters we met earlier, not apparently doctors (he implies, ch. 2.1 J), but different speakers discussing what man is made of, and our indignant author mentions a range of monistic doctrines that they expound. At any rate the charge is that they are able to persuade and therefore win the contest once, but their grasp of facts and evidence is so insecure, their theories so insecurely grounded, that they cannot manage to persuade a second time. This is reminiscent of the criticism Cleon makes of his Athenian audience in Thucydides, that they love listening to political speeches as if they were merely rhetorical contests of the sophists rather than matters to deliberate upon (III 38.7; cf. 38.4[11]). A similar image of verbal contests (*antilogiai* and contests of words, ἀγῶνες λόγων) is envisaged in the more familiar exchange between Protagoras and Socrates in Plato's *Protagoras*, where Socrates tries to ease Protagoras away from his long speech-like answers and from the formal antagonistic

---

[9] *Art* ch. 1, 1 J: ἀλλ' ἱστορίης οἰκείης ἐπίδειξιν ποιεύμενοι, a phrase we return to. Its last chapter refers again to an *epideixis*, but possibly in a play on the usual meaning, talks of *epideixis* through deeds rather than words: after mentioning his own exposition, he adds 'those *epideixeis* of those who know the art, which they demonstrate, more keenly, from deeds than from words' (ἃς ἐκ τῶν ἔργων ἥδιον ἢ ἐκ τῶν λόγων ἐπιδεικνύουσιν) (ch. 13): perhaps distancing himself from *epideixis* by mere words?

[10] *Epideixis* in Hippocratic Corpus: *Art* ch. 1.1 J; ch. 13.1, and the verb also in 13.1 (see n. 9); *Regimen* I 6. 496.8 L; also *Precepts* 9.266.14 L. *Epideiknumi* occurs 11 times: *Art* (above); *Anc. Med.* ch. 2.2 J bis ('I will try to show, saying and demonstrating that the art exists' – ἐγὼ πειρήσομαι ἐπιδεῖξαι, λέγων καὶ ἐπιδεικνύων τὴν τέχνην ὅτι ἐστίν); ch. 20.1 J ('I think I have made sufficient exposition'); *Breaths* 5.2 J; 15.1, 2 J. In later works: *Regimen* I 6. 468.5 L; *On Joints* 4. 158.13 L; *Prog.* 2. 134.1 L ('show').

[11] Cf. III 42.3, mention of an *epideixis*, with Hornblower (1987), 100.

exchanges he is used to, towards the short questioning that Socrates prefers and in which, of course, he excels.[12] According to Diogenes Laertius (IX 52), Protagoras was the one who began such contests. Whether or not we should believe this, these verbal contests (*antilogiai*) seem to belong to the same style and genre as those castigated in the Hippocratic essay.

The early Hippocratic essays which have seemed to scholars to verge scandalously on the rhetorical are particularly interesting for our purposes because they bridge nicely, and with plentiful evidence, the gap between the technical or 'scientific' (pertaining to understanding of the natural world), and the persuasive. Here we have a range of essays which span the detailed, quite technical exposition of theories relating to medicine and health (e.g. *Nat. Man*) to the most flamboyant, rhetorical conceit, *On the Art*, which purports to prove that medicine is indeed a *techne* in its own right. Rhetorical techniques seem to have percolated into a milieu which, for all its unscientific failings by modern standards (e.g. neglect of experimentation), was attempting to set itself up as a *techne* or craft/art, and which used the ideas and notions available, whether purely abstract or based on observation, to attempt to understand the workings of the human body and the pursuit of health. If doctors gave display performances, then the role of the display performance seems to have included the transmission of medical, as well as philosophical, ideas, not merely the rhetorical tricks – admittedly, transmitting formulae for legal arguments – of a mock defence of Gorgias' *Helen*.

Obviously, then, the display piece can be associated with the medical world. It may also be associated with wider types of display – it perhaps need not be equated solely with the epideictic sub-genre of rhetoric, as Demont has shown, but is a term of broader extension.[13] The *epideixis* in the fifth century was, in essence, wider, encompassing a display of excellence by words or by deeds, in which the demonstration of excellence or of a *techne*, was at the forefront. A wider element of visual 'display' is often present, which serves to emphasize the main point about the crucial importance of display of other kinds. The essay *On Joints* goes so far, notoriously, as to describe certain exuberant types of bandages which were to impress rather than to effect medical cure,[14] and medicine was to retain a dramatic, demonstrative element, a display for an audience, for

---

[12] *Protag.* 334–5, esp. 335a4 ff.: 'I've had verbal contests (εἰς ἀγῶνα λόγων ἀφικόμην) with a great many people, and if I had done what you tell me to do, and spoken according to the instructions of my antagonist (ὡς ὁ ἀντιλέγων ἐκέλευέν με διαλέγεσθαι), I should never have got the better of anyone, nor would the name of Protagoras have become known in Greece.' Cf. also 336b–d. Kerferd (1981a), 28–34, discusses sophistic performance.

[13] Demont (1993), for fullest recent discussion, including audience, specialism etc., though occasionally he seems over rigid in his separation of 'specialists' and 'laymen'.

[14] Ch. 35: 4.158–60 L; Demont (1993), 188; cf. G. E. R. Lloyd (1979), 89–93 for similar attractions.

centuries. Galen had strong and restrictive views about who should be allowed to give 'displays' in public areas.[15] The low reputation of the *epideixis* may be either a later development or (in part) a product of Plato's and Socrates' own scorn for at least some of the sophists who delivered them.[16]

The *epideixis* also encompassed written texts as well as oral performances, for the same piece might well have a written version, yet also be presented from memory several times, as Hippias or Prodicus did.[17] Prodicus' story of the choice of Heracles, for instance, was often presented, hence, perhaps, Gorgias' scornful description of his products as 'stale and often repeated', and circulated in a written version,[18] though it cannot necessarily be assumed[19] that this meant Prodicus actually read it out from the text in front of his audience. It seems clear that the display performance might indeed involve both oral performance and written text, the text serving merely as an *aide-mémoire* for the display before an audience. We obviously cannot be sure that the written texts we have exactly replicate the performance of a piece, indeed as Alcidamas points out in his later polemical essay *On Those who Write Written Speeches*, the advantage of being able to improvise around a prepared structure rather than rely on exact memory of a fully prepared text was precisely that the speaker could respond to the interests (or boredom) of his audience. But we should be wary of assuming that a performance had no backing at all in a written text just because it was performed.

What topics, then, do these *epideixeis* deal with? What was their range? The Hippocratic essays are perhaps the clearest, most straightforward evidence for the *epideixis* and the display of specialist knowledge by specialists to lay and specialist audiences. But Plato's dialogues are full of

---

[15] Cf. von Staden (1995) for *epideixis* and display in medicine, esp. anatomy, in Galen's time; note the two-day *agon* in Ephesus in the second century AD, at n. 37, p. 61.

[16] I use 'sophist' here as elsewhere to refer to the individuals conventionally known as Sophists, Protagoras etc., without implying any theory about what they had in common as a group, if group they were (see further, ch. 5). Plato does show respect for some sophists, esp. Protagoras, Prodicus – see Rowe (1984), 151–60, for antidote to standard view.

[17] See Demont (1993); also Cole (1991), esp. 89 (*epideixis* for him is the oral presentation of something prepared beforehand, thus epideictic oratory may originally be 'what *epideixis* is in Xenophon's account of Prodicus: not the showing off of one's talent, but the displaying or revealing (orally) of what was already in existence beforehand' i.e. prememorized or written); ch. 5 for *technai* involving demonstration texts. Guthrie (1971), 41–4 on sophistic displays. O'Sullivan (1996) on written and spoken word in the sophists: he argues that Protagoras and Prodicus (esp. 121–2) were particular devotees of the book and the accuracy of the written word (he does not deal with the *epideixis* itself). The relation of the character of epideixis to 'written' / 'oral style' is not particularly clear.

[18] DK 82 A 24 (Gorgias, in Philostr. *Vit. Soph.* I Proem); for written circulation, DK 84 B 1 (= Σ Ar. *Nub.* 361), B2. Cf. Demont (1993), 186 for other sophistic *epideixeis*.

[19] As does O'Sullivan (1996), 115–27: at 119, 122; contrast Cole (1991), 77.

references to various individuals 'displaying' their knowledge in this way, most of them famous sophists, though we should not, of course, see the sophists as an undifferentiated group.[20] Protagoras is said to have made much money from giving *epideixeis* to people 'of all kinds' – presumably this is a criticism (*Greater Hipp.* 282c7–d5), as did the later Gorgias and Prodicus. At the beginning of the *Euthydemus* in a passage impressively full of the language of display, Euthydemus and Dionysodorus had been 'exhibiting' wisdom and Socrates hoped they would defer the other part of the *epideixis* till later (*Euthyd.* 275a4 ff. – and earlier), one of many ironically critical remarks about such 'displays' on Socrates' part.

For Plato, display performances, *epideixeis*, are like books, they offer a fine display, but cannot answer the simplest question (*Protag.* 329a2–7). Several dialogues refer to the visiting sophist having just given an *epideixis* where the display performance seems at least to have some content worth discussing. That is, they are not treated as merely rhetorical fluff, but the form is frustrating for Socrates for he thinks they seek admiration only and give no opening for dialogue. It may be significant that we tend to hear about these *epideixeis* at the start of a dialogue which then goes on to discuss in more depth or actually to take apart what the *epideixis* has been concerned with. The 'fifty-drachma *epideixis*' of Prodicus mentioned in the *Cratylus* (384b3–6) refers to an exposition which, Socrates declares, would, no doubt, have enlightened him, had he heard it, on 'the truth about correctness of words', though the one-drachma lecture Socrates did hear was less helpful – an early expression of the idea that you get only what you pay for.[21] Prodicus' lecture on Heracles, as mentioned above, was also an *epideixis*.[22] Hippias seems almost to have been a walking *epideixis*, ready at the most inappropriate moments to lauch into an exposition.[23] In the opening of *Hippias Minor*, Hippias has just been giving an *epideixis* to a small group and boring people; he also boasts about giving his prepared *epideixeis* to the assembled Greeks at Olympia (363d2). Nevertheless, Socrates' ironic remarks of respect accompany questions he wants to ask about the content of the *epideixis* – he could not follow all of it, and did not want to ask questions for fear of interrupting the *epideixis* (*Hipp. Min.* 364b6). Socrates' treatment of Hippias' pretentiousness and encyclopaedic knowledge is getting at the fact that these

---

[20] As O'Sullivan, for example, has recently pointed out (1996).

[21] Also *Greater Hipp.* 282c4–5 on the way Prodicus has been giving *epideixeis* for young men as well as pursuing his diplomatic activities.

[22] Demont (1993), 195. Cf. O'Sullivan (1996), esp. 121–3 on Prodicus. Xen. *Mem.* 2.1.21 describes Prodicus' *Choice of Heracles* as an *epideixis* (πλείστοις ἐπιδείκνυται).

[23] E.g. *Protag.* 347a6–b2, Hippias offering to deliver an *epideixis*, mildly rebuked by Alcibiades.They were clearly excessively egocentric too: imitation in Plato, DK 86, sect. c, has numerous first persons.

performances are both prepared in advance and not open to interruption or questioning – moreover, Hippias has not even begun to think about what he is discussing. It is the impossibility of interaction and discussion which seems here to be the essence of Socrates' suspicion; a similar criticism to that of relying on a written text. A similar point emerges in Socrates' interchange with Protagoras, who stresses Protagoras' ability to answer questions, unlike so many others, and the desirability of combining both speaking at length (*makrologia*) and briefer question and answer (*brachylogia*) (*Protag*. 329b1–5, 334e4–335c).[24]

What emerges, however, in most of these cases is that the content of the *epideixis*, however ironically Socrates regards the form they take, deserves discussion or refutation. It may be the peculiarity of Gorgias – at least as presented by Plato – that his display pieces seem to be treated as if devoid of serious content – significant perhaps of his presentation as rhetorician rather than sophist: in the *Gorgias*, Gorgias is said to have been 'exhibiting various fine things', but when Chairephon suggests he give another exhibition (ὥστε ἐπιδείξεται ἡμῖν, 447b2), Socrates asks somewhat shortly whether he will answer our questions: 'he may, as you suggest, defer his general demonstration (*epideixis*) to some other time' (447c3–4). They are still trying to work out the initial question of what, precisely, is Gorgias' art, or *techne*, indeed whether it bears any relation to knowledge and *logos*, as essential for a *techne*, or merely aims at pleasure (cf. 500e–501b). Socrates suggests curtly that Gorgias 'should make an exhibition (*epideixis*) of the shorter method now, the longer one at some other time' (449c4: καὶ μοι ἐπίδειξιν αὐτοῦ τούτου ποίησαι, τῆς βραχυλογίας, μακρολογίας δὲ εἰς αὖθις). The pomposity and formality of the genre arouse most irritation, according to Plato,[25] but things are worse still if you cannot even define the area of knowledge concerned.

Under the general umbrella of 'persuasion', then, we see more specifically the wide range of activities, contexts and applications of certain persuasive techniques current in the latter part of the fifth century: from

---

[24] Cf. O'Sullivan's remarks (1996), 124; though cf. his suggestion (n. 28), that Protagoras rejects Socrates' claims (334e–335a) that Protagoras can speak at length on any subject. Protagoras' Περὶ τῆς ἐν ἀρχῇ καταστάσεως could have been a public lecture, as suggested by Nestle: Guthrie (1971), 63 n. 3. Protagoras' speech in *Protag*. 320c–328d2, is presumably an *epideixis*, since it is described at the start (320c3–4: Protagoras asks, μῦθον λέγων ἐπιδείξω ἢ λόγῳ διεξελθών; – and chooses the first) and end (328d2–3) with the verb *epideiknumi*. Socrates even uses *epideixis* of his own offer 'to exhibit (ἐπίδειξιν ποιήσωμαι) if you like, the method I have followed on the second best mode of enquiring into the cause/ causation' (*Phaedo* 99d2; cf. also, Eupolis fr. 395 K–A, Plato, *Apol*. 22a7, *Theaet*. 158c3) Here *epideixis* shades into wider expression of proof/demonstration.

[25] Cf. Xen. *Mem*. II 1.34: Socrates not wanting to keep to the pompous style of the *epideixis*; *Soph*. 217e2: something the stranger wants to avoid is a 'long soliloquy or address, like an *epideixis*' (οἷον ἐπίδειξιν ποιούμενον).

Prodicus' *epideixeis*, to *epideixeis* on technical subjects (from medicine to characters in Homer) to lay audiences, performances by medical specialists, lectures by Protagoras, mock speeches, and semi-formal debates or *antilogiai*, all of which involved oral performance, some degree of rhetorical skill as well as some technical or philosophical knowledge. We may recollect the sub-categories suggested by Jouanna (1984), from the display *epideixis* to didactic lectures. The *epideixeis* are at the rhetorical and most persuasive end of this spectrum, demonstrative, opinionated, and directed towards a live audience. It is also clear that sophists sometimes told 'myths' or stories to back up their points (as discussed in chapter 6, Introduction), so an *epideixis* might also, presumably, consist of a narrative myth – not only Prodicus', but Protagoras' long speech containing the 'myth', in Plato's dialogue of that name, is introduced and concluded in terms which suggest it was regarded as an *epideixis* (see n. 24). It is also worth noting that even in the hostile Platonic evidence, these display pieces are not always inextricably connected with money: often a sophist is portrayed as using the language of *epideixis*, or has apparently just given one (Protagoras, just mentioned), in a context where the audience has no intention of passing over payment. Let us return to Herodotus.

Herodotus' delivery of 'lectures' is well known, if sometimes doubted. Though the precise testimony that he gave lectures tends to become fuller in later authors, it would be implausible to think that Herodotus, of all writers in this period, did not give public lectures or oral performances of some kind.[26] It is significant that later writers could simply assume he delivered lectures; and after all, even Prodicus, so clearly associated with books, gave many displays, too many for his critics. But modern scholars have been reticent about quite how they envisage these performances.[27]

---

[26] Cf. Lucian, *Herod.* I (who fancies that Herodotus had the idea, copied by sophists); with Momigliano (1978) on historians and their audiences. Cf. also Evans (1991), 89–90; cf. Lattimore (1958), 9–21 for a theory about his method of composing. Johnson (1994) underestimates the extent of evidence for performance (and for serious ideas): for possible compatibility with some written version, see also next note.

[27] I agree entirely with Johnson (1994) that scholars tend to accept Herodotus' lectures without scrutinizing the exact implications. Any idea that the written text exactly replicates a performance neglects what we know about the fluidity and immediacy of performance. Johnson notes (n. 44) that the relation of performance and written text must be fluid: he therefore argues against exact identity, and therefore against the current 'orthodoxy' that Herodotus gave lectures. However, he draws over rigid boundaries between 'historians' and others, sophists and others, and what is appropriate to each genre, and assumes that Herodotus' use of *grapho* (e.g.) means he was not giving performances. See Alcidamas, *On Those Who Write Written Speeches*, for the most articulate, if polemical, near contemporary discussion of the relation of performance and written texts, memorized or not; and Thomas (1992), Kullmann and Althoff (1993), Worthington (1996); cf. Bakker (1997) on Homer.

The world of the *epideixis* in its wider (and earlier?) sense may help give substance to the picture of Herodotean performance, and help interpret some elements of his style. We have been looking at some of the characteristics of Herodotus' polemical style, his penchant for criticizing others and the manner in which he goes about it: in particular his liking of the language of demonstration and proof, a demonstration in particular which in other contexts would be seen as the epitome of the epideictic style, his language of truth or more precisely 'correctness', the energetic and striking presence of his authorial views expressed in the first person. It is noticeable that these features tend to occur together in clusters, along with the claims to have proofs that we looked at in chapter 6. His claims to be able to prove his point also occurred in the first person (chapter 6). They occur overwhelmingly in the geographical and ethnographical descriptions, or at other points of controversy: for some reason it is his geographical and ethnographical enquiries, rather than the sections of narrative where Herodotus seems more likely to slip into this kind of style. These characteristics seem to belong to the polemical style, the discourse, of intellectual debate, often literally debate in public, in the latter part of the fifth century.

I have already suggested elements of rhetorical style and stressed the persuasive nature of Herodotus' language of proof and polemic. But we can perhaps go further and be more precise. To suggest that Herodotus' polemical style has elements of the language of the *epideixis*, or what later became defined as the *epideixis*, the formal display piece, does not necessarily imply that he was offering a sophistic *epideixis* of the Gorgianic kind, as manifestly he was not. Against the range of epideictic activities we have been looking at, which encompass technical and scientific subjects as well as mythical or philosophical, it is not so surprising to find Herodotus using some of the language and methods of presentation that we find in these authors, nor implausible to suggest that he used the same style of delivery, that of the oral presentation. The method was used far more widely and over a wider range of specialisms than it was later; the author of *On the Nature of Man* thought he was giving an *epideixis*. The *epideixis* encompassed far more than the extreme features of Gorgianic rhetoric with its flowery and poetic vocabulary and antithetical style.

In this respect Herodotus might well be on the edge of the specifically medical world of the early Hippocratic writers – as he certainly shows elsewhere some specialist knowledge. However it seems more likely that the close similarities in his polemical style of persuasion to that of essays like *Nat. Man*, are similarities which correspond to a wider intellectual mode, a language of philosophical and intellectual 'discourse', that was more generally current in the intellectual life of this period, especially in the Greek cities on the east coast of the Aegean, and amongst men who originally came from there. Melissos and Diogenes, so far as we can tell, use some of the same language, though also, perhaps, without the panache and rhetorical vigour that we see in, say, *Ancient Medicine* and the more polemical part of the *Histories* (Anaxagoras on the other hand has a far flatter style). Perhaps the state of the fragments forbids one from taking that very far. But it may be tentatively suggested that Herodotus' polemic does have a more rhetorical tinge, one appropriate for oral performance; that we have a glimpse here of the performance lecture, the style and polemical argument of a performance of the kind which was fashionable for the presentation of philosophical debate on *physis*, or on correctness of language, for medical theories, so closely allied with philosophical abstracts, and for the arguments and theories concerned with science, with knowledge and exploration of the nature of the world.

I would suggest, then, that the energetic, polemical first-person style of Herodotus, the language of demonstration and argument, was not simply akin to that of early medicine/science and (to a far lesser degree) some East Greek philosophy, but that it belonged to the style of the live performance of the latter part of the fifth century. In this atmosphere, and the atmosphere evoked by the author of *Nat. Man* (ch. 1), in which there were live debates of contesting and contradictory speakers on the nature of man, the style of the live performance was using the discourse of proof, of *tekmeria* and *marturia*, and the language of early medicine and natural philosophy which sought to prove theories by abstract argument where evidence was lacking.[28] This language was also to become the style of fully developed rhetoric – which was, after all, all about proof, but at this stage it seems to have been acceptable for the presentation of arguments about nature and man which purported to be true, presentation in oral performances with considerable epideictic elements. This helps to explain the immediacy of Herodotus' presence as an author, and how his authorial interventions and claims to truth would be compatible with the sophistication of many of his views, and with that of other writers of the time. It is this style, a style which imparts such vigour and immediacy, that was precisely the style of the oral performance and, as Jouanna has shown, the style of the *epideixis*. It was this style which Thucydides tried to shun, using it only in the speeches, and which became much developed in later rhetoric, in which the presence of the writer/performer/orator is obvious, and in which the speaker rams home the point that he will

---

[28] Demont (1993) makes the interesting suggestion that written *technai* raised the problem that with easier diffusion, anyone might thus become a specialist; hence the need to provide proof.

demonstrate, is demonstrating, and has demonstrated that his view is the correct one. We can be pretty certain that, for different reasons, the flat prose of Pherecydes, Akousilaos or Hecataeus did not share it either.

What exactly does this imply, however, for our understanding of the written text of the *Histories* that we have? In suggesting that Herodotus' demonstrative style was the style characteristic of the oral performance lecture, I would not want to imply that one could slice up the text into sections which were 'oral', that is, repeating the oral presentations that he gave, and sections which were 'written', never delivered as a lecture, meant only for the written page, and for people to read on the page. The rarity of silent reading in any case meant that his written text would probably in the most private of circumstances, have been appreciated from the spoken word as the text was read aloud. The main problem lies in the fact that any oral performance – for prose at least – even if it purports to stick to the words of a written text, will presumably depart from it in some way. We cannot simply divide the text of the *Histories* into possible lectures: we may perhaps presume that his performances might take an episode or section and mould it specially for the particular performance, even if there is a core which remains roughly the same from lecture to lecture. However, there are sections in the *Histories* which would be more suitable for a performance than others; and the language of display and demonstration is more evident, more emphatic in some sections (for example on the Nile; or the habits and customs of the Egyptians). I would prefer to see the written text at these points as replicating elements of the display piece, just as in oratory we see even in the written versions the style of oral persuasion, and in *On the Art* and *Breaths*, the style of the *epideixis*. This implies that there are different modes in the *Histories*, and, since writing by itself does not necessitate a certain style, that the written version is able to repeat and to some extent replicate elements of the oral style of delivery.

The world of the *epideixis* may also help interpret Herodotus' own description of his work in the first sentence as an ἱστορίης ἀπόδεξις. The appearance of *apodexis* in the Proem is usually interpreted from the point of view of archaic and Homeric precedents – toned down translations are offered such as 'a showing forth', or Nagy's 'public display' in the Homeric sense of displaying and perpetuating *kleos*.[29] While there are Homeric echoes in the Proem,[30] it is at least desirable to ask whether Herodotus' opening description of his work might have contemporary

---

[29] Nagy (1987): public display by the *logios* whom he sees in Homeric terms.
[30] See Erbse (1956) on first sentence; Nagy (1987), esp. on *kleos*. Erbse (1992); Pelliccia (1992).

resonances in the mid to late fifth century,[31] and to ask not simply about the root meaning of *apodexis*, but what connotations it might have had to his audience at the time. Lateiner's 'demonstration',[32] or perhaps 'exhibition' or display[33] allow a more contemporary fifth-century nuance.[34] We saw how fond Herodotus is of using the cognate verb *apodeiknumi* to mean 'demonstrate', that is, 'show, prove', with a sense of display, in a manner rather similar to the epideictic language of early science and rhetoric; and that his other uses of *apodeixis* convey the same sense. Modern interpretations of his opening *apodexis* in the light of what the rest of the *Histories* seem to be doing may not always be helpful, and can also be anachronistic.[35] Herodotus is the first attested writer to use the word at all, and the fact that it occurs so prominently in his very first sentence implies deliberate emphasis.

Apodeixis later became the conventional philosophical word for 'proof' or 'demonstration'.[36] Yet while it may not yet have been a fully technical term, Herodotus' use of it in the sense of 'demonstration, proof' would have made sense to at least some of his contemporaries and near contemporaries in the latter part of the fifth century. For *apodeixis* (= proof) appears in Gorgias,[37] Archytas,[38] perhaps Democritus[39] and, rather speciously, in the *Dissoi Logoi*.[40] *Apodeixis* also appears twice in the early

---

[31] Scholars have been unwilling to bring it into connection with other mid or late fifth-century writers. Cf. Drexler (1972), 11–14 on *apodeiknusthai* etc., but without any glance at contemporary usage – stressing Homeric associations; the same problem with Rosén (1993). Pelliccia (1992) on the preface and Gorgias; also Lateiner (1989), 38, 40–3, for a wider sense of its context. See also ch. 7.

[32] E.g. Lateiner (1989), 10, 83–4; briefly, Lateiner (1986), 17.

[33] Marincola (1987), 128: 'The book [II] is an apodexis in the fullest sense, an exhibition to the contemporary audience that superior method has resulted in a significantly fuller and more accurate account'. Marincola's revised Penguin translation (1996): 'displays his enquiry'.

[34] Cf. also Immerwahr (1966), 17, 'the setting forth of his research', with Erbse (1956) on first sentence; cf. 'researches which he publishes' (Rawlinson).

[35] Cf. Lateiner (1989), 18: 'already the noun ἀπόδεξις in the Proem asserts a mediating intelligence'; and pp. 50–1; cf. Lateiner (1986), 10: 'The historian salvages by his construct (ἀπόδεξις) whatever fragment of reality it is that words can transmit'.

[36] Cf. Arist. *Rhet.* I 1.11: 'Since *pistis* is a sort of *apodeixis* (for we most believe when we suppose something to have been demonstrated)'; Kennedy's edn translates *apodeixis* as 'demonstration', here, he believes, denoting more general reasoning, including probable argument (Commentary + translation p. 33). Cf. also *Theaet.* 162e–163c for different forms of demonstration.

[37] DK 82 B 11a (*Palam.*), ch. 29: 'the accuser has given no *apodeixis* (proof) for what he says'.

[38] DK 47, B 4 (*Diatribai*) on geometry: ἀποδείξιας = proof.

[39] Democritus DK 68, B 10b ('by *apodeixis*' implied); B 299 (not genuine in DK).

[40] DK 90, ch. 6, talking of the claim that *sophia* and *arete* cannnot be taught, he mentions 'those who make these claims use these proofs/arguments' (*apodeixis*) (ch. 6.1); and again 6.13 (arguments/demonstrations).

Hippocratic essay *On the Art*, where it seems to denote more broadly
'demonstration' – in the loose sense of informal 'proof':[41]

But about medicine – for this is the subject of this logos – I will make a demonstration of its existence [i.e. the existence of the art] (περὶ δὲ ἰητρικῆς – ἐς ταύτην
γὰρ ὁ λόγος – ταύτης οὖν τὴν ἀπόδειξιν ποιήσομαι.) (*Art* ch. 3.1 J)

And a little later:

In making a demonstration of the existence of the art (ἐν δὲ τῇ τῆς τέχνης ἀπο-
δείξει), I shall at the same time refute the arguments of those who seek to shame it,
on the points where each of them think they have achieved some success. (*Art* ch.
3.3 J)

The whole passage is peppered with the language of demonstration.

On the Art shows most clearly that the claim to present an *apodeixis*
can hover somewhere between the idea of demonstration or proof (logical
proof, proof by argument, inference etc.) and display. The sense of display need not look back only to the Homeric display of deeds in the
pursuit of fame. Both display and demonstration were part of various
important intellectual activities of the later part of the fifth century and
clearly from *On the Art*, part of the rather more flamboyant sophistic
world of the display piece on questions pertaining to various *technai*. This
also hints, crucially, that an *apodeixis* can be very similar to the *epideixis*
(e.g. in *On the Art*), just as we saw (last chapter) that the verbs *apodeiknumi* and *epideiknumi* were sometimes interchangeable; also that like
epideixis, it seems to mean something more special than any type of proof
(cf. *tekmerion*, *ananke*), even if it is not so distinct as to be a separate
genre. Demonstration, proof and display seem to mingle readily here.

This is particularly clear at the beginning of *On the Art*. At the very
beginning the author pitches into his opponents:

There are some who have made an art (*techne*) of vilifying the arts, though they
consider not that they are accomplishing the object I mention, but that they are
making a display of their own enquiry (ἀλλ' ἱστορίης οἰκείης ἐπίδειξιν ποιεύμενοι).[42]

An *histories epideixis* produced by his opponents: 'a display of their own
enquiry' is curiously familiar to any reader of Herodotus, so obviously
reminiscent of Herodotus' famous opening *histories apodexis*. This provides the most vivid suggestion that Herodotus' opening sentence had

---

[41] Also appears in the later *Fleshes*. 8. 596.9 L; *Letters* 9. 392.10 L.
[42] *Art*, ch. 1.1 J: Εἰσίν τινες οἳ τέχνην πεποίηνται τὸ τὰς τέχνας αἰσχροεπεῖν, ὡς μὲν οἴονται
οὐ τοῦτο διαπρησσόμενοι ὃ ἐγὼ λέγω, ἀλλ' ἱστορίης οἰκείης ἐπίδειξιν ποιεύμενοι. See
Jouanna's commentary, pp. 243–4. Jones and Jouanna translate *histories* here as
'knowledge'/'savoir'.

contemporary connotations within the contemporary quest for knowledge. It also implies that the ideas of proof and demonstration might
rapidly imply or shade into display, and then into the display lecture.
Herodotus seems then, in his very first sentence, to be using the fashionable language of the time, language which had precise connotations in a
period where, increasingly, any display of erudition and knowledge could
be made in an oral presentation, an *epideixis*. Here we can enlarge upon
Fowler's cogent and interesting suggestion that it presents Herodotus as a
'sophos' and implies the same combination of experience, learning and
discovery as attributed to Protagoras by Socrates.[43] It is indeed a statement implying wisdom and discovery and couched in terms which are
visibly intellectually significant words – *apodeixis*, and *historie*, which is
particularly associated at this period (chapter 5) with the intellectual enquiries of natural philosophy. Delivering an oral *epideixis* is what Protagoras had done or Hippias – though it is hard to believe Hippias gave
riveting displays – or Gorgias notoriously, who gave the whole genre a
bad name. The author of *Art* uses *epideixis* of his opponents in the opening, *apodeixis* of his own enterprise, then in the last chapter uses *epideixis*
approvingly (see p. 252 with n. 9). Perhaps *apodeixis* and *epideixis* were in
some respects the shadows of each other, and became more and more
opposed as rhetoric developed. Nor would an *apodeixis* in the later fifth
century necessarily preclude oral presentation,[44] especially in a period
when the 'demonstration' and 'proof' of a theory might be presented as
an oral lecture or display piece to a live audience. Herodotus' opening is
not so alien to this world as we might think.

The issue of medical lectures and *apodeixis* recurs in some important
later evidence which I add here because it shows at least that doctors
continued to give lectures to lay audiences. This epigraphic evidence
concerns doctors in the Hellenistic period who are thanked for their lectures to lay audiences. There is an ambiguity, however, for these public
lectures seem to be referred to entirely as giving *apodeixeis*, that is, demonstrations, proofs, of the doctors' skill; the public lectures are themselves
a 'proof' but they are not *apodeixeis* in the sense of 'display pieces', for
which *epideixis* would probably be the usual term by now. One inscription, probably of the second century BC, records two decrees from Pam-
phylian cities in honour of one Asklepiades Muronos of Perge, a doctor,

---

[43] *Protag.* 320b5–c1, with comparison with a fifth-century Theognidean fragment: Fowler
(1996), 86–7.

[44] As has been suggested. Cf. Asheri, *Commentary* on Book I, p. xviii n. 2, 'ἀπόδεξις non
implica oralità', Herodotus is alluding to the written work; also Commentary ad loc. Cf.
Hartog (1988), 276: *apodexis* is part of the world of orality – but it is the orality of epic; it
implies oral publication – Herodotus is a rhapsode, though speaking in his own voice.

who had given many *apodeixeis* of his skill to audiences in the gymnasium.[45] The *apodeixeis* consist of lectures to these audiences, so helpful to the health of the people of Perge, as the inscription charmingly says, and they are accompanied by similar activities singled out by the citizens of the city of Seleuceia, where he had been a doctor. Again 'great *apodeixeis*' of his diligence (*epimeleia*) are praised (lines 26–7), and while this is less obviously connected with public lectures, Wilhelm felt able partially to restore a reference to lectures a little later,[46] for which the honorand received much praise.[47] These provide evidence of public lectures given in the Hellenistic period by doctors to general audiences of laymen. There is clearly an element of display and proof of skill involved in these performances; if the lectures themselves cannot be called *apodeixeis* they remind us of the continuing presence of public performance for technical subjects. Even Galen gave what he calls *epideixeis* on dissection (see n. 15).

There are also hints that Herodotus was well aware of the kind of verbal contest and competing lectures that are vividly castigated by the author of *On the Nature of Man* (ch. 1). He seems familiar with the concept of the *antilogia* or opposed speeches, indeed with the very word itself. He mentions that the Thebans (who medized) hoped for an *antilogie* with King Pausanias after the battle of Plateia (IX 88), and there are several hints at opposite arguments and debates (*antilegein*). For instance in his declaration that he cannot deny the validity of oracles, there are expressions curiously reminiscent of Protagoras' Ἀλήθεια ἢ καταβάλλοντες (*Truth or Refutations*):

---

[45]   καὶ μεταχειριζόμενος τὴν ἰατρικὴν τέχνην ἀ[πο-]
    δείξεις μεγάλας πεποίηται τῆς ἑαυτοῦ ἐνπειρί-
    ας, διά τε τῶν ἐν τῶι γυμνασίωι ἀκροάσεων πολλὰ χρή-
    [σι]μα διατέθειται ἐν αὐταῖς πρὸς ὑγείαν τοῖς πολίται[ς]
    ἀνήκοντα, . . .

Wilhelm, *Neue Beiträge zur griechischen Inschriftenkunde*, IV (1915), 54–5, lines 5–9 = *Mon. Ant.* 23 (1914), no. 48.

[46]   Ibid. (prev. note): lines 34–5. I thank Simon Hornblower for drawing my attention to these inscriptions.

[47]   See Coln-Haft (1956): no.48a + b in his register (Appendix); p. 23 on public lectures; briefly, von Staden (1995), 61. In another inscription from Elatea in Phocis, similar public lectures may have been mentioned: *IG* IX 104 = *SEG* 3.2 (1929) 416 (= Wilhelm *Anz. Ak. Wien* 1924, 130 ff., n. 7), but heavily restored by Wilhelm, including the ref. to ἀκροάσεις – lectures. In a second-century inscription recording an honorary decree for the doctor Onasandros at Halisarna on Cos, the doctor is praised for giving proof (*apodeixis*) over many years of his knowledge of the art, but this is clearly not referring to lectures: *SEG* XLI (1991), no. 680 (*IG* XII 4); transl. with commentary by Jouanna (1992), 524–6. Public lecture at Istros: *Bull.épig.* (*REG* 71, 1958), no. 338, pp. 280–2. Cf. also *SEG* XXXIII 1184.10, an honorary decree from Xanthos for rhetor Themistokles (196 BC) – '*apodeixeis* of rhetorical speeches'. Cf. Marrou (1956), 398–9 n. 16, on ἀπόδειξις διδασκάλων as school examination.

Χρησμοῖσι δὲ οὐκ ἔχω ἀντιλέγειν ὡς οὐκ εἰσὶ ἀληθέες, οὐ βουλόμενος ἐναργέως λέγοντας πειρᾶσθαι καταβάλλειν, ἐς τοιάδε πρήγματα ἐσβλέψας. (VIII 77.1)

I cannot deny (*antilegein*) that there is truth in oracles, not wanting to overturn (*kataballein*) those which express themselves clearly, when I look at the following case.

But we need not see only a Protagorean reference in the *antilogiai*, even though Protagoras is said to have started the practice of opposed/opposing debates.[48] After all, the practice of *antilegein* was wider and reminiscent of more than Protagorean debating; as we have seen, *antilegein* is mentioned in *Nat. Man* (ch. 1),[49] and compare the opening of *On Diseases I*:

He who wishes to ask questions correctly and to answer the questions, and to debate (ἀντιλέγειν) correctly on the subject of healing, must bear in mind the following things. (*Diseases* I ch. 1, VI 140, 1 ff. L)

– here referring to the question and answer sessions encountered earlier in the more hostile environment of the Platonic dialogues, and connected with Protagoras and others.

It may also be relevant here that Herodotus is fond of words of opposition and in some contexts it is hard to see them as reflective merely of an older and simpler sense of balance and opposition.[50] When Herodotus uses the expression ἀντισήκωσις ('compensation, balance') of the Danube evaporation which thus maintains its balance between swelling from melted snow and evaporation from sunshine (IV 50.4: lit. 'by these contrary actions, a compensation occurs' – ἀντιτιθέμενα δὲ ταῦτα ἀντισήκωσις γίνεται), we may be seeing a sense of opposing forces or balances which continues right through the physiological and medical view of the world. The agonistic vision of nature is not confined to the Presocratic philosophers. From many possibilities, we may compare, for instance, the agonistic image of disease as expressed (with verb in *anti-*) in *Prognostic*:[51] of the doctor, 'combating each disease' (πρὸς ἕκαστον νόσημα ἀνταγωνίσασθαι, ch. 1: 2.112. 3 L). Or there is the extraordinary verbal formation perhaps coined to express precisely this kind of counterbalance in *Regimen in Acute Diseases*, which mentions that doctors may think that one violent change should be 'counteracted by another violent change' (μέγα τι κάρτα καὶ ἀντιμεταβάλλειν, ch. 26.2 Joly), where *antimetaballein* is a *hapax*. The 'counter-agonism' of the diseases and treatments is reflected in

---

[48] Nestle sees both Herodotean examples as hints at Protagoras: (1908), 16.
[49] See Jouanna's note, Commentary, p. 235.
[50] Lateiner (1989), 194 (and elsewhere) on importance of balance; also Gould (1989).
[51] On this concept in medicine, see von Staden (1990), 97.

the agonistic context in which the cures and medical theories are presented. We also meet in *On Joints* predictions capable of holding their own in contest – ἀγωνιστικά.[52] Herodotus' more archaic emphasis on *tisis* and balance and retribution, then, is accompanied also by a physiological and scientific sense of balance and counterbalance in the natural world which seems to have remained popular in later (and contemporary) discussions of the nature of the world.

Herodotus mentions opposing arguments in Book VII, where Artabanus opens a speech with the words, 'O king, it is impossible to make choice of the best, if no arguments are uttered in opposition to one another' (μὴ λεχθεισέων μὲν γνωμέων ἀντίεων ἀλλήλῃσι οὐκ ἔστι τὴν ἀμείνω αἱρεόμενον ἑλέσθαι); 'a man is then forced to follow whatever advice he has been given; but if opposing opinions are given ... then one can distinguish (διαγινώσκομεν) the better' (VII 10a 1). This defence of hearing two sides of every argument is strongly reminiscent of the love of opposing arguments of the latter part of the fifth century and of much that went with it. It may be further significant that these arguments are in the mouth of Artabanus whose aim at this point is to defeat Xerxes' interpretation of his dreams with the full force of what are evidently sophistic ideas about dream-interpretation. The idea that Artabanus produces to counter Xerxes' fear, that dreams merely repeat the actions and thoughts of the day-time, is a theory of the late fifth century.[53] Not merely two-way debates either: the constitutional debate (III 80 ff.), a three-cornered debate treating monarchy, oligarchy and democracy, has a form which can be found in other fifth-century debates.[54] An echo of the Protagorean claim to be able to make the weaker argument the stronger may perhaps be visible in Herodotus' description of Themistocles' speech in which he persuades the Greeks to fight: 'His speech throughout contrasted the greater features which occur in human nature and the human condition, with the weaker' (VIII 83.1: τὰ δὲ ἔπεα ἦν πάντα ⟨τὰ⟩ κρέσσω τοῖσι ἥσσοσι ἀντιτιθέμενα, ὅσα δὴ ἐν ἀνθρώπου φύσι καὶ καταστάσι ἐγγίνεται).

Indeed, while Thucydides' speeches are notoriously full of antithesis and oppositional words,[55] so, surprisingly, are Herodotus' *Histories* (e.g. IV 118.2; V 109.2, ἀνταγωνιευμένους, admittedly a military context). More significant, we even glimpse him creating new coinages, such as when he used the remarkable ἀντιγενεηλογεῖν, literally, 'to make a genealogy in

---

[52] *On Joints* ch. 58, 4. 252.15 L; *antimetaballein* is discussed by Jouanna (1980), esp. 310 ff.
[53] *On Regimen* Bk. IV, esp. ch. 88, deals with this idea.
[54] See Demont (1994b) on antilogy.
[55] See Finley (1967), 55–117, esp. 55–88 on antithesis. Aristophanes' *Clouds* has many words in anti-: e.g. for *antilegein/-ia*, 321, 888, 901, 938, 1040, 1173, 1339.

opposition', to describe the Egyptian priests' presentation to Hecataeus of a rival genealogy to beat his mere sixteen generations (II 143.4). There is an exuberance in Herodotus' love for antithesis that may link with his creation of *antilogiai*, or at least with the love of antithesis in this period. He seems to have some familiarity with the world of *antilogiai* in the second half of the fifth century.

It was perhaps this agonistic, display-oriented mode of exchanging and discussing ideas against which Thucydides reacted so energetically when he declared that his work was going to be no mere *agonisma*, no competition piece for the immediate pleasure of the listeners (I 22.4).[56] We do not need to see this as a narrow jab at Herodotus alone, or at the sophistic *epideixis* in its extreme form alone – though if Herodotus also shared this style, the criticism would of course include him too. It should perhaps be understood more widely as a rejection of the agonistic, confrontational and rhetorical mode of intellectual discourse and argument that became popular in the latter part of the fifth century and which Plato also rejected. Perhaps developments during the Peloponnesian War led Thucydides to find this style ever more objectionable, increasing a split perceived between 'rhetoric' and 'truth' that had been less overt before.

The Proem of the *Histories* by this interpretation would present a daring mixture, then, of Homeric reference and hints of the current fashionable language of intellectual activity. Herodotus claims to preserve *kleos*, a claim which has distinct Homeric ancestry and refers also to the evanescence of memory and oral tradition in an oral society. He claims to examine for what cause (δι' ἣν αἰτίην) they went to war with each other, also in an unmistakeable echo of the opening of the *Iliad*,[57] though it may be recalled that natural philosophy also looked for causes. He also emphasizes that his subject includes the great and wonderful deeds of both Greeks and barbarians;[58] and his opening sentence, with its reference to his *histories apodexis*, is couched in the terms of the contemporary language of philosophy and science. This combination is continued in the next chapters which often seem so puzzling (I 1–5), in which he tells myths of women being seized, which supposedly explain the beginning of

---

[56] Thomas (1993); also suggested tentatively by Hornblower, Commentary (1991), 61–2; Boedeker (1995) suggests Thucydides refers to poets like Simonides; Guthrie (1971), 43 took Thucydides to be contrasting himself with the sophists (Johnson (1994) implausibly attempts to separate *agonisma* from the idea of a contest). On the possibility of Thucydides' performances, Hornblower (1991), 60–1, 75; and (1987), 29; and Plut. *De Glor. Ath.* 3. This is not to say, of course, that Thucydides is not competitive and assertive – he is, but in a different way.

[57] For Homeric echoes: Erbse (1992), (1956).

[58] Cf. Hdt. v 97.3 also, on coming evils, for emphasis on Greeks *and* barbarians.

the enmity, only to reject them outright, rejecting along with them much of the mythical and Homeric world. These chapters seem best explained as a parody of the type of history purveyed by Hecataeus and other early prose writers, which focused upon the genealogical and heroic subject matter of Greek myth, and saw the myths and legends as offering sufficient explanation for later events.[59] That these tales are 'a false start' is confirmed further by the style both of the Proem, and of the transition to the serious matter of his enquiry. He moves emphatically to his own account: 'I cannot say whether these events may have happened like this, but I do know who was the first to commit injustice against the Greeks' (I 5.3: ἐγὼ δὲ ...:), and Croesus was the 'first barbarian whom we know' who made some Greeks give him tribute or who made friends with others (I 6.2: οὗτος ὁ Κροῖσος βαρβάρων πρῶτος τῶν ἡμεῖς ἴδμεν ...). In just the same way, as we saw earlier, a later medical writer mentioned the Amazons, only to set them aside for more secure scientific knowledge.[60] A similar distancing occurs in the opening of *Art*, where the author declares (to paraphrase roughly) that some people make an art of vilifying the art; but he thinks (ἐγὼ δὲ ...) that the aim of intelligence is to discover what was unknown before. This seems not to be a wayward ill-structured attempt merely to reach historical time, but a device familiar and more easily recognizable in other writers whom one can readily see as combining persuasive methods and a search for ascertainable knowledge.

The Proem and the opening chapters, seem then, to set out quite deliberately the Homeric precedent and the Homeric and mythical background, only to overlay them with the new language of scientific research and intellectual enquiry – *historie*, *apodexis* and the language of knowledge.[61] The nature of Herodotus' enquiry is thus set out, with a hint of antithesis. This combination of the Homeric and the new is characteristic of the sophists who seem to have seen themselves as the direct successors of Homer, performing at the same festivals as the rhapsodes and even wearing similar purple robes.[62] The combination, then, in Herodotus'

---

[59] Lateiner (1989), 38, 40–3; Fowler (1996), 83; cf. also Pelliccia (1992), making a formal comparison with Gorgias, *Helen*, but also suggesting Herodotus thereby rejects myths about rape and love. Raubitschek (1993) suggests a source for I 1–5 in Phrynichus' *Phoinissai*.

[60] 'If this is true, I do not know. But I do know that the following things would happen if you dislocate the joints of children': *On Joints*. ch. 53 (4. 232. 7–13 L): see chapter 2, pp. 61–2 for comparison with Scythians; chapter 7, p. 245 for first-person distancing.

[61] This is not, however, to deny the clear Homeric echoes, even the form of Homeric structuring, like the catalogues of troops that follow in the rest of the *Histories*.

[62] O'Sullivan (1996), 117, and (1992), 66–7. Richardson (1975) on Homeric professors. O'Sullivan (1996) also cites *Protag*. 316d, Protagoras identifying Homer and Hesiod as sophists who hide the fact. Pelliccia (1992) sees a parallel with Gorgias: I prefer to see the similarity as indicative of wider intellectual patterns of argument.

Histories of identifiably Homeric precedents and influence, and the newer language of contemporary 'enquiry' would seem far from diminishing the importance of either, but to be characteristic precisely of a period in which the poets are giving way as foremost teachers to new generations of experts, pseudo-experts, persuaders, and the prose display piece for oral performance.

9   Epilogue

It is a commonplace that 'history' as a genre was not yet invented when Herodotus was writing, and that his word *historie* denoted something far wider than 'history' in the sense of the rational, critical, study of the past. It is not particularly easy, however, to define or analyse the full implications of this for our interpretation of the *Histories*. In many respects Herodotus was indeed an historian, if we define the historian fairly crudely as someone who makes an enquiry into past events and their causes using critical methods, a variety of sources. But is this all?[1] Obviously the *Histories* encompass far more than this; besides, they also expressly aim to preserve the past (selectively) and celebrate great achievements, following in the tradition of the poets. The expression *historie* is not sufficiently wedded to the study of the past by Herodotus' example for Thucydides to use it. On the contrary, Thucydides talks of his work in terms of 'putting together in writing' (ξυνέγραψε, I 1.1), almost as if he is avoiding the term *historie*, and we should embrace the implications of this. As we have seen (chapter 5), *historie* has indisputable associations and connections with far wider kinds of enquiry: the enquiries of natural philosophy, enquiry into nature and into the nature of man, enquiry into the truth about the world through the kind of methods which would by now be associated with natural philosophy and medicine – that is, a critical relation to predecessors, the use of evidence, argument, theoretical ideas about causations and origins, analysis of the process by which you reached the conclusions. So when Herodotus in the opening line described his work as an *histories apodexis*, he was not appealing to the Muse for truth and knowledge, as Homer did; and his claim says something more than Hecataeus' forthright and critical opening. I have suggested that he was signalling to his audience, present and future, that this was a modern work of *historie* – one might be inclined to translate it as 'science' – using the fashionable and significant language of the time, and overlaying the

---

[1] For an analysis of Herodotus as an historian, see (e.g.): Raaflaub (1987), Meier (1987), Fornara (1971a).

Homeric precedent and expressions with the language of new methods. Hence the ways of shaping the narrative which are clearly Homeric in inspiration which are set alongside passages where he pulls apart the Homeric picture like any later fifth-century sophist. The Homeric image of Helen's presence at Troy, for instance, is comprehensively demolished with the help both of some Egyptian tales and with close argument to show that Helen could not possibly have been at Troy for all that time (II 120). This manner is reminiscent of the sophistic arguments produced for and against Helen and other figures of the heroic age,[2] and it is quite different from the tinkering with the traditional myths to be found in Hecataeus and the playing with heroic genealogies in the other genealogists. Moreover, it is argued through, taking the audience step by step through the stages of deduction.

The self-consciousness, even, at times, ostentation, with which Herodotus stresses his own personal opinion, his enquiries and most important, his methods, are connected, as I have argued. The first-person presence in the text, the expression of personal opinion, the overt disagreement with others, are similar to what we see in the works dealing with medicine, often merging with natural philosophy, and in some (fragmentary) natural philosophers. They are verging towards the more ostentatious style characteristic of the rhetorical end of the spectrum of intellectual activity in the latter half of the fifth century. The language of proof, the very need to cite proofs at all, the arguments and overt presentation of reasons why the audience should believe him, are striking, and they cannot be taken simply as a Herodotean idiosyncrasy, or a sign of his naive enthusiasm.[3] The idea that you have to argue and persuade puts the *Histories* inextricably within the intellectual milieu of the later natural philosophers and medical writers – and as we have seen there are striking connections in style as well as subject matter. In this respect, he is using the intellectual discourse of the latter part of the fifth century, and the *Histories* are themselves partaking of the gradual development of modes of argument, means of expressing why you are right and your opponents are wrong, which were developing in the competitive atmosphere of the latter half of the fifth century.[4]

It is particularly the ethnographical and geographical sections, or the

---

[2] Gorgias' *Helen* and *Palamedes*; cf. Alcidamas, *Odysseus*; and of course Stesichorus long ago suggested that Helen at Troy was a mere phantom.

[3] Cf. Waters (1985), 34: 'It is interesting that the historian does not, as a rule, draw the moral; he leaves the inference to the reader.' A similarity with the poets has been suggested (Thompson 1996, e.g. 65f.) but the style of such competitive manifestations surely belongs elsewhere.

[4] The speeches are also often particularly interesting in this respect and little studied.

sections dealing with questions of customs in more theoretical ways, that show the *Histories* to be part of this milieu. The implications are that Herodotus' narrative history of the Persian Wars in the later books, and his occasional personal comments, are considerably more barbed than sometimes thought, critical, polemical and well aware of alternative damaging versions. It is often, as we have seen, in some of the most involved, controversial questions – involving Hellenism or customs, for instance – that Herodotus used the sustained language of proof and argument, precisely the areas where there is most scope for argument. The heavy guns are directed against those who have mistaken views about Egypt and the division of the world, and those who have extraordinarily ignorant views about Heracles. The self-consciousness with which he parades his own autopsy, the stress he lays on his own enquiries (in pursuit of the ancient Heracles, for instance) are presumably part of the same development of greater awareness of method and evidence. A similar style is visible in the early medical works which also lay enormous emphasis on what has been seen. If some of Herodotus' claims to have seen things, travelled, and observed, seem somewhat too neat for complete comfort, a little too good to be true, it may be that he, like some medical writers, could not quite resist improving upon his researches, and was carried away in stressing the proper nature of their methods precisely because they were at this time new, fashionable, and developing; or that there was all the more demand for this kind of proof because it was part of the necessary intellectual discourse of the time.

As Fowler has suggested plausibly in a comparison with the prose writers who dealt with legend and history, perhaps it was the *problem* of sources that Herodotus discovered.[5] Alternatively, if he is part of an intellectual milieu in which sources, evidence and argument were increasingly being worked out, is it rather, that Herodotus applied the problem of sources to the study of other areas, and to the study of the past amongst them, rather than discovering the whole problem himself?

This is in the Ionian tradition of rational enquiry into the nature of things, the search for causes, and the rejection of an easy divine explanation. But as I hope we have seen, Ionian and East Greek tradition (if we can include those who wrote in Ionic as in the same intellectual tradition) was thriving in the latter part of the fifth century. It was moving into new subject areas, above all, medicine, and spreading beyond Ionian and the East Aegean coast. The vitality of the East Greek intellectual world in the mid and late fifth century may do much to explain the vitality of the *Histories*, and the enormous gap, not to mention the difference in style,

---

[5] Fowler (1996), 86.

between Hecataeus' works and Herodotus'.[6] If we search for an intellectual milieu for the *Histories*, we do not need to confine ourselves to some Ionian writers of fifty years back or more, however interesting they are. Equally, the *Histories* as *historie* could accommodate – indeed, seek out – any topic, all subjects, in a way history could not, from wonders which illustrate the achievements of Greeks and barbarians to wonders which may be part of an understanding of the workings of nature. The voracious nature of the *Histories*, encompassing any knowledge about the human world from India to the Danube and Western Europe to the North African desert and beyond, was accepted, indeed encouraged, by *historie*. As Herodotus says himself, 'my *logos* seeks out additional material' (IV 30.1). A similar breadth, if not quite so extensive a range, is visible in many of the writers of the mid to late fifth century, before 'history' became confined again to the more Homeric subject matter of war. *– Thucy.*

We have seen how Herodotus is often aware of ideas and arguments that one might assume were later than his writing. In particular, we saw how the way he articulates opinions about customs, *nomoi* and describes (or creates) an ethnography, is often close to the more abstracted expressions associated with a few of the major sophists. His reputation as *philobarbaros*, and his openness to barbarian habits and influences seem far removed from at least the popular and official attitudes in Athens of the time. Ethnography also features in medical speculation and research. The very areas of the world which Herodotus chooses to dwell upon at most length are those that have a place in contemporary and later medical ethnography. His ethnography is informed by these wider ideas, which are part of the 'filter' through which he created his accounts. Herodotus seems to be within the milieu of intellectuals who consider the nature of the world – but with a clear preference for the areas of enquiry which bring visible and tangible evidence and experience to bear. His enquiry obviously tends to the human world, the world of human experience and the elements of the visible world that are accessible to human senses, rather than to the totally 'invisible', or to abstract notions favoured by Presocratic cosmologies. So he, like others of the time, employed schemata and a sense of balance in his vision of the world: but it was tempered or sometimes totally destroyed by experience or by information gleaned from others where he could find it (so for instance, his account of Scythia in all its complexity actually breaks down the attractive schematic picture).

Herodotus accepts certain traditional ideas, it is clear, but that does not prevent him from questioning or undermining them at times, and the ac-

---

[6] Given the movement of writers and thinkers, it is not necessary, of course, for Herodotus to be actually living on the Asian coast for much of this time.

ceptance of the traditional view may be held overtly with a hint that he knows of alternatives – for example his affirmation that if the story about the rumour at Mycale is correct, then the gods do indeed intervene in human affairs. His preference for certain divine explanation does not in itself indicate that the rest of the *Histories* must also be highly traditional, and I would prefer to see a far more dynamic relationship between Herodotus and these old or 'traditional' or contemporary views than some scholars see. That there might be a certain disjuncture between 'old' and 'new' at times in Herodotus, is also only what one would expect in a period of rapidly changing styles of knowledge. There is also controversy and polemic within the text which is less openly signalled to the audience but which may have been obvious at the time from the very subject matter, especially in the narrative of events closer to living memory and important in the self-representations of various city-states. Similarly with the Homeric influence: the *Histories* have both Homeric precedents and patterns, but they cannot be interpreted without also a sense that Herodotus – and his generation, *physiologoi* and sophists – were questioning or controverting the world image and agenda set by Homer. The poets celebrated and preserved fame or *kleos*; Herodotus and the prose writers of the late fifth century went considerably further in their different ways. So the opening to the *Histories*, with its series of mythical seizures of various unfortunate women, is either a parody or at least a clever way of starting out on the usual mythical, Homeric and genealogical route, only to set it aside overtly and deliberately, as something that cannot be known.

These characteristics are perfectly illustrated by his theories about the origin of the Greek gods, and I would like to use these for a final case study which will in turn take us to the question of how far Herodotus was really posing, through his enquiries, as a sophist.

The theories about the origins of the Greek gods in Egypt are extraordinarily bold and adventurous: so much so that one is tempted to suggest that in them, as in the whole Egyptian *logos*, he felt he had found the answer to a question of the utmost significance which concerned the earliest nature of mankind and its gods – a similar question about early man as asked by Protagoras, Democritus, Anaxagoras (not to mention Critias), but grounded, he thought, in firm evidence, material monuments, as well as logical argument, and located in another country. Plutarch objected on the grounds that he was using worthless Egyptian stories and undermining all that was best in Greek culture (*de Malig.* 857d–e).

He states early in his Egyptian description that he has a policy about divine matters (*ta theia*), 'I am not keen to describe (or 'expound') those divine accounts which I heard, except only the names (*ounomata*), thinking that all men understand these equally' (II 3.2).[7] He adds that those (i.e. sacred stories?) that he does mention, he mentions because 'forced by my logos' (3.2; cf. II 65.2). 'Names', then, form an exception to his policy of pious religious reticence. And he sets out his ideas about the gods (II 4.2): that the Egyptians were the first to use the 'eponyms' of the Twelve Gods, and that the Greeks took them from them, that the Egyptians were also the first to give altars and images and temples to the gods, and to engrave upon stone the images of animals. It is later that he elaborates and gives reasons. He describes various Egyptian cult practices, in the course of which we learn about the Egyptian Heracles, one of the Twelve Gods, as he discovers in Egypt (II 43–5); Pan and Mendes who are worshipped in a similar way in both Greece and Egypt (II 46.2), and the rites of Dionysus which again are remarkably similar in Egypt to those in Greece (II 48.2–3), and which Herodotus believes were known to Melampous, who must have brought many of these practices to Greek knowledge (II 49). Then we have in summary form what he has been building up to till this point (II 50), supported at greater length later (54–65) amidst further description of Egyptian religious rites:

The names of almost all the gods came from Egypt to Greece. That they came from barbarians, I have discovered in this way; I think they came particularly from Egypt (σχεδὸν δὲ καὶ πάντων τὰ οὐνόματα τῶν θεῶν ἐξ Αἰγύπτου ἐλήλυθε ἐς τὴν Ἑλλάδα. διότι μὲν γὰρ ἐκ τῶν βαρβάρων ἥκει, πυνθανόμενος οὕτω εὑρίσκω ἐόν· δοκέω δ' ὦν μάλιστα ἀπ' Αἰγύπτου ἀπῖχθαι). Apart from Poseidon and the Dioscuri, as I said before, and Hera and Hestia, Themis, the Charites and Nereids, the names (ounomata) of the other gods always existed in Egypt. I say what the Egyptians themselves say. The other gods whose names (οὐνόματα) they say they do not know, I think were named (ὀνομασθῆναι) by the Pelasgians, except for Poseidon; this god they learnt of from the Libyans. No one except the Libyans have used the name (οὔνομα) of Poseidon from the beginning, and they have always honoured this god. The Egyptians do not honour (νομίζουσι) any heroes. (II 50)

This literal translation leaves it clear how frequently Herodotus uses the expression 'the name(s) of the god(s)', where we might be inclined to talk simply of learning about a particular god. He uses as alternatives 'naming a god' and 'learning about a god' from elsewhere: thus, the Pelasgians named all the gods who the Egyptians say they know nothing of, except for Poseidon, of whom they learned from the Libyans. He seems to be using a concept of naming which implies far more than the English

---

[7] II 3.2: τὰ μέν νυν θεῖα τῶν ἀπηγημάτων οἷα ἤκουον, οὐκ εἰμὶ πρόθυμος ἐξηγέεσθαι, ἔξω ἢ τὰ οὐνόματα αὐτῶν μοῦνον, νομίζων πάντας ἀνθρώπους ἴσον περὶ αὐτῶν ἐπίστασθαι.

translation implies. A more fundamental acquisition than simply the proper names seems to be at issue, as is implied by the way Herodotus continues:

Besides these things which I have mentioned, there are many other practices which the Greeks learned from Egypt (ταῦτα μέν νυν καὶ ἄλλα πρὸς τούτοισι, τὰ ἐγὼ φράσω, Ἕλληνες ἀπ᾽ Αἰγυπτίων νενομίκασι·). (II 51.1)

This turns out to involve the Pelasgians as intermediaries (51–2). For they originally gave their gods neither eponym (*eponumie*) nor name (*ounoma*), simply sacrificing to them as '*theoi*', 'for they had not yet heard of them [i.e. the names]' (52.1).

They called them *theoi* because they placed all things in order and assigned each thing to its proper division. Then after a long time they learnt of the names of all the gods, which came from Egypt, but they learned of Dionysus much later. After a while they consulted the oracle at Dodona about the names (*ounomata*) ... whether they should use the names which had come from the barbarians, and the oracle approved. From that time, they sacrificed using the names of the gods. The Greeks received them later from the Pelasgians. (II 52)

Finally, after the Greeks take over the names of the gods from the Pelasgians, Herodotus introduces a further stage, his famous reference to the role of Homer:

Whence each of the gods came, whether they had always existed, what were their forms (*eidea*), these things the Greeks knew nothing of till the other day, so to speak. For Homer and Hesiod, I think, lived only four hundred years before my time, and not more. It was they who constructed a theogony for the Greeks and gave epithets to the gods and apportioned their offices and occupations, and described (lit.: 'showed') their forms (οὗτοι δέ εἰσι οἱ ποιήσαντες θεογονίην Ἕλλησι καὶ τοῖσι θεοῖσι τὰς ἐπωνυμίας δόντες καὶ τιμάς τε καὶ τέχνας διελόντες καὶ εἴδεα αὐτῶν σημήναντες). (II 53)

So, a further stage of development in the work of Homer and Hesiod; the gods are given their eponyms, their honours and *technai* are apportioned, their forms are shown.

This whole theory, then, is tied to Homer and Hesiod, and in setting the achievements of both within the context of his grand theory of Egyptian origin, he thus continues the agenda set by the Homeric poems – and goes somewhat further. The grand sweep of the theory has been remarkably neglected in modern work. He is also seeking the origin of the gods, along with the beginning of human history, and believes he has found it in this country whose depth of human history, it emerges, is greater than most Greeks could possibly contemplate. As he says later in Book II (143–6), the genealogy given by the priests to Hecataeus, and by implication to himself, indicate a chronology for Greek human history which was only about sixteen generations, but Egyptian history purported to go back for 345 generations, and as he claims, the priests point out their rows of statues of earlier priests, each succeeding the other, 'and the line did not go back to either a god or a hero' (II 143.4). Whatever the inaccuracies and misunderstandings which may lie behind Herodotus' own account,[8] Herodotus here uses Egyptian chronology and Egyptian history, which no one could deny was far older than the known history of the Greeks, to give a chronologically differentiated account of when the various gods of the Greek pantheon became known in Greece (note II 145–6 especially).[9] This seems far from the pious protestations of reticence that begin the Egyptian book and which continue at intervals throughout. It is a large exception to his practice, and obviously an important one. He uses first-person argument and presentation, opinionated and highly argumenta-tive, in the style we discussed earlier. Interesting implications also arise from his remarks about the names, and here we return to his intellectual context.

There has been much discussion about what exactly Herodotus could mean by the statement that the Greeks learned of the names of the gods, somewhat at the expense of appreciating the whole theory: could he simply mean that they learned the literal names, the proper nouns, or is something more implied?[10] The internal logic of Herodotus' account indicates that he does mean more than merely the proper names, and that with the 'names' they also acquire knowledge of the personalities: the Pelasgians start with an undifferentiated mass of what they call merely *theoi*: they had not yet heard of the names. When they learnt of the names, it is clear that the naming process must have been accompanied

---

[8] I concentrate on the general results of this argument: for the historicity of the building blocks: see esp. A. Lloyd, Commentary ad loc.; Fehling (1989); West (1991). I take the neat arithmetic (345 generations) as the presentation of someone who is sure their theory is true (and is anxious to persuade others?); and the generation counting itself as a result of the common conflation of successive office-holders with successive generations: for which, see Henige (1974).

[9] His account is buttressed by purporting to be confirmed by the Egyptian priests: there are obviously problems with these priests, their level of expertise and the way they seem to provide very Greek answers, but the solution that Herodotus never went to Egypt, raises more problems than it solves (see A. Lloyd's monumental commentary for the complex-ities of Egyptian society): we do not know what mediators came between Herodotus and any priests, from the many Greeks in Egypt; and critics are excessively literal in their in-terpretation of his account, which is producing a theory rather than a day to day travel-ogue, and which must by definition be interpreting Egypt through Greek eyes: see remarks in Introduction; ch. 2 for examples of theory-led observation; Thomas (1996).

[10] See Lattimore (1939); A. Lloyd, Commentary on II 43, p. 201 ff., esp. 203–5; Diels (1910), 16; Linforth (1926); Linforth (1940); Burkert (1985a), closely focused on the name-problem – who points out the near scholarly silence on the subject; Burkert (1990). Hero-dotus' Greek borrowings from Egypt have been recently publicized by Bernal (1987–91).

with some attribution of personalities and characteristics, the differentiating characteristics. Herodotus is also quite well aware that the gods had Egyptian names as well as Greek. For instance he easily equated Ammon with Zeus (II 42.5: 'For the Egyptians call Zeus "Amoun" (sic)), Demeter with Isis, Dionysus with Osiris (144.2), Pan with Mendes (II 46.4).[11] He cannot be saying that the Greek names ('Dionysus' etc.) themselves came from Egypt. The fact that he occasionally uses 'eponym' instead of *ounomata* (e.g. II 4.2) also indicates that he is thinking of character, attributes and personalities.[12]

We find yet again that one of the more controversial and puzzling passages in Herodotus is in the midst of intellectual debate at the time – and for some time afterwards. The meaning of '*onomata*' was far from being merely a lexicographical issue. Many thinkers of the time, as is well known, were preoccupied with the status of the names of things, whether naming was significant for the character of the object, whether the name indicated something of the essence (a recurrent Greek instinct), or whether it was purely conventional. Hence the debate about whether there existed a 'correctness of names'. It was discussed at most length in the later Platonic dialogue *Cratylus*, but Prodicus treated correctness of names and the related phenomenon of synonyms (*Crat.* 384b; *Euthyd.* 277e); Democritus produced four arguments against the idea of 'natural names'.[13] Anaxagoras may have thought names are apportioned as things develop, but certainly one or two earlier thinkers were concerned about the relation of names and reality.[14] The author of the Derveni papyrus, perhaps influenced by Diogenes of Apollonia, saw the apportioning of names as part of the development and differentiation of the cosmos: 'the things were always there, but once they were distinguished, they were named'.[15] The controversy on the correctness of names was also discussed by Protagoras, to go by the *Cratylus*, and possibly by Hippias and Antiphon.[16]

---

[11] Linforth (1926) on equations with foreign gods.

[12] This was argued by Linforth (1940); Stein Commentary ad loc.; Burkert (1985a). A. Lloyd, Commentary, favours the literal interpretation, but in fact paraphrases to include personalities along with the names (above, n. 10).

[13] DK 68, B 26: 'Democritus [according to Proclus] says that *onomata* are conventional (θέσει), and he tried to establish this by four arguments [which Proclus lists] ... Therefore names are due to chance, not to nature' (τύχῃ ἄρα καὶ οὐ φύσει τὰ ὀνόματα). Note also the social origin of speech, B 5 (Diod. I 8.3–4), B 142 (names of gods), B 145.

[14] For Anaxagoras, see Burkert (1985a), 129. For earlier thinkers, Sluiter (1997), 168–72.

[15] Col. XVII 13f.: ἦμ μὲγ γ[ὰρ καὶ πρ]όσθεν, ὠνομάσθη δὲ γενέσ[θαι] ἐπεὶ διεκρίθ[η]. See Burkert (1970) on this. Text in *ZPE* 47 (1982), 1ff.; recent translation in Laks and Most (1997): col. xxi in the new translation (p. 19, with n. 56); cf. also (new) col. xvii (= *ZPE* col. XIII). Burkert suggests the link with Diogenes of Apollonia.

[16] Hippias: correctness of letters *Hipp. Min.* 368d4–5; cf. *Hipp. Mai.* 285c5–d2; for Protagoras, cf. *Crat.* 391c1–4; for Antiphon, see Morrison (1963), 46. See also Guthrie (1971), 222–4; Kerferd (1981a) ch. 7; Sluiter (1997), 172–88; and Sedley (1998) now on the etymologies in *Cratylus*.

It is difficult to see Herodotus' remarks in relation to the earlier thinkers alone.

Herodotus seems to be of the view that names are part of the process of apportioning, as things, or in this case gods, are differentiated. It seems to be going too far to suggest that he thinks that name-giving is 'correct', that is that names not only differentiate but that they are actually 'correct', in the sense of designating some real essence, as well.[17] On the contrary, he points out that gods do have different names in different places, just as they are worshipped differently.[18] But the modern perplexity surrounding his remarks on names highlights the possibility that he was aware there was a problem and that it was related to the problem of knowledge about the gods.

There are some curious and suggestive links between some remarks made in Book II and in the later, and obviously more philosophically sophisticated *Cratylus* which also brings up the names of the gods in a debate about naming. The Pelasgians in Herodotus, for instance, are given an etymology of '*theoi*', the etymology being that 'they ordered things' (i.e. from *thentes*); in the *Cratylus*, Socrates gives another etymology, from θεῖν, 'to run' and this is linked to the sun, moon and other apparently divine entities, so they are 'correctly named' (*Crat.* 397c–d: ὀρθῶς ἐκλήθησαν). Herodotus' early amorphous gods of the Pelasgians are not even linked to the heavenly bodies, and are thus even more anonymous than these.

Similarly there are a number of suggestive links made between naming and the question of knowledge which may help tease out more of the significance of Herodotus' ideas. Herodotus opened his Egyptian book, as we saw, with a suggestion of scepticism about knowledge of the gods: 'I am not keen to expound those divine matters (*ta theia*) of which I heard, except only the names, thinking that all men understand these equally' (II 3.2). This may well imply a view that all men know very little about the gods – they understand equally, that is, equally badly – and might be a hint of Protagorean scepticism about the possibility of knowledge of the divine.[19] But the sentence (II 3.2) is introduced to explain that

---

[17] As Burkert suggests for Herodotus (1985a), 128–30. Hdt. IV 45 implies, on the contrary, that Herodotus thinks the names of the continents differentiate but have little logic or basis in nature. One needs to distinguish sharply between views of names as distributing agents, and the view that names are 'correct', in the sense which is debated in the *Cratylus*; or they can be 'correct' for each group which uses them. Note, that Herodotus occasionally emphasizes that something has been 'correctly named' – ch. 7, p. 230 – but that would imply that he thinks most names are not, in fact, correct.

[18] A. Lloyd, Commentary vol. II, p. 17, thinks Herodotus would be prepared to accept the names of the gods were conventional; cf. also A. Lloyd (1990), 248.

[19] Cf. Burkert (1985a), who took it as a sceptical statment about knowledge about the gods. It depends on what περὶ αὐτῶν refers to: A. Lloyd's note (Commentary vol. II p. 17) on *ta theia*, for instance, takes it to refer to knowledge of *ta theia*, rather than to knowledge of the names themselves.

he will not talk about *ta theia*, except for the names, unless forced by the exigencies of his *logos*. It may more plausibly be the names that he thinks 'all men know equally'. It is more likely that he is excepting the names because they are, as it were, in the public domain, and accessible to human knowledge – certainly he does go on to talk about the names, while avoiding numerous religious explanations for rituals he observed. Socrates in the *Cratylus* says at one point that they can only really discuss the names of the gods that humans give them: 'since we know nothing about the gods, neither about them, nor about the names which they give themselves'.[20] So this later discussion deals with at least some of the problems signalled or implied in Herodotus and may help elucidate them. It would seem that the names were relatively safe; and if the names of the gods are humanly given, and not necessarily those the gods used themselves, that might explain why Herodotus seems perfectly happy to repeat the Egyptian equivalent names alongside the Greek: names differentiate, but the only names we humans know are the ones used by mankind.

Protagoras' famous opening sentence to his work 'On the gods' expressing scepticism about knowledge of the gods stated that, 'I cannot know about the gods, neither that they exist, nor that they do not exist, nor what they are like in appearance' (*idean*).[21] Herodotus does not go along with this degree of scepticism; indeed he goes out of his way to say that he thinks the gods do, in fact, intervene in human affairs. But the very manner in which he puts this view indicates that he is aware some think otherwise, and the echo of Protagoras led Burkert to suggest that Herodotus was obliquely citing Protagoras.[22] However, the problem of forms and naming again seems to lie in the background: Herodotus told us that it was Homer (and Hesiod) who gave the gods eponyms, and 'showed' their forms (*eidea*). The conjunction of names and forms reappears also in the Hippocratic *On the Art* (ch. 2.3 J) at a point when it was not absolutely necessary for his argument; the author brings up the issue of the relation of names and forms (*eidea*); names he declares are 'institutions' (νομοθετήματα), *eidea* are not institutions but the offspring of nature – that is, names are merely conventional, forms are natural.[23]

---

[20] *Crat.* 400d7–9: ὅτι περὶ θεῶν οὐδὲν ἴσμεν, οὔτε περὶ αὐτῶν οὔτε περὶ τῶν ὀνομάτων, ἅττα ποτὲ ἑαυτοὺς καλοῦσιν.

[21] DK 80, в 4: περὶ μὲν θεῶν οὐκ ἔχω εἰδέναι, οὔθ' ὡς εἰσὶν οὔθ' ὡς οὐκ εἰσὶν οὔθ' ὁποῖοί τινες ἰδέαν·

[22] Burkert (1985a, 131) compares Hdt. II 53.1: ὁκοῖοί τέ τινες τὰ εἴδεα, with Protagoras, в 4: ὁποῖοί τινες ἰδέαν ...

[23] Following the text of Jones as amended by Diels and Gomperz, not Jouanna's – see Jouanna, n. 4 ad loc. (p. 226). Cf. also *Nature of Man* ch. 5.2 J: 'First I assert that the names of these [constituents of man] are separated according to convention, and that none of them has the same name as the others; furthermore, that according to nature, their essential forms (τὰς ἰδέας) are separated, phlegm being quite unlike blood, blood being quite unlike bile, bile being quite unlike phlegm.'

This implies again that the question of the relation of names and forms was sufficiently well known as a problem for it to be brought up even if not strictly necessary to the immediate argument. Herodotus' careful distinctions of chronology and between names and *eidea* – learning of the 'names' of the gods, then of their theogonies and *eidea* – seems designed to provide historical stages and historical explanations for the contemporary manifestations of Greek polytheism.

We seem, then, to find a complex of ideas and problems reappearing in various authors at this time, surrounding naming and names, appearance and its relation to names, and the names and nature of the gods. I would suggest that the very peculiarity of Herodotus' argument about the names of the gods may be a sign that this controversy was current and fashionable when Herodotus was writing and that he was aware of it: propelled in part by this controversy, he was aware that the problem of naming was linked to the problem of the relation of names and reality; and that he left his theory confined to the *names* and eponyms of the gods – despite obvious difficulties in envisaging Greeks learning about gods with Greek names from Egyptians – precisely because as he says, the names of the gods are something we can all know, for (presumably) they are in the human sphere, and belong to the sphere of human worship which is susceptible to human knowledge.[24] It is not merely religious piety at work here in his famous expression of reticence about *ta theia* (divine matters), not merely a reluctance to delve into mysteries and rituals which should not be revealed, but also a consciousness about the possibilities of human knowledge. He is aware of scepticism surrounding matters of the divine, but rather than leave them aside entirely, on the contrary, he goes a considerable way towards 'solving' the problem of the origin of the gods, attributing the gradual discovery of the gods, who are out there unknown and undiscovered, to Egyptians, then certain Greek sages, the names being part of the process of differentiation from the mass of anonymous gods the Pelasgians had accepted. A further process is achieved by Homer and Hesiod, who seem both to 'create' the theogony and honours of the Greek gods, and also to 'show' what their forms are (implying some kind of revelation of the truth): thus there is a distinct human input into religious knowledge. There are difficulties in knowing about the gods, certainly, but Herodotus finds an older history of their knowledge in Egypt and proceeds to create a bold and surely provocative picture of how the Greeks not only received the knowledge of the gods from these various

---

[24] Cf. Burkert (1990) on Herodotus as an anthropologist of religion and his (appropriate) concentration on ritual observance. But this does not prevent Herodotus searching for spectacularly early worship of the gods.

barbarians (Libyans included), but also a great many of their central religious observances.

The whole theory is couched in the first-person style I have argued is a polemical and rhetorical style; some of the dense argument we encountered in earlier discussion (II 43: see chapter 6). It involves extensive enquiries – or purported enquiries – on Herodotus' part, some traditional tales from Dodona and Egypt which are puzzling and strained, and an impressive grasp of a new and immense span of human chronology which lengthens human history to 345 generations, and confines the period in which the gods were actually on earth to the period before that. The gods are located within the long geological time that Herodotus creates from the Egyptian *logos*. It is parallel to some of the anthropological speculations about early human societies associated with several late fifth-century thinkers – Protagoras, Democritus, the author of *On Ancient Medicine* – but grounded firmly in his enquiries in Egypt and in chronologically differentiated time. It seems to be answering the kind of questions asked also by these other thinkers, and in that sense, it is hard to think such a theory could have been produced much earlier. The idea of extensive borrowing – not only of gods, but of whole religious rituals – from barbarians, Egyptians and also other less-admired barbarians, may not have gone down well with many in Herodotus' audience. It certainly links the Greek and barbarian world in a manner which meshes well with Herodotus' remarks about *nomos*, Greek and barbarian (chapter 4), with his announcement in the Proem that he will record the achievements of both Greeks and barbarians, and with his awareness that both Greeks and barbarians had suffered since the Ionian Revolt (v 97.3). We may be tempted to wonder if the machinery of argument, proof and personal enquiry is particularly evident here precisely because these ideas needed all the persuasion they could get: this was part of the lively, ostentatious and persuasive style which belonged to a particular kind of intellectual discourse in the latter part of the fifth century.

We have identified as part of this intellectual style of discourse what is most easily described as the display element, the agonistic, persuasive and epideictic element I would also like to see as belonging to the milieu of 'scientific' enquiry and the pursuit of the truth about the world, and which stands somewhat apart from the narrative. This was an early phase, before the genres of epideictic rhetoric and other types of persuasion had been fully separated, and developed well-defined characteristics of their own – the *Histories* would be at the cusp of this development. It is still, perhaps, something of a free for all, and the *epideixis*, or at least elements of what later became the formalized *epideixis*, was available for the pursuit of scientific enquiries, for argument about the truth about the world, or about the nature of man. It is used by early medical writers, so far as we can see in our extant evidence, but was surely more widely available to those thinkers, natural philosophers, sophists, who could use the vivid style of argument, display and persuasion which was more appropriate to performance in front of a live audience than for a scholarly text to be read in private. It is perhaps this persuasive, argumentative and engaged style of presentation that was growing into fully developed rhetorical tricks of the kind Thucydides so disliked, and which he confined carefully to his speeches. We have seen clear elements of this, I hope, in Herodotus' *Histories*, which would be another reason for Thucydides to avoid this style so consciously. If it tended to be brought into play where overt persuasion, argument and evidence (not always watertight), are meant to draw the audience in, and if it had increasingly close identification with the developing techniques of the orators, it did not present the serious authoritative note that Thucydides sought for his history.

Should we, then, suggest that in the predisciplinary pursuit of *historie*, Herodotus might actually have seen himself as a sophist? It was suggested tentatively at the end of chapter 5 that just as *historie* was part of the 'scientific' vocabulary of the latter part of the fifth century, the *sophos* – literally, 'wise man' – or perhaps the *sophistes* might be the person who pursued it. Coming from a rather different angle, Fowler has suggested attractively that Herodotus considered himself a *sophos*.[25]

The activity of *historie* and the *sophistes* are linked by the neglected writer Alcidamas in the opening to his work '*On Those Who Write Written Speeches, or On the Sophists*', with the following words: '[Since] some of the so-called sophists neglect enquiry (*historia*) and education (*paideia*), and are quite inexperienced at speaking as ordinary men (*idiotai*)', they spend their time writing written speeches, which he thinks should be only an incidental and side skill; as a result they have failed in rhetoric and philosophy and should be called more accurately poets than sophists (chs. 1–2). Written in the early fourth century and probably an attack on further developments in the art of persuasion which do not strictly concern us here, the piece is interesting for our purposes since its polemical opening pairs *sophistai* with *paideia* and *historia*. Some sophists (who, for him, do not deserve the name) are neglecting *historia* and *paideia*: this implies that true sophists engage in both, at least on the level of rhetoric. We meet again the sense that *historia* is a term which embraces a wide spectrum of knowledge and the pursuit of knowledge, but only here is it paired so clearly with the *sophistes*. We also encounter here the attempt to kidnap one or other definition, in a claim of one group to be superior to another.

---

[25] Fowler (1996), esp. conclusion.

What is attractive about this attempt is that its definition of the (true) *sophistes* pairs the recognizable role of the poet as educator and purveyor of wisdom, with *historie* which seems clearly associated with prose works and the enquiry into 'science'. This would reflect Herodotus' own combination in the *Histories* of the authority of the poet in preserving the memory of achievements (*kleos*) as well as the authority of the enquirer into the nature of the world.

Herodotus himself uses the term *sophistes* for Pythagoras, 'not the weakest *sophistes* of the Greeks' (IV 95.2); Solon is mentioned with 'other *sophistai*' as visiting the Lydian Croesus (I 29.1); and he speaks of those *sophistai* later than Melampous who revealed the rites of Dionysus (II 49.1). Pindar uses the term *sophistes* of poets (*Isthm.* V 28), and his most frequent way of referring to poetry is 'wisdom', *sophia*. The *sophistes* appears also in Euripides' *Hippolytus* (v. 921), with irony but not, apparently, in a derogatory sense. This implies that *sophistai* might at this period be synonymous with *sophoi*, wise men, seers, poets, lawgivers, leaders of some intellectual, spiritual or ethical superiority, probably all together. Diogenes is said to use *sophistes* to refer to the *physiologoi* (DK 64, A 4). In the early fourth century Isocrates can do the same, to include Parmenides, Melissos, Empedocles (XV 268); he does also of the 'Seven Sages' (XV 235), just as Plato was enforcing the derogatory sense of sophist upon the term – though of course Isocrates is heavily implicated as he also saw himself as a sophist. These are all non-Platonic or pre-Platonic allusions to the sophists. Indeed, even Plato's Protagoras calls Homer and Hesiod sophists, though Plato makes him admit that they had to conceal the fact (*Protag.* 316d). If there is any common feature in these disparate references, at least it is not the fact of being paid for such wisdom.[26] Payment is not yet a crucial defining issue.

In this sense, then, perhaps Herodotus was a *sophos*, or indeed a *sophistes*, in the sense of the word as it was used before Plato. But it should be said, if so, that this would not be so much in the sense Herodotus himself used it, as Isocrates' usage. For Herodotus' *sophistai* are venerable, ancient seers and sages, and one may be reluctant to suggest Herodotus saw himself as this kind of 'sophist' (cf. Solon's travels: Herodotus uses φιλοσοφεῖν, I 30.2). On the other hand as we saw earlier (pp. 111, 266), the wise adviser in the *Histories* often gives advice which is noticeably

---

[26] For this, see e.g. Guthrie (1971), 27–34 on the term; Kerferd (1981a), ch. 4 ; G. E. R. Lloyd (1987), 93, n. 153 lists the linguistic evidence; most recently, O'Sullivan (1996): sensible caveat about making the definition too broad (116 and n. 8); yet even if 'professional teachers' are essential to the later idea of the sophist, as he stresses, the difficulty for earlier meanings remains in Herodotus' (and others') use of the term. For Pindar and *sophia*, see Davison (1968), ch. 13.

'sophistic' – akin, that is, to views we can relate to certain well-known sophists – and certainly sagacious. The wise adviser, from Solon to Demaratus, Artabanus to Cyrus, provides the narrator's long-term, distant and objective view of events.

Herodotus' *Histories* in their form, style and subject matter seem entwined inextricably with the concerns and styles that are visible in the more extrovert and argumentative representations of *historie* most clearly visible in the early medical writers, but surely characteristic of a wider spectrum of *sophistai* – whether *sophistai* delving into areas of natural philosophy or the study of politics and society. The very way in which his ethnography and geography interlock so well with certain issues that were being discussed in the latter part of the fifth century implies that his enquiries were informed by some of those interests, indeed part of them. This is not to say that the Homeric (and other poetic) background is not present – far from it. Any writer of the mid to late fifth century was conscious of Homeric precedents and influence: the question is what was the reaction to that consciousness. Perhaps we should also consider that in this period competing, sometimes conflicting, ways of seeing the world and of claiming knowledge coexisted, and it is interesting to see how far such models have to share – sometimes uncomfortably – in Herodotus' all-embracing enquiries. Traditional tales also gave their shape to the world and could – and did – clash with these other models. We have not had space to deal with Herodotus' use of traditional tales, the *logoi* about earlier Greek society and the way he welded together the disparate sources and accounts of the Persian Wars. But we have seen enough of the contemporary intellectual context of the *Histories* to see a writer who was in turn mischievous, playful, polemical, controversial, insatiably curious, who was probably quite aware that what he was repeating might not be liked by a prospective audience, and who was all too well aware that it was not enough in the later years of the fifth century simply to repeat 'what was said'.

Appendix: beavers and female ailments

Beavers are a first in Herodotus according to Powell's Lexicon. In Book IV Herodotus treats us to 'an ethnographic logos in miniature'[1] on the Gelonoi and the Boudinoi (chs. 108–9): the Boudinoi are wrongly confused by the Greeks with the Gelonoi, and are autochthonous and nomadic; the Gelonoi on the other hand were originally Greeks (108.2), workers of the land, and they speak part Scythian and part Greek (Boudinoi do not speak the same language). The Boudinoi also eat lice (or pine-seeds?). The land of the Boudinoi, where the Gelonoi also settled, has a large lake, with marshes, and 'in this they catch otters, beavers and other square-faced animals (θηρία τετραγωνοπρόσωπα). The skins they use for clothing, and the testicles are useful to them for the cure of the womb (καὶ οἱ ὄρχιες αὐτοῖσί εἰσι χρήσιμοι ἐς ὑστερέων ἄκεσιν).' (IV 109.2)

An interesting ethnic and cultural mix, then, which Herodotus is keen to describe and sort out, whose different way of life (diaita, 109.1) he expressly points out, in which former Greeks from the emporia chose to live among the Boudinoi in a semi-Greek and Scythian linguistic mélange. What about these otters, beavers and 'square-faced animals'?[2] This intimate piece of medical lore is perhaps surprising in this context, another case of Herodotus' curiosity about medical practice among other peoples, and another case where there is a tantalizing Hippocratic link.

One reaction is to interpret the use of these animal parts in terms of some kind of symbolic balancing, a use of cures which bear more relation to magical, ritual or folk-medicinal notions of health than anything more rational. So in Greek medicine, as it has been argued recently, certain female 'impurities' were dealt with by means of material even more impure.[3]

The curiosity about this particular detail in Herodotus is that it corresponds rather exactly with one aspect of Hippocratic pharmacology, and would have been of great relevance to the Greek doctor. For kastorion or, as it was believed, 'testicles of beaver' was a major ingredient of Hippocratic medicine, an aromatic substance used extensively in salves and unguents, or mixed with wine as a medicinal drink. In the many occasions in which it occurs in the Hippocratic Corpus,

---

[1] Asheri, comm. on IV 108–9 (p. 317).

[2] For a guess as to these latter: Asheri, note ad loc.; Casson (1918/19) who thought (p. 185) they were seals, in the Caspian; cf. also Gardiner-Garden (1987), 331–5, on Boudinoi.

[3] See von Staden (1992b). Brandenburg tentatively suggests (1976, 110–12) it effected a hormonal treatment – he did not know of the Hippocratic parallels.

it is either in the treatises on female health (*Mul. I* and *II*, *Steril.*, *Nat. Mul.*, *Superfet.*) or on the three other occasions, connected with female patients (*Epid. V* and *VII*).

So for instance, a woman with pain in her teeth is given *kastorion* and pepper in her mouth, and the *kastorion* also stops what are called τὰς ἀφ᾽ ὑστερέων κεφα-λαλγίας, literally, 'headaches coming from the womb'.[4] Or in *Nat. Mul.* (VII 316.7 L), if a woman has hysterics and the womb is moving, aromatics are advised, a husband, or a combination of *kastorion* and κόνυζα (inula or 'fleabane') in wine. Or, from many recipes involving *kastorion*, one of the more sensuous lists of aromatics occurs in the treatise *On Superfetation* (VIII 500. 16 + 22 L). Here fumigation is advised to open the uterine opening,[5] and such fumigation involves an extensive list of aromatics, including the lotus, laurel, myrrh, 'testicle of beaver' and rather less aromatic substances including dung of male ass (ὀνίδας ἄρσενος ὄνου) (*Superfet.* ch. 31, VIII. 500, 12–17 L).; for the uterine neck, there comes another aromatic list which includes cardamom, silphium and beaver testicles.

These works are not the earliest in the Corpus, though one would guess that the contexts of these long gynaecological recipes were in a tradition earlier than our first written texts. It has been argued that the gynaecological treatises do seem to have more elements in them which seem older, or more popular and traditional, than some of the others.[6] One might object that almost any pharmacological or botanical product might occur somewhere, since the Hippocratic doctor – and probably others – used the everyday ingredients that were at hand. But *kastorion* is hardly a mundane substance, and it would be a strange coincidence that the Hippocratic recipes not only used it as a remedy, but used it for gynaecological purposes also. The gynaecological slant is particularly striking, since *kastorion* continued later in antiquity to be a drug of major importance, but not one particularly associated with female problems;[7] and since it was being attributed by Herodotus with similar medical properties among the Scythian group too. Wellmann in fact suggested (in 1899) that Hippocrates knew of the Scythian remedy, but he did not pursue it.[8]

There is a further twist. The product called *kastorion* did not actually come from the beaver's testicles at all, as was almost universally believed in antiquity,[9] but from the scent glands in the same region. The process of discovery and commercial marketing stretch the imagination, but as it has been aptly put, 'it seems that some information was lost between the beaver and the market'.[10] Perhaps

---

[4] *Epid. VII*, v 428.14 and 17 L.

[5] For the practice of fumigation or odour therapy, Hanson (1991), esp. 81 ff.; von Staden (1992b) – though this does not discuss the combination of *Dreckapotheke* with aromatics; G. E. R. Lloyd (1983), 119–35, on the use of plants.

[6] Hanson (1991), drawing on Grensemann, *Hippokratische Gynäkologie: die gynäkologischen Texte des Autors C nach den pseudohippokratischen Schriften De muliebribus I, II, und De sterilibus* (Wiesbaden, 1982); G. E. R. Lloyd (1983), 132–4.

[7] See M. Wellmann, *RE* III.1 (s.v. Biber), col. 400–2 (1899), for details of later use when it becomes even more important.

[8] Wellmann, *RE*; Asheri notes (Commentary ad loc.) the Hippocratic use.

[9] Even the sceptical note in Pliny *NH* 32.26, mentioning Sextus Niger's doubts, accepts the usual belief about *kastorion's* provenance.

[10] Majno (1975), 210 (on aromatics).

this was a better way of selling the product. Chemical analysis of *kastorion* even suggests it would have been beneficial in more than psychosomatic ways: it turns out to contain a chemical that is an ingredient of aspirin.[11] There is then further irony in the way Herodotus or his sources transfer the same mistake to the Boudinoi (or Scythians), who were in more of a position to know the true source. Presumably the Hippocratic doctors got their supplies ultimately from the Pontus area.[12] Perhaps some of the information Herodotus got hold of was related in some way to this very trade (a marketing strategy on the Scythians' part?).

At any rate what we seem to be glimpsing in Herodotus' account is a 'medical' practice which may well have been a Greek one in his day, given the Hippocratic evidence, attributed (with alterations) to the Boudinoi north of the Black Sea. It may reflect something of the sources of *kastorion*; the story certainly implies very close resemblance between the medical practice of a Sauromatian tribe and the Hippocratic doctors. It may be that some information about possible use travelled with the drug in question (a suggestion of von Staden's in connection with Egyptian medical substances). Or perhaps it is another area where an essentially Hippocratic treatment was being attributed to another people – or, more precisely, a Hippocratic interpretation or slant was being given to a quite different practice. At any rate it seems to belong to yet another strand of the ethnography of medicine – where *physis* joins with medical attempts to cure – which was perhaps of contemporary interest. Not simply an isolated ethnographic detail, but something that was, or could be, incorporated into medical and physiological discussion – another link between the discussion of ethnography and Hippocratic practice. It suggests not simply a use of ethnographic data in medical circles, but also further connections between ethnographic 'information' related to medicine and the commercial movement of certain of these exotic products.

[11] Salicin and salicylic acid: Majno (1975) citing the chemical analysis of E. Lederer: these are active ingredients of aspirin.

[12] Later, according to Pliny, *NH* xxxii 26 and others, the best *kastorion* came from Pontos, Galatia and then Africa; beavers not in Greece according to Wellmann, but in the North and Africa. Given the patterns of Greek colonization in and by the fifth century, the Black Sea seems the most plausible fifth-century source.

Bibliography

ALLEN, R. E., and FURLEY, D. J. (1975) *Studies in Presocratic Philosophy II, The Eleatics and Pluralists* (London).

ALTHOFF, J. (1993a) 'Herodot und die griechische Medizin', in K. Döring and G. Wöhrle (eds.), *Antike Naturwissenschaft und ihre Rezeption* (Bamberg), 1–16.

(1993b) 'Formen der Wissensvermittlung in der frühgriechischen Medizin', in Kullmann, W., and Althoff, J., *Vermittlung und Tradierung von Wissen in der griechischen Kultur* (Tübingen), 211–23.

ALTY, J. H. M. (1982) 'Dorians and Ionians', *JHS* 102: 1–14.

ALY, W. (1921) *Volksmärchen, Sage und Novelle bei Herodot und seinen Zeitgenossen* (Göttingen).

(1929) *Formprobleme der frühen griechischen Prosa* (*Philologus* Suppl., Leipzig).

ARMAYOR, O. K. (1978) 'Did Herodotus ever go to the Black Sea?', *HSCP* 82: 45–62.

(1980) 'Sesostris and Herodotus' autopsy of Thrace, Colchis, inland Asia Minor and the Levant', *J. Amer. Research Center in Egypt* 15: 59–71.

(1985) *Herodotus' Autopsy of the Fayoum: Lake Moeris and the Labyrinth of Egypt* (Amsterdam).

ASCHERSON, N. (1995) *Black Sea* (London).

ASHERI, D., ed. (1988) *Erodoto, Le Storie, Libro I*, testo e commento (Milan).

(1990) 'Herodotus on Thracian society and history', in *Hérodote et les peuples non-grecs*, Fondation Hardt, XXXV (Geneva), 131–63.

ASHERI, D. and MEDAGLIA, S. M. (eds.) (1990) *Erodoto, Le Storie, Libro III*, testo e commento (Milan).

BAADER, G., and WINAU, R. (eds.) (1989) *Die Hippokratischen Epidemien. Theorie-Praxis-Tradition. Verhandlungen des Ve colloque international hippocratique (1984)* (Stuttgart).

BACKHAUS, W. (1976) 'Der Hellenen-Barbaren-Gegensatz und die hippokratische Schrift περὶ ἀέρων ὑδάτων τόπων', *Historia* 25: 170–85.

BAKKER, E. J. (1997) *Poetry in Speech: Orality and Homeric Discourse* (Ithaca).

BALCER, J. M. (1985) 'Fifth-century Ionia: a frontier redefined', *REA* 87: 31–42.

(1991) 'The East Greeks under Persian rule: a reassessment', in H. Sancisi-Weerdenburg and A. Kuhrt (eds.), *Achaemenid History* VI, 57–65.

BALLABRIGA, A. (1986) 'Les eunuques scythes et leurs femmes', *METIS* 1: 121–38.

BARNES, J. (1987a) 'New light on Antiphon', *Polis* 7: 2–5.

(1987b) *Early Greek Philosophy* (Harmondsworth).

BAXTER, T. M. S. (1992) *The Cratylus. Plato's Critique of Naming* (Leiden).

BEAZLEY, J. D. (1907) *Herodotus at the Zoo* (Oxford).

BECK, I. (1971) *Die Ringcomposition bei Herodot und ihre Bedeutung für die Beweistechnik* (Hildesheim).

BELTRAMETTI, A. (1982) 'Discutere di Erodoto con Hartog', *QS* 15: 235–52.

BENARDETE, S. (1969) *Herodotean Inquiries* (The Hague).

BERNAL, M. (1987–1991) *Black Athena. The Afro-Asiatic Roots of Western Civilization* (vol. I: New Brunswick, 1987; vol. II, London, 1991).

BERTIER, J. (1977) 'L'origine des catégories de grandeur (μέγεθος), d'aspect (εἶδος) et de caractère (ἦθος) dans *l'Histoire des animaux* d'Aristote', in R. Joly (ed.), *Corpus Hippocraticum.Colloque de Mons*, Sept. 1975 (Université de Mons), 327–44.

BETT, R. (1989) 'The sophists and relativism', *Phronesis* 34: 139–69.

BISCHOFF, H. (1932) 'Der Warner bei Herodot' (diss. Marburg) (parts repr. in Marg (1962), 302–19 and 670–6).

BLOEDOW, E. F. (1991) 'On "nurturing lions in the State": Alcibiades' entry on the political stage in Athens', *Klio* 73: 49–65.

BOARDMAN, J. (1964) Review of Cook (1962), in *CR* 14: 82–3.

(1980) *The Greeks Overseas* (new edn, London).

BOEDEKER, D. (1987) 'The two faces of Demaratus', in *Herodotus and the Invention of History*, *Arethusa* 20: 185–201.

(1988) 'Protesilaos and the end of Herodotus' *Histories*', *Class. Ant.* 7: 30–48.

(1995) 'Simonides on Plataea: narrative elegy, mythodic history', *ZPE* 107: 217–29.

BONNEAU, D. (1964) *La Crue du Nil, divinité égyptienne à travers mille ans d'histoire* (322 av.-641 ap.J.-C.) (Paris).

BOURGEY, L. (1953) *Observation et expérience chez les médecins de la collection hippocratique* (Paris).

BOWEN, A. J. (1992) *Plutarch, The Malice of Herodotus*. Translated with an introduction and commentary (Warminster).

BOWRA, C. M. (1956) 'A fragment of the Arimaspea', *CQ* 6: 1–10.

BRANDENBURG, D. (1976) *Medizinisches bei Herodot* (Berlin).

BRAVO, B. (1974) 'Une lettre sur plomb de Berezan: colonisation et modes de contact dans le Pont', *Dialogues d'histoire ancienne* 1: 111–87.

BRIANT, P. (1985) 'Dans de terres et de villes: l'Asie Mineure dans le contexte achaemenide', *REA* 87: 53–72.

(1990) 'Hérodote et la société perse', in *Hérodote et les peuples non-grecs. Fondation Hardt*, Entretiens XXXV (Geneva), 69–104 (105–13 discussion).

BROCK, R. (1991) Review of Woodman (1988), *LCM* 16.7: 97–102.

BROWN, T. S. (1965) 'Herodotus speculates about Egypt', *AJP* 86: 60–76.

(1982) 'Herodotus' portrait of Cambyses', *Historia* 31: 387–403.

BROWN, TRUESDELL S. (1962) 'The Greek sense of time as suggested by their account of Egypt', *Historia* 11: 257–70.

(1988) 'The Greek exiles: Herodotus' contemporaries', *Ancient World* 17: 17–28.

BRUNT, P. (1980) 'On historical fragments and epitomes', *CQ* 30: 477–94.

BURKERT, W. (1970) 'La genèse des choses et des mots', *Les Etudes philosophiques* 25: 443–55.

(1985a) 'Herodot über die Namen der Götter: Polytheismus als historisches Problem', *MH* 42: 121–32.

(1985b) 'Das Ende des Kroisos: Vorstufen einer herodoteischen Gesichtserzählung', in *Catalepton. Festschrift Bernhard Wyss* (Basle), 4–15.

(1990) 'Herodot als Historiker fremder Religionen', in *Hérodote et les peuples non-Grecs*, Fondation Hardt, xxxv (Geneva), with discussion, 1–39.

(1995) 'Lydia between East and West or how to date the Trojan War: a study in Herodotus', in J. B. Carter and S. P. Morris (eds.), *The Ages of Homer. A Tribute to Emily Townsend Vermeule* (Austin), 139–48.

BURNS, A. (1976) 'Hippodamus and the planned city', *Historia* 25: 414–28.

BURNYEAT, M. F. (1982) 'The origins of non-deductive inference', in J. Barnes, J. Brunschwig, M. Burnyeat, M. Schofield (eds.), *Science and Speculation in Hellenistic Theory and Practice* (Cambridge), 193–238.

BUTTI DE LIMA, P. (1996) *L'Inchiesta e la Prova. Immagine storiografica, pratica giuridica e retorica nella Grecia classica* (Turin).

BYL, S. (1995) 'L'aire géographique des médecins hippocratiques', in Ph. van der Eijk et al. (1995), 225–35.

CAGNAZZI, S. (1975) 'Tavola dei 28 *logoi* di Erodoto', *Hermes* 103: 385–423.

CAIZZI, F. D. (1986) 'Il nuovo papiro di Antifonte: POxy LII 3647', in F. Adorno et al. (eds.), *Studi e testi per il Corpus dei papiri filosofici greci e latini*, 2, (Florence), no. 83: 61–9.

CAIZZI, F. D. and BASTIANINI, G. (eds.) (1989) *Corpus dei papiri filosofici greci e latini* (Florence), 176 ff.

CALAME, C. (1996) *Mythe et histoire dans l'antiquité grecque. La création symbolique d'une colonie* (Lausanne).

CAMBIANO, G. (1983) 'Pathologie et analogie politique', in F. Lasserre and P. Mudry (eds.), *Formes de Pensée dans la Collection Hippocratique. Actes du IVe. colloque internationale hippocratique (Lausanne, 1981)* (Geneva), 441–58.

CAREY, C. (1994), 'Rhetorical Means of Persuasion', in Worthington, (1994), 26–45.

CARTLEDGE, P. (1990) 'Herodotus and "the other": a meditation on Empire', *Echoes du Monde classique. Classical Views* 34: 27–40.

(1993) *The Greeks* (Oxford).

CASSON, S. (1918/19) 'Herodotus and the Caspian', *BSA* 23: 175–93.

CHRIST, M. R. (1994) 'Herodotean kings and historical inquiry', *Class. Antiq.* 13: 167–202.

CLASSEN, C. J. (ed.) (1976a) *Sophistik, Wege der Forschung* 187 (Darmstadt).

(1976b) 'The study of language among Socrates' contemporaries', in Classen (ed.), *Sophistik*, 215–47 (orig. *Proc. Afr. Class. Assoc.* 2 (1959), 33–49).

COBET, J. (1971) *Herodots Exkurse und die Frage der Einheit seines Werkes* (*Historia* Einzelschriften 17, Wiesbaden).

(1974) Review of Fehling (1971), in *Gnomon* 46: 737–46.

(1977) 'Wann wurde Herodots Darstellung der Perserkriege publiziert?', *Hermes* 105: 2–27.

COLE, T. (1961) 'The Anonymous Iamblichi and his place in Greek political theory', *HSCP* 65: 127–63.

(1967) *Democritus and the Sources of Greek Anthropology*, Chapel Hill (repr. 1990 Atlanta).

(1991) *The Origins of Rhetoric in Ancient Greece* (Baltimore).

COLN-HAFT, L. (1956) *The Public Physicians of Ancient Greece* (Northampton, Mass.).

CONNOR, W. R. (1993a) 'The Ionian Era of Athenian civic identity', *Proc. Am. Phil. Soc.* 137: 194–206.

(1993b) 'The *Histor* in history', in R. M. Rosen and J. Farrell (eds.), *Nomodeiktes. Greek Studies in honor of Martin Ostwald* (Ann Arbor), 3–15.

COOK, R. M. (1961) 'The Problem of Classical Ionia', *PCPS* 287: 9–18.

(1962) *The Greeks in Ionia and the East* (London).

CORCELLA, A. (1984) *Erodoto e l'analogia* (Palermo).

(1992) 'Sciti ἀροτῆρες e Sciti γεωργοί', *QS* 35: 49–60.

(ed.) (1994) *Erodoto, Le Storie, Libro IV* (Milan).

(1996) 'Ecateo di Mileto cosi dice', *Quad. di Storia* 43: 295–301.

CORSARO, M. (1991) 'Gli Ioni tra Greci e Persiani: il problema dell' identità Ionica nel dibattito culturale e politico del V secolo', in H. Sancisi-Weerdenburg and A. Kuhrt (eds.), *Achaemenid History VI* (Leiden), 41–55.

CRANE, G. (1996) 'The Prosperity of tyrants: Bacchylides, Herodotus and the contest for legitimacy', *Arethusa* 29: 57–85.

DARBO-PESCHANSKI, C. (1987) *Le Discours du particulier. Essai sur l'enquête hérodotéenne* (Paris).

DAVISON, J. A. (1968) *From Archilochus to Pindar* (London).

DAWSON, D. (1992) *Cities of the Gods: Communist Utopias in Greek Thought* (New York and Oxford).

DAWSON, W. R. (1986) 'Herodotus as a medical writer', with notes by F. D. Harvey, *BICS* 33: 87–96.

DEMONT, P. (1983) 'Notes sur le récit de la pestilence athénienne chez Thucydides et sur ses rapports avec la médicine grecque de l'époque classique', in F. Lasserre, and Ph. Mudry (eds.), *Actes du IVe colloq. internat. hippocratique (Lausanne)*, (Geneva), 341–54.

(1988) 'Hérodote et les pestilences, Note sur Hdt. VI 27; VII 171 et VIII 115–117', *Rev. Phil.* 62: 7–13.

(1993) 'Die *Epideixis* über die *Techne* im V. und IV. Jh.,' in W. Kullmann and J. Althoff, *Vermittlung und Tradierung von Wissen in der griechischen Kultur* (Tübingen), 181–209.

(1994a) 'Le *Protagoras* de Platon, Hérodote et la providence', in *Actas del VIII Congreso Español de Estudios Clássicos* (Madrid), 145–58.

(1994b) 'Notes sur l'antilogie au cinquième siècle', in J.-M. Galy and A. Thivel (eds.), *La Rhétorique grecque. Actes du colloque 'Octave Navarre'; troisième colloque international sur la pensée antique organisé par le CRHI (1992)* (Nice), 77–88.

(1995) 'Secours et vengeance: note sur τιμωρίη chez Hérodote', *Ktema* 20 (1995), 37–45.

DESCAT, R. (1985) 'Mnésimachos, Hérodote et le système tributaire Achéménide', *REA* 87: 97–112.

DESCOEUDRES, J.-P. (ed.) (1990) *Greek Colonists and Native Populations: Proceedings of first Australian Congress of Classical Archaeology held in honour of Emeritus Professor A. D. Trendall (Sydney 1985)* (Oxford).

DETIENNE, M. (1977) *The Gardens of Adonis; Spices in Greek Mythology.* Transl. by J. Lloyd (Hassocks, Sussex) (transl. of *Les jardins d'Adonis*, Paris 1972).

DEWALD, C. (1981) 'Women and culture in Herodotus' *Histories'*, in H. P. Foley, *Reflections of Women in Antiquity* (New York), 91–125.

(1985) 'Practical knowledge and the Historian's role in Herodotus and Thucydides', in M. H. Jameson (ed.), *The Greek Historians: Literature and History. Papers presented to A. E. Raubitschek* (Saratoga, Calif.), 47–63.

(1987) 'Narrative surface and authorial voice in Herodotus' *Histories'*, in *Herodotus and the Invention of History*, *Arethusa* 20: 147–170.

(1990) review of F. Hartog, *The Mirror of Herodotus, Class. Phil.* 85: 217–24.

(1993) 'Reading the world: the interpretation of objects in Herodotus' *Histories'*, in R. M. Rosen and J. Farrell (eds.), *Nomodeiktes. Greek Studies in Honour of M. Ostwald* (Ann Arbor), 55–70.

(1997) 'Wanton Kings, pickled heroes and gnomic Founding Fathers: strategies of meaning at the end of Herodotus' *Histories'*, in D. H. Roberts, F. M. Dunn and D. Fowler (eds.), *Classical Closure. Reading the End in Greek and Latin Literature* (Princeton), 62–82.

DEWALD, C. and MARINCOLA, J. (1987) 'A Selective introduction to Herodotean studies', in *Herodotus and the Invention of History*, *Arethusa* 20: 9–40.

DIELS, H. (1887) 'Herodot und Hekataios', *Hermes* 22: 411–44.

(1910) 'Die Anfänge der Philologie bei den Griechen', *Neue Jahrbücher für das Klassische Altertum* 13, 1–25 (repr. in Diels, *Kleine Schriften zur Geschichte der Antike Philosophie* (Darmstadt, 1969), 68–92).

DIERAUER, U. (1977) *Tier und Mensch im Denken der Antike. Studien zur Tierpsychologie, Anthropologie und Ethik* (Amsterdam).

DIHLE, A. (1962a) 'Herodot und die Sophistik', *Philologus* 106: 207–20.

(1962b) 'Aus Herodots Gedankenwelt', *Gymnasium* 69: 22–32.

(1981) 'Die Verschiedenheit der Sitten als Argument ethische Theorie', in G. B. Kerferd (ed.), *The Sophists and their Legacy, Hermes Einzelschriften* 44 (Wiesbaden), 54–63.

(1990) 'Arabien und Indien', in *Hérodote et les peuples non grecs.* Fondation Hardt, Entretiens xxxv (Geneva), 41–61 (discussion 62–7).

DILLER, H. (1932) 'ΟΨΙΣ ΤΩΝ ΑΔΗΛΩΝ ΤΑ ΦΑΙΝΟΜΕΝΑ', *Hermes* 67: 14–42.

(1934) *Wanderarzt und Aitiologie. Studien zur hippokratischen Schrift ΠΕΡΙ ΑΕΡΩΝ ΥΔΑΤΩΝ ΤΟΠΩΝ (Philologus*, Suppl. 26, Leipzig).

(1952) 'Hippokratische Medizin und attische Philosophie', *Hermes* 80: 385–409 (= *Kleine Schriften z.ant. Medizin*, Berlin 1973, 46–70).

(1958) 'Nochmals: Überlieferung und Text der Schrift von der Umwelt', in *Festschrift Ernst Kapp* (Hamburg), 31–49.

(1962) 'Die Hellenen-Barbaren-Antithese im Zeitalter der Perserkriege', in *Grecs et Barbares*, Fondation Hardt, Entretiens VIII: 76 ff.

(1970) *Hippocrates, De aere aquis locis.* Corpus Medicorum Graecorum, vol.I, 1.2. Edition and translation (Berlin).

(1973) 'Ausdrucksform des methodischen Bewusstseins in den hippokratischen Epidemien', in G. Baader and H. Grensemann (eds.), *Kleine Schriften zur antiken Medizin* (Berlin), 106–23.

DILLON, J. (1984) 'Euripides and Antiphon on Nomos and Physis: some remarks', in *H ΑΡΧΑΙΑ ΣΟΦΙΣΤΙΚΗ. The Sophistic Movement (Papers read at the 1.int.symp. on the Sophistic Movement, Athens 27–29 Sept. 1982)*, (Athens, Kardanitsa), 97–107.

DODDS, E. R. (1959) *Plato, Gorgias*, revised text with introduction and commentary (Oxford).

DORNSEIFF, F. (1933) *Die Archaische Mythenerzählungen* (Berlin): Anhang 2, 'Sophistische παίγνια bei Herodot'.

DREWS, R. (1973) *The Greek Accounts of Eastern History* (Cambridge, Mass.).

DREXLER, H. (1972) *Herodot-Studien* (Hildesheim).

DUBOIS, L. (1996) *Inscriptions grecques dialectales d'Olbia du Pont* (Geneva).

DUCATILLON, J. (1977) *Polémiques dans la Collection Hippocratique* (Paris).

DUE, B. (1980) *Antiphon. A Study in Argumentation* (Copenhagen).

EDELMANN, H. (1970) ''Ερημίη und ἔρημος bei Herodot', *Klio* 52: 79–86.

EDELSTEIN, L. (1931) *Περὶ ἀέρων und die Sammlung der Hippokratischen Schriften* (Berlin).
  (1935) 'Hippokrates', in *RE*, Suppl. Bd. 6, cols. 1290–1345.
  (1939) 'The genuine works of Hippocrates', *Bull. Hist. Medicine* 7: 236–48 (repr. in O. and C. l. Temkin (eds.), *Ancient Medicine. Selected Papers of Ludwig Edelstein* (Baltimore 1967), 133–44.
  (1952) 'The Relation of Ancient Philosophy to Medicine', *Bull. Hist. Med.*, 299ff. (repr. in O. and C. L. Tempkin (eds.) *Ancient Medicine. Selected Papers of Ludwig Edelstein*, (Baltimore 1967), 349–66).

EDWARDS, M. J. (1991) 'Being and seeming: Empedocles' reply', *Hermes* 119: 282–93.

EIJK, PH. J. van der (1990) 'The "Theology" of the Hippocratic treatise *On the Sacred Disease*', *Apeiron* 23: 87–119.
  (1991) '*Airs, Waters, Places* and *On the Sacred Disease*: two different religiosities?', *Hermes* 119: 168–76.
  (1997) 'Towards a rhetoric of ancient scientific discourse. Some formal characteristics of Greek medical and philosophical texts (Hippocratic Corpus, Aristotle)', in E. J. Bakker (ed.), *Grammar as Interpretation. Greek Literature in its Linguistic Contexts* (Leiden), 77–129.

EIJK, PH. J. van der, HORSTMANSHOFF, H. F. J., SCHRIJVERS, P. H. (eds.) (1995) *Ancient Medicine in its socio-cultural Context, vol. I and II* (Amsterdam).

EMLYN-JONES, C. J. (1980) *The Ionians and Hellenism* (London).

ERBSE, H. (1956) 'Der erste Satz im Werke Herodots', *Festschrift Bruno Snell* (Munich), 209–22.
  (1961) 'Tradition und Form im Werke Herodots', *Gymnasium* 68: 239–59.
  (1981) 'Die Funktion der Novellen im Werke Herodots', in G. Kurz, D. Müller and W. Nicolai (eds.), *Gnomosyne. Festschrift für Walter Marg zum 70. Geburtstag*, (Munich), 251–69.
  (1991) 'Fiktion und Wahrheit im Werke Herodots', *Nachrichten der Akademie der Wissenschaften im Göttingen. Philologisch-Historische Klasse*, 131–50.
  (1992) *Studien zum Verständnis Herodots* (Berlin, New York).

ERMATINGER, E. (1897) *Die attische Autochthonensage bis auf Euripides* (Berlin).

EVANS, J. A. S. (1965) 'Despotes Nomos', *Athenaeum* 43: 142–53.
  (1968) 'Father of History or Father of Lies; the Reputation of Herodotus', *CJ* 64: 11–17.

(1979) 'Herodotus' publication date', *Athenaeum* 57: 145–9.

(1991) *Herodotus, Explorer of the Past. Three Essays* (Princeton).

FALUS, R. (1977) 'Hérodote III. 108–9', *Acta Antiqua* 25: 371–6.

FEHLING, D. (1989) *Herodotus and his 'Sources'. Citation, Invention and Narrative Art* (Leeds); transl. and revised edn: originally published as *Die Quellenangaben bei Herodot* (Berlin 1971).

FESTUGIÈRE, A.-J. (1948) *Hippocrate. L'ancienne médecine. Introduction, traduction et commentaire* (Paris).

FINLEY, J. (1942) *Thucydides* (Cambridge, Mass.).

(1967) *Three Essays on Thucydides* (Cambridge, Mass.).

FLORY, S. (1980) 'Who read Herodotus' Histories?', *AJP* 101: 12–28.

(1987) *The Archaic Smile of Herodotus* (Detroit).

(1989–90) 'The meaning of τὸ μὴ μυθῶδες (1.22.4) and the usefulness of Thucydides' *History*', CJ 85: 193–208.

FORNARA, C. (1971a) *Herodotus: an Interpretative Essay* (Oxford).

(1971b) 'Evidence for the date of Herodotus' publication', *JHS* 91: 25–34.

(1981) 'Herodotus' knowledge of the Archidamian War', *Hermes* 109: 149–56.

(1983) *The Nature of History in Ancient Greece and Rome* (Berkeley).

(1990) 'Human history and the constraint of fate in Herodotus', in J. W. Allison, *Conflict, Antithesis and the Ancient Historian* (Columbus, Ohio), 25–45.

FOUCART, G. (1943) 'Le soleil d'Hérodote et la cosmophysique des physiologues', *Bull. Inst. Ég.* 25: 93–100.

FOWLER, R. L. (1996) 'Herodotus and his contemporaries', *JHS* 116: 62–87.

FRITZ, K. von (1936) 'Herodotus and the growth of historiography', *TAPA* 67: 315–40.

(1967) *Die griechische Geschichtsschreibung* (Berlin).

FROIDEFOND, C. (1971) *Le mirage égyptien dans la littérature grecque d'Homère a Aristote* (Aix-en-Provence).

FURLEY, D. J. (1981) 'Antiphon's case against justice', in Kerferd (1981b), 81–91.

GAGARIN, M. (1990) 'The ancient tradition on the identity of Antiphon', *GRBS* 31: 27–44.

GARDINER-GARDEN, J. R. (1987) 'Darius' Scythian expedition and its aftermath', *Klio* 69: 326–50.

GEDDES, A. G. (1987) 'Rags and riches. The costume of Athenian men in the fifth century', *CQ* 37: 307–31.

GEORGES, P. (1994) *Barbarian Asia and the Greek Experience* (Baltimore).

GIGANTE, M. (1956) *ΝΟΜΟΣ ΒΑΣΙΛΕΥΣ* (Naples).

(1962) 'Herodot, der erste Historiker des Abendlandes', in Marg (1962), 259–81.

GOEBEL, G. H. (1989) 'Probability in the earliest rhetorical theory', *Mnemosyne.* 42: 41–53.

GOLDHILL, S. (1991) *The Poet's Voice. Essays on Poetics and Greek Literature* (Cambridge).

GOMME, A. W. (1945–81) *A Historical Commentary on Thucydides.* In 5 vols.; vol. IV and V completed by A. Andrewes and K. J. Dover (Oxford).

GOULD, J. (1989) *Herodotus* (London).

(1994) 'Herodotus and religion', in S. Hornblower (1994a), 91–106.

GRAF, F. (1974) 'Das Kollegium der Μολποί von Olbia', *MH* 31: 209–15.

GRAFTON, A. (1992) *New Worlds, Ancient Texts* (Harvard).

GRAHAM, A. J. (1982) 'Colonial expansion of Greece', *CAH* 3.3 (2nd edn, Cambridge), ch. 37.

GRAY, V. (1995) 'Herodotus and the rhetoric of otherness', *AJP* 116: 185–212.

GRECS ET BARBARES. Entretiens sur l'antiquité classique (Fondation Hardt, Geneva, 1961).

GREENBLATT, S. (1991) *Marvelous Possessions. The Wonder of the New World* (Oxford).

GRENSEMANN, H. (1968) *Die hippokratische Schrift 'Über die heilige Krankheit'* (Berlin).

(1979) 'Das 24. Kapitel von *De aeribus, aquis, locis* und die Einheit der Schrift', *Hermes* 107: 423–41.

GRIFFITHS, A. (1987) 'Democedes of Croton: A Greek doctor at the court of Darius', in H. Sancisi-Weerdenburg and A. Kuhrt (eds.), *Achaemenid History II, The Greek Sources* (Leiden), 37–51.

(1989) 'Was Kleomenes mad?', in A. Powell (ed.), *Classical Sparta: Techniques behind her Success* (London), ch. 3.

(forthcoming) 'A grim dairy tale', in N. Luraghi (ed.), *The Dawn of Historiography (Oxford)*.

GRMEK, M. D. (ed.) (1980) *Hippocratica. Actes du colloque hippocratique de Paris 1978* (Paris).

(1983a), *Les maladies à l'aube de la civilisation occidentale* (Paris 1983) (= *Disease in the Ancient Greek World*, transl. M. and L. Muellner (Baltimore and London 1989)).

(1983b) 'Ancienneté de la chirurgie hippocratique', in F. Lasserre and P. Mudry (eds.), *Formes de pensée dans la Collection hippocratique. Actes du IVe colloque internationale Hippocratique, Lausanne, 1981* (Geneva), 285–96.

GSELL, S. (1915) *Hérodote* (Algiers) (repr. 1971, Rome).

GUTHRIE, W. K. C. (1965) *A History of Greek Philosophy. Vol. II. The Presocratic Tradition from Parmenides to Democritus* (Cambridge).

(1971) *The Sophists* (Cambridge) (1st publ. as Part I, of *A History of Greek philosophy, Vol. III*, Cambridge 1969).

HALL, E. (1989) *Inventing the Barbarian. Greek Self-Definition through Tragedy* (Oxford).

(1996) 'When is a myth not a myth? Bernal's "Ancient Model"', in M. R. Lefkowitz and G. M. Rogers, *Black Athena Revisited* (Chapel Hill and London), 333–48 (repr. with revisions, from *Arethusa* 25 (1992), 181–201).

HALL, J. (1997) *Ethnic Identity in Greek Antiquity* (Cambridge).

HANFMANN, G. (1953) 'Ionia: leader or follower', *HSCP* 61: 1–27.

HANSON, A. E. (1987) 'The eight month's child and the etiquette of birth: *obsit omen!*', *Bull. Hist. Med.* 61: 589–602.

(1989) 'Diseases of Women in the Epidemics', in G. Baader and R. Winau, *Die Hippokratischen Epidemien. Theorie-Praxis-Tradition. Verhandlungen des Ve colloque international hippocratique* (1984) (Stuttgart), 38–51.

(1991) 'Continuity and change: three case studies in Hippocratic Gynecological therapy and theory', in S. Pomeroy (ed.), *Women's History and Ancient History* (Chapel Hill), 73–110.

(1992) 'Conception, gestation and the origin of female nature in the Corpus Hippocraticum', *Helios* 19: 31–71.

(1994) 'A division of labor. Roles for men in Greek and Roman births', *Thamyris* 1: 157–202.

(1995) 'Paidopoiïa: Metaphors for conception, abortion and gestation in the Hippocratic Corpus', in Ph. van der Eijk et al. (1995), vol. I, 291–307.

HARMATTA, J. (1990) 'Herodotus, historian of the Cimerians and the Scythians', in *Hérodote et les peuples non grecs*, Fondation Hardt, Entretiens, XXXV (Geneva), 115–30.

HARRISON, E. L. (1964) 'Was Gorgias a sophist?', *Phoenix* 18: 183–92.

HARRISON, T. (1998) 'Herodotus' conception of foreign languages', *Histos* 2.

HART, J. (1982) *Herodotus and Greek History* (London).

HARTOG, F. (1988) *The Mirror of Herodotus. The Representation of the Other in the Writing of History* (Princeton) (transl. by Janet Lloyd of *Le Miroir d'Hérodote: Essai sur la représentation de l'autre*, Paris 1980).

(1996a) *Mémoire d'Ulysse. Récits sur la frontière en Grèce ancienne* (Paris).

(1996b) 'Fondements grecs de l'idée d'Europe', *Quad. di Storia* 43: 5–17.

HARVEY, F. (1966) 'The political sympathies of Herodotus', *Historia* 15: 254–5.

HEIDEL, W. A. (1937) *The Frame of the Ancient Greek Maps* (New York).

HEINIMANN, F. (1945) *Nomos und Physis* (Basle).

(1976) 'Eine Vorplatonische Theorie der Τέχνη', in C. J. Classen (ed.), *Sophistik* (WdF), 127–69 (= *MH* 18 (1961), 105–30).

HENIGE, D. P. (1974) *The Chronology of Oral Tradition. Quest for a Chimera* (Oxford).

HENRICHS, A. (1975) 'Two doxographical notes: Democritus and Prodicus on religion', *HSCP* 79: 93–123.

(1984) 'The sophists and Hellenistic religion: Prodicus as the spiritual father of the Isis Aretologies', *HSCP* 88: 139–58.

HERINGTON, J. (1991) 'The closure of Herodotus' *Histories*', *BICS* 16: 149–60.

HERMANN, J. (1967) 'Nomos bei Herodot und Thukydides', *Gedächtnisschrift Hans Peters* (Berlin), 116–24.

Hérodote et les peuples non-grecs, Fondation Hardt, Entretiens XXXV (Geneva, 1990).

HERTER, H. (1963) 'Die kulturhistorische Theorie der hippokratischen Schrift der Alten Medizin', *Maia* 15, 464–83 (= *Kleine Schriften*, München 1975, 157–74).

HIPPOCRATICA. *Actes du Colloque hippocratique de Paris* (1978), ed. M. D. Grmek (Paris 1980).

HOLLADAY, A. J. (1987) 'Thucydides and the recognition of contagion: a reply', *Maia* 39: 95–6.

HOLLADAY, A. J., and POOLE, J. C. F. (1979) 'Thucydides and the plague of Athens', *CQ* 29: 282–300.

HORNBLOWER, S. (1982a) *Mausolus* (Oxford).

(1982b) 'Thucydides, the Panionian festival and the Ephesia (III 104)', *Historia* 31: 241–5.

(1987) *Thucydides* (London).

(1991) *A Commentary on Thucydides, Volume 1: Books I–III* (Oxford).

(1992) 'Thucydides' use of Herodotus', in J. M. Sanders (ed.), *ΦΙΛΟΛΑΚΩΝ. Laconian Studies in honour of Hector Catling* (Athens), 141–54.

(ed.) (1994a) *Greek Historiography* (Oxford).

(1994b) 'Narratology and narrative techniques in Thucydides', in Hornblower (1994a), 131–66.

(1994c) 'Asia Minor', *CAH* (2nd. edn) vol. VI, ch. 8a.

(1996), *A Commentary on Thucydides. Vol. 2, Books IV–V.24* (Oxford).

HOW, W. W. and WELLS, J. (1928) *A Commentary on Herodotus*, 2nd edn, 2 vols. (Oxford).

HUBER, L. (1965) 'Herodots Homerverständnis', in H. Flashar and K. Gaiser (eds.), *Synusia. Festgabe für W. Schadewaldt* (Neske), 29–52.

HUMPHREYS, S. C. (1987) 'Law, custom and nature in Herodotus', in *Arethusa* 20, *Herodotus and the Invention of History*, 211–20.

(1996) 'From riddle to rigour. Satisfactions of scientific prose in ancient Greece', in S. Marchand and E. Lunbeck (eds.), *Proof and Persuasion. Essays on Authority, Objectivity, and Evidence* (Princeton), 3–24.

(1997) 'Fragments, fetishes and philosophies: towards a history of historiography after Thucydides', in G. W. Most (ed.), *Collecting Fragments/Fragmente sammeln* (Göttingen), 207–24.

HUNT, D. W. (1947) 'Feudal survivals in Ionia', *JHS* 67: 68–76.

HUNTER, V. (1982) *Past and Process in Herodotus and Thucydides* (Princeton).

HUXLEY, G. (1965a) 'Ion of Chios', *GRBS* 6: 29–46.

(1965b) 'A fragment of the Ἀσσύριοι λόγοι of Herodotus', *GRBS* 6: 207–12.

HUYSE, P. (1990) 'Die persische Medizin auf der Grundlage von Herodots Historien', *Ancient Society* 21: 141–8.

IMMERWAHR, H. R. (1954) 'Historical action in Herodotus', *TAPA* 85: 16–45.

(1956) 'Aspects of historical causation in Herodotus', *TAPA* 87: 241–80.

(1960) 'Ergon: history as a monument in Herodotus and Thucydides', *AJP* 81: 261–90.

(1966) *Form and Thought in Herodotus* (Cleveland, Ohio).

IOANNIDI, H. (1989) 'La pratique de l'écriture chez les médecins auteurs des Épidémies (Livres I et III; II, IV, VI)', in G. Baader and R. Winau (1989), 159–65.

JACOB, C. (1991) *Géographie et ethnographie en Grèce ancien* (Paris).

(1996) 'Disegnare la terra', in S. Settis (ed.), *I Greci. Storia Cultura Arte Società*, I Noi e i Greci (Turin), 901–53.

JACOBY, F. (1911) 'Zu Hippokrates π. ἀέρων, ὑδάτων, τόπων', *Hermes* 46: 518–67.

(1912) 'Hekataios' (no. 3), *RE* VII, 2, cols. 2667–2769.

(1913) 'Herodotos', *RE Suppl. II* (Stuttgart), cols. 205–520.

(1956) 'Über die Entwicklung der griechischen Historiographie und den Plan einer neuen Sammlung der griechischen Historikerfragmente', in Jacoby, *Abhandlungen zur griechischen Geschichtschreibung* (Leiden), 16–64.

JOHNSON, W. A. (1994) 'Oral performance and the composition of Herodotus' *Histories*', *GRBS* 35: 229–54.

JOLY, R. (1960) *Recherches sur le traité ps.-hippocratique Du Régime* (Paris).

(1966) *Le niveau de la science hippocratique* (Paris).

(1970) *Hippocrate. De la Génération, De la Nature de l'Enfant, Des Maladies IV, Du Foetus de Huit Mois. Texte et Traduction* (Paris).

(1977) 'Indices lexicaux pour la datation de *Génération, Nature de l'Enfant* et *Maladies IV*', in R. Joly (ed.), *Corpus Hippocraticum. Colloque de Mons, Sept. 1975* (Université de Mons), 136–47.

(1980) 'Un peu d'épistémologie historique pour hippocratisants', in M. D. Grmek (ed.), *Hippocratica. Actes... 1978* (Paris), 285–97.

(1984) *Du Régime.* Edit, traduit et comment, avec la collaboration de S. Byl, *CMG* I 2,4 (Berlin).

JONES, W. H. S. (1923–31) *Hippocrates*, Loeb edition, 4 vols. (London and Cambridge, Mass.)

(1945) '"Hippocrates" and the Corpus Hippocraticum', *Proc. Brit. Acad.* 31 (1945), 103–25.

(1946) *Philosophy and Medicine in Ancient Greece, Suppl.* 8 to the *Bull. Hist. Medicine* (Baltimore 1946).

JOUANNA, J. (1965) 'Rapports entre Mélissos de Samos et Diogène d'Apollonie à la lumière du traité hippocratique', *REA* 67 (1965), 306–23.

(1975), *Hippocrate, De natura hominis.* Corpus Medicorum Graecorum, vol. I 1,3. Edition, translation and commentary (Berlin).

(1978) 'Le médecin modèle du législateur dans les *Lois* de Platon', *Ktema* 3 (1978), 77–91.

(1980) 'Politique et médecine. La problématique du changement dans le *Régime des maladies aiguës*, et chez Thucydides (Livre VI)', in M. D. Grmek (ed.), *Hippocratica. Actes du colloque hippocratique de Paris 1978* (Paris), 299–318.

(1981) 'Les causes de la défaite des barbares chez Eschyle, Hérodote et Hippocrate', *Ktema* 6 (1981), 3–15.

(1984a) 'Collaboration ou résistance au barbare: Artémise d' Halicarnasse et Cadmos de Cos chez Hérodote et Hippocrate', *Ktema* 9: 15–26.

(1984b) 'Rhétorique et médecine dans la Collection Hippocratique', *REG* 97: 26–44.

(1988) *Hippocrate. Des Vents – De l'Art.* (Tome V, 1re partie.) Texte et traduction (Paris).

(1990) *Hippocrate. L'Ancienne médecine* (Tome II, 1re partie). Texte et traduction (Paris).

(1991) 'Un nouveau témoin du traité hippocratique des *Airs, Eaux, Lieux*', *REG* 104: 85–108.

(1992) *Hippocrate* (Paris).

(1994) 'L'eau, la santé et la maladie dans le traité hippocratique des *Airs, Eaux, Lieux*', *BCH Suppl.* 28: 25–40.

(1996) *Hippocrate. Airs, Eaux, Lieux.* (Tome II, 2e partie) Texte et traduction (Paris).

KAHN, C. (1973) 'Language and ontology in the *Cratylus*', in E. N. Lee, A. P. D. Mourelatos and R. M. Rorty (eds.), *Exegesis and Argument: Studies in Greek Philosophy presented to G. Vlastos, Phronesis, Suppl.* 1: 152–76.

(1981) 'The origins of social contract theory in the fifth century B.C.', in G. B. Kerferd (1981b), 92–108.

(1993) 'Plato's *Ion* and the problem of *techne*', in R. M. Rosen and J. Farrell (eds.), *Nomodeiktes. Greek Studies in honor of Martin Ostwald* (Ann Arbor), 369–78.

KENNEDY, G. A. (1959) 'The earliest rhetorical handbooks', *AJP* 80: 169–78.

(1963) *The Art of Persuasion in Greece* (London).

(1991) *Aristotle, on Rhetoric: A Theory of Civic Discourse*. Newly transl. with Introduction, notes and appendices (Oxford, New York).

(1994) *A New History of Classical Rhetoric* (Princeton).

KERFERD, G. B. (1981a) *The Sophistic Movement* (Cambridge).

(ed.) (1981b), *The Sophists and their Legacy*, *Hermes Einzelschriften* 44 (Wiesbaden).

KIENAST, D. (1994) 'Die Auslösung des Ionischen Aufstandes und das Schicksal des Histiaios', *Historia* 43: 387–401.

KONSTAN, D. (1983) 'The stories in Herodotus' *Histories*: Book 1', *Helios* 10: 1–22.

(1987) 'Persians, Greeks and Empire', in *Arethusa* 20, *Herodotus and the Invention of History*, 59–73.

KUDLIEN, F. (1967) *Der Beginn des medizinischen Denken bei den Griechen. Von Homer bis Hippokrates* (Zurich/Stuttgart).

(1968) 'Early Greek primitive medicine', *Clio Medica* 3: 305–36.

(1970) 'Medical education in classical Antiquity', in C. D. O'Malley (ed.), *The History of Medical Education* (Berkeley), 3 ff.

(1974) 'Dialektik und Medizin in der Antike', *Medizinhistorisches Journal* 9: 187–200.

(1977) 'Das Göttliche und die Natur im hippokratischen Prognostikon', *Hermes* 105: 268–74.

KÜHN, J.-H. and FLEISCHER, U. (1986) *Index Hippocraticus* (Göttingen).

KUKOFKA, D.-A. (1991) 'Das μαρτύριον μέγιστον der Sybariten (Herodot 5, 43–46)', *Hermes* 119: 374–80.

KULLMANN, W. and ALTHOFF, J. (1993) *Vermittlung und Tradierung von Wissen in der griechischen Kultur* (Tübingen).

KUPPERMAN, K. O. (1995) *America in European Consciousness, 1493–1750* (Chapel Hill).

KURKE, L. (1995) 'Herodotus and the language of metals', *Helios* 22: 36–64.

LACHENAUD, G. (1978) *Mythologies, religion et philosophie de l'histoire dans Hérodote* (Lille).

LAÍN ENTRALGO, P. (1970) *The Therapy of the Word in Classical Antiquity* (ed. and transl. by L. J. Rather and J. M. Sharp) (New Haven).

LAIRD, A. G. (1933) 'Herodotus on the Pelasgians in Attica', *AJP* 54: 97–119.

LAKS, A. and MOST, G. W. (eds.) (1997) *Studies on the Derveni Papyrus* (Oxford).

LANG, M. (1984) *Herodotean Narrative and Discourse* (Cambridge, Mass.).

LANGHOLF, V. (1990) *Medical Theories in Hippokrates. Early Texts and the 'Epidemics'* (Berlin).

LASSERRE, F. (1976) 'Hérodote et Protagoras: le débat sur les constitutions', *MH* 33: 65–84.

LASSERRE, F. and MUDRY, P. (eds.) (1983) *Formes de Pensée dans la Collection hippocratique. Actes du IVe. colloque internationale hippocratique, Lausanne 1981* (Geneva).

LATEINER, D. (1982a) 'The failure of the Ionian Revolt', *Historia* 31: 129–60.

(1982b) 'A note on the perils of prosperity in Herodotus', *RhM* 125: 97–101.

(1984) 'Herodotean historiographical patterning: the Constitutional Debate', *CQ* 20: 257–84.

(1985a) 'Nicias' inadequate encouragement (Thuc. 7.69.2)', *CP* 80: 201–13.

(1985b) Review of V. Hunter, *Past and Process in Herodotus and Thucydides*, *CP* 80: 69–74.

(1986) 'The empirical element in the methods of early Greek medical writers and Herodotus: a shared epistemological response', *Antichthon* 20: 1–20.

(1989) *The Historical Method of Herodotus* (Toronto).

LATTIMORE, R. (1939) 'Herodotus and the names of Egyptian gods', *Class. Phil.* 34: 357–65.

(1958) 'The composition of the *History* of Herodotus', *CP* 53: 9–21.

LAUROT, B. (1981a) 'Les trois approches de l'Ethiopien par l'opinion gréco-romaine', *Ktema* 6, 69–87.

(1981b) 'Idéaux grecs et barbarie chez Hérodote', *Ktema* 6: 39–48.

LEGRAND, PH.-E. (1932) *Hérodote. Introduction* (Paris) (Introduction to Budé edition).

LESHER, J. H. (1984) 'Parmenides' critique of thinking: the *Polydēris elenchos* of Fragment 7', *Oxf. Stud. Anc. Philosophy* 2: 1–30.

(1991) 'Xenophanes on inquiry and discovery: an alternative to the "Hymn to Progress" reading of fr.18', *Ancient Philosophy* 11: 229–48.

LÉVY, E. (1981) 'Les origines du mirage scythe', *Ktema* 6: 57–68.

(1983) '*Autonomia* et *eleutheria* au Ve siècle', *RPh.* 57: 249–70.

(1984) 'Naissance du concept de barbare', *Ktema* 9: 5–14.

(1991) 'Apparition des notions de Grèce et des Grecs', in Said (1991), 49–69.

LEWIS, D. M. (1977) *Sparta and Persia. Lectures delivered at the University of Cincinnati, Autumn 1976, in memory of Donald W. Bradeen* (Leiden).

LIEBER, E. (1991) 'Herodotus and the Hippocratic "Airs, Waters, Places", on eunuchs – natural and divine', in *Actes du XXXIIe Congrès International d'Histoire de la médicine* (Antwerp), 169–73.

(1996) 'The Hippocratic "Airs, Waters, Places" on cross-dressing eunuchs: "natural" yet also "divine"', in *Hippokratische Medizin und antike Philosophie. VIII Intern. Hippokr. Kolloq.* (Zürich), 451–76.

LIENAU, C. (1973) *Hippokrates: Über Nachemfängnis, Geburtshilfe, und Schwangerschaftesleiden* (= *CMG* I 2.2; Berlin).

LILJA, S. (1967) 'Indebtedness to Hecataeus in Hdt. II 70–71', *Arctos* 5: 85–96.

LINFORTH, I. M. (1926) 'Greek gods and foreign gods in Herodotus', *Univ. of California Publications in Classical Philology* 9: 1–25.

(1940) 'Greek and Egyptian gods', *Class. Phil.* 35: 300–1.

LLOYD, A. B. (1975) *Herodotus, Book II. Introduction* (Leiden).

(1976) *Herodotus, Book II. Commentary 1–98* (Leiden).

(1988a) *Herodotus, Book II. Commentary 99–182* (Leiden).

(1988b) 'Herodotus' account of Pharaonic History', *Historia* 37: 22 ff.

(1990) 'Herodotus on Egyptians and Libyans', in *Hérodote et les peuples non-Grecs*, Fondation Hardt, xxxv (Geneva), with discussion, 215–53.

LLOYD, G. E. R. (1963) 'Who is attacked in *On Ancient Medicine*?' *Phronesis* 8, 108–26 (repr. in his *Methods and Problems*, ch. 3).

(1966) *Polarity and Analogy: Two Types of Argumentation in Early Greek Thought* (Cambridge).

(1975a) 'The role of medicine in the development of early science', *Lampas* 8: 327–33.

(1975b) 'The Hippocratic Question', *CQ* 25: 171–92 (repr. in *Methods and Problems*, ch. 9)

(1975c) 'Aspects of the interrelations of medicine, magic and philosophy in ancient Greece', *Apeiron* 9: 1–17.

(1979) *Magic, Reason and Experience. Studies in the Origin and Development of Greek Science* (Cambridge).

(1982) 'Observational error in later Greek science', in J. Barnes, J. Brunschwig, M. Burnyeat, M. Schofield (eds.), *Science and Speculation* (Cambridge), 128–64 (repr. in *Methods and Problems* (Cambridge 1991), ch. 13).

(1983) *Science, Folklore and Ideology. Studies in the Life Sciences in Ancient Greece* (Cambridge).

(1987) *Revolutions of Wisdom. Studies in the Claims and Practice of Ancient Greek Science* (California).

(1991) *Methods and Problems in Greek Science. Selected Papers* (Cambridge).

(1994) 'Adversaries and authorities', *PCPS* 40: 27–48.

LONGRIGG, J. (1963) 'Philosophy and medicine, some early interactions', *HCSPh* 67: 147–75.

(1983) '[Hippocrates] *Ancient Medicine* and its intellectual context', in F. Lasserre and P. Mudry (1983), 249–56.

(1993) *Greek Rational Medicine. Philosophy and Medicine from Alcmaeon to the Alexandrians* (London).

LONIE, I. M. (1977) 'De Natura Pueri, ch. 13', in *Corpus Hippocraticum, Colloque de Mons, Sept. 1975* (Univ. de Mons), 123–35.

(1981) *The Hippocratic Treatises 'On Generation', 'On the Nature of the Child', 'Diseases IV'* (Berlin).

(1983) 'Literacy and the development of Hippocratic medicine', in F. Lasserre and P. Mudry (1983), 145–61.

LÓPEZ FÉREZ, J. A. (1994) 'Los escritos hipocráticos y el hacimento de la identidad europea', in H. A. Khan (ed.), *The Birth of the European Identity; the Europe-Asia Contrast in Greek Thought, 490–322 BC* (Nottingham), 90–123; with 'Response' by Vivien Nutton, 124–30.

LORAUX, N. (1979) 'L'autochthonie: une topique athénienne. Le mythe dans l'espace civique', *Annales E.S.C.* 34: 1–26.

(1987) *The Invention of Athens: the Funeral Oration in the Classical City* (Cambridge, Mass.) (transl. of *L'Invention d'Athènes*, Paris 1981).

LOVEJOY, A. O. and BOAS, G. (1935) *A Documentary History of Primitivism and Related Ideas in Antiquity* (Baltimore).

LURAGHI, N. (1994) 'Erodoto tra storia e fantasia: la parola alla difesa', *Quaderni di Storia* 40: 181–90.

(forthcoming) 'Local knowledge in Herodotus' *Histories*', in N. Luraghi (ed.), *The Dawn of Historiography* (Oxford).

MACAN, R. W. (1895) *Herodotus: The Fourth, Fifth and Sixth Books* (2 vols., London).

(1908) *Herodotus: The Seventh, Eighth and Ninth Books* (2 vols., London).

MAIER, F. (1985) 'Griechische "Freiheit", – nicht nur ein philologisches Problem. Zu einer Zentralstelle in Herodots Demaratos-Gespräch', in W. Suerbaum and F. Maier (eds.), *Festschrift für Egermann* (Munich), 9 ff.

MAJNO, G. (1975) *The Healing Hand. Man and Wound in the Ancient World* (Cambridge, Mass.).

MANETTI, G. (1993) *Theories of the Sign in Classical Antiquity* (Bloomington, Indiana; Ital. edn 1987).

MANSFELD, J. (1971) *The Pseudo-Hippocratic Tract ΠΕΡΙ 'ΕΒΔΟΜΑΔΩΝ CH. 1– 11 and Greek Philosophy* (Assen).

(1980a) 'Theoretical and empirical attitudes in early Greek scientific medicine', in M. D. Grmek (1980), 371–90.

(1980b) 'Plato and the method of Hippocrates', *GRBS* 21: 341–62.

(1981) 'Protagoras on epistemological obstacles and persons', in Kerferd (1981b), 38–53.

MARG, W. (ed.) (1962) *Herodot. Eine Auswahl aus der neueren Forschung.* (2nd. edn, Munich).

(1965) '"Selbstsicherheit" bei Herodot', in Marg (ed.), *Herodot*, 290–301 (first publ. in *Studies presented to D. M. Robinson on his 70th birthday* (St. Louis, 1953) vol. II, 1103–11).

MARINCOLA, J. (1987) 'Herodotean narrative and the narrator's presence', *Arethusa* 20: 121–37.

MARROU, H. I. (1956) *A History of Education in Antiquity* (London) (6th French edn, Paris 1965).

MASARACCHIA, A. (ed.) (1990) *Erodoto, Le Storie, libro VIII* (2nd edn, Milan).

MAZZARINO, S. (1966) *Il Pensiero storico classico*, vol. I (Bari).

MCNEAL, R. A. (1985) 'How did the Pelasgians become Hellenes? Hdt. I 56–58', *Illin. Class. Stud.* 10: 11–21.

(1988) 'The Brides of Babylon', *Historia* 37: 54–71.

MEIER, C. (1987) 'Historical answers to historical questions: the origins of history in ancient Greece', in *Herodotus and the Invention of History*, *Arethusa* 20: 41–57.

MEIGGS, R. (1972) *The Athenian Empire* (Oxford).

MEJER, J. (1976) 'The alleged new fragment of Protagoras', in Classen (ed.), *Sophistik*, 306–11 (= *Hermes* 100 (1972), 175–8).

MILLER, H. W. (1949) '*On Ancient Medicine* and the origin of medicine', *TAPA* 80: 187–202.

(1952) '*Dynamis* and *physis* in *On Ancient Medicine*', *TAPA* 83: 184–97.

(1955) '*Techne* and discovery in *On Ancient Medicine*', *TAPA* 86: 51–62.

MITCHELL, S. (1989–90) 'Archaeology in Asia Minor 1985–1989', *Archaeological Reports for 1989–90 (JHS)*, 83–131.

MOELLER, C. (1903) *Die Medizin im Herodot. Für Mediziner und Philologen* (Berlin).

MOLES, J. (1996) 'Herodotus warns the Athenians', *Leeds Internat. Latin Seminar* 9: 259–84.

MOMIGLIANO, A. (1966) 'The place of Herodotus in the history of historiography', ch. 8 of *Studies in Historiography* (London) (orig. publ. *History* 43 (1958), 1–13).

(1975) *Alien Wisdom. The Limits of Hellenization* (Cambridge).

304   Bibliography

(1978) 'The historians of the classical world and their audiences; some suggestions', *Ann. d. scuola norm. de Pisa* 8: 59–75.

MORRISON, J. S. (1941) 'The place of Protagoras in Athenian political life (460–
415 B.C.)', *CQ* 35: 1–16.

(1961) 'Antiphon', *PCPhS* 7: 49–58.

(1963) 'The truth of Antiphon', *Phronesis* 8: 35–62.

MÜLLER, C. W. (1967) 'Protagoras über die Götter', *Hermes* 95: 140–59
(= Classen (ed.), *Sophistik* (1976), 312–40).

MÜLLER, D. (1981) 'Herodot – Vater des Empirismus?', in G. Kurz, D. Müller
and W. Nicolai (eds.), *Gnomosyne: menschliches Denken und Handeln in der
frühgriechischen Literatur: Festschrift für Walter Marg zum 70. Geburtstag*
(Munich), 299–318.

(1997) *Topographischer Bildkommentar zu den Historien Herodots. Kleinasien*
(Tübingen).

MÜLLER, K. E. (1972, 1980) *Geschichte der antiken Ethnographie und ethno-
graphischen Theoriebildung*, 2 vols. (Wiesbaden).

MUNSON, R. V. (1988) 'Artemisia in Herodotus', *Class. Ant.* 7: 91–106.

(1991) 'The madness of Cambyses (Herod. 3.16–38)', *Arethusa* 24: 43–65.

(1993a) 'Three aspects of Spartan kingship in Herodotus', in R. M. Rosen and
J. Farrell (eds.), *Nomodeiktes: Greek Studies in honor of Martin Ostwald* (Ann
Arbor), 39–54.

(1993b) 'Herodotus' use of prospective sentences and the story of Rhampsinitus
and the thief in the *Histories*', *AJP* 114: 27–44.

MURRAY, O. (1966) "Ο ἈΡΧΑΙΟΣ ΔΑΣΜΟΣ', *Historia* 15: 142–56.

(1970) 'Hecataeus of Abdera and Pharaonic kingship', *JEA* 56: 143–70.

(1972) 'Herodotus and Hellenistic culture', *CQ* 22: 200–13.

(1973) 'Hecataeus of Abdera and Theophrastus on Jews and Egyptians', *JEA*
59: 163–8.

(1987) 'Herodotus and oral history', in H. Sancisi-Weerdenburg and A. Kuhrt
(eds.), *Achaemenid History II, The Greek Sources* (Leiden), 93–115.

(1988) 'The Ionian Revolt', *CAH* (2nd. edn, Cambridge), vol. IV, ch. 8.

(1993) *Early Greece* (2nd edn, London).

MYRES, J. L. (1896) 'An attempt to reconstruct the maps used by Herodotus',
Geographical Journal 6: 606–31.

(1953) *Herodotus Father of History* (Oxford).

NAGY, G. (1987) 'Herodotus the *logios*', in *Arethusa* 20, *Herodotus and the Invention of History*, 175–184.

NENCI, G. (ed.) (1994) *Erodoto, Le storie, libro V* (Milan).

NESSELRATH, H.-G. (1995) 'Herodot und die Enden der Erde', *Mus. Helv.* 52: 20–44.

NESTLE, W. (1908) *Herodots Verständnis zur philosophie und Sophistik* (Schöntal).

(1938) 'Hippocratica', *Hermes* 73: 1–38.

(1942) *Vom Mythos zum Logos* (Stuttgart; repr. 1966).

NIESCHKE, A. (1891) *De figurarum, quae vocantur σχήματα Γοργίεια, apud Her-
odotum usu* (Münden).

NIPPEL, W. (1990) *Griechen, Barbaren und 'Wilde'. Alte Geschichte und Sozialan-
thropologie* (Frankfurt).

NUTTON, V. (1994) 'Response' [to López Férez 1994], in Khan (1994), 124–30.

OSTWALD, M. (1986/7) *From Popular Sovereignty to the Sovereignty of Law. Law, Society and Politics in Fifth-Century Athens* (Berkeley).

(1991) 'Herodotus and Athens', *Illin. Class. Stud.* 16: 137–48.

(1992) 'Athens as a cultural centre', ch. 8h, *Cambridge Ancient History* (2nd edn), vol. V (Cambridge).

O'SULLIVAN, N. (1992) *Alcidamas, Aristophanes and the Beginnings of Greek Stylistic Theory. Hermes* Einzelschriften, vol. 60.

(1996) 'Written and Spoken in the First Sophistic', in I. Worthington (ed.), *Voice into Text* (Leiden), 115–27.

PACKMAN, Z. M. (1991) 'The incredible and the incredulous: the vocabulary of disbelief in Herodotus, Thucydides and Xenophon', *Hermes* 119: 399–414.

PARKE, H. W. (1946) 'Citation and recitation: a convention in early Greek historians', *Hermathena* 67: 80–92.

PARKER, R. (1987) 'Myths of early Athens', in J. Bremmer (ed.), *Interpretations of Greek Mythology* (London), 187–214.

PEARSON, L. (1939) *Early Ionian Historians* (Oxford).

(1941) 'Credulity and scepticism in Herodotus', *TAPA* 72: 335–55.

PELLICCIA, H. (1992) 'Sappho 16, Gorgias' *Helen,* and the preface to Herodotus' *Histories*', *YCS* 29: 63–84.

PELLING, C. (1996) 'The urine and the vine: Astyages' dreams at Herodotus I.107–8', *CQ* 46: 68–77.

(1997) 'East is East and West is West – or are they? National Stereotypes in Herodotus', *Histos* 1.

PERNOT, L. (1993) *La Rhétorique de l'éloge dans le monde gréco-romain.* 2 vols. (vol I: Histoire et technique) (Paris).

PETIT, T. (1985) 'L'integration des cités ioniennes dans l'Empire Achaemenide (VIe siècle)', *REA* 87: 43–52.

PFEIFFER, R. (1976) 'Die Sophisten, ihre Zeitgenossen und Schüler', in Classen (ed.), *Sophistik,* 170–214.

PHILLIPS, E. D. (1973) *Greek Medicine* (London).

PIGEAUD, J.-M. (1980) 'Quelques aspects du rapport de l'âme et du corps dans le corpus hippocratique', in Grmek (1980), 417–32.

(1983) 'Remarques sur l'inné et l'acquis dans le Corpus hippocratique', in F. Lasserre & P. Mudry (1983), 41–56.

(1988) 'Le style d'Hippocrate ou l'écriture fondatrice de la médicine', in M. Detienne (ed.), *Les Savoirs de l'écriture. En Grèce ancienne* (Lille), 305–29.

PIPPIDI, D. M. (1960) 'Sur la philosophie de l'histoire d'Hérodote', *Eirene* 1: 75–92.

POHLENZ, M. (1937) *Herodot. Der Erste Geschichtschreiber des Abendlandes* (Leipzig–Berlin).

(1953) 'Nomos und Physis', *Hermes* 81: 418–38 (repr. in *Kleine Schriften* (1965), 341–60).

(1938) 'Hippokratesstudien', in *Nachrichten von der Gesellschaft der Wissenschaften zu Göttingen,* Neue Folge, Fachgruppe I: 67–102.

PÖHLMANN, E. and GAUER, W. (eds.) (1994) *Griechische Klassik. Vorträge bei der interdisziplinären Tagung des Deutschen Archäologie Verbandes und der Mommsengesellschaft vom 24.–27.10.1991 in Blaubeuren* (Nuremberg).

POOLE, J. C. F. and HOLLADAY, A. J. (1979) 'Thucydides and the Plague of Athens', *CQ* 29: 282–300.

POTTER, P., MALONEY, G., DESAUTELS, J. (1990) *La Maladie et les maladies dans la collection hippocratique. Actes du VI e. colloque intern. hippocratique (Québec 1987)* (Quebec).

POWELL, J. E. (1937) 'Puns in Herodotus', *CR* 51: 103–5.

(1966) *A Lexicon to Herodotus* (2nd edn, Hildesheim; orig. 1938).

PRITCHETT, W. K. (1975) *Dionysius of Halicarnassus, On Thucydides*. English Translation and Commentary (Berkeley).

(1993) *The Liar School of Herodotus* (Amsterdam).

RAAFLAUB, K. (1987) 'Herodotus, political thought, and the meaning of history', in *Arethusa* vol. 20, *Herodotus and the Invention of History*, 221–48.

(1990) 'Contemporary Perceptions of Democracy in Fifth-Century Athens', in Connor et al., *Aspects of the Athenian Democracy* (*Class. et Med.* Diss., Copenhagen), 32–70.

RADERMACHER, L. (1951) *Artium Scriptores, Reste der voraristotelischen Rhetorik* (Vienna).

RAUBITSCHEK, A. E. (1993) 'The *Phoinissai* of Phrynichos', *Tyche* 8: 143–4.

REDFIELD, J. (1975) *Nature and Culture in the Iliad* (Chicago).

(1985) 'Herodotus the tourist', *CP* 80: 97–118.

REGENBOGEN, O. (1930) 'Herodot und sein Werk', *Antike* 6: 202–48; repr. in Marg (ed.), *Herodot* (1962), 57–108.

(1961) 'Eine Forschungsmethode antiker Naturwissenschaft', *Kleine Schriften* (Munich), 141–94. (orig. in *Quellen und Studien zur Geschichte der Mathematik* I 2 (1930), 131–82).

RICHARDSON, N. J. (1975) 'Homeric professors in the age of the Sophists', *PCPhS* 21: 65–81.

ROBINSON, J. M. (1973) 'On Gorgias', in *Exegesis and Argument, Studies ... Vlastos, Phronesis* Suppl. vol. I (Assen), 49–60.

ROBINSON, T. M. (1979) *Contrasting Arguments. An edition of the Dissoi Logoi* (Salem, New Hampshire).

ROEBUCK, C. (1953) 'The economic development of Ionia', *CP* 48: 9–16.

ROLLE, R. (1989) *The World of the Scythians* (Batsford; transl. of *Die Welt der Skythen*).

ROLLE, R. et al. (1991) *Gold der steppe. Archäologie der Ukraine* (Schleswig).

ROLLINGER, R. (1993) *Herodots babylonischer Logos: eine kritische Untersuchung der Glaubwürdigkeitsdiskussion an Hand ausgewählter Beispiele* (Innsbruck).

ROMM, J. (1987) 'Dragons and gold at the edges of the earth; a folktale motif developed by Herodotus', *Wonders and Tales* 1: 45–55.

(1989) 'Herodotus and mythic geography: the case of the Hyperboreans', *TAPA* 119: 97–113.

(1992) *The Edges of the World in Ancient Thought* (Princeton).

ROSELLINI, M. and SAÏD, S. (1978) 'Usages des femmes et autres nomoi chez les "sauvages" d'Hérodote: Essai de lecture structurale', *Annali della Scuola Normale Superiore di Pisa*, ser. 3, 8: 949–1005.

ROSÉN, VON HAIIM B. (1993) "Ἱστορίης ἀπόδεξις. Ein Problem der herodotischen Textkritik', *Glotta* 71: 146–53.

ROSENMEYER, T. G. (1955) 'Gorgias, Aeschylus and *apate*', *AJP* 76: 225–60.

ROSIVACH, V. (1987) 'Autochthony and the Athenians', *CQ* 37: 294–306.

RÖSLER, W. (1990) '*Mnemosyne* in the symposium', in O. Murray (ed.), *Sympotica. A Symposium on the Symposium* (Oxford), 230–7.

ROWE, C. (1984) *Plato* (Brighton).

RUBINSON, K. S. (1975) 'Herodotus and the Scythians', *Expedition* 17: 4.16–25.

RUDENKO, S. I. (1970) *Frozen Tombs of Siberia. The Pazyryk Burials of Iron Age Horsemen.* Transl. and pref. by M. W. Thompson (London; orig., Moscow 1953).

SAÏD, S. (1980) 'Guerre, intelligence et courage dans les *Histoires* d'Hérodote', *Ancient Society* 11: 83–117.

(1981) 'Darius et Xerxes dans les Perses d'Eschyle', *Ktema* 6: 17–38.

(1984) 'Grecs et barbares dans les tragédies d' Euripide. La fin des différences?', *Ktema* 9: 27–53.

(ed.) (1991) *Hellenismos. Quelques jalons pour une histoire de l'identité grecque.* (Leiden – New York – Copenhagen).

STE. CROIX, G. E. M. DE (1954–5) 'The character of the Athenian Empire', *Historia* 3: 1–41.

(1972) *The Origins of the Peloponnesian War* (London).

SANDERS, T. J. (1977/8) 'Antiphon the sophist on natural law (B44 DK)', *Proc. Aristot. Soc.* 78: 215–36.

SANSONE, D. (1985) 'The date of Herodotus' publication', *Illin. Class. Stud.* 10: 1–9.

SAUGE, A. (1992) *De l'épopée à l'histoire. Fondement de la notion d'historié* (Frankfurt).

SCHENKEVELD, D. M. (1992a) 'Prose usages of ΆΚΟΥΕΙΝ', *CQ* 42: 129–41.

(1992b) Review of Cole (1991), *Mnemosyne* 45: 387–92.

SCHEPENS, G. (1975) 'Some aspects of source theory in Greek historiography', *Ancient Society* 6: 257–74.

(1980) *L' 'autopsie' dans la méthode des historiens grecs du Ve siècle avant J.- C.* (Brussels).

SCHUPP, F. (1926) 'Zur Geschichte der Beweistopik in der älten griechischen Gerichtsrede', *Wien.Stud.* 45: 17–28, 173–85.

SCHWARTZ, S. B. (1994) *Implicit Understandings. Observing, Reporting and Reflecting on the Encounters between Europeans and Other Peoples in the Early Modern Era* (Cambridge).

SEALEY, R. (1957) 'From Phemios to Ion', *REG* 70: 312–51.

SEDLEY, D. (1998) 'The etymologies in Plato's *Cratylus*', *JHS* 118: 140–54.

SEGAL, C. P. (1962) 'Gorgias and the psychology of the logos', *HSCP* 66: 99–155.

(1983) '*Kleos* and its ironies in the *Odyssey*', *AC* 52: 22–47.

SEKUNDA, N. (1985) 'Achaemenid colonization in Lydia', *REA* 87: 7–29.

SHERK, R. (1992) 'The eponymous officials of Greek cities IV. The Register. Part III: Thrace, Black Sea area, Asia Minor (continued), *ZPE* 93: 223–72.

SHERWIN-WHITE, S. (1978) *Ancient Cos: An Historical Study from the Dorian Settlement to the Imperial Period, Hypomnemata* 51 (Göttingen).

SHIMRON, B. (1989) *Politics and belief in Herodotus, Historia* Einzelschriften 58.

SHRIMPTON, G. S. (1997) *History and Memory in Ancient Greece*, with Appendix on Herodotus' source citations by G. S. Shrimpton and K. M. Gillis (Montreal & Kingston).

SLUITER, I. (1997) 'The Greek Tradition', in W. van Bekkum, J. Houben, I. Sluiter, and K. Versteegh (eds.), *The Emergence of Semantics in Four Linguistic Traditions* (Amsterdam), Part III.

SMELIK, K. A. D. and HEMELRIJK, E. A. (1984) ' "Who knows not what monsters demented Egypt worships?" Opinions on Egyptian animal worship in Antiquity as part of the ancient conception of Egypt', *ANRW* II 17.4, ed. W. Haase (Berlin), 1852–2000.

SMITH, W. D. (1979) *The Hippocratic Tradition* (Ithaca).

(1983) 'Analytical and catalogue structure in the Corpus Hippocraticum', in F. Lasserre and P. Mudry (1983), 277–84.

SNELL, B. (1924) *Philologische Untersuchungen: die Ausdrücke für den Begriff des Wissens in der vorplatonischen Philosophie* (Berlin).

SOLMSEN, F. (1975) *Intellectual Experiments of the Greek Enlightenment* (Princeton).

SOLOMON, J. (1985) 'Thucydides and the recognition of contagion', *Maia* 37: 121–3.

SOURVINOU-INWOOD, C. (1988) ' "Myth" and history: on Hdt. III 48 and 50–53', *Opuscula Atheniensia* 17: 167–82.

STADEN, H. von (1989) *Herophilos. The Art of Medicine in Early Alexandria* (Cambridge).

(1990) 'Incurability and hopelessness: the Hippocratic Corpus', in P. Potter et al. (eds.), *La Maladie et les maladies dans la collection hippocratique. Actes du VIe colloque international hippocratique* (Quebec), 75–112.

(1992a) 'Affinities and elisions. Helen and hellenocentrism', *ISIS* 83: 578–95.

(1992b) 'Women and dirt', *Helios* 19: 7–30.

(1994) 'Author and authority. Celsus and the construction of a scientific self', in M. E. Vázquez Buján (ed.), *Tradición e Innovación de la Medicina Latina de la Antigüedad y de la Alta Edad Media. Actas del IV Coloquio Internacional sobre los 'textos médicos latinos antiguos'* (Santiago de Compostela), 103–17.

(1995) 'Anatomy as rhetoric: Galen on dissection and persuasion', *Journal Hist. of Medicine and Allied Sciences* 50: 47–66.

STADTER, P. A. (1992) 'Herodotus and the Athenian *arche*', *Annali della Scuola Normale Superiore di Pisa* 22: 781–809.

STAHL, H.-P. (1975) 'Learning through suffering? Croesus' conversations in the *History* of Herodotus', *YCS* 24: 1–36.

STASZAK, J.-F. (1995) *La géographie d'avant la géographie. Le climat chez Aristote et Hippocrate* (Paris).

STEIN, H. (ed.) (1882–93), *Herodotos* 5 vols. (Berlin, 5th edn).

STERN, J. (1991) 'Scapegoat narratives in Herodotus', *Hermes* 119: 304–11.

STIER, H. E. (1928) 'Nomos Basileus', *Philologus* 83: 225–58.

STRASBURGER, H. (1955) 'Herodot und das perikleische Athen', *Historia* 4: 1–25 (repr. Marg (1962), 574–608).

(1972) *Homer und die Geschichtsschreibung* (Heidelberg).

STROHEKER, K. F. (1953/4) 'Zu den Anfängen der monarchischen Theorie in der Sophistik', *Historia* 2: 381–412.

STÜCKELBERGER, A. (1984) *Vestigia Democratea. Die Rezeption der Lehre von den Atomen in der antiken Naturwissenschaft und Medizin* (Basle).

SWAIN, S. (1994) 'Man and medicine in Thucydides', *Arethusa* 27: 303–27.

THIVEL, A. (1981) *Cnide et Cos? Essai sur les doctrines medicales dans la collection hippocratique* (Paris).

THOMAS, R. (1989) *Oral Tradition and Written Record in Classical Athens* (Cambridge).

(1992) *Literacy and Orality in Ancient Greece* (Cambridge).

(1993) 'Performance and written publication in Herodotus and the Sophistic generation', in W. Kullmann and J. Althoff, *Vermittlung und Tradierung von Wissen in der griechischen Kultur* (Tübingen), 225–44.

(1995a) 'The place of the poet in Archaic society', in A. Powell (ed.), *The Greek World*, (London), ch. 5.

(1995b) 'Review of Sauge (1992)', *CR* 45: 456–7.

(1996) 'Review article I: Herodotus' (review of Erbse (1992), Pritchett (1993), Rollinger (1993)), *JHS* 116: 175–8.

(1997a) 'Ethnography, proof and argument in Herodotus' *Histories*', *PCPhS* 43: 128–48.

(1997b) 'Introduction' to Herodotus, *The Histories* translated by G. Rawlinson (Everyman Library, reprint, London).

THOMPSON, N. (1996) *Herodotus and the Origins of the Political Community. Arion's Leap* (New Haven, London).

THOMSON, J. O. (1948) *History of Ancient Geography* (Cambridge).

THORDARSON, F. (1988) 'The Scythian funeral customs: some notes on Hdt. IV 71–75', in *A Green Leaf. Papers in Honour of Prof. Jes P. Asmussen* (Leiden, Acta Iranica 28), 539–47.

TOYE, D. L. (1995) 'Dionysius of Halicarnassus on the first Greek historians', *AJP* 116: 279–302.

TOZER, H. F. (1935) *History of Ancient Geography*, 2nd edn with notes by M. Cary (Cambridge).

TRUDINGER, K. (1918) *Studien zur Geschichte der griechischen-römischen Ethnographie* (Basle).

TSETSKHLADZE, G. R. (1998) 'Who built the Scythian and Thracian royal and elite tombs?', *Oxford Journal of Archaeology* 17: 55–92.

TULIN, A. (1993) 'Xenophanes Fr.18 D–K and the origins of the idea of progress', *Hermes* 121: 129–38.

VANDIVER, E. (1991) *Heroes in Herodotus. The Interaction of Myth and History* (Frankfurt).

VANICELLI, P. (1993) *Erodoto e la storia dell' alto e medio archaismo (Sparta – Tessaglia – Cirene)* (Rome).

VANSINA, J. (1973) *Oral Tradition. A Study in Historical Methodology* (Harmondsworth; orig. publ. in French, 1961; 1st English edn, 1965).

(1985) *Oral Tradition as History* (London and Nairobi).

VEEN, J. E. VAN DER (1996) *The Significant and the Insignificant. Five Studies in Herodotus' View of History* (Amsterdam).

VERDENIUS, W. J. (1981) 'Gorgias' doctrine of deception', in Kerferd (1981b), 116–28.

VERDIN, H. (1971) *De Historisch-Kritische Methode van Herodotus* (Brussels).

(1975) 'Hérodote historien? Quelques interprétations récentes', *L'Antiquité Classique* 44: 668–85.

VLASTOS, G. (1970) Review of Cornford, *Principium Sapientiae*, in D. Furley and R. Allen, *Studies in Presocratic Philosophy* I (London 1970), 42–55 (= *Gnomon* 27 (1955), 65–76).

(1975) 'Ethics and physics in Democritus', in R. E. Allen and D. Furley, *Studies in Presocratic Philosophy II. The Eleatics and Pluralists* (London), 381–408 (= *Philos. Rev.* 54 (1945), 578–92 and 55 (1946), 53–64).

(1976) 'Protagoras', in C. J. Classen (ed.), *Sophistik* (Darmstadt), 271–89.

WALBANK, F. (1962) 'Polemic in Polybius', *JRS* 52: 1–12.

WALLINGA, H. T. (1987) 'The Ancient Persian Navy and its predecessors', in H. Sancisi-Weerdenburg and A. Kuhrt (eds.), *Achaemenid History* vol. I (Leiden), 47–77.

WATERS, K. H. (1985) *Herodotos the Historian: his Problems, Methods and Originality* (London).

WEBER, H. A. (1976) *Herodots Verständnis von Historie: Untersuchungen zur methodologie und Argumentationsweise Herodots* (Frankfurt and Munich).

WEIDAUER, K. (1954) *Thukydides und die hippokratischen Schriften* (Heidelberg).

WELLS, J. (1923) 'Herodotus and the intellectual life of his age', in Wells, *Studies in Herodotus* (Oxford), 183–204.

WENSKUS, O. (1983) 'Vergleich und Beweis im Hippokratischen Corpus', in F. Lasserre and P. Mudry (1983), 393–406.

WEST, S. (1985) 'Herodotus' epigraphical interests', *CQ* 35: 278–305.

(1987) 'And it came to pass that Pharaoh dreamed: Notes on Herodotus 2.139, 141*', *CQ* 37: 262–71.

(1988) 'The Scythian ultimatum (Herodotus IV 131, 132)', *JHS* 108: 207–11.

(1991a) 'Herodotus' portrait of Hecataeus', *JHS* 111: 144–60.

(1991b) Review of Lateiner (1989), in *CR* 105: 23–5.

WILCOX, S. (1942) 'The scope of early rhetorical instruction', *HSCP* 53: 121–55.

WILL, E. (1956) *Doriens et Ioniens* (Paris).

WITTERN, R. (1974) *Die hippokratische Schrift De Morbis I, Ausgabe, Übersetzung und Erlaüterungen* (Hildesheim, New York).

(1994) 'Die Anfänge des wissenschaftlichen Denkens am Beispiel der Medizin des 5. Jahrhunderts', in E. Pöhlmann, and W. Gauer (1994), 153–66.

WOLFF, E. (1964) 'Das Weib des Masistes', *Hermes* 92: 51–8.

WOODMAN, A. J. (1988) *Rhetoric in Classical Historiography* (London).

WORTHINGTON, I. (ed.) (1994) *Greek Rhetoric in Action* (London).

(ed.) (1996) *Voice into Text. Orality and Literacy in Ancient Greece* (Leiden).

Index locorum

Aelian, *NH*
(vi 60) 128; (xii 16) 139; (xii 18–20) 139
Aeschylus
Choeph. (523–50) 144 n.32; *Eum.* (700–3)
55, 66 n.91; *Persai* (759–86) 56; *Suppl.*
(692) 142 n.26; (frag. 229R) 49 n.44
Alcidamas
On Those who Write Written Speeches
(chs.1–2) 283–4
Alcmaeon, DK 24
(A2) 161; (A5) 158; (B1) 205–6; (B3) 151
Anaxagoras, DK 59
(A105) 159; (B4) 239 n.74; (B4.5) 174, 226
  n.27; (B12) 174, 226 n.27, 239 n.74;
  (B17) 84 n.18, 230; (B21a) 206
Andocides
(iii 2) 199 n.69
Antiphon, DK 87
(B13) 231 n.44; (B22–39) 161; (B44, frag. A)
  231 n.44; (B44, frag. B) 131–3, 199
  n.67; (B45) 127; (B46) 89 n.32, 127–8;
  (B54) 174; (B58) 231 n.44; (B60) 231
  n.44
Antiphon (orator)
Tetral. (i 4. 8, 10) 199 n.69, 227 n.31;
  Tetral. (ii 4.8, 9–10) 234 n.59; *Tetral.*
  (iii 1.1) 234 n.59
(i 3) 245 n.91; (v 88–91) 234 n.59; (vi 15)
  245 n.91; (vi 30–1) 199 n.69; (vi 33)
  245 n.91; (frags. 35 and 72 Blass) 199
  n.69; (frag. B1, col. iv) 234 n.59
Archytas, DK 47
(A14) 231 n.42; (B1) 231 n.42; (B4) 261 n.38
Aristophanes
Acharnians (85–7, 92) 20 n.59; (v.523 ff.) 20
  n.59; (1030–2) 23, 250 n.2
Clouds (227 ff.) 158–9, 233 n.57; (233) 52
  n.50; (236) 52 n.50; (321) 266 n.55;
  (360) 161; (659) 231 n.43, 233 n.57;
  (679) 231 n.43, 233 n.57; (742) 233
  n.57; (888, 901, 938) 266 n.55; (1421–
  31) 3

Knights (1232) 199 n.70
Peace (1253) 72
Wasps (1076–7) 118 n.30
frags. (577–89 K–A) 217 n.5
Aristotle
Gen. Anim. (736a10 ff.) 30 n.3; (759a8–
  761a2) 150 n.48; (771a14 ff.) 144 n.31;
  (771b27 ff.) 144 n.31; (773a33 ff.) 146
  and n.36; (774a) 146 n.38; (783b) 77
  n.2
Hist. Anim. (501b19 ff.) 138; (523a17 ff.) 30
  n.3; (579b2 ff.) 144 n.32; (579b–580a)
  146 n.35; (606a18 ff.) 152; (606b)
  53 n.54, 89 n.31; (606b17 ff.) 96,
  139
Meteor. (362b11 ff.) 215
Pol. (1252b5 ff.) 93; (1255a28–b4) 93;
  (1266a39 ff.) 129 n.61; (1267b22 ff.) 13;
  (1327b23 ff.) 93, 95 and n.48
Prior Anal. (B27) 191 n.54
Problemata (892a–b3) 144–5, 146
Rhet. (i 1.11, 1355a) 261 n.36; (1357b7 ff)
  191 n.54
On Marvellous Things Heard (830b, 837b)
  163; (846b18 ff.) 144 n.32, 163; (847b)
  163

Cicero
De leg. (i 5) 1
De orat. (3.32. 127–8) 147

Democritus, DK 68
(A1) 12 n.33; (A99) 136; (A99a) 52 n.52, 138;
  (A135) 159n.82; (A150a) 128; (A150a–
  155) 52 n.52; 139, 143 n.29, 150–1;
  (A151) 139, 143
(B5) 278 n.13; (B5.2) 231 n.42; (B10b) 261
  n.39; (B15) 215; (B20a) 230; (B26) 84,
  278; (B26b, c, d) 159; (B40) 231; (B58)
  231 n.42; (B116) 12; (B142, 145) 278
  n.13; (B148) 159; (B246) 12 n.33; (B259)
  239 n.74; (B299) 12, 166 n.102, 261
  n.39

311

General index

Agrippaioi, 30, 35 n.9
Alcidamas, 251 n.8, 254, 257, 271 n.2, 283–4
Alcmaeon, 151, 154, 158, 161, 199, 205
Amasis, 224 n.22
Amazons, 56, 61–2, 88, 245
Anacharsis, 55, 65 n.90
analogy, 112, 170, 175, 185, 200–11
ananke, 169, 184, 185, 186, 191, 197, 221 and n.14
Anaxagoras, 7, 8 n.21, 13, 16, 49 n.42, 52 n.51, 84 n.18, 136, 143, 156 n.70, 159, 166, 174, 196, 202, 206, 210, 226, 230, 231–2, 239 n.74, 259, 274, 278
Anaximander, 78, 135 n.1
Androphagoi, 64, 129
animals: analogy with humans, 2–3, 128, 129–30; of Asia, 96; of Libya, 53–4, 96; of Scythia, 65, 70–1, 96; *see also* generation, nature
antilogiai, 250, 252–3, 264–7
Antiphon 'orator', 199 n.69, 227 and n.31, 234, 245
Antiphon 'sophist', 16, 125, 127–8, 131–3, 161, 174, 199, 231, 278
apodeixis, apodeiknumi, 169, 191, 200, 221–2, 223, 224–5, 249–69 esp. 250, 260–4
Arabia: animals, 139, 163; snakes, 139–45, 149; spices, 72–3, 140
Archelaos of Miletus, 13
Archytas, 261
arete, 109–12
argument: 19, 21; deductive, 175–90, 212; methods of, 168–213 esp. 168–90
Aristagoras, 113
Aristophanes: 147 n.42, 158–9, 199; *Ach.* 23; *Clouds*, 3, 52, 233, 266 n.55
Aristotle: on barbarians, 71, 93; on geography, 215; on natural world, 138, 139, 147, 152; on proof, 191
Artabanus, 266, 285

Asia: extent of, 81–4; fertility of, 54 n.56; in world division, 80–6, 177–8; inhabitants of, 75, 79, 86–100; *see also* Asia Minor
Asia Minor, Greeks of, 90–1, 92–5, 99, 100–1
Atarantes, 53, 129
Athens: as cultural centre, 10–13; democracy, 114–17, 118; empire, 14–15, 90, 95–6, 114, 116; energy of, 92 and n.37; and Ionia, 118 n.29, 120; origins of, 117–22, 195, 216; Persian victory, 190; *see also* autochthony
autochthony, 117–22
autonomy, effect of, 90–3, 94, 95, 115

Babylonians, 29, 129
barbarians: 29, 54 n.57, 71; and Greeks, 75, 79, 90–1, 92–5, 97, 103, 113, 121 and n.43, 131–4, 267–8, 282; in Hippocratic Corpus, 72 n.99, 90, 92; and *physis*, 28–74 esp. 42–74
beavers, 41, 63, 72, 286–8
bile, 41, 62–3
bitumen, 138, 153
Black Sea, 8, 43 and n.31, 47, 48 n.37, 55 and n.58, 58, 65 n.90, 78, 288
Borysthenes, 66
Boudinoi, 63, 286, 288

Cambyses, 29, 30, 34–5, 229
Carians, 9–10, 44, 224
cinnamon, 73
Clazomenae, 13, 15
Cleomenes, 33, 55
Cleon, 250, 252
climate: and animals, 150–2; and ethnic character, 7 n.18, 23, 32, 86–98, 100–1, 104–14; and health, 37–9, 40, 42–72; and natural philosophy, 68, 69–71, 74, 76
Colchians, 90, 171 n.14, 193–4

Lightning Source UK Ltd.
Milton Keynes UK
UKOW050505010812

196869UK00002B/10/A